"Written in the same spirit of creat[...]
'third wave therapies' into the mainstream, Levin, Hayes, [...]
tributors compellingly illustrate how acceptance, mindfulness, and context are vital resources in reducing the seemingly intractable suffering caused by addictive behavior."

—Zindel Segal, PhD, author of *The Mindful Way through Depression*

"The addiction field is blessed with a variety of paths to recovery, and this volume presents cutting-edge, theory-based alternatives to traditional approaches. It explores some frontiers from which a next generation of addiction treatments is likely to emerge."

—William R. Miller, PhD, emeritus-distinguished professor of psychology and psychiatry at the University of New Mexico

"Steven C. Hayes and Michael E. Levin have put together a must-read for researchers, clinicians, and students of addictive behaviors and their treatment. This very substantive book is refreshingly diverse in both theoretical perspectives and clinical contexts of varying addictive behaviors. Held together by contextual cognitive behavioral therapy as a unifying theme, perspectives discussed include acceptance and commitment therapy (ACT), dialectic behavior therapy (DBT), mindfulness-based relapse prevention (MBRP), motivational interviewing (MI), and meta-cognitive therapy (MCT), among others. Clinical problem areas range from detoxification, problem drinking, problem gambling, substance dependence (including borderline personality disorder), binge eating, shame and stigma associated with addictions, pornography addiction, and smoking cessation. With the unifying theme of teaching clients new ways of relating to their experiences, including distressing thoughts, feelings, and sensations, this book marks the progress that already has been achieved in these areas, while at the same time providing a roadmap for exciting future directions."

—Richard A. Brown, PhD, professor in the department of psychiatry and human behavior at Alpert Medical School of Brown University and director of addictions research at Butler Hospital

THE
MINDFULNESS & ACCEPTANCE
PRACTICA SERIES

As mindfulness and acceptance-based therapies gain momentum in the field of mental health, it is increasingly important for professionals to understand the full range of their applications. To keep up with the growing demand for authoritative resources on these treatments, *The Mindfulness and Acceptance Practica Series* was created. These edited books cover a range of evidence-based treatments, such as acceptance and commitment therapy (ACT), cognitive behavioral therapy (CBT), compassion-focused therapy (CFT), dialectical behavioral therapy (DBT), and mindfulness-based stress reduction (MBSR) therapy. Incorporating new research in the field of psychology, these books are powerful tools for mental health clinicians, researchers, advanced students, and anyone interested in the growth of mindfulness and acceptance strategies.

Visit www.newharbinger.com for
more books in this series.

MINDFULNESS & ACCEPTANCE FOR ADDICTIVE BEHAVIORS

Applying Contextual CBT to Substance Abuse & Behavioral Addictions

Edited by
STEVEN C. HAYES, PhD
& MICHAEL E. LEVIN, MA

CONTEXT PRESS
An Imprint of New Harbinger Publications, Inc.

Publisher's Note

This publication is designed to provide accurate and authoritative information in regard to the subject matter covered. It is sold with the understanding that the publisher is not engaged in rendering psychological, financial, legal, or other professional services. If expert assistance or counseling is needed, the services of a competent professional should be sought.

Library of Congress Cataloging-in-Publication Data

Mindfulness and acceptance for addictive behaviors : applying contextual CBT to substance abuse and behavioral addictions / edited by Steven C. Hayes and Michael E. Levin.

   p. cm. -- (The context press mindfulness and acceptance practica series)
  Includes bibliographical references and index.
  ISBN 978-1-60882-216-4 (pbk. : alk. paper) -- ISBN 978-1-60882-217-1 (pdf e-book) -- ISBN 978-1-60882-218-8 (epub) 1. Compulsive behavior--Treatment. 2. Substance abuse--Treatment. 3. Mindfulness-based cognitive therapy. I. Hayes, Steven C. II. Levin, Michael E.
  RC533.M57 2012
  616.89'1425--dc23

2012020870

To my loving father, Charles Aloysius Hayes, Jr., who showed such courage and humanity in his struggle with addiction.

—SCH

In memory of my brother, David Brian Levin, who reminds me how precious every day is.

—MEL

Contents

Part 1
Treatment Models

Part 2
Clinical Issues and Populations

Alphabetical List of Contributors

Sarah Bowen, *University of Washington*

Jonathan B. Bricker, *Fred Hutchinson Cancer Research Center and University of Washington*

Gabriele Caselli, *London South Bank University and Studi Cognitivi Cognitive Psychotherapy School*

Neha Chawla, *University of Washington*

Jesse M. Crosby, *Utah State University and McLean Hospital/Harvard Medical School*

Linda A. Dimeff, *Behavioral Tech Research, Inc.*

Maureen K. Flynn, *University of Mississippi*

Steven C. Hayes, *University of Nevada, Reno*

Karen S. Ingersoll, *University of Virginia*

Barbara S. Kohlenberg, *University of Nevada School of Medicine*

A. Solomon Kurz, *University of Mississippi*

Michael E. Levin, *University of Nevada, Reno*

Jason Lillis, *Weight Control and Diabetes Research Center, The Miriam Hospital/Brown Alpert Medical School*

Jason B. Luoma, *Portland Psychotherapy Clinic, Research, and Training Center*

Akihiko Masuda, *Georgia State University*

Stephen Rollnick, *Cardiff University*

Jennifer H. R. Sayrs, *Evidence Based Treatment Centers of Seattle*

Lindsay W. Schnetzer, *University of Mississippi*

Marcantonio M. Spada, *London South Bank University and North East London NHS Foundation Trust*

Angela L. Stotts, *University of Texas Medical School at Houston*

Tony Toneatto, *University of Toronto*

Michael P. Twohig, *Utah State University*

Christopher C. Wagner, *Virginia Commonwealth University*

Adrian Wells, *University of Manchester*

Kelly G. Wilson, *University of Mississippi*

Katie Witkiewitz, *Washington State University*

Christopher M. Wyszynski, *Fred Hutchinson Cancer Research Center*

INTRODUCTION

Contextual Cognitive Behavioral Therapies for Addictive Behaviors

Michael E. Levin

Steven C. Hayes

University of Nevada, Reno

I t is commonplace for books or articles on addiction to begin with what can only be called a tale of woe. The entire area of addiction involves difficulties. The problem is enormous; the cases are complex; the treatment resources are limited. That is a bad combination.

The enormity of the problem can hardly be overstated. Lifetime prevalence rates of substance use disorders (SUDs) are estimated to be around 14.6% (Kessler, Chiu, Demler, Merikangas, & Walters, 2005), and about 8.7% of individuals over twelve years of age in the United States reported a substance use disorder in the previous year (Substance Abuse and Mental Health Services Administration, 2011). The present volume expands its scope from substance use disorders to addictive behaviors of all kinds, which increases those numbers. Compulsive gamblers approach 5% of the population, and that number is growing as gambling becomes more accessible and widespread (Welte, Barnes, Tidwell, & Hoffman, 2011). About 6% of the population views pornography online more than eleven hours per week, and these people often state that doing so jeopardizes major life domains (Levin, Lillis, & Hayes, in press). Binge eating and other compulsive eating patterns affect another 3% to 5% (e.g., Hudson, Hiripi, Pope, & Kessler, 2007). Most of these problems tend to co-occur, with comorbidity rates as high as 50%

depending on the specific comparison (Barnes, Welte, Hoffman, & Tidwell, 2011), and that is one reason we have included them in the present volume under the general term "addictive behaviors." Indeed, that co-occurrence is even cross-generational. For example, children of problem gamblers have been shown to have higher levels of tobacco, alcohol, and drug use and overeating than their classroom peers (Gupta & Derevensky, 1997).

These comorbidity statistics themselves suggest the level of case complexity, but the problem is even more extensive. Addiction problems of all kinds tend to co-occur with mental health problems more generally. A few examples show the extent of the issue. Severely mentally ill persons have lifetime prevalence rates of substance use disorder of about 50% (e.g., Jablensky, McGrath, & Morgan, 1999). Rates of comorbid SUDs are even higher among subgroups of people with severe mental illness, such as the homeless (Mueser et al., 1999). Similar findings exist for personality disorders or Axis I disorders (Kessler et al., 2005). Some of this is because the use of substances actually can *induce* mental disorders such as stimulant- or cannabinoid-induced psychoses, substance-induced mood disorders, and substance-induced anxiety conditions (Schuckit, 2006).

The problem of case complexity does not end there, however. Addiction problems are associated with impaired occupational and social functioning, medical problems, and legal problems (Kessler, Nelson, & McGonagle, 1996; Kessler et al., 2005). They tend to be associated with interpersonal violence (Pernanen, 1991), increased HIV risk behavior (Donovan & McEwan, 1995), and suicide (Grant & Hasin, 1999). We could continue, but all thoughtful readers take the point: addictive behaviors are keystones in the creation of human misery.

Given that context, it is a bit shocking how poor the treatment resources are for people with addiction problems. Substance use disorders tend to be chronic conditions (McLellan, Lewis, O'Brien, & Kleber, 2000), yet treatment resources tend to be limited by time, setting, and access. Although almost every primary care practice, mental health clinic, school, or criminal justice facility constantly makes contact with those suffering from addictions, these entities typically lack the staff or expertise to screen, assess, and refer such cases. Those who are referred will often be denied care, and those who access care will find agencies that are understaffed, underfunded, and so organizationally unstable that they find it difficult to implement evidence-based care (McLellan & Meyers, 2004). This is the case despite the fact that drug and alcohol treatment is becoming more professionalized and is increasingly turning toward evidence-based methods.

Such is the state of the tale of woe.

But something is happening in evidence-based care that is hopeful. Some of the very challenges faced by addiction treatment providers and agencies have placed this treatment area, which has long been pushed to the sidelines in terms of funding, scientific attention, and implementation, on the cutting edge of psychosocial treatment development, dissemination, and implementation. The present volume is meant to leverage that historical coincidence. There is a synergy that is made possible by the connection between two important streams: the creativity, vision, and sensitivities of treatment providers in the addictions field, and broadly focused innovations occurring in evidence-based care across the behavioral health disciplines.

Turning Problems into Assets: Advances in the Psychosocial Treatment of Addiction

Addiction treatment has been an innovator in behavioral health in many ways. Due to the nature of the problem it is addressing, the addiction field has long been interested in perspectives that go beyond a strictly medical model to focus on treating the whole person. For example, while issues involving spirituality have traditionally been barely mentioned in the evidence-based treatment of mental health problems, those issues are commonplace in addiction treatment and always have been. The importance of personal values, the creation of social and interpersonal recovery resources, and the role of self-acceptance were on the radar of addiction counselors long before they became mainstream in other behavioral health areas. The long list of comorbidities documented earlier has limited any tendency of addiction treatment providers to push human beings into narrow diagnostic categories, as if a human life could be captured by a syndromal label. The problems clients face are too numerous and too broad for that to appear to be useful. As a result, there has been more interest in treatment methods that have a broad focus, as well as more interest in digging down to the smaller set of key processes that underlie multiple problem areas. Providers want to cut to the chase—to focus on what is essential. Arcane details of diagnosis or complicated sequences of intervention simply are not central.

Treatment demand is so high and the number of treatment personnel so limited that the addictions field has had to emphasize modes of treatment delivery that are highly efficient. As a result, this field has pioneered in group treatments, in treatments that facilitate the use of self-help resources, and in very short interventions that empower long-term personal involvement in recovery. By necessity, the addictions field has become more comfortable with a kind of stepped-care model and has been more open to creating treatment programs that integrate professionals and paraprofessionals across a range of levels of expertise.

The 12-step tradition includes elements of community, spirituality, self-acceptance, honesty, conscious contact with spirituality, examination of values, willingness to make amends, compassion toward others, and action in the service of others. In a 12-step tradition these themes are generally cast in terms of "God as we understood him," but the themes and steps are not specifically religious or sectarian.

Although there are useful agonist and antagonist medications in some areas, such as smoking, alcohol addiction, and opiate addiction, there are no medications that claim to be cures, and even the medications that exist require psychosocial interventions. The federal funding apparatus has spent billions on medications for substance use, perhaps even more disproportionately over the last decade, but by a huge margin, providers utilize psychosocial approaches for addictive behaviors. In contrast to fairly widespread beliefs in regard to some mental health issues, few people seem to believe that a pill will soon arrive that will solve the problem of addictive behavior.

All of these features have made the addictions field well prepared for the message contained in this volume. Over the last decade or two, a set of evidence-based methods in the area of acceptance, mindfulness, motivation, and values have emerged that can empower existing traditions in addiction treatment. Some of these, such as motivational interviewing (MI; see Wagner, Ingersoll, & Rollnick, chapter 5 of this volume), emerged first in the addictions area. Others, such as dialectical behavior therapy (DBT; Linehan, 1993; see also Dimeff & Sayrs, chapter 2 of this volume) and acceptance and commitment therapy (ACT; Hayes, Strosahl, & Wilson, 1999, 2011; see also Wilson, Schnetzer, Flynn, & Kurz, chapter 1 of this volume), emerged first in mental health areas and then moved to the addictions field. Regardless of their original area of development, advocates for contextual methods arrive to the addiction area to find counselors who have been working with acceptance, mindfulness, motivation, and values for a long time. Indeed, the universally known Serenity Prayer is a virtual archetype of the centrality of the dialectic of acceptance and change—a central theme that is critical to these new methods based in acceptance, mindfulness, motivation, and values.

While these methods echo long-held sensitivities in the addictions field and some, such as MI, are already widely implemented there, as a body of work they bring something new to the table for addiction treatment providers. Other behavioral health approaches have learned things about acceptance, mindfulness, motivation, and values that haven't been widely discovered in the addictions field. Many of the major developments that have occurred in other areas of behavioral health regarding acceptance- and mindfulness-based methods could be helpful to drug and alcohol treatment providers and researchers.

That is a major purpose of the present volume. For the first time, a single volume gathers experts in dialectical behavior therapy (DBT; Dimeff & Sayrs, chapter 2), acceptance and commitment therapy (ACT; Wilson et al., chapter 1), motivational interviewing (MI; Wagner et al., chapter 5), mindfulness-based relapse prevention (MBRP; Bowen, Witkiewitz, & Chawla, chapter 3), and metacognitive therapy (MCT; Spada, Caselli, & Wells, chapter 4). They describe their model of addiction and the co-occurring disorders commonly seen in addiction, and link this model to their theoretical model of intervention. In addition, these experts provide a practical, step-by-step description of how the approach would typically treat addictive behaviors, and describe how the treatment approach is best integrated into addiction treatment settings. In these chapters, which comprise part 1 of the book, the authors also provide a summary of evidence relevant to the model and treatment approach, and address how the data inform such issues as the impact on co-occurring disorders. The sections that follow then bring these ideas to bear on a range of general and specific clinical topics. We will review these later in this chapter.

Contextual Cognitive Behavioral Therapy

The overarching label we are using for the methods in the present volume is "contextual cognitive behavioral therapy," or "contextual CBT." By *contextual CBT*, we mean therapies within an empirical, principle-focused approach that examine psychological events in terms of their context and functions (Hayes, 2004). These methods tend to emphasize contextual and experiential change strategies in addition to more direct and didactic ones, and seek the construction of broad, flexible, and effective repertoires over eliminative approaches to narrowly defined problems or syndromes. Further, most of these methods emphasize the relevance of such issues for clinicians as well as clients.

We are not trying to assert some primacy for CBT per se in using this label. This orientation touches upon other traditions, especially humanistic, existential, and other approaches that have long emphasized such uniquely human issues as values, purpose, meaning, self, and self-acceptance. What justifies calling them part of CBT is that many of these methods emerged from CBT, and that CBT is a broad umbrella that traditionally has covered most empirical, principle-focused approaches dealing with situated action. Some, however, insist that CBT should be limited to perspectives that adopt the view that thoughts are causal (e.g., Hofmann, 2010). That construction will not easily cover some of the methods discussed in this introduction, including ACT. To the extent that these methods are considered part of CBT, it is clear that they reformulate and synthesize previous generations of behavioral and cognitive therapy and carry that tradition forward into deeper or more complex questions, issues, and domains that were previously addressed primarily by other, less empirical traditions.

As will be seen in the chapters in part 1, these treatments take a functional and contextual approach to understanding psychological and behavioral problems (understanding the contextual factors that contribute to and maintain problems), often leading to principles that can apply to a range of topographically distinct problems. Thus, these approaches tend to apply equally across a whole range of problems counselors are likely to see.

The distinction between content and context is often made by developers of the methods discussed in this introduction. For example, Segal, Teasdale, and Williams have stated, "Unlike CBT, there is little emphasis in MBCT [mindfulness-based cognitive therapy] on changing the content of thoughts; rather, the emphasis is on changing awareness of and relationship to thoughts" (2004, p. 54). The developer of MCT has emphasized that while "CBT is concerned with testing the validity of thoughts...MCT is primarily concerned with modifying the way in which thoughts are experienced and regulated" (Wells, 2008, p. 652). ACT developers have stated that "the ACT model points to the context of verbal activity as the key element, rather than the verbal content. It is not that people are thinking the wrong thing—the problem is thought itself and how the verbal community supports its excessive use as a mode of behavioral regulation" (Hayes et al., 1999, p. 49).

This focus on contextual principles and process is reflected in the use of interventions based on acceptance, mindfulness, and values within contextual CBTs. These treatments focus on the role of motivational processes and how individuals relate to their own thoughts, feelings, and bodily sensations, rather than the specific content of these experiences, in understanding the development, maintenance, and exacerbation of psychological and behavioral problems. Acceptance and mindfulness methods are used to teach clients a more open, aware, and flexible way of relating to their internal experiences, seeking to alter the function of internal experiences, rather than their appearance or frequency (Hayes, 2004). These interventions are combined with methods that seek to identify and contextualize targets for behavioral change within clients' larger life context, delving into issues such as motivation, purpose, and meaning.

In the following sections we examine the common core features of contextual CBT that unite the various treatments discussed in this volume. We provide examples from each of the chapters to highlight these commonalities and introduce the chapters to come. We encourage you to continue to note common contextual themes between these approaches, as well as points of divergence, as you read through the chapters that follow.

Encouraging Mindfulness of the Present Moment

The contextual CBTs reviewed in this book share a common focus on helping clients develop an awareness of experiences in the present moment in a way that is flexible, nonjudgmental, and nonreactive, a process that is generally referred to as *mindfulness*.

Individuals struggling with addiction often develop habitual patterns in which addictive behaviors occur automatically in response to triggers, with little active intention or awareness. Breaking patterns of use is difficult when clients are unaware of situations where they are likely to use and when they impulsively engage in addictive behaviors in reaction to triggers before they have an opportunity to even consider abstaining. Mindfulness interventions seek to interrupt this process by encouraging a flexible and nonreactive awareness of triggers, providing a space from which clients can notice when triggers occur, and actively choose how to respond to them. For example, Bowen and colleagues (chapter 3) describe how meditation exercises are used in MBRP to increase clients' mindful awareness of internal experiences, beginning with focusing on the breath and, over time, moving to urges, cravings, and other internal experiences related to substance use. Clients are taught to apply these mindfulness skills outside of session when triggers actually occur. For example, clients are taught to use the *SOBER* breathing space technique in which they are instructed to *stop* when encountering a trigger, *observe* the internal experiences, focus on the *breath*, *expand* awareness to other experiences in the present, and finally *respond* mindfully to the situation.

Individuals who struggle with addictive behaviors are frequently unaware of the effects and consequences of their addiction. They may hold unrealistic beliefs about how an addictive behavior works for them, and fail to notice negative consequences that might otherwise lead to a decision to abstain. Mindfulness-based interventions can increase clients' sensitivity to the effects and consequences of addictive behaviors and how those behaviors fit with their goals. Spada and colleagues (chapter 4) describe one such strategy in MCT, called *situational attentional refocusing*, which seeks to increase clients' awareness of important features of the present moment. For example, clients might be asked to focus on noticing the effects of drinking, which can help them identify when a goal for a drinking episode has been reached, which could support more moderate use, or to notice the actual effects of alcohol relative to their expectancies and metacognitions. Wagner and colleagues (chapter 5) similarly describe how MI counselors seek to elicit client discussion of the consequences and effects of addictive behaviors, and whether their behavior and its consequences are consistent with their lower- and higher-order goals and values.

In some cases, a lack of present-moment awareness may be due to being lost in one's thoughts, such as ruminating about the past or worrying about the future. In addition to taking attention away from the present, these cognitive patterns can increase a whole host of distressing thoughts and emotions, particularly when clients become judgmental of their experiences or themselves. This can serve as a further trigger for addictive behaviors. Mindfulness interventions seek to improve clients' ability to step out of these maladaptive cognitive patterns by observing the process of thinking (i.e., to notice a thought as just a thought), rather than being caught up in the content of thoughts. For example, Wilson and colleagues (chapter 1) describe how, in ACT, counselors help clients notice when they are caught up in thoughts and self-stories and then reorient to the present moment, such as through a breathing meditation exercise. Spada and colleagues (chapter 4) similarly describe how detached mindfulness is applied in MCT as a means of disengaging from rumination and worry through approaches such as the free-association task, in which clients practice noticing their reactions to a series of words recited by the counselor as just thoughts and emotions, rather than as representations of reality.

These interventions fit within the umbrella of contextual treatments, because they focus on altering the context in which clients relate to their environment and internal experiences. They shift from automatically reacting to their thoughts and feelings without awareness of the consequences of doing so, to being present and aware of their experiences in the moment in a way that provides more flexibility and choice in how to respond. Although the form and intensity of the internal experiences themselves may not change with these interventions, the context in which they are experienced is altered in a way that allows clients to be more aware, nonreactive, and compassionate toward whatever is present.

Encouraging Acceptance of Internal Experiences

A typical approach in traditional treatments is to focus on identifying and altering the internal experiences that contribute to addictive behaviors, and to mental health problems more generally. This may include restructuring irrational cognitions or pharmacotherapy designed to reduce cravings, withdrawal symptoms, and negative affect.

Contextual CBTs are united by a common emphasis on alternative ways of relating to these experiences, involving consciously attending to and opening up to difficult internal experiences, rather than rigidly focusing on trying to avoid, distract, change, or otherwise control their occurrence. Clients learn to allow difficult internal experiences to be there, without acting on or wallowing in them, or trying to fight with or change them directly. This emphasis on acceptance is based on theoretical models and empirical evidence indicating that unwillingness to experience thoughts, feelings, cravings, and other internal experiences plays a key role in addiction.

Addictive behaviors can often serve as a means of avoiding or otherwise trying to control difficult internal experiences. Distressing thoughts and feelings are a common precipitant to use and relapse (Baker, Piper, McCarthy, Majeskie, & Fiore, 2004; Witkiewitz & Villarroel, 2009), and using substances to cope with difficult internal experiences is a strong predictor of addiction (Kuntsche, Knibbe, Gmel, & Engels, 2005). Although addictive behaviors can sometimes provide temporary relief from aversive internal experiences, they often lead to an exacerbation of these experiences over time, due in part to the negative consequences of addiction (e.g., relationship difficulties, stigma from others, shame, or withdrawal symptoms).

Contextual CBTs seek to alter the functional relationship between difficult internal experiences and addictive behaviors through acceptance-based interventions, such that distressing thoughts and feelings can be compassionately acknowledged without necessitating avoidance strategies such as substance use. For example, Bowen and colleagues (chapter 3) describe how meditation is used in MBRP to teach participants to mindfully notice difficult thoughts and feelings without reacting to them (e.g., giving in or fighting). Consistent with this approach,

MBRP has been found to decrease the relationship between depressed mood and cravings, which subsequently predicts lower substance use rates (Witkiewitz & Bowen, 2010). Stotts and Masuda (chapter 8) provide examples of acceptance interventions in ACT, such as an exercise in which clients carry a card with them throughout the week that represents a difficult internal experience, which helps them learn how to make room for such experiences while continuing to engage in chosen activities. Lillis (chapter 11) provides similar examples from DBT for binge eating, including opposite action, in which clients engage in behaviors that are directly opposite to urges associated with emotions (e.g., making behavioral approaches in the face of anxiety, despite the urge to avoid or escape).

Clients may be unwilling to accept the reality of their current life situation, past events, or even themselves. Addictive behaviors may be turned to as a means of trying to escape this reality. Wagner and colleagues (chapter 5) describe how MI practitioners encourage acceptance of oneself and one's situation in therapeutic interactions by having an open, empathic, and accepting stance toward clients and wherever they are in the process of considering change. Luoma and Kohlenberg (chapter 7) describe a number of acceptance and mindfulness strategies that can be used to promote clients' self-acceptance and self-compassion within the context of treating self-stigma and shame, such as an exercise in which clients wear a name tag with a difficult self-judgment as a way to practice willingness and defusion from self-evaluations. It is important to note that accepting oneself and the reality of one's situation does not imply giving up; rather, it means acknowledging what is there as part of the process of looking toward changes one wants to make.

A common strategy that clients use for attempting abstinence is to try to suppress cravings and urges. However, attempting to cope with craving cues through suppression can paradoxically lead to an increase in their occurrence (e.g., Palfai, Colby, Monti, & Rohsenow, 1997). Furthermore, responding to cravings in this manner reinforces the notion that cravings are bad and must be avoided at all costs or else one will use, which can actually increase the chances that cravings lead to substance use in the future. Alternatively, researchers have found that when people are more accepting of these automatic motivations for substance use, they are less likely to engage in substance use, even when automatic motivations are relatively strong (e.g., Ostafin & Marlatt, 2008).

Acceptance interventions seek to encourage clients to notice cravings and urges for what they are, without trying to control them or giving in to them. For example, the DBT chapter by Dimeff and Sayrs (chapter 2) describes urge surfing, in which individuals ride out their urges to use like a surfer on a wave, staying in contact with the urges while not falling into them. Similarly, Spada and colleagues (chapter 4) describe how MCT targets clients' use of suppression strategies to cope with thoughts about alcohol through a variety of metacognitive approaches, such as exploring the workability of suppression and teaching detached mindfulness as an alternative stance in regard to alcohol-related thoughts.

Clients are often uncomfortable, or even unwilling, to practice acceptance at first, given that they typically have a long history of avoidance. Wagner and colleagues (chapter 5) describe how, from a MI approach, acceptance is treated the same as other behavior change targets, and clinicians therefore use the same strategies in promoting acceptance as they employ with other targets for change. This shares similarities with the approach often taken in ACT in which counselors openly explore the workability of trying to control one's internal experiences to help clients determine whether their experiential avoidance strategies actually create more distress and take them further away from their values.

These acceptance-based interventions play a key role within a contextual approach. Such interventions create a focus on altering the function of internal experiences within the larger behavioral context; for example, they establish shame and anxiety as emotions to simply notice and acknowledge, rather than "bad" experiences that must be avoided through substance use. The use of such strategies is an important aspect of why the therapies reviewed in this volume are considered contextual CBTs.

Focusing on Values and Motivation

Another core feature of contextual CBTs is an emphasis on clients' personal values and motivation. These therapies seek to meet clients where they are in regard to their addictive behavior and to help them find motivation for change within their unique life situations. Although reducing or eliminating an addictive behavior is generally a primary target, this is often subsumed under an overarching goal of helping the person live a valued, meaningful life.

Addictive behaviors occur within a larger life context in which motivators for both continued use and abstinence are probably present. At times, this contributes to resistance or ambivalence toward change in therapy. Navigating this dialectic between opposing motivations and helping clients identify how the addictive behavior stands in relation to their values and goals is central in many contextual CBTs. Wagner and colleagues (chapter 5) provide a theoretical model for understanding this process based on MI. The authors highlight how MI counselors work inside this process to resolve ambivalence and increase commitment to change. Examples of such strategies include exploring clients' values and goals in relation to current actions and their consequences, and helping clients notice discrepancies between what they care about and want versus what they are doing.

This highlights a common strategy for enhancing motivation for change that is used in many contextual CBTs: examining the workability of one's actions relative to one's personal goals and values. For example, Spada and colleagues (chapter 4) describe how metacognitive beliefs about coping strategies can be targeted by having clients consider the advantages and disadvantages of the coping behavior and whether alternatives would be more effective for their goals. Similarly, Wilson and colleagues (chapter 1) describe ACT exercises in which clients are asked to explore how their addiction has impacted living consistently with personal values. Such an approach requires counselors to take an open stance toward clients' behaviors, using clients' values and experiences as a guide in identifying targets for behavior change, rather than what the counselor believes is most effective or thinks clients should do.

Clients' personal values provide a context for motivating changes and guiding courses of action. However, some clients may have difficulty identifying their values, or their values may not be highly salient to them. In these cases, values clarification interventions can be helpful. Luoma and Kohlenberg (chapter 7) provide examples of ACT values clarification interventions, such as the tombstone exercise, in which clients are asked what they would want their epitaph to say, if they could choose.

Clarifying and highlighting clients' values can provide a useful motivator for acceptance work and persisting in actions despite difficult internal barriers. For example, Stotts and Masuda (chapter 8) describe the importance of revisiting clients' values during difficult stages of detoxification, when withdrawal symptoms, difficult emotions, and thoughts about quitting are likely to occur. Similarly, Bricker and Wyszynski (chapter 9) describe how values are explored in relation to quitting smoking, which helps frame the difficult path of quitting within the context of what motivates and matters to the client.

Often, clients have engaged in addictive behaviors at the cost of other valued patterns of activity. As meaningful and pleasant activities and events decrease, they may then turn to their addiction even more as a source of comfort and to avoid the pain associated with lost values. Ultimately, the goal of many contextual CBTs is to help clients reengage in valued activities and build the life they want to live. Engaging in valued living can further establish a context that supports abstinence, and working toward abstinence, or at least healthy use, can further support valued living.

Thus, contextual CBTs include a focus on identifying and engaging in valued activities. For example, Wilson and colleagues (chapter 1) describe ACT exercises in which clients are asked to mindfully reflect on their values, meditating on ways they haven't been engaging in values within important life domains, what is meaningful to them in these domains, and what they would want to bring more of to each domain. Exercises are used to identify specific actions that clients can take that are in line with their values, such as the Valued Action Worksheet, which asks clients to list a number of values-based actions, both small and large, that they might engage in. Bowen and colleagues (chapter 3) describe a similar process within the later sessions of MBRP in which clients focus on increasing engagement in what they term "nourishing" activities and use mindfulness meditation to enhance positive experiences.

This focus on clients' personal values and motivation represents another core feature within a contextual approach. These interventions place an emphasis on how current behaviors and potential targets for behavior change fit within the larger context of clients' lives and higher-order goals and values. Bringing such issues to bear in therapy provides a powerful method for identifying treatment goals that ring true with clients, and a touchstone that can be continuously revisited to help motivate and sustain meaningful changes in clients' lives.

Taking a Broad, Functional Approach

Addictive patterns of behavior can develop in a remarkable variety of areas beyond substance use, including eating, gambling, sex, shopping, and Internet use, among many others. Clients struggling with addiction are often experiencing a range of other psychological, behavioral, and life problems that can both contribute to and occur as a result of their addiction. This presents a challenge to treatment providers in terms of both prioritizing treatment targets and having the necessary interventions at hand to meet the range of problems to be addressed.

An advantage of focusing on contextual principles such as mindfulness, acceptance, and values is that these processes are likely to apply to a broad range of topographically distinct but functionally similar problems. Contextual CBT methods provide models that can deal with the complexity and variety of problems within addiction. For example, although Spada and colleagues (chapter 4) focus on applying the self-regulatory executive function model specifically to problem drinking, it has also been successfully applied to a range of issues, including depression and a number of anxiety disorders. Wagner and colleagues (chapter 5) describe how MI can be applied to a range of addictive behaviors and co-occurring disorders using the same general approach of targeting motivation and commitment to goals for behavior change. Wilson and colleagues (chapter 1) also note that psychological flexibility is a transdiagnostic model that applies to a broad range of psychological problems. In line with this, many of the contextual CBTs included in this volume have been found to be effective for a broad range of problems that may co-occur with addictive behaviors, including depression, anxiety disorders, eating disorders, chronic health problems, and, in the case of some contextual CBTs, even borderline personality disorder and psychosis (see Hayes, Villatte, Levin, & Hildebrandt, 2011, for a review of the empirical evidence for contextual CBTs).

Thus, many contextual CBTs provide methods that can target a broad array of problems within a single treatment approach. These therapies apply not just to drug and alcohol use, but to the full range of addictive behaviors and even many co-occurring problems, which is important because drug and alcohol counselors are often called upon to help in these areas. One advantage of bringing this way of thinking into addiction work is that the conceptual and technological skills required are transportable when dealing with people with a dual diagnosis (those also dealing with mental health issues), without having to assemble complex teams, which can be hard to set up for a variety of reasons, including limited financial and staff resources.

We have highlighted this unique feature of contextual CBTs in the current volume by including a series of chapters in part 2 of the book describing how such treatments can be applied to a number of specific problems. Chapters are provided on applying contextual CBTs to self-stigma and shame (Luoma and Kohlenberg, chapter 7), detoxification (Stotts & Masuda, chapter 8), smoking (Bricker & Wyszynski, chapter 9), gambling (Toneatto, chapter 10), binge eating (Lillis, chapter 11), and pornography addiction (Crosby & Twohig, chapter 12), and even on applying such methods to counselors themselves (Sayrs, chapter 6). In these chapters, the authors describe how theoretical models within contextual CBTs, including ACT, DBT, MI, and other mindfulness-based therapies, can be applied to these particular problem areas and provide specific examples of treatment interventions.

The chapters in part 2 of this volume also provide an opportunity to explore unique issues in applying contextual CBTs to treating specific addictive behaviors. For example, Stotts and Masuda (chapter 8) describe how therapy can be integrated within the stages and context of detoxification, as well as issues related to working in a multidisciplinary team. Lillis (chapter 11) highlights features specific to treating binge eating, such as coping with the near-constant availability of unhealthy food and dealing with weight-related stigma. Crosby and Twohig (chapter 12) describe clinical issues in treating pornography addiction, including navigating the frequent high-stakes context in which any relapse is perceived as devastating, and working with religious clients who hold the belief that thoughts related to pornography are as bad as the actual behavior of viewing pornography.

Taking a contextual approach to understanding human difficulties, defined more in terms of principles and processes than topographical symptoms and syndromes, has allowed the development of theoretical models that apply to the complex and multiproblem clients often encountered in addiction treatment. This highlights a key feature and advantage of contextual CBTs and a theme of these approaches that is observable throughout the chapters in this volume.

Applying Therapies to Difficult to Treat and Novel Problems

Empowered by a contextual approach to understanding behavior, there has also been a tendency to apply contextual CBTs to areas that are particularly difficult to treat or have traditionally been outside of a CBT approach. For example, Luoma and Kohlenberg (chapter 7) provide a model for the role of acceptance, mindfulness, and values processes in treating self-stigma and shame, outlining a specific ACT protocol based on this model. Dimeff and Sayrs (chapter 2) describe how dialectical behavior therapy for substance use disorders (DBT-SUD) can be applied to a population that's particularly difficult to treat: clients with comorbid borderline personality disorder and substance use disorders. Crosby and Twohig (chapter 12) describe another innovative application of ACT: treating pornography addiction, an area that has received little attention from treatment development researchers thus far.

The contextual principles and processes outlined in these chapters can serve as analytical tools for understanding and treating a range of presenting problems, including the more challenging or unique clinical populations and issues within addiction. We have purposefully included chapters on some of the more difficult-to-treat problem areas and novel treatment applications to highlight this point.

Applying Contextual CBTs to Counselors Themselves

The broad application of contextual CBTs has also moved beyond various client presentations to considering the role of acceptance, mindfulness, and values processes with counselors themselves. This application of contextual CBTs seeks to both enhance the effectiveness of counselors with their clients and improve counselors' health and well-being more generally.

A common way contextual CBTs are applied to counselors is within the therapeutic relationship. By applying acceptance, mindfulness, and values processes to themselves within therapeutic interactions, counselors can model skills with clients and also create meaningful therapeutic moments that make transformative changes possible for clients. The therapy transcripts provided by Wilson and colleagues (chapter 1) provide a number of examples in which the counselor brings a present-focused and accepting approach to interacting with clients as they work with difficult thoughts and feelings and explore personal values. A curious and compassionate attention is brought to bear on understanding the client's experiences, while the counselor also models a willingness to make room for whatever difficult experiences might show up in this process. Similarly, Bowen and colleagues (chapter 3) provide examples of how MBRP facilitators model a mindful stance toward internal experiences in group discussions, guiding participants to notice experiences in the present moment for what they are, rather than getting lost in thoughts. Wagner and colleagues (chapter 5) outline a structured set of communication skills (OARS: Open questioning, Affirming, Reflective listening, and Summarizing) that MI practitioners use to model empathy, openness, and acceptance toward clients and to facilitate collaborative therapeutic interactions.

Some contextual CBTs encourage therapists to maintain some form of personal mindfulness practice or other similar practice to further heighten their skill and expertise in applying these processes to themselves and their clients. For example, Bowen and colleagues (chapter 3) state that MBRP practitioners typically have a significant history of formal meditation practice. This provides an important experiential understanding of acceptance and mindfulness, which can help clinicians more effectively guide their clients in engaging in these processes.

Another important reason for applying contextual CBTs to counselors is to tackle the problem of burnout. Addiction counselors often work in stressful environments with limited resources and challenging clients. In this context, counselors can easily start to feel overwhelmed and as though there is a lack of rewarding experiences in their work. Some contextual CBTs approach this problem head-on by including an explicit focus on maintaining counselor motivation and well-being within the therapy model. For example, Dimeff and Sayrs (chapter 2) describe an entire modality within DBT-SUD that focuses on counselor burnout and motivation, primarily through the functions of the consultation team. The chapter by Sayrs (chapter 6) has an in-depth focus on this issue specifically, giving practical suggestions on how counselors can apply acceptance, mindfulness, and values to reduce burnout and increase well-being both in and out of work situations.

Embracing a contextual approach means that the counselor's psychological process is part of the equation in effectively treating clients. Bringing the counselor's own process into the case conceptualization and therapeutic model can be a challenge, but it is supported by the assumption that the factors thought to contribute to clients' suffering and growth are likely to apply to counselors as well. This creates unique clinical opportunities to demonstrate and work through processes in the room with clients for the sake of instigating and modeling how clients can do the same in their lives, while also enhancing the therapeutic relationship. At an even broader level, this brings counselors' own well-being into the picture, helping them move toward what they value in clinical work and in their lives more broadly, while also working with stress and burnout when they impede clinical work or quality of life.

Integrating Acceptance, Mindfulness, and Values with Other Interventions

Many contextual CBTs incorporate traditional cognitive and behavioral techniques and principles. These additions are purposeful and driven by theoretical models that specify how such interventions fit within the context of other treatment components and the overall therapeutic approach.

A common addition is evidence-based behavior change methods targeted to a specific problem area. This provides the advantage of taking a transdiagnostic approach to treatment focused on common psychological processes while still including targeted behavior change interventions known to be effective for specific clinical problems being treated. For example, Bowen and colleagues (chapter 3) describe how MBRP incorporates skills found to be helpful in traditional relapse prevention, including identifying situations that may trigger substance use and learning alternative behaviors for these situations. Similarly, Dimeff and Sayrs (chapter 2) describe a number of additional intervention strategies that are included in DBT when treating substance use disorders, some of which were developed in other treatments, such as urge surfing and stimulus control strategies for substance use cues.

Additional cognitive and behavioral interventions are sometimes integrated into contextual CBTs for purposes other than those for which they are classically used. For example, behavioral activation strategies may be used in ACT, but in the service of building values-based patterns of activity rather than as a means to eliminate symptoms per se. Similarly, many contextual CBTs include some exposure-like procedures related to cues and cravings for the addictive behavior. However, the goal of these exercises is to increase clients' awareness and flexibility in responding to stimuli that often have precipitated substance use in the past, rather than to try to reduce the intensity of cravings and urges through habituation, as has sometimes been the goal in traditional cue exposure interventions. It is also important to note that not all traditional CBT or other treatment technologies are consistent with contextual CBTs, and that technologies that directly contradict a treatment model (e.g., cognitive disputation or thought stopping) may have to be abandoned if they cannot be changed to fit the underlying model (e.g., linking cognitive reappraisal strategies to the promotion of cognitive flexibility or linking relaxation techniques to letting go rather than winning a war with anxiety).

Some contextual CBTs have integrated acceptance strategies with methods that explicitly target changing thoughts, feelings, and sensations. The potential for inconsistencies and confusion from these two opposing strategies is avoided by providing a coherent model for how acceptance and change can be integrated. For example, Dimeff and Sayrs (chapter 2) describe how DBT takes a dialectical approach, which balances and synthesizes the opposing processes of accepting one's internal experiences while engaging in change strategies to improve these conditions. The authors note the consistency between this approach and the Serenity Prayer, which is also consistent with many other contextual CBT approaches, where the use of acceptance or change strategies is dictated by what works—accepting what can't be changed while working to change what can be.

Within the approaches reviewed in this book, MI is somewhat unique. As Wagner and colleagues (chapter 5) describe it, MI is a cousin to contextual CBTs, with some similarities even though it originally emerged from a distinct philosophy and treatment approach. The chapters by Wagner and colleagues (chapter 5)and by Bricker and Wyszynski (chapter 9) provide an in-depth discussion of the similarities and differences between these approaches. Given the consistencies noted between the two approaches, the authors suggest that MI might actually be used in combination with some of the other contextual CBTs; for example, MI could be used to engage clients early in treatment, prior to taking a more skills-based approach.

Many of the chapters describe how contextual CBTs can be integrated within a larger addiction treatment program. Contextual CBTs are consistent with a number of treatment approaches. For example, Wilson and colleagues (chapter 1) describe how ACT is consistent with and can be integrated with a number of therapies, including 12-step treatments. Similarly, Dimeff and Sayrs (chapter 2) describe how pharmacotherapy can serve a useful role within DBT-SUD. In addition, contextual CBTs can fit well within a variety of settings. For example, Stotts and Masuda (chapter 8) describe the use of ACT within a detoxification setting, and Luoma and Kohlenberg (chapter 7) describe an ACT protocol that was integrated within a residential addiction treatment program. In some cases, contextual CBTs can be integrated as a relatively small part of a larger treatment program through brief interventions, which have been shown to have a substantial impact on addiction outcomes (e.g., Bricker, Mann, Marek, Liu, & Peterson, 2010; Burke, Arkowitz, & Menchola, 2003; Luoma, Kohlenberg, Hayes, & Fletcher, 2012). For example, the group treatment described by Luoma and Kohlenberg (chapter 7) involves only three two-hour sessions yet has long-lasting effects on substance use, making it a brief approach that can easily be integrated within a residential program. Similarly, Bricker and Wyszynski (chapter 9) highlight how both ACT and MI can be conducted in a brief intervention format, including via alternative modalities to face-to-face therapy, such as phone or web-based interventions.

The contextual CBTs reviewed in this book thus seem promising not only in meeting the needs of addiction counselors working with difficult and complex patients, but also in providing approaches that can be integrated within existing practices and programs.

Summary

This volume represents the first attempt in a book-length form to synthesize and review the variety of contextual CBTs that have been developed and applied to addiction. The following chapters describe cutting-edge treatment approaches rooted in acceptance, mindfulness, and values work. Reviews of the current research evidence for these approaches is provided by experts in the field, along with suggestions and comments on future directions that need to be taken in this work. The chapters also provide examples of how to apply these approaches to a variety of addictive behaviors and issues.

We hope this book will serve as a motivator and guide for applying contextual CBTs within the field of addiction, broadly defined. We have attempted to serve the interests of addiction counselors and other practitioners, providing useful strategies and case conceptualization tools that are helpful in practice. We have tried to address the needs of researchers wanting to understand the underlying theoretical models for these contextual CBTs, the state of evidence supporting them, and how such approaches can be brought to bear on the complex problems faced in addiction. Finally, we hope to motivate students to continue to learn about contextual CBTs for addictive behaviors and to consider how these approaches might fit within their training and career goals. As such, this book is not meant to be an ending for any of the major audiences we are trying to serve; rather, it is meant to serve as a door into a major wing of evidence-based addiction practice and research. The contextual CBTs hold out great promise for an area in which the problems are enormous, the cases are complex, and the treatment resources are limited. That is indeed a bad combination, but if we work together, it may not be an insurmountable one.

References

Baker, T. B., Piper, M. E., McCarthy, D. E., Majeskie, M. R., & Fiore, M. C. (2004). Addiction motivation reformulated: An affective processing model of negative reinforcement. *Psychological Review, 111,* 33-51.

Barnes, G. M., Welte, J. W., Hoffman, J. H., & Tidwell, M. C. O. (2011). The co-occurrence of gambling with substance use and conduct disorder among youth in the U.S. *American Journal on Addictions, 20,* 166-173.

Bricker, J. B., Mann, S. L., Marek, P. M., Liu, J., & Peterson, A. V. (2010). Telephone-delivered acceptance and commitment therapy for adult smoking cessation: A feasibility study. *Nicotine and Tobacco Research, 12,* 454-458.

Burke, B. L., Arkowitz, H., & Menchola, M. (2003). The efficacy of motivational interviewing: A meta-analysis of controlled clinical trials. *Journal of Consulting and Clinical Psychology, 71,* 843-861.

Donovan, C., & McEwan, R. (1995). A review of the literature examining the relationship between alcohol use and HIV-related sexual risk-taking in young people. *Addiction, 90,* 319-328.

Grant, B. F., & Hasin, D. S. (1999). Suicidal ideation among the United States drinking population: Results from the National Longitudinal Alcohol Epidemiological Survey. *Journal of Studies on Alcohol, 60,* 422-429.

Gupta, R., & Derevensky, J. L. (1997). Familial and social influences on juvenile gambling behavior. *Journal of Gambling Studies, 13,* 179-192.

Hayes, S. C. (2004). Acceptance and commitment therapy, relational frame theory, and the third wave of behavior therapy. *Behavior Therapy, 35,* 639-665.

Hayes, S. C., Strosahl, K. D., & Wilson, K. G. (1999). *Acceptance and commitment therapy: An experiential approach to behavior change.* New York: Guilford Press.

Hayes, S. C., Strosahl, K., & Wilson, K. G. (2011). *Acceptance and commitment therapy: The process and practice of mindful change* (2nd ed.). New York: Guilford Press.

Hayes, S. C., Villatte, M., Levin, M., & Hildebrandt, M. (2011). Open, aware, and active: Contextual approaches as an emerging trend in the behavioral and cognitive therapies. *Annual Review of Clinical Psychology, 7,* 141-168.

Hofmann, S. G. (2010). *An introduction to modern CBT: Psychological solutions to mental health problems.* New York: Wiley-Blackwell.

Hudson, J. I., Hiripi, E., Pope, H. G., & Kessler, R. C. (2007). The prevalence and correlates of eating disorders in the National Comorbidity Survey Replication. *Biological Psychiatry, 61,* 348-358.

Jablensky, A., McGrath, J., & Morgan, V. (1999). Australians living with psychotic illness, 1997-1998. Preliminary results of the study on low-prevalence disorders as part of the Australian National Mental Health Survey. *Australian and New Zealand Journal of Psychiatry, 33,* A30.

Kessler, R. C., Chiu, W. T., Demler, O., Merikangas, K. R., & Walters, E. E. (2005). Prevalence, severity, and comorbidity of 12-month *DSM-IV* disorders in the National Comorbidity Survey Replication. *Archives of General Psychiatry, 62,* 617-627.

Kessler, R. C., Nelson, C. B., & McGonagle, K. A. (1996). The epidemiology of co-occurring addictive and mental disorders: Implications for prevention and service utilization. *American Journal of Orthopsychiatry, 66,* 17-31.

Kuntsche, E., Knibbe, R., Gmel, G., & Engels, R. (2005). Why do young people drink? A review of drinking motives. *Clinical Psychology Review, 25,* 841-861.

Levin, M., Lillis, J., & Hayes, S. C. (in press). When is online pornography viewing problematic among college males? Examining the moderating role of experiential avoidance. *Sexual Addiction and Compulsivity.*

Linehan, M. M. (1993). *Cognitive behavioral therapy of borderline personality disorder.* New York: Guilford Press.

Luoma, J. B., Kohlenberg, B. S., Hayes, S. C., & Fletcher, L. B. (2012). Slow and steady wins the race: A randomized clinical trial of acceptance and commitment therapy targeting shame in substance use disorders. *Journal of Consulting and Clinical Psychology, 80,* 43-53.

McLellan, A. T., Lewis, D. C., O'Brien, C. P., & Kleber, H. (2000). Drug dependence, a chronic medical illness: Implications for treatment, insurance, and outcomes evaluation. *Journal of the American Medical Association, 284,* 1689-1695.

McLellan, A. T., & Meyers, K. (2004). Contemporary addiction treatment: A review of systems problems for adults and adolescents. *Biological Psychiatry, 56,* 764-770.

Mueser, K. T., Rosenberg, S. D., Drake, R. E., Miles, K. M., Wolford, G., Vidaver, R., et al. (1999). Conduct disorder, antisocial personality disorder, and substance use disorders in schizophrenia and major affective disorders. *Journal of Studies on Alcohol, 60,* 278-284.

Ostafin, B. D., & Marlatt, G. A. (2008). Surfing the urge: Experiential acceptance moderates the relation between automatic alcohol motivation and hazardous drinking. *Journal of Social and Clinical Psychology, 27,* 404-418.

Palfai, T. P., Colby, S. M., Monti, P. M., & Rohsenow, D. J. (1997). Effects of suppressing the urge to drink on smoking topography: A preliminary study. *Psychology of Addictive Behaviors, 11,* 115-123.

Pernanen, K. (1991). *Alcohol in human violence.* New York: Guilford Press.

Schuckit, M. A. (2006). Comorbidity between substance use disorders and psychiatric conditions. *Addiction, 101,* 76-88.

Segal, Z. V., Teasdale, J. D., & Williams, J. M. G. (2004). Mindfulness-based cognitive therapy: Theoretical rationale and empirical status. In S. C. Hayes, V. M. Follette, & M. M. Linehan (Eds.), *Mindfulness and acceptance: Expanding the cognitive-behavioral tradition.* New York: Guilford Press.

Substance Abuse and Mental Health Services Administration. (2011). *Results from the 2010 National Survey on Drug Use and Health: Summary of National Findings.* Rockville, MD: Substance Abuse and Mental Health Services Administration.

Wells, A. (2008). Metacognitive therapy: Cognition applied to regulating cognition. *Behavioral and Cognitive Psychotherapy, 36,* 651-658.

Welte, J. W., Barnes, G. M., Tidwell, M. C. O., & Hoffman, J. H. (2011). Gambling and problem gambling across the lifespan. *Journal of Gambling Studies, 27,* 49-61.

Witkiewitz, K., & Bowen, S. (2010). Depression, craving, and substance use following a randomized trial of mindfulness-based relapse prevention. *Journal of Consulting and Clinical Psychology, 78,* 362-374.

Witkiewitz, K., & Villarroel, N. (2009). Dynamic association between negative affect and alcohol lapses following alcohol treatment. *Journal of Consulting and Clinical Psychology, 77,* 633-644.

PART 1

Treatment Models

CHAPTER 1

Acceptance and Commitment Therapy for Addiction

Kelly G. Wilson

Lindsay W. Schnetzer

Maureen K. Flynn

A. Solomon Kurz

University of Mississippi

*A*cceptance and commitment therapy (ACT, pronounced as a word) is an approach designed to increase psychological flexibility—a way of living characterized by openness, awareness, and engagement (Hayes, Strosahl, & Wilson, 2011). Psychological flexibility can be described as willingness to accept all aspects of one's experience without engaging in unnecessary avoidance behaviors, when doing so serves the development of patterns of values-congruent activity.

ACT is grounded in traditional behavior analysis and relational frame theory (RFT)—a contemporary behavioral model of language and cognition (Hayes, Barnes-Holmes, & Roche, 2001; Törneke, 2010). The psychological flexibility model describes a set of six functional processes underlying much human suffering and adaptability: acceptance, defusion, present-moment awareness, self processes, values-based living, and committed action. The model describes functioning along a continuum, and the processes that are cultivated during treatment to promote psychological flexibility are aimed at the prevention of psychological difficulties in the future.

The psychological flexibility model is *transdiagnostic*, meaning it identifies common mechanisms underlying an array of psychological difficulties. Transdiagnostic models are becoming increasingly common in the cognitive behavioral treatment development community (Barlow, Allen, & Choate, 2004; Mansell, Harvey, Watkins, & Shafran, 2009) and offer an alternative to the dominant diagnostic system based on syndromal classification (American Psychiatric Association, 2011).

One advantage of a transdiagnostic approach is that it allows researchers and clinicians to address the problem of comorbidity in a more effective and efficient way, in terms of both diagnosis and treatment. Among those who meet criteria for a substance use disorder, rates of comorbidity are quite high, approaching 18% for co-occurring anxiety disorders and 20% for co-occurring mood disorders (Grant et al., 2006). Whereas a clinician using syndromal classification may attempt to treat one diagnosis before addressing the other, a clinician using a transdiagnostic approach would attempt to identify and treat core processes that have led to a variety of symptom clusters. In this approach, many problems that are formally distinct become functionally unitary.

A description of the psychological flexibility model follows, with specific attention to addiction and related symptom presentation or patterns of dysfunction. Next, cultivation of the positive pole of each process is delineated as an approach to assessment and treatment.

A Psychological Flexibility Model of Addiction

Within the psychological flexibility model, addiction is conceived as a learned pattern of behavior. Although the etiology of addiction is somewhat controversial, few would argue against the idea that addiction involves entrenched patterns of behavior that require modification.

Although the six core processes are presented here as relatively distinct, it is important to note that there is a considerable degree of interaction among them. Any given stream of behavior could be viewed in terms of any of the six processes. For instance, when examining values, it is often necessary to consider the ways in which fears, vulnerabilities, and avoidance (nonacceptance) and thoughts of inevitable failure (fusion) may distance people from behaving in accordance with their values. Therefore, intervention strategies might focus on one or several processes.

Difficulties with Present-Moment Processes

Difficulties with flexible and focused attention to the present moment often involve rigid focus on the past or future—in other words, rumination and worry. When the attention of a person with substance abuse problems is captured by evaluative stories about past or future failures, the result is detachment from experiences in the present and an inability to respond with sensitivity to events in the present moment and, ironically, to long-term consequences of behavior in the future. There is a paradox in rumination and worry. Both seem to hold promise and contain the seed of a solution (*If I go over the past or future carefully enough, I will avoid making or repeating mistakes*). However, neither is correlated with good functioning. For example, rumination has been shown to be predictive of drinking behavior in problem drinkers (Caselli, Bortolai, Leoni, Rovetto, & Spada, 2008; Caselli et al., 2010; Willem, Bijttebier, Claes, & Raes, 2011).

Some substance abuse patterns appear to be exquisitely focused on the present moment. Individuals may be acutely aware of moment-by-moment physical sensations and cravings. However, while sensitive to those particular physical sensations, they may be very insensitive to other aspects of their current situation. The cultivation of present-moment processes within the ACT model of psychological flexibility involves flexibility of attention. Fixed attention on a narrow range of present circumstances can have negative effects similar to those of fixation on past and future events.

Attention to the present moment is an important component of mindfulness. Jon Kabat-Zinn defines mindfulness as involving "paying attention in a particular way: on purpose, in the present moment, and nonjudgmentally" (1994, p. 4). Although mindfulness involves more than merely present-moment processes, its relation to problems seen in addiction is highly relevant (see Wilson, 2009, for a book-length examination of mindfulness in the context of the therapeutic interaction from an ACT perspective). Both within and outside of ACT, mindfulness has received increased empirical scrutiny and has been found to be associated with the alleviation of symptoms concomitant with substance abuse, including depression and anxiety. Rumination has been shown to be predictive of relapse of major depressive disorder after mindfulness-based cognitive therapy (MBCT; Michalak, Hölz, & Teismann, 2011), and reductions in brooding have been found to mediate outcomes in MBCT (Shahar, Britton, Sbarra, Figueredo, & Bootzin, 2010). Mindfulness-based treatments have been shown to be effective in reducing worry in both clinical and nonclinical samples (Delgado et al., 2010; Evans et al., 2008; Vøllestad, Sivertsen, & Nielsen, 2011).

Difficulties with Self Processes

Consistent with the larger tradition of cognitive behavioral therapy (CBT), ACT emphasizes the importance of self processes in problems with addiction. From a CBT perspective, deficits in self-esteem or self-efficacy are thought to contribute to the etiology and/or maintenance of problems with addiction (Beck, Wright, Newman, & Liese, 1993). Generally, however, ACT highlights three distinct ways of relating to the self: self-as-content, self-as-process, and self-as-context (Hayes et al., 2011), each of which may be implicated in problems with addiction.

The first of the three processes, self-as-content, aligns most closely with mainstream conceptualizations of the self. Also known as "conceptualized self," this perspective involves categorization and evaluation through a narrative about one's personal attributes and roles. Becoming overly attached to the conceptualized self may reduce the likelihood of behaving in a flexible manner. For example, an individual attached to a role of being an addict may not be sensitive to opportunities to behave in ways uncharacteristic of addicts. From an ACT perspective, what is considered problematic is not the content of self-conceptualization, but the ways the conceptualized self can constrain behavior. The target of intervention is not the content, but the constraint.

The second way of relating to the self, self-as-process, is the ongoing awareness of one's internal experience (thoughts, feelings, urges, memories, and so forth). Problems related to self-as-process may arise when people have difficulty attending to their ongoing internal experience in a flexible way. Many forms of therapy incorporate skill building in the area of self-awareness. For example, cognitive therapy for substance abuse involves keeping thought and mood records and developing an ability to notice and challenge urges (Beck et al., 1993). ACT practitioners emphasize this skill to perhaps a greater degree, encouraging their clients to cultivate an ongoing sense of mindful awareness of internal experience without being fixed on or defined by particular aspects of that experience. This ongoing awareness is often practiced directly in therapy sessions.

The third way of relating to the self, self-as-context, is also referred to as perspective taking. This way of relating to the self involves contacting a sense of self that observes or notices one's experience, and cultivating the ability to adopt the perspective of the self in the past, present, and future, as well as the perspective of others. Difficulties in processes related to self-as-context may take the form of inflexibility in perspective taking. Those who struggle with psychological difficulties such as substance abuse, depression, and anxiety often expend substantial inward-focused energy on attempts to problem solve and manage their experience.

This internal focus may interfere with several forms of perspective taking that could potentially help curb destructive addictive behavior. One issue is that a strong internal problem-solving focus may interfere with effectively taking the perspective of others, which may manifest as deficits in empathy or inability to consider others' perspectives when making decisions. Another issue is that a rigid internal problem-solving focus may impair temporal perspective taking. For example, those struggling with addiction often have considerable difficulty making contact with the sense of self that existed before the addiction and possible selves that might exist in the future. Fixed attention to momentary events, like strong physical cravings, can cause addicts to lose contact with a sense of self that transcends momentary events.

A recent study by Luoma, Kohlenberg, Hayes, and Fletcher (2012) demonstrates the disruption of the functional relationship between negative self-narrative and substance abuse. Interesting differences emerged between participants who received the standard twenty-eight-day residential treatment and those receiving an additional six hours of ACT during the same twenty-eight-day treatment. At post-treatment, shame scores in the standard treatment condition were highly correlated with subsequent drinking. The shame scores of those who received ACT, though worse than those in the control condition, were not correlated with drinking at follow-up. Scores on measures of shame crossed over during the follow-up period such that ACT participants had improved in negative self-evaluations as compared to controls. These data suggest that positive self-evaluations *followed*, rather than *produced*, good substance use outcomes.

Experiential Avoidance

According to Hayes and colleagues (2011), "Experiential avoidance occurs when a person is unwilling to remain in contact with particular private experiences (e.g., bodily sensations, emotions, thoughts, memories, behavioral predispositions) and takes steps to alter the form, frequency, or situational sensitivity of these experiences even though doing so is not immediately necessary" (pp. 72-73). In other words, experiential avoidance is nonacceptance of one's inner experience. When people's existence is largely characterized by attempts to modify or avoid aversive internal stimuli, they become disconnected from engaging in the world; the effect is often a sense of emptiness and loss of vitality (Hayes et al., 2011).

Experiential avoidance is associated with multiple psychological difficulties, including substance abuse (Chawla & Ostafin, 2007; Hayes, Luoma, Bond, Masuda, & Lillis, 2006). It is not difficult to imagine how someone with an avoidant repertoire might become trapped in a pattern of substance abuse. Initial substance use might have many sources, including social inclusion, recreation, or coping with unwanted internal experiences (e.g., the self-medication hypothesis; see Khantzian, 1997). Persistent use can create life difficulties that, in turn, precipitate avoidant drug use, which may provide immediate, albeit temporary, escape from compounding stress. Moreover, once use is well established, attempts to quit may cause uncomfortable withdrawal symptoms, which, again, can be attenuated temporarily by continued use (Baker, Piper, McCarthy, Majeskie, & Fiore, 2004). Whether attempts to regulate these aversive internal stimuli take the form of using a substance or trying to suppress thoughts, feelings, or urges, individuals become trapped within a futile struggle to avoid their own experience.

Research has demonstrated the causal role of coping motives with regard to substance abuse (Cooper, Russell, & George, 1988). Additionally, research has shown that attempts to suppress substance-related thoughts tend to result in increases in the frequency of such thoughts (Palfai, Monti, Colby, & Rohsenow, 1997; Salkovskis & Reynolds, 1994; Toll, Sobell, Wagner, & Sobell, 2001). Conversely, acceptance of ongoing experience has been shown to weaken the link between urges and consumption (Bowen, Witkiewitz, Dillworth, & Marlatt, 2007; Ostafin & Marlatt, 2008).

Perhaps one reason treatment of addiction is so challenging is that the primary avoidance strategy—substance use—is so immediately effective. Drugs and alcohol produce a double bind: they can cause great difficulties, yet, over the short term, they are remarkably effective at helping people avoid those difficulties. Treatments often include engagement with difficult internal and external events (e.g., negative self-evaluations, memories of wrongdoings, emotional or physical discomfort, or damage to career or relationships).

Fusion

"Fusion" is a term used to indicate a tight functional linkage between a word and its referent (Hayes et al., 2011). Cognitive fusion becomes problematic when people attend solely to verbal events, rather than flexibly attending to a wider variety of internal and external events (Hayes et al., 2011). Potentially problematic cognitions might include thoughts about the efficacy of drugs in alleviating physical discomfort, doubts about success at quitting, doubts about the necessity or importance of quitting, and doubts about coping, among others.

The cognitive tradition emphasizes the importance of problematic thoughts. Beck's concept of the cognitive triad regarding depression applies similarly to those with substance abuse disorders; according to the cognitive model of addiction, negative thoughts about the self, the world, and the future may contribute to keeping someone stuck in addiction. As such, treatment involves helping clients identify and dispute or otherwise modify problematic thoughts (Beck et al., 1993). Contrary to the cognitive perspective, from an ACT perspective the problem is not the content of thoughts; rather, it is the rigidity with which these thoughts organize behavior.

While the causal role of fusion has not yet been the target of systematic investigation in individuals abusing substances, studies have examined the role of defusion as a mechanism of change in patients with depression (Zettle, Rains, & Hayes, 2011) and psychosis (Bach, Gaudiano, Hayes, & Herbert, in press). Data from cognitive therapy for depression support this conception of the role of cognition in recovery. Jarrett, Vittengl, Doyle, and Clark (2007) found that changes in cognition followed, rather than preceded, improvements in depressive symptomology. In other words, contrary to the cognitive hypothesis, changes in cognitive content do not appear to be the causal mechanism responsible for improved outcomes. ACT interventions are aimed directly at producing this delinking of cognition and action. Paired with the data from Luoma and colleagues (2012) described above, this suggests that negative thoughts do not need to improve in frequency or form prior to good addiction outcomes; what is more important is to change the client's relationship to entangling thoughts.

Disruption of Values

In ACT, *values* are defined as "freely chosen, verbally constructed consequences of ongoing, dynamic, evolving patterns of activity, which establish predominant reinforcers for that activity that are intrinsic in engagement in the valued behavioral pattern itself" (Wilson, 2009, p. 66). Therefore, and stated more simply, disengagement with values can be considered a disconnection from life areas that one deems important.

Since deeply painful thoughts and feelings are often associated with valued domains, difficulties with values may involve avoidance of such aversive states and fusion with negative thoughts about the past and future. For example, an alcoholic might reduce his interactions with his wife because feelings of guilt and shame are likely to surface when they are together. Additional difficulties may take the form of an inability to verbalize what one values or confusion surrounding what one values. Repertoire-narrowing fusion may also occur in some valued domains.

For example, an individual may be so fused with parenting failures that resulted from drinking that she becomes insensitive to parenting opportunities that are currently available.

Values are also emphasized in motivational interviewing (MI), an approach used when individuals experience ambivalence regarding behavior change (Miller & Rollnick, 2002; see also Wagner, Ingersoll, & Rollnick, chapter 5 of this volume). According to MI, change is motivated by a perceived discrepancy between behavior and values. MI involves helping clients choose values and identify discrepancies between these values and current behavior, and in this regard MI is similar to ACT.

Some evidence suggests that attention to values may help with substance-related outcomes. For example, in a smoking cessation study, health concerns and wanting to set a good example for one's children were associated with successful quitting (Halpern & Warner, 1993). Intrinsic motivations to quit smoking (e.g., concerns about health) are predictive of greater success in cessation than extrinsic motivations (e.g., responding to social pressures to quit), which suggests that freely choosing values may promote cessation efforts (Curry, McBride, Grothaus, Louie, & Wagner, 1995; Curry, Wagner, & Grothaus, 1990).

Difficulties with Committed Action

Committed action involves engaging in valued patterns of activity and returning to that engagement upon noticing that actions have drifted from values (Hayes et al., 2011; Wilson, 2009). Although committed action is similar to the values process, there is a key distinction. The values process involves establishing qualities of ongoing patterns of activity as reinforcers, whereas committed action involves active, moment-to-moment engagement and reengagement in those patterns and their construction. An important feature of committed action is the gentle return to valued action upon noticing that one has veered off course.

Relapse to substance abuse provides a good example of the ACT approach to committed action. Once an individual has relapsed, engaging in committed action would involve returning to abstaining in the service of some value or values. In the ACT model, relapse to substance abuse is treated in the same way as any other lapse in important valued action. First, the ways abstinence (or a goal of moderation) relates to a variety of valued domains is examined. Next, a pattern of activity that would make subsequent relapse less likely is generated. And finally, the client reengages in the valued pattern.

Depending upon the severity of substance abuse problems, individuals may have reduced or completely stopped engaging in committed action in multiple areas. For example, searching for the next fix or getting high may interfere with going to work, spending time with one's children, or eating a well-balanced diet. In addition, co-occurring depressive symptoms often contribute to general behavioral suppression, rendering committed action even more challenging. For some people, a low level of committed action may have preceded their problems with substances. It is possible that low levels of valued action increase attempts to avoid unpleasant thoughts and feelings that are exacerbated by the lack of valued action and the consequences of the inaction.

Other treatments also emphasize the importance of increasing activity. Behavioral activation (BA) is primarily used to treat depression by increasing contact with potential reinforcers (Martell, Dimidjian, & Herman-Dunn, 2010). Because depressive symptomology is common among people with substance abuse problems, these strategies are highly relevant. Cognitive therapy for substance abuse incorporates BA as a component of treatment (Beck et al., 1993). Activity monitoring and scheduling techniques are used to promote engagement in activities that are related to life goals clients were neglecting while using substances. MacPherson and colleagues (2010) examined the efficacy of BA in a sample of smokers with elevated depression symptoms. They found that smokers in the BA condition reported greater smoking abstinence and lower depressive symptoms than those in the standard treatment condition, which included nicotine replacement therapy and smoking cessation strategies. Such evidence lends support to ACT's emphasis on regular, ongoing behavioral engagement in valued activities.

Assessment and Intervention

In order to examine assessment and intervention, we will begin with a case study and partial opening dialogue with a client being treated using

ACT. We will then draw upon the hypothetical client to demonstrate ACT processes in treatment.

Case Study

Andrea is a thirty-seven-year-old, single, Caucasian female who is currently employed as an English teacher at a community college. Andrea has an older brother and a younger sister, and her parents are still married. All of her relatives reside in another state. After becoming employed at age sixteen, she started smoking marijuana on a daily basis and drinking alcohol on a near-daily basis. This pattern continued in her college and graduate-school years. During the past five years, the quantity of alcohol she consumes has increased.

Although she has engaged in this pattern of substance use over a long period, she has experienced few academic or employment problems. Her primary difficulties are most apparent in the interpersonal realm. This is not generally apparent to fellow students and coworkers, other than that they find her somewhat reserved. She reports no romantic relationships apart from extremely brief encounters, lives alone, and reports a markedly limited social life other than her interactions at work.

ACT Informed Consent and an Opening Session

A good and ethical place to begin any therapy is to provide a bit of informed consent so that the client has an idea of the direction and content of treatment. The following dialogue is an example of what shape this discussion might take when using ACT to treat substance abuse problems:

Therapist: Andrea, I know that you have become more and more concerned about your increase in drinking and your profound sense of isolation. The way you have described it, it is as if your life is sort of closing in on you—like it has gone from small but sufferable to a sort of prison. And in the midst of all of that, I hear a tiny kernel of longing, as if there is an old, old sense that there would be more to life, maybe even a hope that you gave up on a long time ago.

Andrea: I don't know what you mean. I don't understand.

Therapist: I know I can be a little obscure. Sometimes I am feeling my way along in therapy, feeling for something that has a sense of life in it. That can be confusing. Would you look at me for a moment…right here, in
my face, in my eyes? Can you see that I am sincere in this? Can you see that even though we have only begun our conversation, it matters to me that your life open up to something richer? So, without completely understanding just yet, can I ask a few more questions and speak to you a bit about what to expect in treatment with me?

Andrea: I guess so. I can't stand where I am.

Therapist: Yes, I get that.

Andrea: But richness? I don't get that at all.

Therapist: Yes, I understand that too. And, what if I am right about this sense? What if there is something more, something richer, just out of sight? Wouldn't that be worth a few more questions—a little more work for you and me? Here? Now?

Andrea: Sure. Let's do it.

Therapist: Some treatments for alcohol and drugs go pretty directly after the drug and alcohol use itself. Sometimes problems with drug and alcohol use get treated as if they are free-standing troubles, other than perhaps some recognition that they mess with your life. Acceptance and commitment therapy is focused on enriched living, on people living the freest and richest lives possible. I do not mean rich in conventional terms; I mean rich on your own terms—a life that you would call rich and meaningful. During, treatment we will cultivate a set of practices. I will not kid you about drugs and alcohol. When people have struggled with them, especially people who have struggled as long and hard as you, the possibility of letting them go entirely may be necessary in the service of living well. However, I want you to note here that I will not be the one to determine if letting them go entirely is necessary. You will be making that choice on your own. I will offer invitations persistently throughout our therapy. If you give them a try, your own experience will tell you about their importance. However, I will ask that you persist with them for a while. Sometimes if we judge things on a very immediate basis, we miss their long-term effects. It's like going to the gym; sometimes it hurts at first. Sometimes you need to learn the difference between pain that is taking you to a better place and pain that is destructive. Part of our work will be about learning to notice that difference. In fact, right now we can check it out with getting drunk itself.

Andrea:　Okay. What do you mean?

Therapist:　When you get home, I am guessing that sometimes you have promised yourself not to drink that night.

Andrea:　Sure.

Therapist:　And how does that go?

Andrea:　Well, sometimes it works, but I guess if it worked really great, I wouldn't be here, right?

Therapist:　Right. So for this little inquiry, tell me about when it has not worked so we can explore a bit of unworkability.

Andrea:　Well, I come home planning to not drink, but later I drink anyway.

Therapist:　And let's slow down and get curious about the moment when you make the shift from not drinking to drinking. Tell me about that moment.

Andrea:　Well, sometimes I just drink and don't even think about it until later. And sometimes I have sort of a fight with myself about drinking.

Therapist: And how is that fight? What is it like?

Andrea: It sucks. Sometimes I feel like my chest is about to crack open because it gets so tight.

Therapist: And when you shift and take that first drink?

Andrea: Well, at least I can breathe. I feel it wash all warm down my throat, and I can breathe.

Therapist: Anything else?

Andrea: Well, it doesn't make any sense, but I get this feeling like *Tomorrow I am going to cut drinking loose forever and just move on with my life.*

Therapist: That sounds nice—really nice. I can almost feel my own breath fill me to the brim as you say it.

Andrea: Well, it doesn't last. I always end up stupid drunk. I just feel so weak and stupid.

Therapist: Well, hold on a minute. I want to check out a couple of things. Remember how I said that I would ask you to practice some things and to watch what happens both over the short term and over the long term? First let's look at this: Notice how over the short term, that drink feels great; but over the long term, it feels awful and it's getting worse.

Andrea: I know. I must be stupid. Over and over, even when I know better. That's the story of my life. I'm not like other people. I see them and think, *What is wrong with me?* I can't do the simplest thing. I can't talk to people—just talk to them! I just stand there like an idiot. I have always been like that. I can't do anything.

Therapist: Wow! I mean… Did you see what just happened? I just asked you about drinking over the short term and the long term, and… *(Therapist gets quiet.)* It was like this wave of hurt and judgment washed over our conversation.

Andrea: I'm sorry. I shouldn't have said anything.

Therapist: No, that really helps me actually. Are those the kinds of things you are thinking as you sit alone in your apartment?

Andrea: That's it. Over and over and over.

Therapist: Wow. And when you drink, you get a little easing of that.

Andrea: But it doesn't last.

Therapist: Okay, this is really going to help me explain the therapy. Perfect, really. There is something that got lost in all that sense of doom that washed over our conversation that I want to touch on. Let's look at those moments after that first drink, when you get that sense of peace, of something being possible.

Andrea: But it's a lie.

Therapist: I get that there is a piece of it that always seems to go wrong, but let's check and see if there is something else there too.

Andrea: What? What else?

Therapist: I want to check out that moment of peace and possibility. What if in that moment is a glimpse of what I was talking about earlier—a life lived with freedom and richness and meaning, a life where you could choose.

Andrea: But it's a lie.

Therapist: Well, it has not happened. I get that. But in a world where that was possible—a life lived with richness, freedom, and purpose—what would such a life mean to you? What would be the shape of that life?

Andrea: I just don't know.

Therapist: If our work was about making a place where possibilities could be kindled, would that work be worth doing? That is the work I want to do with you. What if there were practices we could do here and that you could do at home and at work that could open up that sense of possibility and purpose without your taking a drink?

Andrea: Well… But, how?

Therapist: This is a little like swimming, Andrea. I can tell you some, but I could talk all day and you would not know what it is like to get in the water. But to tell you a bit, if you decide to come along, we will make six practices the center of our work together. The first practice involves learning to come to stillness, to notice the richness and complexity of each moment. The second practice will involve learning to shift perspectives on things—on the world and on ourselves, past, present, and future. The third practice will be the practice of acceptance. It will be up to you, always, but we will practice noticing the difference between pain that moves us toward well-being and pain that is destructive, and we will also practice opening up to pain that is in the service of living. The fourth practice will be letting go of unhelpful stories. This is not about true and false stories. It is about helpful and unhelpful. This brings us to the fifth practice. If the stories are not in charge, then what is? The fifth practice will be the practice of authoring a valued sense of direction. It is perfectly fine for this to be fuzzy at first. We will simply begin that process and allow it to develop over time. The sixth and last practice is where, in the smallest and simplest ways, we put our lives in motion in a direction that we could love.

Assessment in Motion

In an important sense, every ACT session is an assessment. This opening session contains many of the elements we will continually assess and treat over the course of therapy. In what follows, we examine the ways that treatment can address these behavioral excesses and deficits by building practices to support growth and development in the treatment of clients with substance use problems.

Structured Exercises to Promote Psychological Flexibility

There are a number of ACT protocols specific to addiction available on the website of the Association for Contextual Behavioral Science (ACBS; www.contextualpsychology.org), and numerous general protocols in the form of books. All of these can provide structure and guidance in the use of ACT in treating addictions. The following set of exercises, Practicing Our Way to Stillness (POWS) have been excerpted with minor adaptations from *The Wisdom to Know the Difference: An Acceptance and Commitment Therapy Guide to Recovery from Substance Abuse* (Wilson & DuFrene, 2012). The exercises and inventories can be spread across treatment as the client is prepared to engage them. They provide opportunities to practice all six ACT processes. After presenting the four parts of the POWS exercise, we will discuss cultivation of the six core ACT processes fundamental to psychological flexibility.

Practicing Our Way to Stillness— Part 1

In this inventory, you'll be asked to notice places in your life where you have been absent or perhaps less present in some way. See if you can let go of self-condemnation for now. There will be plenty of time for that if you decide you need to give yourself a beating. For now, let this be more like an exercise in noticing.

Below you'll find a list of twelve aspects of life. Some may be important to you, and some may not. These are areas of living that some people care about. Let your eyes come to rest on each one:

- *Family (other than your spouse or partner and your children)*

- *Marriage and intimate relationships*

- *Parenting*

- *Friends and social life*

- *Work*

- *Education and learning*

- *Recreation and fun*

- *Spirituality*

- *Community life*

- *Physical self-care, exercise, sleep, and nutrition*

- *The environment and nature*

- *Art, music, literature, and beauty*

You'll be invited to reflect on some of these areas. You can eventually reflect on all twelve, if you like, but start with only three or four that resonate with you the most.

Let yourself become aware of the first area you choose to reflect on. Slowly and gently, allow yourself to become aware of ways you've been absent, of times when you could have been present to this area of your life and just weren't. Don't judge or evaluate. Just notice.

You may not be able to think of any examples of not showing up that relate to a particular area. That's fine. This is an inventory. There are no right or wrong answers, and the exercise isn't about doing anything. It is about learning how to notice and gently shift your attention and, ultimately, about learning how to be still. See if you can bring your gentlest self to the task.

When you're ready, move on to the next area. Slowly and gently, once again allow yourself to become aware of ways you've been absent, of times when you could have been present to this area of your life and just weren't. Take your time. Slow down. Breathe. There is nothing to accomplish here, nothing to be done other than notice. Whatever happens, breathe through it and let yourself come to rest.

Practicing Our Way to Stillness— Part 2

As we continue, remember that this isn't an exercise in what's wrong with you, although those kinds of thoughts may well be called up. Just allow yourself to show up for those thoughts, even if they are very hard to bear. Remember that our purpose here is to help you practice coming to stillness when hard things are in front of you. This is about learning to notice any tendencies you have to hide, run, or fight when things get ugly.

Hiding may show up as I don't need to do this. Running may show up as I'll do this later. Fighting may show up as Why do I need to do this? You can't make me do this! That's all true. You don't need to do this work at all, and you can certainly put this work off until later. No one can make you do anything. But if you can learn to slow down and to pause in the face of hard things, you will be better practiced at pausing later, when we talk about choosing a path.

To continue this inventory, I want you to go back over the areas that you reflected upon in the first part of this exercise. Ponder each of these three questions in relation to that area of your life:

- What does this area mean to you?

- What would you hope for it to mean?

- In a world where you could take time, in a world where you could offer yourself a gift in this area, what gift might you offer?

The last question is especially important. If you're willing to give yourself one small gift in an area of your life that matters to you, you start down a path that holds the possibility of leading to a richer, more fulfilling life.

Practicing Our Way to Stillness— Part 3

In a notebook, set up a separate page for each of the following substances that you've used:

- *Alcohol*

- *Marijuana*

- *Hallucinogens (LSD, mushrooms, peyote, and so forth)*

- *Depressants (Xanax, valium, barbiturates, and so forth)*

- *Stimulants (speed, cocaine, ecstasy, ephedrine, and so forth)*

- *Inhalants (glue, gasoline, aerosol propellants, and so forth)*

- *Opiates (heroin, Vicodin, codeine, OxyContin, Percodan, and so forth)*

For each substance, write down the following information:

- *The age you started using*

- *How long you used*

- *The frequency of use (in times per week, month, or whatnot)*

- *How you used the substance (smoked, drank, ate, injected, and so forth)*

Begin with the first time you remember using any mood-altering substance, no matter how little the amount. It is important that you be painstakingly thorough in this task. You can use a format like the one in the sample below, or just write a description of your age and usage.

Example: Stimulants

Age	Quantity and frequency	How used
12 to 15 years	amphetamines 2-3 tablets, 6-8 times per year	oral
16 years	a few lines of cocaine, about 4 times that year	snorted
17 years	about 1/4 gram of cocaine, about 3-6 times per week	snorted, some smoked

Practicing Our Way to Stillness— Part 4

After you've made a thorough inventory of your past use of substances, write down any problems or changes in your life that were associated with using alcohol or drugs in each of the twelve areas listed in the first part of this exercise. In some ways, this is a harder review than what you did in part 1 of this exercise. In part 1, you were just looking for general ways you might have been less than fully present. For many people, drugs and alcohol are an important way to check out. If that's true for you, there are likely to have been consequences. Those consequences are what you're going to reflect on in this final part of the exercise.

If there were no consequences, write, "None." However, I encourage you to list any consequences, even if they were small. For example, you may not have been fired from a job, but you may have gone to work with a hangover and been less effective as a result. Number each section and keep the twelve areas separate from each other as much as possible. It is absolutely okay to be repetitive, writing the same consequence in several different areas. Pay special attention to times when, as a result of drinking or using (or seeking alcohol or drugs), you did things that violate your personal values (concealing, rationalizing, being secretive, being violent, and so on). Give a few very specific examples in each section.

Present-Moment Processes and Practices

As suggested to the client in the opening session, an intervention may begin by assessing and building present-moment practices and processes. This can be done via relatively formal mindfulness practices, but it can also be done moment-by-moment in therapy. When helping clients build skills in present-moment processes, it's important to acknowledge related processes that pull us out of the present moment.

Interventions to build more flexible present-moment repertoires involve training for fluid transitioning to and from engagement with past, present, and future. They also involve breaking up fused storytelling to build sensitivity to the richness of experience in the moment. In the dialogue above, take note of the inflexible, fused quality in Andrea's description of her social interactions: "I must be stupid. Over and over, even when I know better. That's the story of my life… I can't do the simplest thing. I can't talk to people—just talk to them! I have always been like that. I can't do anything." This sort of fused narrative is likely to recur in and out of therapy.

Rather than engage the client in evidence gathering or refutation, use the reemergence of this theme in therapy as an ideal moment to notice the familiarity and repetitiveness of the story and then drop into a brief, simple present-moment practice such as Six Breaths on Purpose (Wilson & DuFrene, 2012). In Andrea's case, if the same pattern reemerged in a discussion of the POWS inventory, the following dialogue might occur:

Therapist: Andrea, I want to interrupt you for just a moment. I want you to notice this story of self-judgment that has washed over you. Take just a moment and notice the quality of what you are saying—as if you are trying to convince me. Can you notice a sort of urgency in your speech? Stop for a moment and notice whether you feel it in your body.

Andrea: What? I wasn't thinking about how my body felt at all. I don't know.

Therapist: This would be a good time to practice reconnecting with the present moment. We don't need to make that story go away, but let's try taking six breaths on purpose and see what happens. Here's how it works: Our breath enters and leaves all the time, but we seldom notice it. So what we are going to do right now is just come to rest and take six breaths slowly and deliberately, noticing all of the small sensory details of the rise and fall of the breath.

The therapist would then ask Andrea to close her eyes, settle into her chair, and take a moment to notice the physical details of the rise and fall of the breath—the stretch of muscles as the belly and chest rise, the warmth of the exhalation, and the coolness of the inhalation. After giving that direction, the therapist counts out six breaths and then asks Andrea to allow her eyes to open. After clients have done this practice a few times, little coaching is needed beyond the suggestion to stop and take six breaths together on purpose.

This is a practice clients can carry with them into virtually any area of daily living. It is brief enough to do in line at the grocery store, sitting in the office, or lying in bed in the evening. The exercise is not aimed at eliminating troubling thoughts, though it often has the effect of softening their hold. The purpose is to practice fluid transitions to flexible, focused attention.

It is useful to practice present-moment processes using varied content, including benign, challenging, and sweet. This is more likely to generate breadth, flexibility, and generalizability in the practice. Practicing only in the context of troubling thoughts may result in present-moment processes being used as an avoidance strategy, whereas the practice we want to cultivate involves the ability to fluidly allocate attention in a wide variety of circumstances.

Self Processes

Within the area of self processes, intervention efforts are aimed at diluting fixed, conceptualized views of the self, improving ongoing self-awareness, and building perspective-taking skills. When individuals are fused with stories containing categorical assessments, laden with evaluations and comparisons, they are encouraged to loosen the hold of such stories by engaging in defusion exercises. The POWS inventories described above provide many opportunities for transitioning to different perspectives and letting go of rigid, negative self-evaluation as an exclusive perspective. Each inventory, when undertaken without flinching from careful examination of mistakes or losses, invites the adoption of a compassionate and mindful perspective.

In practice, clients are reminded to use descriptive, nonevaluative statements while focusing on moment-to-moment experience (self-as-process). Once the self is encountered as more of a stream of ongoing experiences, clients can practice taking the perspective of the observer self (self-as-context). Exercises such as Leaves on a Stream (Hayes et al., 2011) ask clients to close their eyes and picture their thoughts moving past them on leaves floating down a stream. Such exercises serve to increase skills in adopting a perspective consistent with self-as-context and the ability to see thoughts as an ongoing flow moving through an awareness that has constancy.

Other exercises might involve actively shifting perspective. Once the therapist and client have settled into an alert, mindful state, the therapist may engage the client in the following way:

Therapist: What thoughts are coming up for you now?

Andrea: When I was writing about family, I found myself thinking they would be better off without me. I deserve to be alone so I don't hurt people anymore.

Therapist: If you let your eyes close for a moment, I wonder if you can allow yourself to travel back through time and see if you can see your own face at different times when you felt this strong sense that there was something wrong with you, that your family and others would be better off without you. How young were you when you first had that sense?

Andrea: Forever. I have always felt wrong—just not like other people.

Therapist: Do you remember feeling that as far back as six or seven years old?

Andrea: Yes, always.

Therapist: I ask that you call to mind the image of that younger you—that six- or seven-year-old you. Notice the way she holds her body, the way the hair falls around her face. Can you look into those eyes and see that sense of being off? Maybe it is something other people wouldn't see, but can you see it? See if you can know something about that child's inner experience that others do not know. Take a moment and let your eyes linger on the child's face. *(Pauses.)* Imagine that you could reach out and gently lay your hand on that child's cheek—feeling the softness of that skin at your fingertips. Imagine that you could say to that child, "I know." Imagine that as that child looks into your eyes, she sees into the eyes of someone who knows her. Just stay with those eyes for a moment. *(Pauses.)*

And breathe. Bring your attention to bear on the gentle rise and fall of your chest as you inhale and exhale, here in this room with me. Notice any tension you may be holding in your shoulders, back, or legs. And breathe a sense of softness into these places.

Now I ask that you call to mind an image of yourself twenty years from now. Let it be an older, wiser version of you. Even if you cannot imagine how, let it be that, somehow, you found your way to an older and wiser place. Let yourself see it. Can you see the outline of her face? The same face that you wore as a little girl, that you wear now, still visible in those eyes. Those deep-brown eyes that have known pain and profound sadness… Imagine that she knows something you don't know now—something about how things will turn out for you. Imagine that she could reach out to you, laying her hand gently on your cheek. Imagine that she could whisper a message to you—a message from the future, something to carry you forward. *(Pauses.)* What message does she have for you? *(Pauses.)*

And, once again, become aware of the rise and fall of your breath. Allow those images to well up around you, without struggle. And breathe, deep and full.

The predominant focus of this visualization is taking multiple perspectives, though it also has significant acceptance and present-moment components. Taking the perspective of a younger self and an older and wiser self allows the same content to be viewed from different perspectives. Secondary but important aspects of the exercise involve practicing intentional mindful movement of awareness—from the visualizations suggested in the exercise, to the rise and fall of the breath, back to the visualizations, and finishing with the breath.

Acceptance

The substance use components of the POWS (parts 3 and 4) are often a great place for people with substance use problems to practice acceptance. Working through the extent of a substance use history allows both client and therapist to look at patterns of use and any changes in patterns of use over time. For example, in Andrea's case, the therapist's review of part 3 of the POWS would show that Andrea increased her alcohol use about five years ago. The therapist might then ask questions about what was going on in her life at that point in time, noticing function and workability over the short term and long term.

In part 4 of the POWS, clients are asked to write descriptions of specific consequences of their substance use in valued domains such as work, self-care, and a variety of interpersonal domains. The purpose of this work is not to punish or to generate insight. The purpose is to use these often painful life experiences as opportunities to practice acceptance. The assumption is that life has, and will, contain many painful experiences, and that increased acceptance can allow for more effective living. The following dialogue between Andrea and the therapist illustrates Andrea's experiential avoidance and an initial introduction of acceptance as an alternative.

Therapist: So in the area of family, you wrote that you drifted apart from your siblings. Tell me more about that.

Andrea: For the past few years, if I wasn't at work I was home drinking. I didn't feel like talking to anyone, so I didn't. I drank instead. If you don't talk to people, you drift apart.

Therapist: Tell me about one particular instance where you chose to drink instead of calling one of your siblings. Tell me about it in as much detail as you can.

Andrea: I didn't call my brother on his birthday. I knew it was his birthday. It had probably been a month since I'd last talked with him. It was a particularly dark day for me—one of those days when saying just one word hurts. I thought about calling him, and then I thought about how absent I've been, which made me feel worse. I just kept drinking instead of calling him.

Therapist: What thoughts were you having?

Andrea: That I am a horrible person, so uncaring and selfish. That I don't deserve them, and it would be better for everyone if I never left my apartment and didn't talk to anyone.

Therapist: Yes. And what kind of feelings are you having at this moment?

Andrea: I feel guilty and ashamed. I feel anger at myself for ruining my relationships with them, and sadness because I really miss them. This feels terrible.

Therapist: What do you do when these types of thoughts and feelings come up?

Andrea: I shut myself away in my apartment and drink.

Therapist: And how has that been working?

Andrea: Not well.

Therapist: What if the way out of the struggle is stepping out of the fight with your thoughts and feelings? If trying to avoid them or reduce them hasn't worked, what if the job is to notice the negative thoughts and feelings when they come up, acknowledge them, and then return to activities that are important in your life, like calling your brother?

Clients often engage in other unworkable behaviors, in addition to substance use, in an effort to avoid aspects of their experience. Coming into contact with the unworkability of previous strategies makes way for a new approach. It is important to speak of acceptance as an ongoing practice, rather than an all-or-nothing matter. Part of the practice involves letting go of avoidance, and part of it involves becoming curious about what might be possible in the absence of that struggle.

Defusion

The purpose of engaging in defusion exercises is to loosen the functional hold of stories on behaviors when those stories prevent movement in valued directions. Stories about self, touched on in the section on self processes above, are a subset of fusion. Verbal formulations of how the world works can also sometimes function as a sort of verbal prison. Beck's central insight was that people do not simply live in the world; they live in a version of the world built on stories (Beck, Rush, Shaw, & Emery, 1979), including stories about themselves. ACT is beholden to Beck for pressing this issue to the forefront of the CBT movement. However, ACT differs from cognitive therapy in that the primary response to unhelpful thoughts is not to attempt to replace them with more accurate thoughts. Instead, ACT interventions aim at loosening the grip these stories have on living effectively. Many stories about the wreckage created in the midst of substance abuse will be true, and stories about the likelihood of wreckage in the future may be highly probable. Yet sometimes very unlikely things happen. Holding stories lightly is a practice that allows change regardless of whether the stories change. We see this dynamic reflected in the findings of Luoma and colleagues (2012) described above. Even though participants in the ACT condition had higher shame scores at post-treatment, they drank less and used more aftercare treatment resources than those in the control condition. At follow-up their shame scores had continued to drop. Thus, loosening the grip of stories appears to be both teachable and useful.

Clinicians should listen for words like "should," "shouldn't," "always," "never," "possible," "impossible," "right," "wrong," "fair," "unfair," "but," "everyone," and "no one," as these are common indicators of fusion (Wilson, 2009). Defusion exercises involve practice discriminating between thoughts and direct moment-by-moment experience (Hayes et al., 2011). The goal is to create space between individuals and the thoughts they are experiencing, enabling direct contact with environmental contingencies, and even the thoughts themselves, in a more flexible and articulated way.

Many defusion exercises involve practicing mindful observation of thoughts and noticing when awareness is hooked by them. In some regards, acceptance, present-moment, and self process interventions almost always contain an element of defusion. They involve taking a nonjudgmental stance toward cognitive processes and engaging in state-ments that are descriptive, rather than evaluative. Many exercises have been developed to promote the cultivation of defusion. One involves labeling thoughts as thoughts (e.g., *I'm having the thought that I'm a hope-less case*; Hayes et al., 2011, p. 266). In another, distressing words can be repeated until the strong functional hold of the word fades (Titchener's repetition; Titchener, 1916; see also Hayes et al., 2011, p. 248). A variety of defusion exercises found in ACT treatment manuals can be adapted to troubling thoughts related to substances and substance use.

Values

Walking away from substances is difficult. Withdrawal symptoms are uncomfortable and often painful. Some individuals who give up sub-stances are also giving up the only peace they know. In ACT, values are emphasized from the beginning. In fact, the original ACT values proto-cols were generated in the context of a treatment development grant for polysubstance abusers. Values serve as a compass, indicating the direc-tion in which the client wishes to travel, and therefore serving as a guide in treatment. In ACT for substance use problems, treatment is not just about getting sober; it is about creating a full, rich, meaningful life. Part 4 of the POWS asks clients to come into contact with areas in their lives that they care about and with how using substances has affected those areas. Sometimes behavior while using substances results in the loss of things that matter to the individual. In Andrea's case, in the process of hiding away and drinking alone in her apartment, she neglected her rela-tionship with family members and missed opportunities to have mean-ingful experiences with them. Andrea's behavior also made the develop-ment of friendships difficult.

Sometimes the losses identified in part 4 of the POWS are the result of inappropriate behavior while using (e.g., showing up at work drunk, getting a DUI, hitting a loved one), and sometimes the losses are the result of a reduction in engagement in activities related to valued areas, as in Andrea's case. Part 4 of the POWS can help people see ways their behavior harms the very things and people they care about. In the fol-lowing example, the therapist reviews this material with Andrea and uses it as a guide for further conversation:

Therapist: I see that you didn't write down any consequences related to physical or health problems that are related to drinking.

Andrea: That's correct. My drinking hasn't caused any physical damage to my body.

Therapist: Okay. Direct physical consequences of alcohol are only one kind of damage that can happen. Have you treated your body the way you would treat the body of someone you really love?

Andrea: No. Probably not.

Therapist: Tell me a little more about that.

Andrea: I haven't really given my body much thought at all. I don't think about what I put in my body. I don't exercise.

Therapist: Is this something you would like to do? Take better care of yourself physically?

Andrea: I haven't really thought about it. I don't think it's possible. I've tried to eat better and exercise before, but it never lasts.

Therapist: I didn't ask whether it was possible or how it has worked out in the past. Imagine a world where it was possible. In that world, would you choose to take better care of your body?

Andrea: Yes.

The point of coming into contact with the consequences of drinking is not to condemn past actions or lead clients to ruminate about them. The purpose is to examine how using substances takes them away from the things and people that matter to them and to illuminate a path forward. During treatment, clients are encouraged to act in service of their values despite negative thoughts and feelings. Helping clients get in contact with what they value and how to act in service of those values are important aspects of treatment.

Another way to explore and expand on values is through the use of instruments like the Valued Living Questionnaire – 2 (VLQ-2; Wilson, 2009; also available at www.actforaddiction.com). The questionnaire provides a systematic format for the client and therapist to examine the twelve valued domains listed in part 1 of the POWS and to explore the client's sense of importance, concerns, and sense of possibility across those domains of living. Patterns of growth cultivated in the resulting clinical conversations can then be used to cultivate the final psychological flexibility process: committed action.

Committed Action

Clients often want to know if, once abstinent, they will ever drink or use again. The simple fact is, we don't know. The only way to answer that question with certainty is to drink. Each moment is a choice to drink or not drink. That is all there is, a commitment in this moment. If a person who chose abstinence relapses, committed action involves the gentle return back to not drinking. Committed action in other life areas works the same way.

Clients with substance abuse problems are often trying to rebuild their lives, and the wreckage of their past may seem massive and impossible to overcome. The key is to ask them to start small. Initial committed actions could be something as simple as making a phone call to a sibling, going to an AA meeting, going for a walk, or filling out one job application. This work is about slow and steady movements toward values:

Therapist: Tell me a value you hold.

Andrea: I value having an engaged relationship with my siblings.

Therapist: Okay. Let your eyes gently close. I'm going to ask you to imagine a few things and ponder a few questions. There is no need to answer these questions out loud. Begin by imagining a pantry with empty shelves. If you were going to stock your pantry with acts related to being the sister you want to be, what would those acts be? Think both big and small. It could be a phone call to your brother on your way home from work or sending your sister a card in the mail. It might be listening attentively during a conversation or making a surprise visit. What kind of acts could you fill your pantry shelves with? Remember, for now these are not things you must do. Let some items be things you may never do but can leave open as possibilities—maybe you would retire to the same town or take a holiday together in Mexico. Be playful. Don't forget to think small too. See if you can think of a few things that you could do in a few minutes, like sending a text message.

After engaging clients in this sort of visualization, let them sit in stillness with their experience for a moment. Then ask them to open their eyes and use a form like the Valued Action Worksheet (available at www.actforaddiction.com). For your reference, we include the following abbreviated sample of that worksheet.

Valued Action Worksheet

Below, please describe who you want to be and what you want to do in regard to a value that's important to you. The focus of the question is on you and your role in these areas. Please write a short sentence describing the value, including a few qualities you'd like to have in that area. Then list various actions that you could take that would be consistent with that value. Try to come up with a variety of actions, large and small, including some very small, simple but meaningful acts. You don't have to list eight different actions, but give it a try.

My value is: *Being a loving, available, and connected sister.*

1. Make a Facebook post once a week.	5. Send some recent pictures of myself.
2. Call once a week just to talk.	6. Answer the phone when they call me.
3. Call on birthdays.	7. Invite them to visit.
4. Fly to visit on spring break.	8. Talk about things I'm doing in my life.

The activities generated in this exercise can form the core of a plan for values-consistent behavioral activation. Clients should be encouraged to proceed gently. The purpose is to create a steady process of building healthy patterns of living.

For some clients, domains such as family may be precisely where they are prepared to start. For others, direct work on certain areas of living will need to be delayed. For example, parents separated from their children by court order may need to demonstrate a period of stability in residence and employment. Also, some clients may not be prepared to immediately take on development in certain areas. For example, in Andrea's case it might make sense to devote time to cultivating less challenging social relationships before plunging into intimate relations. For some clients, a commitment to attend regular 12-step meetings or to engage in some form of physical exercise might be an appropriate starting point. The critical feature of this work is that sustainable life engagement is good medicine. We believe this to be consistent with findings in behavioral activation and with data demonstrating that psychosocial dysfunction predicts increased depressive symptoms (Vittengl, Clark, & Jarrett, 2009). As suggested by the ACT model and by ongoing work in motivational interviewing, the best behavioral targets are the ones that clients themselves endorse.

Integration into Current Treatment Settings

In considering the integration of ACT into current treatment settings, two central considerations emerge: structural elements of treatment, and procedural, theoretical, and philosophical compatibilities. As to structural elements, ACT appears quite flexible in implementation. It has been successfully delivered in inpatient treatment (e.g., Bach & Hayes, 2002), outpatient treatment (e.g., Batten & Hayes, 2005), and residential treatment (e.g., Luoma et al., 2012). ACT has been used in individual therapy (e.g., Twohig, Shoenberger, & Hayes, 2007), group therapy (e.g., Kocovski, Fleming, & Rector, 2009), and mixed individual and group therapy (Gifford et al., 2004; Hayes et al., 2004). It has been executed in medical settings (e.g., Branstetter-Rost, Cushing, & Douleh, 2009; Wicksell, Melin, & Olsson, 2007), as bibliotherapy (Muto, Hayes, & Jeffcoat, 2011), and as a single-day workshop (Gregg, Callaghan, Hayes, & Glenn-Lawson, 2007; Lillis, Hayes, & Levin, 2011). Duration and intensity of treatment have likewise been quite varied. For example, the trial with polysubstance-abusing methadone clients by Hayes and colleagues (2004) involved sixteen weeks, with participants assigned to receive two individual and one group session per week. In others, such as Bach and Hayes (2002), clients received just three one-hour sessions of ACT. Although the variability in intervention structure specifically for substance abuse is necessarily smaller than in the broader ACT treatment development effort, this demonstrated breadth of effective protocols suggests that the treatment can accommodate many real-world circumstances.

ACT has some unique theoretical and philosophical assumptions (Hayes et al., 2011). However, at a more practical level, ACT and ACT components have been successfully blended with a relatively wide variety of treatments with promising results. For example, ACT has been combined with elements of dialectical behavior therapy (Gratz & Gunderson, 2006) and functional analytic psychotherapy (Gifford et al., 2011). Substantial ACT components are mixed with more traditional CBT components in acceptance-based behavior therapy for generalized anxiety disorder (Orsillo, Roemer, & Holowka, 2005). ACT values components can be found in some variants of behavioral activation (Lejuez, Hopko, & Hopko, 2001). ACT has been added as a component to a residential drug and alcohol treatment with significant 12-step components in two studies (Luoma, Kohlenberg, Hayes, Bunting, & Rye, 2008; Luoma et al., 2012; Peterson & Zettle, 2009). These latter data are particularly important for integration in the United States, where many programs continue to have a 12-step focus. ACT has long been argued to be compatible with many 12-step sensibilities (Wilson, Hayes, & Byrd, 2000; see also Wilson & DuFrene, 2012, for a book-length self-help treatment that integrates these approaches).

ACT is theoretically consistent with the motivational interviewing approach, commonly employed with clients experiencing ambiguity about changing substance-related behaviors (Miller & Rollnick, 2002). Like ACT, MI is a collaborative approach, fostering a partnership between therapist and client (See Bricker & Wyszynski, chapter 9 of this volume, for an in-depth discussion of similarities between ACT and MI). Another common approach, harm reduction, is compatible with ACT in many respects. Marlatt and Witkiewitz (2002) describe the harm reduction approach as based upon three core objectives: to reduce detrimental substance-related consequences, to provide a treatment alternative to abstinence-only approaches, and to lower the treatment threshold for those unready or unwilling to cease all using. These three pragmatic harm reduction goals are entirely congruent with those of ACT.

Finally, ACT is closely related to and compatible with mindfulness-oriented interventions. Like ACT, mindfulness interventions have only recently begun to be studied empirically with regard to their application to substance use disorders (Bowen et al., 2009; Bowen, Chawla, & Marlatt, 2010). ACT's relationship to these interventions is twofold. First, from an ACT perspective, mindfulness is the convergence of four core processes: present-moment awareness, perspective taking, acceptance, and defusion (Hayes et al., 2011; Wilson, 2009). Because of this overlap, it would not be difficult to add substantial mindfulness training components to an ACT protocol. Likewise, the addition of ACT exercises that involve mindfulness could fit readily into a primarily mindfulness-based treatment. A second overlap between ACT and mindfulness-based treatments is the idea, widely held in both treatment development communities, that a personal practice on the part of the practitioner will allow the practitioner to deliver the treatment with sensitivity and integrity (see comments on this issue in Segal, Williams, & Teasdale, 2001).

Summary of Evidence: The State of the Research

Although the collective body of research pertaining to ACT and substance abuse is relatively new, it has received increased attention and is gaining momentum. In 2010, ACT was added to SAMHSA's National Registry of Evidence-Based Programs and Practices (Substance Abuse and Mental Health Services Administration, 2010). Generally, as an approach for smoking cessation, ACT has been shown to produce results comparable to those of CBT (Hernández-López, Luciano, Bricker, Roales-Nieto, & Montesinos, 2009) and results significantly better than those of nicotine replacement treatment (Gifford et al., 2004) or, when combined with bupropion, compared to the results of bupropion alone (Gifford et al., 2011). A pilot study found preliminary support for a treatment package combining ACT, nicotine replacement therapy, exposure, and relapse prevention to improve distress tolerance in early-lapse smokers (Brown et al., 2008). One recent study found preliminary support for a brief (five sessions, ninety minutes total) ACT intervention for smoking cessation delivered via telephone (Bricker, Mann, Marek, Liu, & Peterson, 2010).

With regard to alcohol abuse, a study conducted by Petersen and Zettle (2009) demonstrated quicker releases for inpatients experiencing comorbid depression and substance abuse compared to treatment as usual (which was couched within a 12-step program). Additionally, a case study published in 2003 described improved quality of life and a consumption rate that dropped to nearly zero in a male client diagnosed with alcohol dependence (Heffner, Eifert, Parker, Hernandez, & Sperry, 2003).

A study conducted by Twohig and colleagues (2007) provided preliminary evidence for the effectiveness of ACT with individuals dependent on marijuana. In terms of severe drug abuse, there is evidence that ACT performs as well or better compared to other efficacious treatments, including 12-step facilitation, methadone maintenance, and CBT (Hayes et al., 2004; Smout et al., 2010). A case study published in 2009 produced positive immediate and long-term (one-year) outcomes in a client receiving methadone maintenance in combination with twenty-four weekly ACT sessions (Stotts, Masuda, & Wilson, 2009). In a recent study on methadone detoxification, nearly double the number of participants in ACT condition were successfully detoxified from methadone (37%) as compared to those in drug counseling (19%), with no increase in risk for opiate use (Stotts et al., in press). Further, beyond showing reductions in substance use, recent studies have demonstrated the efficacy of ACT interventions in reducing self-stigma and shame surrounding substance abuse (Luoma et al., 2008; Luoma et al., 2012).

Research Directions and the Way Forward

Although preliminary evidence is promising, the majority of the work lies ahead. Consistent with the contextual behavioral science model (Hayes et al., 2011), we recommend that the development effort proceed across multiple strategic fronts. First, we should continue to test variants of ACT protocols both as freestanding treatments and as added components within existing institutionalized treatment efforts. We should continue to experiment with different levels of treatment duration and intensity in order to establish empirically optimal effective and intensive treatment protocols. In addition to the examination of efficacy, funding priorities ought to go to studies that sample theoretically relevant change processes over multiple time points. Contemporary CBT has focused too strongly on treatment outcomes and insufficiently on the necessity of various components and the processes of change through which they work. Because ACT suggests different mechanisms of change than have been common in mainstream traditional CBT, development of measures should be a priority. Behavioral and self-report measures assessing putative change processes will allow us to develop and teach efficient and effective treatment strategies. Also, in support of the increased process-focused research and treatment development agenda, we need to see experimental psychopathology that examines the impact of micro-interventions extracted from larger ACT protocols. Such studies can be done relatively quickly and inexpensively, and will provide steps that can set up later, far more expensive and burdensome dismantling studies. Finally, development of the model should continue to be executed in broad contexts, including applied contexts. Deep within the contextual behavioral science mode is the idea that the breadth of the treatment development effort and the involvement of a large and diverse treatment development community is the best way to ensure the creation of a broadly applicable, acceptable, and useful model.

The future will see how far these developments go, but in the meantime ACT and its underlying model are now at a place where they can begin to be deployed in treatment programs for addiction problems. The ACT approach seems to be flexible enough to work in a variety of settings, for a variety of problems, and with a variety of protocols. It can be combined with other elements commonly found in treatment facilities for substance use disorders. ACT is now part of the range of methods that should be considered for use by drug and alcohol counselors and other professionals who work with problems of addiction.

References

American Psychiatric Association. (2011). *Draft diagnostic and statistical manual of mental disorders* (5th ed.; *DSM-V*). Washington, DC: American Psychiatric Association. Retrieved January 11, 2011, from www.dsm5.org.

Bach, P., Gaudiano, B. A., Hayes, S. C., & Herbert, J. D. (in press). Acceptance and commitment therapy for psychosis: Intent to treat hospitalization outcome and mediation by believability. *Psychosis.*

Bach, P., & Hayes, S. C. (2002). The use of acceptance and commitment therapy to prevent the rehospitalization of psychotic patients: A randomized controlled trial. *Journal of Consulting and Clinical Psychology, 70,* 1129-1139.

Baker, T. B., Piper, M. E., McCarthy, D. E., Majeskie, M. R., & Fiore, M. C. (2004). Addiction motivation reformulated: An affective processing model of negative reinforcement. *Psychological Review, 111,* 33-51.

Barlow, D. H., Allen, L. B., & Choate, M. L. (2004). Toward a unified treatment for emotional disorders. *Behavior Therapy, 35,* 205-230.

Batten, S. V., & Hayes, S. C. (2005). Acceptance and commitment therapy in the treatment of comorbid substance abuse and post-traumatic stress disorder: A case study. *Clinical Case Studies, 4,* 246-262.

Beck, A. T., Rush, A. J., Shaw, B. F., & Emery, G. (1979). *Cognitive therapy of depression.* New York: Guilford Press.

Beck, A. T., Wright, F. D., Newman, C. F., & Liese, B. S. (1993). *Cognitive therapy of substance abuse.* New York: Guilford Press.

Bowen, S., Chawla, N., Collins, S., Witkiewitz, K., Hsu, S., Grow, J., et al. (2009). Mindfulness-based relapse prevention for substance use disorders: A pilot efficacy trial. *Substance Abuse, 30,* 205-305.

Bowen, S., Chawla, N., & Marlatt, G. A. (2010). *Mindfulness-based relapse prevention for addictive behaviors: A clinician's guide.* New York: Guilford Press.

Bowen, S., Witkiewitz, K., Dillworth, T. M., & Marlatt, A. (2007). The role of thought suppression in the relationship between mindfulness meditation and alcohol use. *Addictive Behaviors, 32,* 2324-2328.

Branstetter-Rost, A., Cushing, C., & Douleh, T. (2009). Personal values and pain tolerance: Does a values intervention add to acceptance? *Journal of Pain, 10,* 887-892.

Bricker, J. B., Mann, S. L., Marek, P. M., Liu, J., & Peterson, A. V. (2010). Telephone-delivered acceptance and commitment therapy for adult smoking cessation: A feasibility study. *Nicotine and Tobacco Research, 12,* 454-458.

Brown, R. A., Palm, K. M., Strong, D. R., Lejuez, C. W., Kahler, C. W., Zvolensky, M. J., et al. (2008). Distress tolerance treatment for early-lapse smokers: Rationale, program description, and preliminary findings. *Behavior Modification, 32,* 302-332.

Caselli, G., Bortolai, C., Leoni, M., Rovetto, F., & Spada, M. M. (2008). Rumination in problem drinkers. *Addiction Research and Theory, 16,* 564-571.

Caselli, G., Ferretti, C., Leoni, M., Rebecchi, D., Rovetto, F., & Spada, M. M. (2010). Rumination as a predictor of drinking behaviour in alcohol abusers: A prospective study. *Addiction, 105,* 1041-1048.

Chawla, N., & Ostafin, B. (2007). Experiential avoidance as a functional dimensional approach to psychopathology: An empirical review. *Journal of Clinical Psychology, 63,* 871-890.

Cooper, M. L., Russell, M., & George, W. H. (1988). Coping, expectancies, and alcohol abuse: A test of social learning formulations. *Journal of Abnormal Psychology, 97,* 218-230.

Curry, S. J., McBride, C., Grothaus, L. C., Louie, D., & Wagner, E. H. (1995). A randomized trial of self-help materials, personalized feedback, and telephone counseling with nonvolunteer smokers. *Journal of Consulting and Clinical Psychology, 6,* 1005-1014.

Curry, S. J., Wagner, E. H., & Grothaus, L. C. (1990). Intrinsic and extrinsic motivations for smoking cessation. *Journal of Consulting and Clinical Psychology, 58,* 310-316.

Delgado, L., Guerra, P., Perakakis, P., Vera, M., del Paso, G., & Vila, J. (2010). Treating chronic worry: Psychological and physiological effects of a training programme based on mindfulness. *Behaviour Research and Therapy, 48,* 873-882.

Evans, S., Ferrando, S., Findler, M., Stowell, C., Smart, C., & Haglin, D. (2008). Mindfulness-based cognitive therapy for generalized anxiety disorder. *Journal of Anxiety Disorders, 22,* 716-721.

Gifford, E. V., Kohlenberg, B. S., Hayes, S. C., Antonuccio, D. O., Piasecki, M. M., Rasmussen-Hall, M. L., et al. (2004). Acceptance-based treatment for smoking cessation. *Behavior Therapy, 35,* 689-705.

Gifford, E. V., Kohlenberg, B. S., Hayes, S. C., Pierson, H. M., Piasecki, M. P., Antonuccio, D. O., et al. (2011). Does acceptance and relationship focused behavior therapy contribute to bupropion outcomes? A randomized controlled trial of functional analytic psychotherapy and acceptance and commitment therapy for smoking cessation. *Behavior Therapy, 42,* 700-715.

Grant, B. F., Stinson, F. S., Dawson, D. A., Chou, S., Dufour, M. C., Compton, W., et al. (2006). Prevalence and co-occurrence of substance use disorders and independent mood and anxiety disorders: Results from the National Epidemiologic Survey on Alcohol and Related Conditions. *Alcohol Research and Health, 29,* 107-120.

Gratz, K. L., & Gunderson, J. G. (2006). Preliminary data on an acceptance-based emotion regulation group intervention for deliberate self-harm among women with borderline personality disorder. *Behavior Therapy, 37,* 25-35.

Gregg, J. A., Callaghan, G. M., Hayes, S. C., & Glenn-Lawson, J. L. (2007). Improving diabetes self-management through acceptance, mindfulness, and values: A randomized controlled trial. *Journal of Consulting and Clinical Psychology, 75,* 336-343.

Halpern, M. T., & Warner, K. E. (1993). Motivations for smoking cessation: A comparison of successful quitters and failures. *Journal of Substance Abuse, 5,* 247-256.

Hayes, S. C., Barnes-Holmes, D., & Roche, B. (2001). *Relational frame theory: A post-Skinnerian account of human language and cognition.* New York: Plenum Press.

Hayes, S. C., Luoma, J. B., Bond, F. W., Masuda, A., & Lillis, J. (2006). Acceptance and commitment therapy: Model, processes, and outcomes. *Behaviour Research and Therapy, 44,* 1-25.

Hayes, S. C., Strosahl, K. D., & Wilson, K. G. (2011). *Acceptance and commitment therapy: The process and practice of mindful change* (2nd ed.). New York: Guilford Press.

Hayes, S. C., Wilson, K. G., Gifford, E. V., Bissett, R., Piasecki, M., Batten, S. V., et al. (2004). A preliminary trial of twelve-step facilitation and acceptance and commitment therapy with polysubstance-abusing methadone-maintained opiate addicts. *Behavior Therapy, 35,* 667-688.

Heffner, M., Eifert, G. H., Parker, B. T., Hernandez, D. H., & Sperry, J. A. (2003). Valued directions: Acceptance and commitment therapy in the treatment of alcohol dependence. *Cognitive and Behavioral Practice, 10,* 378-383.

Hernández-López, M., Luciano, M., Bricker, J. B., Roales-Nieto, J. G., & Montesinos, F. (2009). Acceptance and commitment therapy for smoking cessation: A preliminary study of its effectiveness in comparison with cognitive behavioral therapy. *Psychology of Addictive Behaviors, 23,* 723-730.

Jarrett, R. B., Vittengl, J. R., Doyle, K., & Clark, L. (2007). Changes in cognitive content during and following cognitive therapy for recurrent depression: Substantial and enduring, but not predictive of change in depressive symptoms. *Journal of Consulting and Clinical Psychology, 75,* 432-446.

Kabat-Zinn, J. (1994). *Wherever you go, there you are: Mindfulness meditation in everyday life.* New York: Hyperion.

Khantzian, E. J. (1997). The self-medication hypothesis of substance use disorders: A reconsideration and recent applications. *Harvard Review of Psychiatry, 4,* 231-244.

Kocovski, N. L., Fleming, J. E., & Rector, N. A. (2009). Mindfulness and acceptance-based group therapy for social anxiety disorder: An open trial. *Cognitive and Behavioral Practice, 16,* 276-289.

Lejuez, C. W., Hopko, D. R., & Hopko, S. D. (2001). A brief behavioral activation treatment for depression: Treatment manual. *Behavior Modification, 25,* 255-286.

Lillis, J., Hayes, S. C., & Levin, M. E. (2011). Binge eating and weight control: The role of experiential avoidance. *Behavior Modification, 35,* 252-264.

Luoma, J. B., Kohlenberg, B. S., Hayes, S. C., Bunting, K., & Rye, A. K. (2008). Reducing self-stigma in substance abuse through acceptance and commitment therapy: Model, manual development, and pilot outcomes. *Addiction Research and Theory, 16,* 149-165.

Luoma, J. B., Kohlenberg, B. S., Hayes, S. C., & Fletcher, L. (2012). Slow and steady wins the race: A randomized clinical trial of acceptance and commitment therapy targeting shame in substance use disorders. *Journal of Consulting and Clinical Psychology, 80,* 43-53.

MacPherson, L., Matusiewicz, A. K., Strong, D. R., Hopko, D. R., Brown, R. A., Tull, M. T., et al. (2010). Randomized controlled trial of behavioral activation smoking cessation treatment for smokers with elevated depressive symptoms. *Journal of Consulting and Clinical Psychology, 78,* 55-61.

Mansell, W., Harvey, A., Watkins, E., & Shafran, R. (2009). Conceptual foundations of the transdiagnostic approach to CBT. *Journal of Cognitive Psychotherapy: An International Quarterly, 23,* 6-19.

Marlatt, G. A., & Witkiewitz, K. (2002). Harm reduction approaches to alcohol use: Health promotion, prevention, and treatment. *Addictive Behaviors, 27,* 867-886.

Martell, C. R., Dimidjian, S., & Herman-Dunn, R. (2010). *Behavioral activation for depression: A clinician's guide.* New York: Guilford Press.

Michalak, J., Hölz, A., & Teismann, T. (2011). Rumination as a predictor of relapse in mindfulness-based cognitive therapy for depression. *Psychology and Psychotherapy: Theory, Research, and Practice, 84,* 230-236.

Miller, W. R., & Rollnick, S. (2002). *Motivational interviewing: Preparing people for change.* New York: Guilford Press.

Muto, T., Hayes, S. C., & Jeffcoat, T. (2011). The effectiveness of acceptance and commitment therapy bibliotherapy for enhancing the psychological health of Japanese college students living abroad. *Behavior Therapy, 42,* 323-335.

Orsillo, S. M., Roemer, L., & Holowka, D. W. (2005). Acceptance-based behavioral therapies for anxiety: Using acceptance and mindfulness to enhance traditional cognitive-behavioral approaches. In S. M. Orsillo & L. Roemer (Eds.), *Acceptance and mindfulness-based approaches to anxiety: Conceptualization and treatment.* New York: Springer.

Ostafin, B. D., & Marlatt, G. A. (2008). Surfing the urge: Experiential acceptance moderates the relation between automatic alcohol motivation and hazardous drinking. *Journal of Social and Clinical Psychology, 27,* 404-418.

Palfai, T. P., Monti, P. M., Colby, S. M., & Rohsenow, D. J. (1997). Effects of suppressing the urge to drink on the accessibility of alcohol outcome expectancies. *Behaviour Research and Therapy, 35,* 59-65.

Petersen, C. L., & Zettle, R. D. (2009). Treating inpatients with comorbid depression and alcohol use disorders: A comparison of acceptance and commitment therapy versus treatment as usual. *Psychological Record, 59,* 521-536.

Salkovskis, P. M., & Reynolds, M. (1994). Thought suppression and smoking cessation. *Behaviour Research and Therapy, 32,* 193-201.

Segal, Z. V., Williams, M. G., & Teasdale, J. D. (2001). *Mindfulness-based cognitive therapy for depression.* New York: Guilford Press.

Shahar, B., Britton, W. B., Sbarra, D. A., Figueredo, A., & Bootzin, R. R. (2010). Mechanisms of change in mindfulness-based cognitive therapy for depression: Preliminary evidence from a randomized controlled trial. *International Journal of Cognitive Therapy, 3,* 402-418.

Smout, M. F., Longo, M., Harrison, S., Minniti, R., Wickes, W., & White, J. M. (2010). Psychosocial treatment for methamphetamine use disorders: A preliminary randomized controlled trial of cognitive behavior therapy and acceptance and commitment therapy. *Substance Abuse, 31,* 98-107.

Stotts, A. L., Green, C., Masuda, A., Grabowski, J., Wilson, K., Northrup, T., et al. (in press). A stage I pilot study of acceptance and commitment therapy for methadone detoxification. *Drug and Alcohol Dependence.*

Stotts, A. L., Masuda, A., & Wilson, K. G. (2009). Using acceptance and commitment therapy during methadone dose reduction: Rationale, treatment description, and a case report. *Cognitive and Behavioral Practice, 16,* 205-213.

Substance Abuse and Mental Health Services Administration. (2010, July). *Acceptance and commitment therapy.* Retrieved March 7, 2012, from www.nrepp.samhsa.gov/ViewIntervention.aspx?id=107.

Titchener, E. B. (1916). *A text-book of psychology.* New York: Macmillan.

Toll, B. A., Sobell, M. B., Wagner, E. F., & Sobell, L. C. (2001). The relationship between thought suppression and smoking cessation. *Addictive Behaviors, 26,* 509-515.

Törneke, N. (2010). *Learning RFT: An introduction to relational frame theory and its clinical application.* Oakland, CA: New Harbinger.

Twohig, M. P., Shoenberger, D., & Hayes, S. C. (2007). A preliminary investigation of acceptance and commitment therapy as a treatment for marijuana dependence in adults. *Journal of Applied Behavior Analysis, 40,* 619-632.

Vittengl, J. R., Clark, L., & Jarrett, R. B. (2009). Deterioration in psychosocial functioning predicts relapse/recurrence after cognitive therapy for depression. *Journal of Affective Disorders, 112,* 135-143.

Vøllestad, J., Sivertsen, B., & Nielsen, G. (2011). Mindfulness-based stress reduction for patients with anxiety disorders: Evaluation in a randomized controlled trial. *Behaviour Research and Therapy, 49,* 281-288.

Wicksell, R. K., Melin, L., & Olsson, G. L. (2007). Exposure and acceptance in the rehabilitation of adolescents with idiopathic chronic pain—A pilot study. *European Journal of Pain, 11,* 267-274.

Willem, L., Bijttebier, P., Claes, L., & Raes, F. (2011). Rumination subtypes in relation to problematic substance use in adolescence. *Personality and Individual Differences, 50,* 695-699.

Wilson, K. G., with DuFrene, T. (2009). *Mindfulness for two: An acceptance and commitment therapy approach to mindfulness in psychotherapy.* Oakland, CA: New Harbinger.

Wilson, K. G., & DuFrene, T. (2012). *The wisdom to know the difference: An acceptance and commitment therapy guide to recovery from addiction.* Oakland, CA: New Harbinger.

Wilson, K. G., Hayes, S. C., & Byrd, M. R. (2000). Exploring compatibilities between acceptance and commitment therapy and 12-step treatment for substance abuse. *Journal of Rational-Emotive and Cognitive-Behavior Therapy, 18,* 209-234.

Zettle, R. D., Rains, J. C., & Hayes, S. C. (2011). Processes of change in acceptance and commitment therapy and cognitive therapy for depression: A mediation reanalysis of Zettle and Rains. *Behavior Modification, 35,* 265-283.

CHAPTER 2

Dialectical Behavior Therapy for Substance-Dependent Individuals

Linda A. Dimeff

Behavioral Tech Research, Inc.

Jennifer H. R. Sayrs

Evidence Based Treatment Centers of Seattle

*D*ialectical behavior therapy for substance use disorders (DBT-SUD) is a comprehensive treatment for individuals with borderline personality disorder and substance use disorders (BPD-SUD; Linehan & Dimeff, 1997). DBT-SUD is heavily based on standard DBT, a treatment developed by Marsha M. Linehan, PhD, at the University of Washington, for chronically suicidal individuals with BPD (Linehan, 1993a, 1993b). With sixteen published randomized controlled trials to date supporting its efficacy, DBT meets the "well-established" criteria described by Chambless and Hollon (1998). With more evidence supporting its efficacy than any other approach for BPD, DBT is considered the gold-standard treatment for BPD (National Institute for Health and Clinical Excellence [NICE], 2009). Like standard DBT, DBT-SUD is a comprehensive, multimodal psychosocial treatment for a population of individuals with multiple, complex, and severe behavioral problems. Most of standard DBT was adopted into DBT-SUD, but with a number of specific adaptations to more fully address substance dependence (McMain, Sayrs, Dimeff, & Linehan, 2007). Three randomized controlled trials now support the efficacy of DBT-SUD (Linehan et al., 2002;

Linehan, Korslund, Lynch, Harned, & Rosenthal, 2009; Linehan, Lynch, et al., 2009; Linehan, Schmidt, et al., 1999).

Our intent in this chapter is to provide an overview of the DBT-SUD approach, as well a brief summary of the research to date on this treatment. While our focus will be on comorbid BPD and SUDs, elements of DBT seem to be of broad relevance for emotion dysregulation and SUDs more generally, and might be useful in specific cases.

Scope of the Problem

SUDs commonly co-occur with BPD (Trull, Sher, Minks-Brown, Durbin, & Burr, 2000) and result in serious and complex behavioral problems. In their extensive review of BPD and SUD comorbidity data, Trull and colleagues (2000) found that among those seeking substance abuse treatment, rates of BPD ranged from 5.2% to 65.1%. Prevalence of current SUDs among patients receiving treatment for BPD range from approximately 25% (Miller, Belkin, & Gibbons, 1994) to 67% (Dulit, Fyer, Haas, Sullivan, & Frances, 1990). Dulit and her colleagues (1990) found that only a small portion of the overlap (10%) can be accounted for by the fact that substance abuse is a criterion for BPD.

Individuals with BPD-SUD are more difficult to treat and have a wider range of problems compared to those with either SUD or BPD alone (Links, Heslegrave, Mitton, van Reekum, & Patrick, 1995). For example, rates of suicide and suicide attempts, already high among people with BPD (Stone, 2009) and people with substance abuse problems (Links et al., 1995; Rossow & Lauritzen, 1999) are even higher for individuals with both disorders (Rossow & Lauritzen, 1999). Furthermore, studies comparing people with substance abuse problems with and without personality disorders have reported that those with personality disorders have significantly more behavioral, legal, and medical problems, including alcoholism and depression, and are more extensively involved in substance abuse than patients without personality disorders (e.g., Cacciola, Alterman, Rutherford, McKay, & Mulvaney, 2001; McKay, Alterman, Cacciola, Mulvaney, & O'Brien, 2000). Those with BPD and SUD also have more severe psychiatric problems than patients with other personality disorders (Skinstad & Swain, 2001).

Biosocial Model

From a DBT perspective, the core problem in BPD and BPD-SUD is pervasive emotion dysregulation (Linehan, 1993a). This core concept guides all elements of the treatment. Indeed, BPD criterion behaviors are understood in this context as either functioning to regulate emotions (e.g., suicidal and substance use behaviors) or as a consequence of dysregulation (e.g., a significant interpersonal fight). Linehan's theory posits that pervasive emotion dysregulation develops and is maintained by biological factors that facilitate vulnerability to emotion and by environmental factors, namely an invalidating environment.

Vulnerability to Emotion

Linehan's model posits that individuals with BPD and BPD-SUD experience greater vulnerability to emotion than those without BPD due to a number of possible factors (e.g., genes, intrauterine factors, or temperament). This vulnerability is characterized by heightened emotional sensitivity, heightened emotional reactivity, and a slow return to baseline (Linehan, 1993a). Recent findings from basic research demonstrate that those with BPD do indeed experience more frequent, more intense, and more long-lasting aversive states (Stiglmayr et al., 2005), and that this vulnerability may directly contribute to challenges in regulating emotion (e.g., Ebner-Priemer et al., 2005; Juengling et al., 2003).

Invalidating Environment

Biologically based vulnerability to emotional sensitivity and intensity is not, by itself, problematic. It is when a biologically vulnerable individual and an invalidating environment transact, or interact repeatedly over an extended period of time, that problems can arise (Linehan, 1993a). In an invalidating social or familial environment, an individual's communication of private experiences (e.g., thoughts, feelings, and physiological experiences that are not observable to others) are pervasively met by messages such as "You shouldn't feel that way," "You're manipulating," "You're paranoid," or other communications that the individual's private experiences are inaccurate. Other examples of invalidating environments include families that favor controlling or inhibiting emotional expressiveness, that disapprove of expressed negative affect, or that restrict demands the child may make on the environment ("If you want something, you may only ask when I invite you to").

The consequences of growing up in an environment that pervasively, consistently communicates that experiences and expressions are invalid are considerable. Such environments contribute to emotional dysregulation by failing to teach the child to label and modulate arousal, tolerate distress, and trust his or her own emotional responses as valid interpretations of events. When the child's own experiences are invalidated, the child learns instead to scan the environment for cues about how to act and feel. By exaggerating the ease with which life's problems can be solved, the environment fails to teach the child how to form realistic goals. By punishing the expression of negative emotion and responding erratically to emotional communication only after escalation by the child, the family shapes a style of emotional expression in which the child vacillates between extreme inhibition and suppression of emotional experience, on the one hand, and expression of extreme emotions, on the other. Because the child does not learn to label, predict, or understand his or her emotions and is punished for displaying them, the experience of an emotion can be highly distressing. Myriad strategies to regulate or eliminate emotions may develop, which for BPD-SUD clients include substance use, suicidal behavior, and/or nonsuicidal self-injurious behavior.

Dialectical Philosophy and DBT

DBT is defined in part by its philosophical base in dialectics. Commonly associated with the teachings of Marx and Hegel, *dialectics* refers to a process of change, a method of logic or argumentation, and a particular understanding of the nature of reality (Linehan & Schmidt, 1995). As a process of change, dialectics posits that every idea or event (thesis) contains its opposite (antithesis), the presence of which transforms the thesis and ultimately leads to a reconciliation of opposites (synthesis).

Importantly, synthesis seldom is achieved through quiet mediation or accommodation of differences (for example, adding black to white pigment to achieve a medium gray), but instead occurs through a dynamic process of movement and, often, complete inclusion of opposing forces.

The overriding dialectic in DBT-SUD is the need to radically accept reality as it is (including pain and suffering) while at the same time working to change it. It is within this dialectic that the Zen practices of mindfulness, including observing, taking a nonjudgmental stance, and accepting the current moment, are integrated with a technology of change using cognitive and behavioral techniques. This dance between the two core poles in DBT is, in many respects, consistent with the notion of acceptance and change practiced within 12-step programs and embodied in the Serenity Prayer that is recited at 12-step meetings: "God, grant me the serenity to accept the things I cannot change, courage to change the things I can, and wisdom to know the difference."

Core assumptions about the nature of reality in dialectics also form the nucleus of DBT. First, in dialectics reality is characterized by whole-ness and connection. Parts are important only in relation to one another and in relation to the whole that they help create, define, and give meaning to. Given the interconnectedness of all things, changes any-where in the system result in changes throughout the system. Second, change is considered continuous; one can never step in the same river twice, so to speak, as each moment is changed by the moments before it. Third, change occurs through dynamic interactions between polarity, as captured in the movement from tension between thesis and antithesis to synthesis to the next thesis, and so on.

The spirit of a dialectical perspective is to never accept a final truth or an undisputed fact, and to always consider the question, "What is being left out of our understanding?" Truth is neither absolute nor rela-tive but is always evolving, developing, and constructed over time. The ability to see the validity of both sides of an argument, as well as to reach a synthesis of both sides (which is different from a compromise), demands skills that most patients with BPD-SUD lack when they enter treatment. Teaching clients how to think dialectically provides a way out of dichoto-mous, black-or-white thinking patterns that limit their options and moves them from an "either-or" perspective to a "both-and" position.

Modes and Functions of Treatment

DBT-SUD is a principle-driven, voluntary treatment that balances problem-solving and other change-based strategies with acceptance-based strategies. It is comprised of four treatment modes: weekly individual therapy, weekly skills training group, weekly therapist consultation team, and as-needed phone consultation. Ancillary services that often augment DBT-SUD include case management, vocational rehabilitation, and drug-replacement pharmacotherapy. More important than the modes are their corresponding functions, or what DBT seeks to accomplish in a particular mode. To ensure fidelity to the model, a DBT-SUD program will need to satisfy all five of its functions—enhancing motivation, enhancing capabilities, skills generalization, structuring the treatment environment, and enhancing therapist motivation and capability—as detailed below.

Enhancing Motivation

Enhancing clients' motivation refers to the strategic effort, throughout treatment, to align important controlling variables to maximize the likelihood that clients will engage in effective behavior and minimize the likelihood that they will engage in ineffective behaviors. From a behavioral perspective, motivation emphasizes the probability of effective behavior, not getting clients to enjoy engaging in therapy or skills. This function is typically relegated to the realm of individual therapy because of the unique role the individual therapist plays in working collaboratively with clients in developing and updating their treatment plan, and because of the therapist's intimate understanding of the individual client's problems. In milieu settings, however, this function may be largely subsumed by the milieu. For example, skillful behavior can be reinforced with increased privileges. In essence, the task of the primary treatment provider in particular and the treatment as a whole is to identify and execute those conditions most likely to produce functional behavior from the client in those situations where skillful behavior is most needed.

Enhancing Capabilities

DBT-SUD assumes that clients begin treatment with significant skills deficits. In many instances, clients simply lack the behavioral skills to act in accordance with their goals. In other instances, they may know what is required in a situation but simply cannot produce the behavior in a particular context (e.g., when severely depressed or when with family members who are judgmental about their addiction). Enhancing capabilities can take many forms in DBT, the most common of which is participating in DBT skills training, in which clients are introduced to a variety of skills in four skills modules: mindfulness, emotion regulation, interpersonal effectiveness, and distress tolerance (Linehan, 1993b). Emphasis is placed on learning new skills through didactic presentation of information (skills acquisition) and modeling, rehearsal, and feedback to improve their capacity to use the skill (skills strengthening). Enhancing capability can also be achieved through the effective use of pharmacotherapy.

Skills Generalization

The challenge faced by many SUD treatments is relapse following discharge. Although clients are able to act skillfully when removed from their daily stressors and the environmental cues that saturate their daily lives, they may have difficulty maintaining abstinence once they leave the controlled treatment environment. For this reason, skills generalization is an imperative function of DBT-SUD to ensure that the newly acquired skills necessary to maintain abstinence emerge when needed in the context of the client's life.

There are several ways to accomplish generalization, including audio-recording sessions and having clients listen to them at home, and assigning homework for practice in the natural environment. In outpatient settings, an important means of generalization involves after-hours phone contact with the therapist for purposes of DBT skills coaching in real time. Within residential environments, an important method of skills generalization involves coaching as needed and on the fly (i.e., outside of structured, planned therapeutic activities when it is evident to the client and/or staff that behavioral skills are required to avert an incident but are not being produced). Displaying DBT skills posters (often made by residents) throughout the milieu is another milieu-based method for facilitating generalization of skills.

Structuring the Treatment Environment

There are two key objectives with respect to structuring the treatment environment. The first objective is to maximize the efficiency and effectiveness of treatment. This can take the form of lining up other ancillary treatments, self-help programs, and services, including pharmacotherapy (such as drug-replacement services), vocational rehabilitation, case management, probation, an AA or NA sponsor, and family members who can actively assist in their loved one's treatment. The second objective is to minimize factors that compromise DBT-SUD's impact. This can involve key individuals, programs, or systems that interfere with the effective delivery of DBT-SUD or dilute its strength. Common examples include barring clients from utilizing services under the influence of drugs (a policy at odds with the DBT-SUD approach, which states that clients need to learn new skills in all contexts, including under the influence, as long as their behavior does not interfere with the learning of other group members); probation officers expecting to receive weekly results of parolees' drug testing, which are likely to cause harm to the client and interfere with treatment; an NA sponsor objecting to the high dose of methadone the client is receiving to manage withdrawal symptoms; or clients' parents continuing to provide them with excessive financial assistance following every aversive event caused by drug use, such as giving a client a new car after he or she totaled a previous car while intoxicated.

Enhancing Therapist Motivation and Capability

Clients with BPD-SUD are among the most difficult, challenging, and stressful to treat precisely because of the nature and severity of their behavioral problems. Most of these patients present with a myriad of other disorders, face a number of complex life challenges (e.g., unstable housing, intimate partner violence, compromised physical health, warrants out for their arrest, or few if any stable friends or family members who don't abuse drugs). Most have previously "failed" in other treatments. Making matters worse, the increased risk of death by suicide, unintentional overdose, or homicide creates further stress on their treatment providers. Not surprisingly, many therapists are reluctant to treat these multidiagnostic, severe, and high-risk patients, and burnout among those who do is not uncommon. For these reasons, therapists treating such high-risk, complex clients need consultation and support to remain effective and motivated (Linehan, 1993a; NICE, 2009). Linehan (1993a) initially developed the mode of the DBT consultation team with the specific intent to enhance therapists' capabilities and motivation to deliver the best possible treatment for the patients. The DBT consultation team was envisioned as therapy for the therapist, providing dedicated time and focus on those issues that directly impact clients' care.

The importance of this function and its corresponding mode when working with BPD-SUD patients cannot be overstated. Indeed, this function is best fulfilled when DBT-SUD is understood as a treatment delivered by a community of providers working as a seamless team. Where teams are unavailable, such as in rural areas or settings where only one DBT therapist is employed, webcam meetings, phone consultation, and supervision may also serve this function. It is extremely important to note that, just as in DBT, participation in a DBT team must be voluntary, where therapists willingly agree to follow the principles of DBT.

DBT-SUD Target Hierarchy, Clear Mind, and the Path to Clear Mind

The DBT hierarchy (Linehan, 1993a) provides clinicians and clients with clear principles to help organize and prioritize the client's problems and topics in session. It is not uncommon for a BPD-SUD client to come to session with four or more high-priority clinically relevant situations. For example, a client, who happens to show up twenty minutes late to session and missed the previous group because she couldn't get a ride, gets free rent from her boyfriend in exchange for sex on demand, continues to binge and purge, is drinking excessively (over thirty drinks a week total), has steady but reasonably high suicidal ideation, continues to use heroin, has near-daily flashbacks associated with the murder of a friend, and has ongoing conflicts with her boyfriend that have escalated to include pushing and shoving. When faced with multiple severe and unique problems, how do you decide where to start? The DBT target hierarchy provides a clear path.

DBT's target hierarchy begins with decreasing imminent life-threatening behaviors, (e.g., suicidal, nonsuicidal self-injurious, and homicidal behaviors); followed by decreasing client and therapist behaviors that interfere with therapy (e.g., not attending therapy, dissociating during session, arriving late, attending sessions significantly intoxicated, or not engaging during the session), decreasing behaviors that interfere with quality of life (e.g., homelessness, probation, Axis I behavioral problems, or domestic violence), and increasing behavioral skills. The logic is simple: the client has to stay alive in order to receive the treatment, so all behaviors associated with imminent risk of dying go to the top of the behavioral hierarchy list. Next, it is important that the client remain in treatment, attend and actively participate in session, and engage in behaviors that do not interfere with treatment. The same set of expectations is also true for the clinician. Rather than waiting for the client to drop out or for the therapist to get burnedout, the idea is to proactively treat behaviors that interfere with therapy. Next, in standard DBT, quality-of-life targets are typically chosen and prioritized by clients in collaboration with their DBT individual therapist to meet their most important goals for therapy. In DBT-SUD, decreasing drug use and behavioral patterns associated with drug use is typically the highest-order behavioral target within the category of behaviors that interfere with quality of life. The final target is increasing behavioral skills—something that the therapist should be doing while treating the higher-order targets to, in effect, "replace pills with skills."

It is important to note that although this is a hierarchy, it does not suggest rigidity. It is not necessary to ignore lower-level targets when higher-order targets are present. Severe drug use, a behavior that interferes with quality of life, may be targeted in each session. The DBT-SUD therapist must simply ensure that higher-order targets are attended to, and the hierarchy provides the structure needed to organize and address such essential targets.

Clear Mind

Clear mind is the ultimate goal of the substance abuse targets in DBT. It is a prerequisite to getting into wise mind (Linehan, 1993a, 1993b), in which the patient can synthesize the poles of reasonable mind (where one is influenced only by logic without the benefit of emotion) and emotion mind (where one is influenced only by emotions without the benefit of logic) to incorporate all ways of knowing. *Wise mind* is, by definition, a state where one is able to make the wisest decisions possible, knowing just what is needed in any given moment. *Clear mind* is a dialectic within itself; it is the synthesis of addict mind and clean mind. Substance-abusing patients start treatment in addict mind, in which their thoughts, beliefs, actions, and emotions are controlled by craving drugs, finding drugs, and using drugs. This is the state where one is "chasing the bag," impulsive, and willing to sacrifice what is important just to obtain and use the desired substance. After some clean time, patients often move to clean mind. In *clean mind*, the patient is not using but forgets that she or he may be in danger of using again. This state can be thought of as being "blinded by the light," or having one's judgment clouded by the fact that one has finally managed to get off drugs. Patients in this state may become reckless, thinking they are immune from future problems because they have succeeded in getting clean. As a result, they may fail to manage pain appropriately, ignore temptations or cues that increase their vulnerability to using, and keep options to use drugs open.

In clear mind, the patient has achieved a state of clean mind *and* remains very aware that addict mind could return at any time. Cues may still lead to intense cravings and, without intervention, to actual drug use. The patient not only stops to enjoy success, but also prepares for future problems and has plans for what to do if staying clean becomes difficult. A metaphor that may help patients understand this point is as follows: Being in clear mind is like going for a hike up a mountain. As you near the peak, you may get excited and feel that the hard work is done. When you get to the top, you stop working, rest, and enjoy the view. Without taking away from the thrill and relief of reaching the top, to be effective you need to remember that there is still a return trip. You need to leave the peak while there is still enough daylight to get back to the car; you need to make sure you have enough food and water for the return trip; and you need to be sure you have enough energy to get back safely. The point is, while you are enjoying your success, you must also remember and prepare for the remaining challenges of hiking down the mountain. Thus, in clear mind, you work hard at getting clean and really appreciate the success of being clean, but you do not forget that getting clean isn't the end point. There is still a journey after getting clean that involves staying clean. Additionally, planning for the return trip can't be put off until you reach the top of the mountain. If you make it to the peak and then realize you don't have enough food or energy for the return trip, you will be in trouble. Planning for staying clean needs to occur from the start, just as planning for the entire hike begins before you leave home.

Path to Clear Mind

The Path to Clear Mind is a unique set of behavioral targets for substance abuse aimed at helping clients get off drugs and stay off, nestled within the subset of targets that interfere with quality of life. The path begins with the overarching target of decreasing substance abuse, then places equal focus on other important steps necessary in becoming and staying clean. The behavioral targets specific to substance abuse include decreasing substance abuse, decreasing physical discomfort, decreasing urges and cravings to use, decreasing options and cues to use, decreasing capitulation to drug use, and increasing community reinforcement of clear mind behaviors. In contrast to the standard DBT hierarchy, the targets that form the Path to Clear Mind are not hierarchically arranged with the exception of the first, logical target: decreasing substance abuse.

DECREASING SUBSTANCE ABUSE

The highest-order target of DBT-SUD is decreasing use of illegal and legal drugs of abuse, as well as misuse of prescription and over-the-counter medications. The majority of BPD-SUD patients we have treated have historically abused many drugs, and when they enter treatment, they frequently meet dependence criteria for more than once substance. One of the first considerations faced is which drugs should be targeted with a goal of abstinence and which should be (for now, and potentially forever) ignored. There are three principles that govern this selection.

First, target the primary substance of abuse—the drug or drugs most significantly compromising the individual's quality of life. In our experience, it is readily apparent to both the client and clinician which drug or drugs are causing the greatest havoc. Second, target those drugs that are on the path to higher-order targets, such as suicidal or nonsuicidal self-injurious behavior or using the primary drug of abuse. Finally, the goal must be pragmatic and attainable. Clients with both BPD and SUD typically have a myriad of problem behaviors. Realistically, there is only so much a severely disordered individual with BPD and SUD can be expected to change at one time. While a client's weekly consumption of alcohol, for example, may far exceed recommended guidelines for safe use, unless the client states an explicit interest in stopping alcohol use, unless alcohol is the primary drug causing the individual problems, or unless alcohol is reliably associated with use of the primary drug of choice or another higher-order target (e.g., the client only attempts suicide when drunk), DBT may not choose to target it as a treatment goal or may postpone focusing on it until other gains are made.

DECREASING PHYSICAL DISCOMFORT

The target of decreasing physical discomfort is particularly focused on reducing discomfort due to abstinence or withdrawal symptoms but also includes other causes of physical discomfort. Drug use and abstinence from drugs both involve a great deal of physical discomfort. Many chronic drug users have damaged their body's ability to regulate pain, so pain itself may be much more acute for them than it would be for people who don't use drugs. Therefore, these clients are often significantly more afraid of pain and withdrawal. DBT-SUD places strong emphasis on helping clients manage pain, both by using DBT skills (e.g., distraction, self-soothing, and mindfulness skills; Linehan, 1993b) and via medical interventions (such as supervised detox, replacement medication or other forms of pharmacotherapy that help them deal with ending drug use, and so on).

DECREASING URGES AND CRAVINGS TO USE

Training clients to recognize and manage urges, cravings, and temptations to use is extremely important. Many BPD-SUD clients believe that urges will continue to build in force and will not cease unless they use drugs; most have never ridden out an urge and are simply unaware that urges will subside over time if ignored. The fact that drug urges do not automatically lead to drug use is, for many, an important revelation. Clients are taught a variety of skills to manage urges. These include observing and labeling an urge as "only an urge," urge surfing (described below), reviewing the long-term pros and cons of using, distracting from the urge to use, self-soothing, tolerating the urge just for a moment, immersing one's face in ice water to elicit the dive response to help regulate emotion (Porges, Doussard-Roosevelt, & Maiti, 1994), and conveying the concept that urges and cravings are temporary and need not result in action. Clients are also taught how they might extinguish urges over time by not acting on them or focusing on them, and how they might strengthen urges by focusing intensely on them or having an unwritten rule that once an urge gets to a certain strength, it is acceptable to use. Clients' urge patterns are analyzed carefully, and plans for resisting intense urges are carefully created and followed.

DECREASING OPTIONS AND CUES TO USE

The behavioral target of decreasing options and cues for drug use involves attending to a variety of behaviors associated with using drugs, including getting rid of drug paraphernalia, changing phone numbers, moving, changing jobs, changing bus routes, being public about getting clean, and changing how one dresses and one's general appearance. The overarching concept is to completely shut the door to all avenues and situations associated with using drugs, leaving no route to use available whatsoever. It is as if clients intentionally paint themselves into a drug-free corner during moments of high willingness to stop using drugs (often at the start of treatment and following a slip) by actively burning bridges to all avenues to drug use.

An important subcategory of decreasing options to use is decreasing lying. Not all SUD clients lie, and DBT-SUD clinicians generally assume that clients are honest, but some BPD-SUD clients acquire a habit of lying in order to get drugs, use, and hide drug use. Because of this, lying is actively targeted in DBT-SUD in several ways. One is that DBT-SUD clinicians directly assess whether clients lie, when and how they lie, and how they are likely to lie directly to the clinician. In another strategy, lying is directly targeted on the DBT diary card where clients record the number of incidents of lying per day (including whether they are lying about lying). DBT-SUD clinicians also directly ask their BPD-SUD clients if they are lying in situations that rouse their suspicion. In addition, drug screens are actively incorporated into the treatment to reduce the temptation to lie about drug use. And finally, the therapist may use strategic naiveté, a form of extending whereby the therapist takes a lie more seriously than the client had expected (e.g., spending a significant amount of session time on how to avoid the person who "put drugs in the client's coffee," which eventually becomes frustrating to the client and may thereby lead to a more direct and honest dialogue or direct behavioral change).

DECREASING CAPITULATION TO DRUG USE

Capitulation refers to surrendering, giving up, and acting as though future use is inevitable. Targeting every instance of capitulation is very important in training clients to avoid drugs. When a client stops using but keeps needles "just in case," this must be targeted as a case of capitulating to drug use. Another example is when clients are presented with drugs from a friend or partner and assume they cannot say no—that it is simply inevitable that they will use in that situation. Heavy focus on how to navigate those situations or avoid them altogether is essential in therapy.

INCREASING COMMUNITY REINFORCEMENT OF CLEAR MIND BEHAVIORS

Clients who succeed in getting clean will not stay clean if their new, skillful behaviors are not reinforced. It is important for them to arrange their environments so that they receive reinforcement, not punishment, for engaging in these changes. A patient who manages to get clean but still spends time with friends who use is likely to experience punishers that can threaten treatment success (e.g., statements such as "I can't believe you're seeing a therapist" or "This won't last"). This target focuses on helping the client find new friends, social activities, vocational settings, and other environments that will provide support for clean behaviors and withdraw support or even punish behaviors related to drug use.

The interpersonal effectiveness skills (Linehan, 1993a) are particularly helpful in building these new relationships.

Achieving Abstinence Dialectically

A dialectical approach to abstinence balances two prevailing and diametrically opposed approaches to drug treatment: absolute abstinence (e.g., pushing for clients to stop using drugs immediately and completely) and harm reduction (e.g., teaching clients to identify specific strategies to minimize the harmful effects of using should they lapse or to use drugs in safer and more controlled ways). In dialectical abstinence, a synthesis is sought in which there is recognition that, on the one hand, harm reduction approaches such as relapse prevention are effective in reducing the frequency and intensity of relapses following periods of abstinence from drug use (Marlatt & Donovan, 2005; Marlatt & Gordon, 1985) and, on the other hand, absolute abstinence approaches are effective in lengthening the interval between periods of use (Hall, Havassy, & Wasserman, 1990). Dialectical abstinence is a synthesis of unrelenting insistence on total abstinence before drug use with an emphasis on radical acceptance, nonjudgmental problem-solving, and effective relapse prevention after drug use, followed by a quick return to the unrelenting insistence on abstinence.

Absolute abstinence involves a variety of self-management and other strategies intended to achieve abstinence while simultaneously decreasing the probability of momentary waffling or capitulating. The emphasis on absolute abstinence begins in the first session of DBT, when the therapist communicates an expectation of abstinence by asking for a commitment from the client to stop using drugs now. Because a lifetime of abstinence can seem out of reach, clients are encouraged to make a commitment to absolute abstinence, but only for a length of time they know they are 100% certain they will be able to achieve. The commitment to 100% abstinence may be for a month, a day, or five minutes. The client then commits to the next achievable time interval after completing the previous length. Abstinence is ultimately achieved through piecing together manageable moments of time. This concept is no different from the 12-step slogan "just for today," used as a cognitive strategy to reach a particular end—a lifetime of abstinence achieved one moment at a time.

A second absolute abstinence strategy involves teaching clients to cope ahead (Linehan, 2012)—a behavioral skill of looking ahead to the future to anticipate potential cues in the moments, hours, and days ahead, and then proactively problem solving and rehearsing solutions to high-risk situations that may otherwise threaten their abstinence. Clients are also encouraged to burn bridges to drug use so they no longer have access to drugs (essentially the target of decreasing options and cues to use, discussed above). Woven throughout the absolute abstinence pole of the dialectic is the clear message that use of drugs would be a complete disaster and must be avoided.

With no allegiance to a particular ideology or approach other than achieving the ultimate treatment goal (i.e., a drug-free life that is worth living), the focus shifts rapidly from the absolute abstinence pole to relapse prevention once a slip has occurred. The lapse is then viewed simply as a problem to solve (rather than evidence of treatment failure), and emphasis shifts to failing well—dusting oneself off after the fall and getting back up. As with Marlatt's concept of prolapse in relapse prevention (Marlatt & Gordon, 1985), the focus becomes gleaning all that can be learned from the lapse by means of a thorough behavioral chain analysis in the service of preventing a full relapse and reducing the probability of future lapses. This cognitive reframing of the lapse also functions as treatment for the intense negative emotions and associated maladaptive cognitions (e.g., *What's the point?* or *I've already blown it. I might as well really go for it*) that comprise what Marlatt and Gordon (1985) have described as the abstinence violation effect, which can interfere with effective problem solving following the lapse.

In addition, failing well also involves repairing the harm caused to others and oneself during the lapse. This concept of assuming responsibility for the damage done during the period of drug use is similar to making amends in 12-step approaches (steps 8 and 9; Alcoholics Anonymous, 2006) and serves two functions: It increases awareness and memory of the negative consequences when the person use drugs. And it directly treats a component of the abstinence violation effect—namely, justified guilt. This may be particularly important for individuals with BPD and SUD, given their proneness to emotion dysregulation. Once the individual has resumed abstinence, the therapist returns to the opposite pole (absolute abstinence).

The concept of dialectical abstinence is similar to the actions of a quarterback in football. In each play, the quarterback is never fully content to obtain a few extra yards for a first down; he is always striving to score a touchdown, and all plays are organized in the service of a touchdown. The DBT-SUD therapist takes a similar approach, running with the client in the direction of the goal, stopping only if clients fall and only long enough to get clients back on their feet, and ready to resume full intent to score a touchdown in the next play. Importantly, DBT does not make continuation of treatment (e.g., receipt of replacement medications when prescribed or attendance at sessions) contingent on abstinence. Rather than punishing the client for having the very problems treatment was sought for in the first place, the assumption is instead that clients are doing the best they can but nonetheless must work harder to achieve a life worth living.

A common misunderstanding in DBT involves the scope of abstinence required. Does DBT, for example, view "a drug as a drug as a drug," as is the case in many 12-step programs, and require abstinence from all drugs and alcohol? As discussed above, DBT-SUD, like relapse prevention, does not require abstinence from all substances. Instead, it uses an ideographic approach that is guided by principle and based on thorough behavioral assessment of the drug use and its consequences. To review, the principles determining the scope of abstinence are threefold. First, target abstinence from the primary drugs of abuse (those that are causing the most significant problems for the client). Second, target abstinence from other drugs that appear to reliably precipitate use of the primary drug of abuse, suicidal behavior, or other higher-order targets. Third, make sure that the treatment goals are attainable.

Attachment Strategies

As is often the case with clients with drug abuse problems, some clients with BPD are difficult to hook into treatment. In contrast to those who attach easily to their primary treatment providers, they instead behave like butterflies, flying frequently into and out of the therapist's hand, departing at just the very moment when the therapist believes they are landed for good (Linehan, 1993a). We've found that this is particularly the case with drug-dependent clients with BPD. Common "butterfly" problems include engaging in therapy only episodically, not returning phone calls or not participating in treatment, and, ultimately, terminating treatment early. Additionally, the therapist of an unattached, "butterfly" client has less power to persuade the client to do things he or she prefers not to do (including staying alive and forestalling a suicide attempt) and may therefore have less motivation to stay close to such a client.

Approaches for how best to treat unattached BPD-SUD clients range along the continuum from not intervening at all and allowing clients to hit bottom (e.g., using until the natural aversive consequences of drug use are directly experienced) to bringing the therapy directly to clients in their environment. How assertive the DBT therapist is in getting the client to engage in treatment is entirely dependent on the factors controlling the client's "butterfly" behavior and on the most effective strategy to ultimately assist the client in getting off drugs and building a life worth living. Often, particularly early in treatment, the DBT therapist is extremely active in building and retaining attachment.

DBT includes a number of strategies that address the problem of client ambivalence about treatment and change, as well as strategies for reaching clients who would otherwise be difficult to engage. In addition, a set of strategies tailored to address the specific challenges faced by people with BPD and SUD has been developed. These attachment strategies function to increase the positive valence of therapy and the therapist, to reengage "lost" clients, and to prevent deleterious consequences that commonly occur during periods when clients fall out of contact with their therapists. Until an attachment is secured and the substance-dependent individual with BPD is out of significant danger of relapse, DBT therapists are typically active (rather than assuming a wait-and-see stance) in finding "lost" clients and getting them reengaged in treatment.

Beginning in the initial individual therapy sessions after the client has agreed to participate in DBT, the therapist orients the client to the attachment problem, and the two discuss the likelihood that the client may fall out of contact with the therapist during the course of treatment. A "just in case" plan is established—including generating a list of all the places the therapist might look for the client should he or she disappear (including addresses and phone numbers of drug-using friends and places where the client goes to use drugs), as well as supportive family members and friends who can be counted on to help the therapist and client should this occur. Other strategies include increasing contact with the client during the first several months of treatment (e.g., having scheduled check-in phone calls between sessions or exchanging voice mail or e-mail messages), conducting therapy in vivo (e.g., at the client's home, in a park or car, or at a diner), shortening or lengthening therapy sessions, and actively finding clients when they disappear. This may also include some humor, such as mailing a bottle of glue with a note saying, "Stick with me!"

Increasing Skills for Avoiding Illicit Drug Use

As in standard DBT, skills training in DBT-SUD is designed to remediate behavioral skills deficits typical of those with BPD. Four groups of DBT skills—core mindfulness skills, distress tolerance skills, emotion regulation skills, and interpersonal effectiveness skills—are taught in a structured format. These skills are outlined and described in great detail in Linehan's *Skills Training Manual for Treating Borderline Personality Disorder* (Linehan, 1993b). Self-management skills, a requisite skill set for learning all other skills, are taught as needed throughout the treatment. The standard DBT skills are easily applicable to problems faced by those with BPD and SUDs.

Mindfulness

Mindfulness skills are central to DBT-SUD, so much so that they are referred to as core skills. The skills are a psychological and behavioral translation of meditation skills usually taught in Eastern spiritual practices. Drawn most heavily from the practice of Zen, the skills are compatible with most Western contemplative and Eastern meditation practices. Mindfulness skills include three "what" core skills (observing, describing, and participating) and three "how" core skills (nonjudgmentalness, one-mindfulness, and effectiveness). As a whole, they are intended to help cultivate wise mind, wherein actions are governed by wisdom and intuition in accordance with one's values and long-term goals.

Mindfulness in its totality has to do with the quality of awareness one brings to activities (Linehan, 1993b). The goal is to learn to focus the mind and awareness in the current moment, rather than splitting attention between several activities or thoughts. Mindfulness requires control of attention, a crucial capability for achieving and sustaining abstinence— and one that often is often lacking in BPD-SUD clients. It is not uncommon for these clients to be distracted by urges, cravings, and distressing moods, emotions, and thoughts (e.g., thoughts about the past or worries about the future, including where the next fix will come from). DBT mindfulness skills help cultivate the ability to be fully awake, alert, and aware in the present moment and to act in ways that are skillful.

Distress Tolerance

Until recently, treatment of mental health problems has paid little attention to simply accepting, finding meaning in, and tolerating distressing situations in life; rather, the focus has been on changing distressing situations, cognitions, and behaviors. Borrowing again from Zen and other acceptance-based traditions, DBT places an equal emphasis on bearing pain skillfully and on changing (reducing) pain. Given that pain is a part of life, particularly for those with BPD-SUD, and cannot be avoided, the ability to tolerate and accept pain is an essential survival skill. Indeed, the inability to tolerate pain often creates conditions that cause more pain and suffering to arise. Distress tolerance skills, which incorporate the use of mindfulness skills, involve the ability to fully accept oneself and one's situation in a nonevaluative and nonjudgmental fashion, to perceive one's environment without wanting or demanding that it be different, and to notice one's thoughts, desires, and urges without attempting to control or act on them (Linehan, 1993b; Linehan & Dimeff, 1997). Distress tolerance skills include crisis survival skills to help clients get through short-term distressing moments without making the situation worse, as well as radical acceptance skills that include turning the mind toward willingness and full, total acceptance.

Emotion Regulation

The core of DBT-SUD's treatment model assumes that patients are exquisitely emotionally sensitive and have profound difficulties regulating their painful emotions. The inability to effectively manage extreme and distressing emotions often leads to a variety of dysfunctional behaviors that help stop the pain. Indeed, both suicidal behaviors and substance abuse behaviors can function to regulate emotions. For this reason, the emotion regulation module provides a wide array of skills intended to help clients identify their emotions, reduce their vulnerability to extreme emotions, increase pleasant emotions, change distressing emotions they wish to change by acting opposite to the emotion's expressive and behavioral action tendencies, and, most centrally, experience current emotions skillfully (Linehan, 1993b).

Interpersonal Effectiveness

Many individuals with BPD have a variety of interpersonal skill deficits that interfere with their ability to ask for what they want and say no to requests in an effective manner that preserves relationships as well as their own self-respect. The DBT interpersonal effectiveness module focuses on specific skills intended to help clients achieve an objective, build or maintain relationships, and preserve their own self-respect. Additionally, interpersonal effectiveness skills teach clients how to determine the level of urgency or intensity that would be most effective in an interpersonal situation, and how to identify and respond to obstacles that interfere with such interpersonal skills. These skills are particularly important for helping clients with BPD-SUD move away from drug situations and build a nondrug community.

Skills Specific to DBT-SUD

To keep the focus of DBT-SUD more tightly on reducing drug use, six new skills were developed: burning bridges, urge surfing, (adaptive) denial, alternate rebellion, avoiding or eliminating cues to use, and building a life worth living.

Burning Bridges

Burning bridges involves eliminating connections to clients' world of drugs. Examples include deleting phone numbers of friends who use drugs and drug dealers; telling drug-using friends that until they are clean, they are not welcome in the client's home; telling parents and significant others all the ways in which they have hidden drug use; and telling drug dealers that their families are monitoring their moves closely and, for the dealers' own safety, they should completely ignore the client and any future efforts to buy drugs.

Urge Surfing

Urge surfing, a technique described by Marlatt (Marlatt & Gordon, 1985), involves helping clients detach from urges by using DBT "observe" and "describe" skills (Linehan, 1993b) in a nonjudgmental, effective way. This makes urges more tolerable and reminds the client that urges will simply pass with time. The surfing metaphor captures the strategies necessary to successfully cope with urges. Surfing requires the individual to be fully attuned to the constantly changing wave and make subtle adjustments to ride the wave without wiping out. If one can stay with the wave, it will gradually diminish and ultimately fully fade. In addition, ignoring waves will not make them go away; rather, it will leave the individual more at risk for being overtaken by the urge.

(Adaptive) Denial

(*Adaptive*) *denial* involves blocking, denying, or pushing away something that is too painful or overwhelming to accept. This skill takes advantage of clients' well-honed ability to deny and uses it for skillful purposes—to simply not know that which is otherwise too painful to know. There are many times when it is extremely adaptive for clients to convince themselves that something is true or not true. A common example is the 12-step saying, "just for today." Those who find comfort in this slogan know that, ultimately, their resolve to abstain extends far beyond just this day; however, saying "just for today" allows the individual to adaptively deny the otherwise overwhelming reality of remaining abstinent forever. Another form of (adaptive) denial is demonstrated by the protagonist of the popular television series *Kojak*, a New York detective who was frequently seen sucking lollipops—a substitution for his real desire to smoke cigars. An example of this approach is one of our clients with marijuana dependence who developed a "habit" of brewing special teas. When an urge would arise to smoke pot, she denied it and replaced it with the belief that she wanted tea. She would then engage in an elaborate ritual of preparing her tea (not unlike the ritual she engaged in when she smoked pot).

Alternate Rebellion

Alternate rebellion involves satisfying the wish to rebel without doing harm by using drugs or engaging in other behaviors that compromise a person's wise mind goals. For some people with BPD-SUD, drug use functions as the ultimate means of rebelling against family, peers, or society at large. It can be very difficult for BPD-SUD clients to give up the thrill or meaning of the rebellion when trying to get clean. Finding some behavior that truly feels like a rebellion but does not involve drugs or other harmful behavior can be quite a challenge, yet it is very helpful in maintaining abstinence. Examples include dressing in offbeat or edgy clothes, breaking low-risk societal norms (e.g., making eye contact with strangers in elevators), riding a motorcycle, parachuting for the adrenaline rush, coloring one's hair, getting a tattoo in a hidden location, or wearing racy underwear under work clothes.

Avoiding and Eliminating Cues to Use

A common intervention is to remove drug cues: stimuli in the environment that lead to drug-related responses, including urges and cravings, drug use, and even withdrawal symptoms. For example, clients can stop driving past their favorite bar or stop riding the bus that goes near a dealer's house. This approach receives heavy emphasis in DBT-SUD. A careful examination of what sets off drug behavior is conducted, and all cues that can be removed or altered become a target. However, these cues may be difficult to identify. One client figured out that the way the light hit his ceiling in the morning when he woke up and was lying in bed was the signal to him that it was time to use. He had to rearrange his bedroom and wake at a different time to successfully avoid the cue and eliminate morning drug use.

Building a Life Worth Living

The goal in DBT-SUD is not actually to stop drug use or other dysfunctional behavior, but to build a life worth living—one that the individual wants to wake up for, stay clean for, and be engaged in. Of course, all of the DBT skills outlined above must be targeted in order to build that life. While this is the overarching goal in DBT (Linehan, 1993a), this notion receives even more overt attention in DBT-SUD skills training. For BPD-SUD clients, the problem with using drugs and engaging in other dysfunctional behaviors is that often these behaviors directly interfere with achieving life goals. For example, it is impossible to have stable housing, content and secure children, and a loving, caring relationship that will last over the long haul unless individuals are able to act in skillful ways (e.g., regulating their emotions; tolerating distress; engaging with others fairly, evenhandedly, and compassionately; and self-regulating their behavior in the interest of their long-term goals).

It is important to note the transaction between achieving abstinence and building functionality and a life worth living. They propel one another: gaining traction on abstinence helps propel actions that build a life worth living (e.g., applying for jobs, passing a vocational occupation test, or expressing gratitude to a loved one), taking concrete steps to build a life worth living further creates conditions for abstinence, and so on. The essential point is this: the work of beginning to build a life worth living—building a bridge to a new life—begins the moment treatment begins and occurs in a parallel fashion with getting off drugs and staying off. This approach stands in contrast to the sequential approach: waiting to begin building a life worth living until after abstinence has been fully achieved.

Using Drug Testing and Replacement Medication

For people with BPD-SUD, the importance of using drug testing and replacement medication when possible cannot be overstated. Many of our clients with BPD-SUD have indicated that both of these strategies helped them achieve abstinence. In our own research at the University of Washington, urinalyses were performed three times a week by a technician who fully observed the client during the urinalysis procedure. Additionally, because of the preponderance of evidence supporting the use of opiate replacement medication (National Institute on Drug Abuse, 2009), opiate-dependent patients were placed on a replacement medication, most recently Suboxone, a medication that combines buprenorphine and naloxone. Principles for their use are defined below.

While urinalyses are not always feasible outside of a research trial, saliva screens are. Ideally, drug screens for the primary drugs of abuse are gathered three times weekly, and clients are tested at random for other drugs of abuse (typically once weekly or biweekly). Because clients with BPD-SUD may only be visiting the clinic twice weekly (for individual therapy and group), the question is how best to ensure that a third screening is conducted. In some cases, having a supportive family member or friend conduct the drug screen may be helpful; in other instances, the client may prefer to return to the clinic.

With respect to the use of opiate replacement medications, several principles are critical to their use. First and foremost, it is imperative that drug induction occur as swiftly as is medically safe and that the maintenance dose is sufficient to prevent breakthrough withdrawal symptoms. Second, until the individual has gained behavioral stability (e.g., has maintained abstinence for a number of months, has burned bridges to drug use, and is actively building a life worth living—one characterized by drug-incompatible behaviors), use of opiate replacements should be directly and fully observed by the DBT-SUD therapist or supportive loved ones who are themselves stable.

Research to Date

To date, sixteen published randomized controlled trials conducted across eight independent research institutions support DBT's efficacy for a number of behavioral problems, including suicide attempts and self-injurious behaviors (Bohus et al., 2004; Carter, Willcox, Lewin, Conrad, & Bendit, 2010; Koons et al., 2001; Linehan, Armstrong, Suarez, Allmon, & Heard, 1991; Linehan et al., 2006; Linehan, Heard, & Armstrong, 1993; McMain et al., 2009; van den Bosch, Koeter, Stijnen, Verheul, & van den Brink, 2005; Verheul et al., 2003), substance abuse (Linehan et al., 2002; Linehan, Korslund, et al., 2009; Linehan, Lynch, et al., 2009; Linehan, Schmidt, et al., 1999), bulimia (Safer, Telch, & Agras, 2001), binge eating (Telch, Agras, & Linehan, 2001), and depression (Feldman, Harley, Kerrigan, Jacobo, & Fava, 2009; Lynch et al., 2007; Lynch, Morse, Mendelson, & Robins, 2003). These and other studies have demonstrated the cost-effectiveness of DBT compared to treatment as usual (TAU) in reducing treatment dropouts, hospitalization, emergency room visits, medical severity of suicide attempts, and utilization of crisis or respite beds (American Psychiatric Association, 1998; Linehan, 1999; Linehan, Kanter, & Comtois, 1999).

Three randomized controlled trials have evaluated the efficacy of DBT-SUD for individuals with BPD-SUD (Linehan et al., 2002; Linehan, Korslund, et al., 2009; Linehan, Lynch, et al., 2009; Linehan, Schmidt, et al., 1999). The length of treatment in all three trials was twelve months, followed by at least one follow-up assessment.

The initial randomized controlled trial sought to evaluate whether DBT was superior to standard treatment delivered for BPD-SUD in the community (TAU). Comorbid women with BPD and SUD were randomized to DBT-SUD (n = 12) or to community-based TAU (n = 16; Linehan, Schmidt, et al., 1999). In comparison to subsequent studies, inclusion criteria did not narrowly define the primary drug of abuse, resulting in a relatively heterogeneous population of subjects. In comparison to those receiving TAU, those who received DBT-SUD were significantly more likely to remain in treatment (64%, as opposed to 27%), had significantly reduced their drug use as measured by structured interviews and urinalyses throughout the treatment year, and attended significantly more individual therapy sessions. Additionally, while subjects in both conditions demonstrated significant improvement in social and global adjustment during the treatment year, only DBT subjects continued to show improvements on these variables at the sixteen-month follow-up.

The second efficacy trial of DBT-SUD (Linehan et al., 2002; $n = 23$) included a rigorous control condition (comprehensive validation therapy with 12-step; CVT + 12-step). CVT + 12-step is a manualized approach that includes the major acceptance-based strategies used in DBT-SUD in combination with participation in a 12-step program, such as Narcotics Anonymous (NA). In contrast to the earlier trial, all subjects were required to meet criteria for opiate dependence in addition to BPD. All subjects were provided an opiate replacement medication throughout the treatment and subsequent assessment-only follow-up year. Three major findings emerged: First, both treatments were effective in significantly reducing opiate use; however, only DBT subjects maintained these reductions during the last four months of treatment. Second, both conditions retained subjects in treatment; however, the CVT + 12-step condition was exceptional as it retained 100% of subjects (compared to 64% in DBT-SUD). And third, at both post-treatment and the four-month follow-up assessment, subjects in both treatment conditions showed statistically significant overall reductions in levels of psychopathology relative to baseline.

The third randomized controlled trial, a multisite efficacy trial ($n = 125$), sought to compare DBT-SUD ($n = 62$) to a well-validated treatment for drug dependence, individual and group drug counseling (IGDC; $n = 63$; Mercer & Woody, 2000). In contrast to earlier research, in which subjects were solely women, subjects included both women and men. All subjects were again required to meet criteria for opiate dependence and qualify for use of Suboxone. Preliminary results from this study indicate that while both treatments are effective at reducing drug abuse, DBT appears to be superior to IGDC on mental health outcomes, including depression and anxiety, and may also be superior to IGDC on reducing substance use over time (Linehan, Korslund, el al., 2009; Linehan, Lynch, et al., 2009).

Ongoing research in DBT includes dismantling studies, including investigating the usefulness of DBT skills without the presence of other DBT treatment components. The efficacy of DBT with individuals with emotion dysregulation who do not meet criteria for BPD is another important area of focus. In addition to the need for replication of the existing trials on DBT-SUD, future DBT-SUD research is likely to move into these domains as well.

Summary

Over the past decade, Linehan and her colleagues have developed, refined, and evaluated a modification of DBT for substance-dependent individuals with BPD. DBT-SUD does not seek to replace the need for a thorough understanding and use of standard DBT. Instead, it adds additional components that allow for greater precision and treatment of SUD in those with BPD who also suffer from substance dependence. These modifications include specific behavioral targets for treating SUD, dialectical abstinence, attachment strategies, skills specific to DBT-SUD, and use of drug testing and opiate replacement medication. To date, three randomized controlled trials have been conducted on DBT-SUD; each has provided further support of DBT in general and DBT-SUD in particular for those with BPD-SUD. Importantly, all studies of DBT-SUD involve the comprehensive delivery of DBT, where all treatment modes and functions are included. DBT-SUD is a promising approach for those suffering from BPD-SUD.

References

Alcoholics Anonymous. (2006). A.A. fact file. Retrieved March 1, 2012, from http. alcoholics-anonymous.org/en_pdfs/m-24_aafactfile.pdf.

American Psychiatric Association. (1998). Gold award: Integrating dialectical behavior therapy into a community mental health program. *Psychiatric Services, 49,* 1138-1340.

Bohus, M., Haaf, B., Simms, T., Limberger, M. F., Schmahl, C., Unckel, C., et al. (2004). Effectiveness of inpatient dialectical behavioral therapy for borderline personality disorder: A controlled trial. *Behaviour Research and Therapy, 42,* 487-499.

Cacciola, J. S., Alterman, A. I., Rutherford, M. J., McKay, J. R., & Mulvaney, F. D. (2001). The relationship of psychiatric comorbidity to treatment outcomes in methadone maintained patients. *Drug and Alcohol Dependence, 61,* 271-280.

Carter, G. L., Willcox, C. H., Lewin, T. J., Conrad, A. M., & Bendit, N. (2010). Hunter DBT project: Randomized controlled trial of dialectical behavior therapy in women with borderline personality disorder. *Australian and New Zealand Journal of Psychiatry, 44,* 162-173.

Chambless, D. L., & Hollon, S. D. (1998). Defining empirically supported therapies. *Journal of Consulting and Clinical Psychology, 66,* 7-18.

Dulit, R. A., Fyer, M. R., Haas, G. L., Sullivan, T., & Frances, A. J. (1990). Substance use in borderline personality disorder. *American Journal of Psychiatry, 147,* 1002-1007.

Ebner-Priemer, U. W., Badeck, S., Beckmann, C., Wagner, A., Feige, B., Weiss, I., et al. (2005). Affective dysregulation and dissociative experience in female patients with borderline personality disorder: A startle response study. *Journal of Psychiatric Research, 39,* 85-92.

Feldman, G., Harley, R., Kerrigan, M., Jacobo, M., & Fava, M. (2009). Change in emotional processing during a dialectical behavior therapy–based skills group for major depressive disorder. *Behaviour Research and Therapy, 47,* 316-321.

Hall, S. M., Havassy, B. E., & Wasserman, D. A. (1990). Commitment to abstinence and acute stress in relapse to alcohol, opiates, and nicotine. *Journal of Consulting and Clinical Psychology, 58,* 175-181.

Juengling, F. D., Schmahl, C., Hesslinger, B., Ebert, D., Bremner, J. D., Gostomzyk, J., et al. (2003). Positron emission tomography in female patients with borderline personality disorder. *Journal of Psychiatric Research, 37,* 109-115.

Koons, C. R., Robins, C. J., Tweed, J. L., Lynch, T. R., Gonzalez, A. M., Morse, J. Q., et al. (2001). Efficacy of dialectical behavior therapy in women veterans with borderline personality disorder. *Behavior Therapy, 32,* 371-390.

Linehan, M. M. (1993a). *Cognitive behavioral treatment of borderline personality disorder.* New York: Guilford Press.

Linehan, M. M. (1993b). *Skills training manual for treating borderline personality disorder.* New York: Guilford Press.

Linehan, M. M. (1999). Development, evaluation, and dissemination of effective psychosocial treatments: Stages of disorder, levels of care, and stages of treatment research. In M. G. Glantz & C. R. Hartel (Eds.), *Drug abuse: Origins and interventions.* Washington, DC: American Psychological Association.

Linehan, M. M. (2012). *Dialectical behavior therapy skills training manual.* Manuscript in preparation.

Linehan, M. M., Armstrong, H. E., Suarez, A., Allmon, D., & Heard, H. L. (1991). Cognitive-behavioral treatment of chronically parasuicidal borderline patients. *Archives of General Psychiatry, 48,* 1060-1064.

Linehan, M. M., Comtois, K. A., Murray, A. M., Brown, M. Z., Gallop, R. L., Heard, H. L., et al. (2006). Two-year randomized controlled trial and follow-up of dialectical behavior therapy vs. therapy by experts for suicidal behaviors and borderline personality disorder. *Archives of General Psychiatry, 63,* 757-766.

Linehan, M. M., & Dimeff, L. A. (1997). *Dialectical behavior therapy manual of treatment interventions for drug abusers with borderline personality disorder.* Seattle: University of Washington.

Linehan, M. M., Dimeff, L. A., Reynolds, S. K., Comtois, K. A., Welch, S. S., Heagerty, P., et al. (2002). Dialectical behavior therapy versus comprehensive validation therapy plus 12-step for the treatment of opioid dependent women meeting criteria for borderline personality disorder. *Drug and Alcohol Dependence, 67,* 13-26.

Linehan, M. M., Heard, H. L., & Armstrong, H. E. (1993). Naturalistic follow-up of a behavioral treatment for chronically parasuicidal borderline patients. *Archives of General Psychiatry, 50,* 971-974.

Linehan, M. M., Kanter, J. W., & Comtois, K. A. (1999). Dialectical behavior therapy for borderline personality disorder: Efficacy, specificity, and cost-effectiveness. In D. S. Janowsky (Ed.), *Psychotherapy: Indications and outcomes.* Washington, DC: American Psychiatric Press.

Linehan, M. M., Korslund, K. E., Lynch, T. R., Harned, M. S., & Rosenthal, Z. (2009, November). *Randomized controlled trial of DBT vs. drug counseling for opiate dependent BPD men and women.* Paper presented at the annual convention of the Association for Behavioral and Cognitive Therapies, New York, NY.

Linehan, M. M., Lynch, T. R., Harned, M. S., Korslund, K. E., Rosenthal, M. Z., Whalley, B., et al. (2009, November). *Dialectical behavior therapy for substance abuse in individuals with borderline personality disorder: Results from a multicenter randomized controlled trial.* Paper presented at the annual convention of the Association for Behavioral and Cognitive Therapies, New York, NY.

Linehan, M. M., & Schmidt, H. (1995). The dialectics of effective treatment of borderline personality disorder. In W. O. O'Donohue & L. Krasner (Eds.), *Theories in behavior therapy: Exploring behavior change.* Washington, DC: American Psychological Association.

Linehan, M. M., Schmidt, H., Dimeff, L. A., Craft, J. C., Kanter, J., & Comtois, K. A. (1999). Dialectical behavior therapy for patients with borderline personality disorder and drug-dependence. *American Journal on Addictions, 8,* 279-292.

Links, P. S., Heslegrave, R. J., Mitton, J. E., van Reekum, R., & Patrick, J. (1995). Borderline personality disorder and substance abuse: Consequences of comorbidity. *Canadian Journal of Psychiatry, 40,* 9-14.

Lynch, T. R., Cheavens, J. S., Cukrowicz, K. C., Thorp, S., Beyer, J., & Bronner, L. (2007). Treatment of older adults with comorbid personality disorder and depression: A dialectical behavior therapy approach. *International Journal of Geriatric Psychiatry, 22,* 131-143.

Lynch, T. R., Morse, J. Q., Mendelson, T., & Robins, C. J. (2003). Dialectical behavior therapy for depressed older adults: A randomized pilot study. *American Journal of Geriatric Psychiatry, 11,* 33-45.

Marlatt, G. A., & Donovan, D. M. (2005). *Relapse prevention: Maintenance strategies in the treatment of relapse prevention* (2nd ed.). New York: Guilford Press.

Marlatt, G. A., & Gordon, J. R. (1985). *Relapse prevention: Maintenance strategies in the treatment of addictive behaviors.* New York: Guilford Press.

McKay, J. R., Alterman, A. I., Cacciola, J. S., Mulvaney, F. D., & O'Brien, C. P. (2000). Prognostic significance of antisocial personality disorder in cocaine-dependent patients entering continuing care. *Journal of Nervous and Mental Disease, 188,* 287-296.

McMain, S. F., Links, P. S., Gnam, W. H., Guimond, T., Cardish, R. J., Korman, L., et al. (2009). A randomized trial of dialectical behavior therapy versus general psychiatric management for borderline personality disorder. *American Journal of Psychiatry, 166,* 1365-1374.

McMain, S., Sayrs, J. H. R., Dimeff, L. A., & Linehan, M. M. (2007). Dialectical behavior therapy for individuals with borderline personality disorder and sub-stance dependence. In L. A. Dimeff & K. Koerner (Eds.), *Dialectical behavior therapy in clinical practice: Applications across disorders and settings.* New York: Guilford Press.

Mercer, D., & Woody, G. (2000). *An individual drug counseling approach to treat cocaine addiction.* Rockville, MD: National Institute on Drug Abuse.

Miller, N. S., Belkin, G. M., & Gibbons, R. (1994). Clinical diagnosis of substance use disorders in private psychiatric populations. *Journal of Substance Abuse and Treatment, 11,* 387-392.

National Institute for Health and Clinical Excellence. (2009). Borderline personal-ity disorder: Treatment and management. NICE Clinical Guideline 78. *Computerised Cognitive Behaviour Therapy for Depression and Anxiety.* London: National Institute for Health and Clinical Excellence.

National Institute on Drug Abuse. (2009, September). Info facts: Treatment approaches for drug Addiction. Retrieved March 9, 2012, from www.nida.nih.gov/infofacts/treatmeth.html.

Porges, S. W., Doussard-Roosevelt, J., & Maiti, A. K. (1994). Vagal tone and the physiological regulation of emotion. *Monographs of the Society for Research in Child Development, 59,* 167-186.

Rossow, I., & Lauritzen, G. (1999). Balancing on the edge of death: Suicide attempts and life-threatening overdoses among drug addicts. *Addiction, 94,* 209-219.

Safer, D. L., Telch, C. F., & Agras, W. S. (2001). Dialectical behavior therapy for bulimia nervosa. *American Journal of Psychiatry, 158,* 632-634.

Skinstad, A. H., & Swain, A. (2001). Comorbidity in a clinical sample of substance abusers. *American Journal of Drug and Alcohol Abuse, 27,* 45-64.

Stiglmayr, C. E., Grathwol, T., Linehan, M. M., Ihorst, G., Fahrenberg, J., & Bohus, M. (2005). Aversive tension in patients with borderline personality disorder: A computer-based controlled field study. *Acta Psychiatrica Scandinavica, 111,* 372-379.

Stone, M. H. (2009, August). *Forty-year follow-up of borderline patients.* Paper pre-sented at the international congress of the International Society for the Study of Personality Disorders, New York, NY.

Telch, C. F., Agras, W. S., & Linehan, M. M. (2001). Dialectical behavior therapy for binge eating disorder. *Journal of Consulting and Clinical Psychology, 69,* 1061-1065.

Trull, T. J., Sher, K. J., Minks-Brown, C., Durbin, J., & Burr, R. (2000). Borderline personality disorder and substance use disorders: A review and integration. *Clinical Psychology Review, 20,* 235-253.

Van den Bosch, L. M. C., Koeter, M., Stijnen, T., Verheul, R., & van den Brink, W. (2005). Sustained efficacy of dialectical behavior therapy for borderline personality disorder. *Behaviour Research and Therapy, 43,* 1231-1241.

Verheul, R., van den Bosch, L. M. C., Koeter, M. W., Ridder, M. A., Stijnen, T., & van den Brink, W. (2003). Dialectical behaviour therapy for women with borderline personality disorder: 12-month randomized clinical trial in the Netherlands. *British Journal of Psychiatry, 182,* 135-140.

CHAPTER 3

Mindfulness-Based Relapse Prevention: Integrating Meditation into the Treatment of Problematic Substance Use

Sarah Bowen

University of Washington

Katie Witkiewitz

Washington State University

Neha Chawla

University of Washington

The *mindfulness-based relapse prevention program* (MBRP; Bowen, Chawla, & Marlatt, 2010; Witkiewitz, Marlatt, & Walker, 2005) is an integration of practices and principles from the mindfulness meditation tradition and exercises and components from relapse prevention therapy (Daley & Marlatt, 2006; Marlatt & Gordon, 1985), which has a cognitive behavioral orientation. It was designed to reduce the probability and severity of substance abuse relapse for individuals in early abstinence and has been used as an aftercare program for individuals who have completed inpatient or intensive outpatient treatment and are working to maintain their treatment goals.

Traditional relapse prevention therapy focuses on helping clients develop and use effective coping responses in high-risk situations, and on challenging cognitions that arise due to perceived failures or lapses. It views problematic substance use as a learned behavior that has biological, psychological, and social antecedents and consequences. Within this framework, relapse is conceptualized as a series of responses to a high-risk situation (Larimer, Palmer, & Marlatt, 1999), and intervention involves identifying the interpersonal, intrapersonal, and environmental characteristics of these high-risk situations (Witkiewitz & Marlatt, 2004). Relapse prevention therapists use several intervention strategies, including training in coping skills, specifically how to effectively cope with high-risk situations and enhance self-efficacy; cognitive therapy approaches such as viewing habit change as a learning process and introducing coping imagery to deal with cravings; and lifestyle modifications such as exercise and spiritual practices (Larimer et al., 1999).

Historically, the cognitive behavioral approach and Buddhist psychology seldom mingled, much less joined together in a single treatment program. Recently, however, a new relationship between these two traditions is manifesting in numerous areas of psychology. Today, several treatments incorporate Western psychological approaches such as cognitive behavioral therapy or behavior therapy with mindfulness practices—for example, dialectical behavior therapy (DBT; Linehan, 1993; see also Dimeff & Sayrs, chapter 2 of this volume) and acceptance and commitment therapy (ACT; Hayes, Strosahl, & Wilson, 1999; see also Wilson, Schnetzer, Flynn, & Kurz, chapter 1 of this volume). Some such treatments also incorporate formal mindfulness meditation—for example, mindfulness-based stress reduction (MBSR; Kabat-Zinn, 1990) and mindfulness-based cognitive therapy (MBCT; Segal, Teasdale, & Williams, 2002). These treatments are each supported by an underlying integrative theoretical foundation joining two traditionally disparate traditions. MBRP follows in this tradition.

A Mindfulness Perspective on Addiction

The MBRP theoretical model focuses on three key aspects in understanding addiction and its treatment: nonacceptance, negative reinforcement, and positive reinforcement. In the sections below we will address how each of these aspects of addiction relates to mindfulness and MBRP.

Nonacceptance: Looking for a "Fix"

From the perspective of mindfulness traditions and practices, we might view addiction as a manifestation of a universal human desire to want what we don't have and be free from what we don't want. In other words, we often want to either fix or escape our present experience to make it fit our idea of how things should be. Addiction might thus be viewed as a nonwillingness or perceived inability to accept what exists in the present moment. There is a grasping for something that we think will deliver the experience we yearn for instead of the one we currently have.

Through meditation and mindfulness practice, we begin to observe the constantly changing nature of thoughts, emotions, and physical sensations. We recognize whatever arises, even if it is not what we might have chosen, and practice relating to it with curiosity, patience, and compassion, rather than reactively attempting to either escape from it or cling to it. Through repeated practice and honing of skills, we raise our awareness of the mind's tendency to habitually react, and we reduce the tendency to grasp at or push away affective, cognitive, or physical experiences. We train the mind to recognize and accept both internal and external events as they are.

Negative Reinforcement: Addiction as a False Refuge

The desire to escape uncomfortable emotional states has been identified as the most common proximal trigger for relapse (Baker, Piper, McCarthy, Majeskie, & Fiore, 2004; Marlatt & Gordon, 1985; Witkiewitz & Villarroel, 2009). This is apparent in the high rates of relapse among individuals with comorbid affective disorders (Curran, Flynn, Kirchner, & Booth, 2000; Greenfield et al., 1998; Hasin et al., 2002; Kessler, Crum, Warner, & Nelson, 1997). From a Western psychological view, the self-medication hypothesis describes substance use as an attempt to cope with or alleviate psychological distress (Khantzian, 1997). The cycle is perpetuated through a process of negative reinforcement, or alleviation of an unwanted experience. This may be quite effective in the short run, providing immediate relief from the discomfort. In the long run, however, it leads to increased suffering, often trapping the individual in a vicious cycle of self-medication followed by feelings of shame, depression, or anxiety in reaction to the behavior, leading to continued self-medication to alleviate these aversive affective states. Developing increased awareness of triggers and the behavioral patterns that follow, and learning to stay with uncomfortable emotions rather than seek escape, may thus be helpful in breaking this cycle. As suggested by Breslin, Zack, and McMain (2002), helping clients recognize their emotional and cognitive responses to triggers for substance use may interrupt the previously automatic response of using substances. Furthermore, reducing avoidance may desensitize clients to the discomfort of cognitive and emotional states that previously led to substance use.

MBRP includes practices that address recognition of triggers and provide alternatives to self-medication, increasing participants' recognition of challenging affective states and helping them tolerate the associated discomfort (Witkiewitz & Bowen, 2010). Specifically, these exercises and practices encourage nonjudgmental awareness and acceptance of current experience, including aversive states such as affective discomfort or cravings. Through increased awareness and acceptance of difficult internal experiences, participants begin to see that it is futile (and unnecessary) to attempt to fix or escape these experiences, and that these ineffective strategies actually bring further suffering. This awareness and acceptance not only may encourage greater tolerance of negative emotional states, which are often strongly related to initial relapse (Witkiewitz & Villarroel, 2009), but also may directly counter the conditioned automatic response of substance use, providing a method of being with and moving through the seemingly intolerable experience of craving. Thus, mindfulness may serve as a form of counterconditioning, in which awareness and acceptance replace the response previously associated with engaging in the addictive behavior.

In addition to engaging in practices centered on increasing awareness of and ability to tolerate discomfort, clients are also repeatedly encouraged to practice, as best they can, a nonjudgmental stance toward themselves and their experiences. This helps them begin to detach from some of the critical and evaluative self-statements that may either serve as triggers to use or exacerbate initial reactions to triggering events. The nonjudgmental aspect of mindfulness practice may further undo some of the deeply internalized self-criticism and shame often characteristic of individuals struggling with substance use and relapse. Through repeated mindfulness practice, participants cultivate a more compassionate view of themselves and their actions, loosening the strong identification with their past and present behaviors.

Positive Reinforcement: Attachment and Clinging

Addiction is not always driven by a need to escape affective discomfort. It may also be driven by a pursuit of excitement, elation, or other appetitive experiences. This, of course, is just another manifestation of wanting things to be other than they are, but in this case, rather than attempting to fix an aversive experience, the desire is to heighten a positive mood or body state, such as joy or rapture. In addition to shedding light on these deeply entrenched behaviors, mindfulness practice may help clients find the naturally reinforcing or nourishing aspects of day-to-day life that are often deemed trivial and thus unworthy of attention or presence. By bringing purposeful attention to what gives us pleasure, not only is contact with natural positive reinforcers increased, but we may also notice pleasure where previously we had missed it. This might be as simple as stepping out of the automatic ruminative thought cycle that often occurs when we are engaged in seemingly mundane activities, such as washing dishes. We might instead pause and intentionally bring focus to the sensations created by the soap or the sound of splashing water. While this doesn't promise sudden euphoria, it may create an increase in pleasurable experiences and an easing of the stress that is often caused by what our minds do during these activities. In this way, we may discover the very simple and gratifying experience of simply being present while engaging in an activity.

Mindfulness-Based Relapse Prevention

After many years of witnessing the benefits of two independent traditions of substance abuse treatment, meditation and mindfulness-based treatment (e.g., Marlatt, Pagano, Rose, & Marques, 1984; Bowen et al., 2009) and cognitive behavioral relapse prevention therapy (e.g., Marlatt & Gordon, 1985; Irvin, Bowers, Dunn, & Wang, 1999; Carroll, 1996), our research team began to envision a treatment that could provide the benefits of both traditions. What elements could we take from each of these promising approaches? And how could we integrate them so that each would augment the other to help our clients maintain their treatment goals? We began to articulate the commonalities of the approaches while also navigating their differences.

Witkiewitz and colleagues (2005) first proposed a treatment combining relapse prevention and meditation and mindfulness skills based on those found in MBSR (Kabat-Zinn, 1990) and MBCT (Segal et al., 2002). Throughout the following months and years, we role-played sessions together in the lab, feeling our way through the integration of practices and themes. In the multiple trials and numerous clients that followed, the two traditions began to naturally integrate. We started to see that, despite the different topographies, the underlying themes and foundations of these therapies were more often than not pointing at the same truths.

The resulting MBRP program (Bowen et al., 2010; Witkiewitz et al., 2005) uses an eight-session, manualized, structured protocol that includes in-session meditations and skills training, along with practices designed for use between sessions. It includes specific relapse prevention strategies rooted in Marlatt and colleagues' cognitive behavioral model of relapse (Larimer et al., 1999; Marlatt & Gordon, 1985) within a program that has mindfulness practice as its foundation. Similar to traditional relapse prevention, MBRP involves identifying precipitants of problematic substance use, such as substance-related cues (e.g., people associated with substance use or favorite bars), and emphasizing personal choice with regard to overall goals for treatment, as well as specific situations and behaviors. In MBRP, however, mindfulness practice is used to help clients raise their awareness of specific triggers (e.g., thoughts, emotions, or sensations) and the "automatic" responses that often follow, to recognize early warning signs for relapse, and to increase an ability to be with the discomfort (e.g., cravings or negative affect) that often leads to substance use.

The structure and format of MBRP closely resemble those of MBSR for chronic pain (Kabat-Zinn, 1990) and MBCT for relapse of depression (Segal et al., 2002), both of which have considerable empirical support (e.g., Baer, 2003; Grossman, Niemann, Schmidt, & Walach, 2004; Kilpatrick et al., 2011; Teasdale et al., 2000). MBRP has benefited from the wisdom in these practices, their order and presentation, and the overall course structure.

Mindfulness practices in the MBRP program include both formal meditation (e.g., the body scan and sitting meditation) and informal practices (e.g., engaging in "mini meditations" in triggering situations and practicing mindfulness during daily activities). The practices take several forms but center on the same core intentions that form the foundation of the program. The first of these is to cultivate awareness of cues previously associated with substance use, creating opportunities to respond to triggering events rather than reacting in self-defeating ways. Second, clients practice reducing the self-judgment and criticism often associated with these reactions. Finally, MBRP provides training and practice in being with affective, cognitive, or physical discomfort through a curious, approach-oriented exploration and nonavoidance, rather than a reactive attempt to escape.

Through regular practice, clients increase their ability to make more skillful behavioral choices, which in turn increases their self-efficacy when confronted with substance use cues or cravings. Clients are taught to increase their awareness of automatic thoughts, how to relate to thoughts differently, and how to relate to all of their experiences and themselves with more compassion. Additionally, they learn concrete cognitive and behavioral skills and also learn to make more skillful lifestyle choices, all in support of maintaining recovery in the face of the inevitable challenges that arise. Relapse prevention components further enhance identification of triggers and high-risk situations, and provide concrete alternative activities and coping skills to decrease contact with high-risk situations and to employ when such situations are encountered (Bowen, Witkiewitz, Chawla, & Grow, in press).

MBRP in Session

MBRP is designed to be an experiential exploration, raising awareness of inner and outer environments and increasing present-centered, nonjudgmental living to allow for more intentional and skillful choices. At the core of the eight-session program is mindfulness practice itself. Discussions, rationale, and theory are in place to facilitate mindfulness practice but are intentionally minimized. An essential aspect of the MBRP program is the style in which groups are facilitated. The group facilitators, who have a strong foundation and established personal history in mindfulness meditation, practice a nonjudgmental, curious, and open approach to whatever arises in each session, using a facilitation style largely inspired by motivational interviewing (W. R. Miller & Rollnick, 2002; see also Wagner, Ingersoll, & Rollnick, chapter 5 of this volume). They facilitate a process of exploration, rather than teaching or processing content. Thus, they are often referred to as "facilitators," and clients are often referred to as "participants."

A central feature of MBRP is inquiry, or the discussion that follows each exercise or practice. This discussion, which is inspired by a similar practice in MBCT (Segal et al., 2002), involves helping participants observe and identify present-moment experience. Discussions are focused on the experience of individuals in the present moment, rather than veering into stories about the past or the future. Thus, facilitators' attitude toward what arises in the group models the stance they are asking participants to adopt toward the experience of their own physical, cognitive, and emotional experiences. The focus of the discussion is on direct experience, with the goal of differentiating between what is actually arising in the moment and ideas about or reactions to that experience. For example, if a participant offers a comment such as "That was great," the facilitator might explore the comment further: "Tell me more about 'great.' What did you experience?" The facilitator would help the participant identify the direct sensations, thoughts, or emotions that arose during the practice, as well as reactions to them (e.g., relaxation, identifying specific thoughts that arose about the experience, or liking the experience and labeling it "great"). Facilitators also inquire about the familiarity or novelty of participants' experiences (e.g., "In the past, have you ever noticed this tendency of your mind to wander when you ask it to focus on something?") and attempt to relate these experiences to the relapse process (e.g., "What does the practice we just engaged in have to do with relapse?").

Week 1: Automatic Pilot and Relapse

Similar to MBSR and MBCT, the MBRP course begins with an experiential introduction to the tendency to operate on automatic pilot. This is contrasted with practices intended to bring more mindful awareness into daily life. The role of automatic pilot in the relapse process is then discussed, with therapists eliciting participants' experiences or thoughts regarding this process. The first session also introduces formal meditation practice with the body scan, an exercise that involves bringing awareness to sensations in different parts of the body, progressing from the toes up thorough each area of the body and to the top of the head. Participants are asked to continue practicing the body scan during the week and to note not only experiences while engaging in the practice, but also challenges that arise or barriers that keep them from engaging in the practice. In this way, facilitators invite all experiences and behaviors as potential objects of awareness, dropping any valence or judgment that might typically be attached to particular behaviors. As part of home practice, participants are also invited to bring intentional interest and attention to seemingly mundane daily activities and to notice the sensations, thoughts, and even emotions that might be present while engaging in actions that are often performed on autopilot, such as brushing teeth, eating, or getting dressed in the morning.

Week 2: Awareness of Triggers and Craving

In week two, the focus shifts to include situations that tend to elicit cravings or habitual reactive behaviors. Using guided exercises and imagined scenarios, participants are invited to bring attention to their personal triggers and observe the emotions, thoughts, and body sensations that often accompany these events. The second session also introduces the practice of being with discomfort without reacting. Participants call to mind a situation in which they might feel or have felt cravings or an urge to behave reactively. They are given instructions to observe what is happening in their bodies, to notice any thoughts that might be present, and to note emotions that arise. Discussion following the exercise centers on the purpose of staying with these aversive experiences versus avoiding, distracting, or struggling against discomfort specifically related to cravings for alcohol and other substances. Participants also explore what might be underneath the craving or urge, investigating the positive and negative reinforcement they receive from substance use by examining what they are seeking from the substance or behavior. They might be yearning for relief from anxiety or emotional pain, searching for comfort or peace, or wanting to experience joy or celebration. They hope to find these experiences in a substance; although this may provide short-term relief or excitement, ultimately it is unsustainable and has many costs.

In this second session, participants also begin to discuss the challenges often associated with meditation practice. These typically include drowsiness, discomfort, the experience of a wandering mind, and doubts about the practice itself or one's ability to engage in it. Thus, an important piece of session two is clarifying misconceptions and expectations about meditation practice (e.g., that one should feel a sense of peace, calm, or bliss). Participants often expect to feel relaxation at the very least. Throughout the program, they are continually reminded that the intention isn't necessarily relaxation or some idealized state. Rather, the intention is to get to know the mind a little better; to become aware of thoughts, emotions, and body states; and to notice reactions to these experiences without adding additional layers of self-evaluation and judgment. Through the meditations and other exercises, participants practice observing experiences rather than reacting to them habitually.

Week 3: Mindfulness in Daily Life

The third session introduces a sitting meditation practice that begins with bringing attention to the physical sensations of breathing (e.g., the belly rising and falling or the sensations of air entering and leaving the nostrils). When the mind inevitably wanders away from the breath, the instruction is to simply notice this occurrence and bring the attention back to the sensations of breathing. This noticing and returning to the breath is repeated again and again. By this third week, participants have had two weeks of formal practice observing physical sensations, have been introduced to meditation focused on the breath, and have been introduced to several practices that involve noticing personal triggers and reactions. Participants are now offered a practice intended to foster continued incorporating of these practices into daily living through a mini meditation adapted from the breathing space exercise in MBCT, here called the SOBER breathing space. This exercise can be done within the span of a few minutes, or even a few seconds, if necessary. SOBER is an acronym outlining the steps of this practice:

- **Stop:** The first step is simply to stop, or take a pause, particularly in the midst of a stressful or triggering situation. This is the most important step, as it creates an opportunity to interrupt a previously automatic reaction.

- **Observe:** The second step is to observe whatever sensations, thoughts, or emotions are currently arising.

- **Breath:** The third step is to gather the awareness and bring it to the sensations of the breath, even for just one or two breaths, as a way to step out of the story or cascade of thoughts and reactions that may be occurring and anchor the awareness in experiencing just whatever is happening in the present moment.

- **Expand:** Participants then expand their awareness back out to the body, the mind, and the situation, while also noticing that this expanded sense of awareness has the capacity to hold all of their current experiences.

- **Respond:** Finally, participants bring awareness to the array of behavioral choices they have in that moment. Even with the existing sensations, emotions, thoughts, and perhaps urges that may be present, they still have the choice to respond with greater awareness and compassion for themselves, rather than reacting automatically.

Week 4: Mindfulness in High-Risk Situations

As participants progress through the remainder of the course, the target of observation begins to shift from physical sensations throughout the body and the specific focus on the physical sensations of breathing to include other aspects of experience, such as sound, sight, emotional states, and thoughts. Beginning in session four, they are also asked to define the individual factors and situations that put them at greater risk for relapse. They are encouraged to continue applying the practices they have learned to triggers and urges in daily life and to continue practicing stepping out of automatic mode, both in typical day-to-day situations and in acute, high-risk situations. Additional forms of mindfulness practice, such as walking meditation, are also introduced.

Week 5: Acceptance and Skillful Action

In session five, participants explore the balance between accepting what is arising, particularly challenging emotional, mental, and physical experiences, and taking skillful action to support their well-being. Misconceptions about acceptance as a passive stance are discussed. Rather than being equated with tolerating situations or circumstances, acceptance is viewed as an intention to simply be with whatever is already arising in the moment, including one's reactions to what has arisen. Acknowledgment and acceptance of what already *is* allows for skillful action, rather than a retrospective disagreement with or struggle against things as they already are.

Week 6: Seeing Thoughts as Thoughts

In week six, participants are guided to begin bringing a specific focus to identifying and stepping back from thoughts and to develop a greater understanding of the role of thoughts in the relapse process. They are instructed to, as best they can, practice observing thoughts as they arise, noticing any associated body sensations or emotions that may accompany these thoughts while also repeatedly returning to the present moment each time they notice that the mind has gotten involved in the content of a thought. In the second half of this session, participants engage in an exercise called the Relapse Cycle, in which they walk through examples of recurring relapse triggers or past experiences of relapse, identifying specific thoughts following the trigger and preceding the relapse. Particular attention is given to self-critical and "tricky" thoughts that are likely to exacerbate cravings or increase the likelihood of a relapse (e.g., *I've already screwed this up. Why even bother trying?* or *I can have just a sip to see how it feels*). This recognition of their common and often automatic thoughts may help participants step out of a previously rote cycle of behavior, creating the space to make more skillful choices. Participants identify points along the way where they might pause, perhaps use a SOBER breathing space, and notice thoughts that are arising. This helps them see that the further they travel down the path, the stronger the tendencies to behave reactively or automatically are likely to be, but that they do indeed have choice points all along the way, even though the mind may be telling them that it is too late.

Week 7: Self-Care and Lifestyle Balance

The final two sessions widen the focus to maintaining a lifestyle that will support both recovery and mindfulness practice. In session seven, exercises and practices designed to encourage greater self-care and self-compassion are introduced, including loving-kindness meditation, which involves cultivating friendliness and well wishes toward oneself and others. In an exercise based on an MBCT practice, participants examine the activities in which they engage on a typical day and look at whether these activities tend to be nourishing or tend to deplete their energy or resources. They then identify what part of the nourishing or depleting qualities may be due to their relation to the activity, rather than inherent in the activity itself. The purpose here is twofold: First, participants bring awareness to how their activities on a typical day may be affecting their overall pool of resources. Second, they begin to look at what role the mind or their reactive behavior may play in how they are affected by these circumstances. They are encouraged to add nourishing activities to their schedule where possible, and also to pay attention to what they are bringing to the depleting activities that may be exacerbating their negative effects.

Week 8: Social Support and Continuing Practice

In the final session, participants are invited to reflect upon their experience in the program and articulate their intentions around maintaining an ongoing practice. They are given a list of written, web-based, audio, and community resources to support ongoing practice and are encouraged to be realistic when setting intentions and in regard to the common barriers and challenges to maintaining a practice. The group concludes with a closing meditation including an appreciation for their own efforts and those of their fellow group members. Participants are invited once again to practice kindness in relating to their own experiences, both in meditation and in daily life, and in their interactions with others.

Integrating MBRP into Current Addiction Treatment

In the long term, development and research in the field of mindfulness-based treatment for substance use disorders should include integration of such programs into existing addiction treatment settings. Thus far, this has taken several different forms but has primarily been achieved by adding mindfulness meditation groups to existing treatment programs. For example, both Bowen and colleagues (2009) and Zgierska and colleagues (2008) integrated mindfulness groups into the aftercare programming of community treatment programs. Other studies have incorporated mindfulness meditation interventions into therapeutic communities (Alterman, Koppenhaver, Mulholland, Ladden, & Baime, 2004; Garland, Gaylord, Boettiger, & Howard, 2010; Liehr et al., 2010; Marcus et al., 2009) and residential treatment programs (Amaro et al., 2010; Chen, Comerford, Shinnick, & Ziedonis, 2010). A few recent studies have recruited individuals for outpatient mindfulness treatment groups directly from clinical and community referrals (e.g., Brewer et al., 2009; Vieten, Astin, Buscemi, & Galloway, 2010). Finally, several treatments that incorporate mindfulness components (e.g., spiritual self-schema therapy, ACT, and DBT) have been delivered in a group format in combination with therapist-led individual intervention sessions (e.g., Avants, Beitel, & Margolin, 2005; Hayes, Follette, & Linehan, 2004; Linehan et al., 2002).

Mindfulness meditation as a stand-alone individual intervention for substance use disorders has not been examined in a randomized trial, and it is unclear whether individual mindfulness interventions will be as powerful as group-based intervention. Several studies of group versus individual psychotherapy have found no differences in outcomes across formats (see McRoberts, Burlingame, & Hoag, 1998, for a meta-analysis), although there is some evidence that group-delivered interventions for substance use might be associated with greater levels of perceived social support following treatment (e.g., Graham, Annis, Brett, & Venesoen, 1996). Given the strong associations between social support and substance use outcomes following treatment (Longabaugh, Wirtz, Zywiak, & O'Malley, 2010), along with the cost savings associated with delivering interventions in group format (see Sobell, Sobell, & Agrawal, 2009), it may be that group-delivered mindfulness interventions are preferable to individual intervention, although future research would be necessary to examine this.

Group-delivered mindfulness-based interventions also provide an opportunity for individuals within the group to form a community of mindfulness practitioners. In Buddhism, the spiritual community (referred to by the Pali word *sangha*) is considered one of the three refuges, which Buddhists can look toward for guidance (Bodhi, 2000). The group format provides the opportunity for each individual to identify common struggles and empathize with the experiences of other group members. The mindfulness community formed via group-delivered mindfulness intervention might provide benefits similar to those seen in 12-step groups, such as Alcoholics Anonymous (AA). Importantly, the degree of social support attained via AA group attendance and participation has been consistently shown to mediate alcohol use outcomes following treatment (see Groh, Jason, & Keys, 2008, for a review).

Another potential value of the group format in MBRP is the commonality participants see with their peers. As the group progresses and participants are increasingly able to identify patterns of their minds, they see similarity in what others are reporting. This illustrates that processes of the mind are not necessarily personal, which can lessen identification with and judgment of the mind's tendencies.

To our knowledge, no empirical studies have examined the use of mindfulness-based telephone, computerized, or Internet interventions for substance use problems or disorders. We are aware of several programs that have been designed to deliver mindfulness treatment via these modalities (e.g., L. D. Miller, 2011), but the efficacy of delivering mindfulness-based interventions via these formats has not been established. However, the efficacy of other psychosocial interventions, such as cognitive behavioral therapy, for substance use disorders delivered via telephone, computer, or the Internet has been demonstrated in numerous studies (e.g., Blankers, Koeter, & Schippers, 2011; Carroll et al., 2009; Hester, Delaney, & Campbell, 2012; see also Gainsbury & Blaszczynski, 2010, for a review). Likewise, Ljótsson and colleagues (2011) described an Internet-based mindfulness intervention for irritable bowel syndrome, and Thompson and colleagues (2010) examined mindfulness-based cognitive therapy for depression delivered in the home via telephone. Based on these recent studies, the development of telephone, computerized, or Internet mindfulness interventions for substance use disorders might provide greater dissemination and access, particularly for individuals in smaller cities or rural areas who do not have immediate access to practitioners trained in mindfulness-based interventions.

Current Research in Meditation and Mindfulness-Based Addiction Treatment

From early research by Marlatt and colleagues on mindfulness and other forms of meditation to the current research on mindfulness-based therapies, studies consistently offer a promising perspective on treatment of problematic substance use. One of the earliest attempts to assess the application of meditation for substance use was a study conducted by Marlatt and Marques (1977), who evaluated Transcendental Meditation as an intervention for high-risk college-student drinkers. Subsequently, two separate randomized trials compared Transcendental Meditation with muscle relaxation and daily quiet recreational reading (Marlatt et al., 1984) and with daily aerobic exercise (Murphy, Pagano, & Marlatt, 1986). In both trials, results indicated that all interventions (including the muscle relaxation and aerobic exercise control conditions) were effective in reducing alcohol use and associated problems. More recently, Bowen and colleagues (2006) evaluated the effectiveness of a ten-day course in vipassana, or "insight" meditation (a practice upon which many of the present mindfulness practices are based), among inmates in a minimum-security jail. Those who completed the course reported significantly less alcohol and drug use three months following release from incarceration, as compared to inmates who did not take the vipassana course.

Since the early studies on Transcendental Meditation and vipassana meditation, numerous studies have examined mindfulness-based interventions in the treatment of substance use disorders. Zgierska and colleagues (2009) provided a narrative review of studies that integrated mindfulness training into treatment for substance use disorders, including eight randomized controlled trials, thirteen noncontrolled or nonrandomized trials, two qualitative studies, and one case report, and concluded that mindfulness approaches produced mostly positive outcomes, but that further systematic research was necessary.

However, research on programs integrating formal meditation practice with evidence-based cognitive behavioral therapies specifically for substance use disorders is still relatively young, and only five independent studies over the past three years have evaluated the effectiveness of MBRP or MBRP-based interventions in the treatment of substance use disorders. In the paragraphs that follow, we outline the results of those studies.

Zgierska and colleagues (2008) examined the feasibility of implementing a manualized eight-week meditation course based on MBRP as part of an intensive outpatient treatment program for alcohol dependence. Fifteen individuals (out of nineteen recruited) completed the course, and all who completed the course reported at least some meditation up to two months following the eight-week course, with 53% of participants meditating four or more days per week. An examination of pre- to post-treatment outcomes indicated that those who completed the course reported significantly fewer days of heavy drinking one month following the course, and significant reductions in stress, depression, and anxiety up to two months after the course. Participants also reported high satisfaction with the course.

Vieten and colleagues (2010) recently developed a manualized eight-session intervention—acceptance-based coping for relapse prevention program—pulling from several mindfulness-based treatments, including MBRP. The twenty-three individuals who completed the course reported significant decreases in cravings, negative affect, emotional reactivity, and perceived stress, as well as significant increases in positive affect, psychological well-being, and mindfulness immediately following the intervention. Participants did not report significant reductions in drinking frequency.

Similarly, Garland and colleagues (2010) conducted a randomized pilot trial of a ten-session mindfulness-based treatment for alcohol dependence in a sample of fifty-three adults and found that, compared to an active control group, mindfulness training appeared to lessen the impact of several key cognitive, affective, and physiological factors shown to be related to relapse, such as stress, thought suppression, physiological recovery following alcohol-related cues, and attentional bias toward brief visual alcohol cues.

In the largest controlled trial conducted to date, the efficacy of MBRP was examined in comparison to standard care at a private, non-profit agency that provided a continuum of care for substance use disorders (Bowen et al., 2009). Facilitators were trained by and received ongoing supervision from the treatment developers. Participants ($n = 168$) were recruited following completion of inpatient or intensive outpatient treatment programs and then randomized to receive eight weeks of MBRP (provided in group format, with 120 minutes per session) or eight weeks of the standard aftercare programming provided by the agency, which consisted of psychoeducational, process-oriented, and 12-step-based groups. Results indicated that individuals who were assigned to MBRP had significantly fewer days of alcohol or other drug use two months following the intervention (MBRP mean = 2.1 days of use; standard care mean = 5.4 days of use). Reductions in use were maintained at the four-month follow-up, although the difference between groups was no longer significant. The MBRP group also reported significant decreases in cravings and greater increases in acceptance, as measured by the Acceptance and Action Questionnaire (AAQ; Hayes, Strosahl, et al., 2004), compared to the standard care condition. The majority of MBRP participants (86%) reported practicing meditation post-intervention, and at the four-month follow-up, 54% reported continued practice for an average of 4.7 days per week and 29.9 minutes per session. The MBRP participants also reported that they were highly satisfied with the course and rated the course as highly important.

The first study evaluating mindfulness training as a primary, versus aftercare, treatment for substance use disorders was conducted by Brewer and colleagues (2009) using a manualized protocol adapted from the MBRP manual. The mindfulness-based treatment was compared to cognitive behavioral treatment, an established, empirically supported treatment for substance use disorders. Thirty-six individuals who had alcohol or cocaine use disorders or both were recruited via media advertisements and clinical referrals and were randomized to either nine weeks of group mindfulness training ($n = 21$) or twelve weeks of group cognitive behavioral treatment ($n = 15$). Treatment completion was low across both groups, with only nine individuals completing mindfulness training (43%) and only five individuals completing cognitive behavioral treatment (33%). Differences between treatment groups on substance use during treatment were not significant; however, psychological and physiological reactivity measures indicated that individuals who received mindfulness training were significantly less reactive to stress provocation following the intervention, as compared to individuals who received cognitive behavioral treatment.

The effect of mindfulness training on reducing reactivity to stress provocation described by Brewer and colleagues (2009) was similar to secondary analyses of data from the study by Bowen and colleagues (2009), which found that individuals who received MBRP were less likely to experience cravings in response to depressed mood (Witkiewitz & Bowen, 2010). The decrease in strength of the relation between depressed mood and subsequent cravings also predicted fewer days of substance use up to four months following treatment for those who received MBRP. Thus, reducing reactivity to negative affect (including depressed mood and psychological stress) could be an important mechanism of change following mindfulness-based treatments. Mindfulness-based treatments may also be particularly well-suited for individuals with co-occurring disorders, particularly when symptoms and behaviors related to one disorder (e.g., depressed mood) are a risk factor for symptoms and behaviors related to another disorder (e.g., substance use).

Several researchers have identified potential mechanisms by which these mindfulness practices and programs may affect problematic substance use. Hayes, Wilson, Gifford, Follette, and Strosahl (1996) suggest that substance use, as well as other maladaptive behaviors, may be maintained by the temporary relief they provide from aversive internal experiences. Continued use is reinforced by the negative reinforcement it provides, in the form of relief from contact with uncomfortable sensations, thoughts, or emotions. Marlatt (1994) discusses the "mindful mind's" ability to realize the impermanent nature of things, and to allow experience to arise and pass without clinging to any one state or attempting to avoid discomfort by searching for escape. "Mindfulness in this sense is learning to let go of the desired outcome, to practice 'nondoing' as an alternative to the addictive fix" (Marlatt, 1994, p. 180).

Empirically, several mechanisms of change in substance use with treatment using mindfulness-based approaches have been identified. For example, a shift in locus of control from external (feeling at the mercy of environmental circumstances) to internal (having a sense of personal agency related to one's behavior) accounted for some of the subsequent changes in substance use following a meditation course (Bowen, Dillworth, Witkiewitz, & Marlatt, 2004). Decreasing efforts to suppress thoughts has also been identified as a mechanism of change, in that individuals may still experience unwanted, intrusive thoughts but begin to relate to those thoughts differently, without attempting to suppress them (Bowen, Witkiewitz, Dillworth, & Marlatt, 2007; Garland et al., 2010). Reductions in stress, increased physiological recovery from alcohol cues, and modulated alcohol attentional bias are also hypothesized mechanisms (Garland et al., 2010). Finally, decreases in cravings following mindfulness-based treatment appear to partially explain changes in substance use (Bowen et al., 2009). This research is young, however, and there is much yet to be discovered on the specific mechanisms by which mindfulness practices affect change in addictive behaviors.

Directions for Future Research

In the review of twenty-five studies that integrated mindfulness training into treatment for substance use disorders (Zgierska et al., 2009), the authors identified three major areas for future research: refinement and standardization of research methods, development of a conceptual model of mindfulness interventions and an examination of the underlying mechanisms of change, and implementation and dissemination in clinical and community settings. The controlled trials of mindfulness-based interventions conducted to date have been limited by small sample sizes, high attrition rates, nonstandardized control groups, brief follow-up assessments, and lack of control for adherence and competence in treatment delivery (however, see Chawla et al., 2010, for adherence and competence ratings of the Bowen et al., 2009, study). Similarly the mindfulness-based interventions for substance use disorders studied to date generally have not been rigorously evaluated in comparison to other active treatments (however, see Brewer et al., 2009). To address some of these limitations, Bowen and colleagues are currently completing a full-scale randomized controlled trial of MBRP in comparison to cognitive behavioral relapse prevention therapy (an active treatment comparison) and a standard care control group. Treatment was provided over eight weeks, and participants in the trial ($n = 291$) are being assessed at two-, four-, six-, and twelve-month follow-ups. Of particular interest are the common and unique mechanisms of action of the MBRP and cognitive behavioral relapse prevention approaches, and for whom each of the treatments may be more or less effective.

The development of a conceptual model and the evaluation of mechanisms of change during and following MBRP are additional areas that are important for future research (Zgierska et al., 2009). We have some evidence that MBRP and related therapies are helpful, but we still have very little data on how they work. Numerous conceptual models of the mechanisms of mindfulness-based treatment have been put forward (e.g., Breslin et al., 2002; Hoppes, 2006), and more recently, Brewer and colleagues (Brewer, Bowen, Smith, Marlatt, & Potenza, 2010) developed an integrated theoretical model of mindfulness-based treatments for co-occurring depression and substance use disorders that provides a framework for targeting physiological, behavioral, and neurobiological processes that are common to co-occurring depression and substance abuse or dependence. As noted above, two studies have empirically assessed reduced reactivity to negative affective states and stress as one potential mechanism of change following MBRP (Brewer et al., 2009; Witkiewitz & Bowen, 2010). Other potential mechanisms of change, including changes in neural connectivity, cognitive biases, and cue reactivity, are currently being examined in two ongoing studies funded by the National Institute on Drug Abuse (grant #R01-DA025764, principal investigators Marlatt and Bowen, and grant #K18-DA031464, principal investigator Lustyk).

It is also critical for future research to evaluate the specific active ingredients of mindfulness-based interventions (DiClemente, 2010; Zgierska et al., 2009). All of the mindfulness-based interventions described in this chapter incorporate multiple components (e.g., formal and informal mindfulness practice, skills training, and lifestyle balance), and it is unclear which of these components have the greatest impact on the process of successful behavior change. Dismantling studies that attempt to isolate each of the components independently would provide a greater understanding of how and why mindfulness-based treatments are effective at reducing substance use. There may be only a few active ingredients that are responsible for the majority of changes observed following mindfulness-based treatment. Isolating these ingredients would help further refine treatments, and this could facilitate dissemination efforts by providing clinicians with training and information regarding only the most active ingredients (Glasner-Edwards & Rawson, 2010). For example, if daily formal meditation practice, group attendance, and training in coping with urges were identified as the three essential ingredients of MBRP, then a streamlined version of the treatment (possibly delivered in fewer sessions) or a stronger focus on specific elements or skills of the existing structure could be disseminated to community treatment providers and clinical settings.

Research to date in the field of mindfulness-based treatment of addictions is promising, but it is still relatively young. Developing a better understanding of the active mechanisms of change, for whom MBRP is best suited, and at what point in recovery the treatment is most effective are areas that deserve further attention. Research by our team and by several of our colleagues is beginning to look through the lens of neuropsychology, psychophysiology, and cognitive psychology to develop a more sophisticated model of how mindfulness practices and treatments may be effecting change in problematic substance use. Additionally, with further studies and larger sample sizes, we will be able to assess the influences of individual characteristics such as gender, drug of choice, addiction severity, psychological history, and other conditions on treatment outcomes to help determine for whom MBRP and related treatments may be most helpful.

References

Alterman, A. I., Koppenhaver, J. M., Mulholland, E., Ladden, L. J., & Baime, M. J. (2004). Pilot trial of effectiveness of mindfulness meditation for substance abuse patients. *Journal of Substance Use, 9*, 259-268.

Amaro, H., Magno-Gatmaytan, C., Meléndez, M., Coréts, D. E., Arevalo, S., & Margolin, A. (2010). Addiction treatment intervention: An uncontrolled prospective pilot study of spiritual self-schema therapy with Latina women. *Substance Abuse, 31*, 117-125.

Avants, S. K., Beitel, M., & Margolin, A. (2005). Making the shift from "addict self" to "spiritual self": Results from a stage I study of spiritual self-schema (3-S) therapy for the treatment of addiction and HIV risk behavior. *Mental Health, Religion, and Culture, 8*, 167-177.

Baer, R. A. (2003). Mindfulness training as a clinical intervention: A conceptual and empirical review. *Clinical Psychology: Science and Practice, 10*, 125-143.

Baker, T. B., Piper, M. E., McCarthy, D. E., Majeskie, M. R., & Fiore, M. C. (2004). Addiction motivation reformulated: An affective processing model of negative reinforcement. *Psychological Review, 111*, 33-51.

Blankers, M., Koeter, M. J., & Schippers, G. M. (2011). Internet therapy versus Internet self-help versus no treatment for problematic alcohol use: A randomized controlled trial. *Journal of Consulting and Clinical Psychology, 79*, 330-341.

Bodhi, B. (2000). *The connected discourses of the Buddha.* Boston: Wisdom Publications.

Bowen, S., Chawla, N., Collins, S., Witkiewitz, K., Hsu, S., Grow, J., et al. (2009). Mindfulness-based relapse prevention for substance use disorders: A pilot efficacy trial. *Journal of Substance Abuse, 30*, 295-305.

Bowen, S., Chawla, N., & Marlatt, G. A. (2010). *Mindfulness-based relapse prevention for substance use disorders.* New York: Guilford Press.

Bowen, S., Dillworth, T. M., Witkiewitz, K., & Marlatt, G. A. (2004, November). *Locus of control as a mediator between vipassana meditation and substance use in an incarcerated population.* Poster presented at the annual conference of the Association for Advancement of Behavioral Therapies, Boston, MA.

Bowen, S., Witkiewitz, K., Chawla, N., & Grow, J. (in press). Integrating mindfulness and cognitive behavioral practices and traditions for the prevention of relapse. *Journal of Clinical Outcomes Management.*

Bowen, S., Witkiewitz, K., Dillworth, T. M., Chawla, N., Simpson, T., Ostafin, B., et al. (2006). Mindfulness meditation and substance use in an incarcerated population. *Psychology of Addictive Behaviors, 20,* 343-347.

Bowen, S., Witkiewitz, K., Dillworth, T. M., & Marlatt, G. A. (2007). The role of thought suppression in the relationship between mindfulness meditation and alcohol use. *Addictive Behaviors, 32,* 2324-2328.

Breslin, F. C., Zack, M., & McMain, S. (2002). An information-processing analysis of mindfulness: Implications for relapse prevention in the treatment of substance abuse. *Clinical Psychology: Science and Practice, 9,* 275-299.

Brewer, J. A., Bowen, S., Smith, J. T., Marlatt, G., & Potenza, M. N. (2010). Mindfulness-based treatments for co-occurring depression and substance use disorders: What can we learn from the brain? *Addiction, 105,* 1698-1706.

Brewer, J. A., Sinha, R., Chen, J. A., Michalsen, R. N., Babuscio, T. A., Nich, C., et al. (2009). Mindfulness training and stress reactivity in substance abuse: Results from a randomized, controlled stage I pilot study. *Substance Abuse, 30,* 306-317.

Carroll, K. M. (1996). Relapse prevention as a psychosocial treatment: A review of controlled clinical trials. *Experimental and Clinical Psychopharmacology, 4,* 46-54.

Carroll, K. M., Ball, S. A., Martino, S., Nich, C., Babuscio, T. A., & Rounsaville, B. J. (2009). Enduring effects of a computer-assisted training program for cognitive behavioral therapy: A six-month follow-up of CBT4CBT. *Drug and Alcohol Dependence, 100,* 178-181.

Chawla, N., Collins, S., Bowen, S., Hsu, S., Grow, J., Douglas, A., et al. (2010). The mindfulness-based relapse prevention adherence and competence scale: Development, interrater reliability, and validity. *Psychotherapy Research, 20,* 388-397.

Chen, K. W., Comerford, A., Shinnick, P., & Ziedonis, D. M. (2010). Introducing qigong meditation into residential addiction treatment: A pilot study where gender makes a difference. *Journal of Alternative and Complementary Medicine, 16,* 875-882.

Curran, G. M., Flynn, H. A., Kirchner, J., & Booth, B. M. (2000). Depression after alcohol treatment as a risk factor for relapse among male veterans. *Journal of Substance Abuse Treatment, 19,* 259-265.

Daley, D., & Marlatt, G. A. (2006). *Overcoming your drug or alcohol problem: Effective recovery strategies.* New York: Oxford University Press.

DiClemente, C. C. (2010). Mindfulness—Specific or generic mechanisms of action. *Addiction, 105,* 1707-1708.

Gainsbury, S., & Blaszczynski, A. (2010). A systematic review of Internet-based therapy for the treatment of addictions. *Clinical Psychology Review, 31,* 490-498.

Garland, E. L., Gaylord, S. A., Boettiger, C. A., & Howard, M. O. (2010). Mindfulness training modifies cognitive, affective, and physiological mechanisms implicated in alcohol dependence: Results of a randomized controlled pilot trial. *Journal of Psychoactive Drugs, 42,* 177-192.

Glasner-Edwards, S., & Rawson, R. (2010). Evidence-based practices in addiction treatment: Review and recommendations for public policy. *Health Policy, 97,* 93-104.

Graham, K., Annis, H. M., Brett, P. J., & Venesoen, P. (1996). A controlled field trial of group versus individual cognitive-behavioral training for relapse prevention. *Addiction, 91,* 1127-1139.

Greenfield, S. F., Weiss, R. D., Muenz, L. R., Vagge, L. M., Kelly, J. F., Bello, L. R., et al. (1998). The effect of depression on return to drinking: A prospective study. *Archives of General Psychiatry, 55,* 259-265.

Groh, D. R., Jason, L. A., & Keys, C. B. (2008). Social network variables in alcoholics anonymous: A literature review. *Clinical Psychology Review, 28,* 430-450.

Grossman, P., Niemann, L., Schmidt, S., & Walach, H. (2004). Mindfulness-based stress reduction and health benefits: A meta-analysis. *Journal of Psychosomatic Research, 57,* 35-43.

Hasin, D., Liu, X., Nunes, E., McCloud, S., Samet, S., & Endicott, J. (2002). Effects of major depression on remission and relapse of substance dependence. *Archives of General Psychiatry, 59,* 375-380.

Hayes, S. C., Follette, V. M., & Linehan, M. M. (Eds.). (2004). *Mindfulness and acceptance: Expanding the cognitive-behavioral tradition.* New York: Guilford Press.

Hayes, S. C., Strosahl, K. D., & Wilson, K. G. (1999). *Acceptance and commitment therapy: An experiential approach to behavior change.* New York: Guilford Press.

Hayes, S. C., Strosahl, K. D., Wilson, K. G., Bissett, R. C., Pistorello, J., Taormino, D., et al. (2004). Measuring experiential avoidance: A preliminary test of a working model. *Psychological Record, 54,* 553-578.

Hayes, S. C., Wilson, K. G., Gifford, E. V., Follette, V. M., & Strosahl, K. D. (1996). Experiential avoidance and behavioral disorders: A functional dimensional approach to diagnosis and treatment. *Journal of Consulting and Clinical Psychology, 64,* 1152-1168.

Hester, R. K., Delaney, H. D., & Campbell, W. (2012). The college drinker's checkup: Outcomes of two randomized clinical trials of a computer-delivered intervention. *Psychology of Addictive Behaviors, 26,* 1-12.

Hoppes, K. (2006). The application of mindfulness-based cognitive interventions in the treatment of co-occurring addictive and mood disorders. *CNS Spectrums, 11,* 829-851.

Irvin, J. E., Bowers, C. A., Dunn, M. E., & Wang, M. C. (1999). Efficacy of relapse prevention: A meta-analytic review. *Journal of Consulting and Clinical Psychology, 67,* 563-570.

Kabat-Zinn, J. (1990). *Full catastrophe living: Using the wisdom of your body and mind to face stress, pain, and illness.* New York: Delacorte.

Kessler, R. C., Crum, R. M., Warner, L. A., & Nelson, C. B. (1997). Lifetime co-occurrence of *DSM-III-R* alcohol abuse and dependence with other psychiatric disorders in the National Comorbidity Survey. *Archives of General Psychiatry,* *54,* 313-321.

Khantzian, E. J. (1997). The self-medication hypothesis of substance use disorders: A reconsideration and recent applications. *Harvard Review of Psychiatry, 4,* 231-244.

Kilpatrick, L. A., Suyenobu, B. Y., Smith, S. R., Bueller, J. A., Goodman, T., Creswell, J., et al. (2011). Impact of mindfulness-based stress reduction training on intrinsic brain connectivity. *NeuroImage, 56,* 290-298.

Larimer, M. E., Palmer, R. S., & Marlatt, G. A. (1999). Relapse prevention: An overview of Marlatt's cognitive-behavioral model. *Alcohol Research and Health, 23,* 151-169.

Liehr, P., Marcus, M. T., Carroll, D., Granmayeh, L., Cron, S. G., & Pennebaker, J. W. (2010). Linguistic analysis to assess the effect of a mindfulness intervention on self-change for adults in substance use recovery. *Substance Abuse, 31,* 79-85.

Linehan, M. M. (1993). *Skills training manual for treatment of borderline personality disorder.* New York Guilford Press.

Linehan, M. M., Dimeff, L. A., Reynolds, S. K., Comtois, K., Welch, S., Heagerty, P., et al. (2002). Dialectical behavior therapy versus comprehensive validation therapy plus 12-step for the treatment of opioid dependent women meeting criteria for borderline personality disorder. *Drug and Alcohol Dependence, 67,* 13-26.

Ljótsson, B., Hedman, E., Lindfors, P., Hursti, T., Lindefors, N., Andersson, G., et al. (2011). Long-term follow-up of Internet-delivered exposure and mindfulness based treatment for irritable bowel syndrome. *Behaviour Research and Therapy, 49,* 58-61.

Longabaugh, R., Wirtz, P. W., Zywiak, W. H., & O'Malley, S. S. (2010). Network support as a prognostic indicator of drinking outcomes: The COMBINE study. *Journal of Studies on Alcohol and Drugs, 71,* 837-846.

Marcus, M. T., Schmitz, J., Moeller, G., Liehr, P., Cron, S. G., Swank, P., et al. (2009). Mindfulness-based stress reduction in therapeutic community treatment: A stage 1 trial. *American Journal of Drug and Alcohol Abuse, 35,* 103-108.

Marlatt, G. A. (1994). Addiction, mindfulness, and acceptance. In S. C. Hayes, N. S. Jacobson, V. M. Follette, & M. J. Dougher (Eds.), *Acceptance and change: Content and context in psychotherapy.* Reno, NV: Context Press.

Marlatt, G. A., & Gordon, J. R. (Eds.). (1985). *Relapse prevention: Maintenance strategies in the treatment of addictive behaviors.* New York: Guilford Press.

Marlatt, G. A., & Marques, J. K. (1977). Meditation, self-control, and alcohol use. In R. B. Stuart (Ed.), *Behavioral self-management: Strategies, techniques, and outcomes.* New York: Brunner/Mazel.

Marlatt, G. A., Pagano, R. R., Rose, R. M., & Marques, J. K. (1984). Effects of meditation and relaxation training upon alcohol use in male social drinkers. In D. H. Shapiro & R. N. Walsh (Eds.), *Meditation: Classic and contemporary perspectives.* New York: Aldine.

McRoberts, C., Burlingame, G. M., & Hoag, M. J. (1998). Comparative efficacy of individual and group psychotherapy: A meta-analytic perspective. *Group Dynamics: Theory, Research, and Practice, 2,* 101-117.

Miller, L. D. (2011). Stay sober mindfully! Mindfulness-based relapse prevention (MBRP). Retrieved August 20, 2011, from www.lisadalemiller.com/mbrp.htm.

Miller, W. R., & Rollnick, S. (2002). *Motivational interviewing: Preparing people for change.* New York: Guilford Press.

Murphy, T. J., Pagano, R. R., & Marlatt, G. A. (1986). Lifestyle modification with heavy alcohol drinkers: Effects of aerobic exercise and meditation. *Addictive Behaviors, 11,* 175-186.

Segal, Z., Teasdale, J. D., & Williams, M. (2002). *Mindfulness-based cognitive therapy for depression.* New York: Guilford Press.

Sobell, L., Sobell, M. B., & Agrawal, S. (2009). Randomized controlled trial of a cognitive-behavioral motivational intervention in a group versus individual format for substance use disorders. *Psychology of Addictive Behaviors, 23,* 672-683.

Teasdale, J. D., Segal, Z. V., Williams, J. M. G., Ridgeway, V. A., Soulsby, J. M., & Lau, M. A. (2000). Prevention of relapse/recurrence in major depression by mindfulness-based cognitive therapy. *Journal of Consulting and Clinical Psychology, 68,* 615-623.

Thompson, N. J., Reisinger, W. E., Obolensky, N., Winning, A., Barmon, C., DiIorio, C., et al. (2010). Distance delivery of mindfulness-based cognitive therapy for depression: Project UPLIFT. *Epilepsy and Behavior, 19,* 247-254.

Vieten, C., Astin, J. A., Buscemi, R., & Galloway, G. P. (2010). Development of an acceptance-based coping intervention for alcohol dependence relapse prevention. *Substance Abuse, 31,* 108-116.

Witkiewitz, K., & Bowen, S. (2010). Depression, craving, and substance use following a randomized trial of mindfulness-based relapse prevention. *Journal of Consulting and Clinical Psychology, 78,* 362-374.

Witkiewitz, K., & Marlatt, G. A. (2004). Relapse prevention for alcohol and drug problems: That was Zen, this is Tao. *American Psychologist, 59,* 224-235.

Witkiewitz, K., Marlatt, G. A., & Walker, D. D. (2005). Mindfulness-based relapse prevention for alcohol use disorders. *Journal of Cognitive Psychotherapy, 19,* 211-228.

Witkiewitz, K., & Villarroel, N. (2009). Dynamic association between negative affect and alcohol lapses following alcohol treatment. *Journal of Consulting and Clinical Psychology, 77,* 633-644.

Zgierska, A., Rabago, D., Chawla, N., Kushner, K., Koehler, R., & Marlatt, A. (2009). Mindfulness meditation for substance use disorders: A systematic review. *Substance Abuse, 30,* 266-294.

Zgierska, A., Rabago, D., Zuelsdorff, M., Miller, M., Coe, C., & Fleming, M. F. (2008). Mindfulness meditation for relapse prevention in alcohol dependence: A feasibility pilot study. *Journal of Addiction Medicine, 2,* 165-173.

CHAPTER 4

The Metacognitive Therapy Approach to Problem Drinking

Marcantonio M. Spada

London South Bank University and North East London NHS Foundation Trust

Gabriele Caselli

London South Bank University and Studi Cognitivi Cognitive Psychotherapy School

Adrian Wells

University of Manchester

*M*etacognition refers to cognition applied to cognition (or thinking about thinking) and can be defined as any knowledge or cognitive process that is involved in the appraisal, control, or monitoring of thinking (Flavell, 1979; Moses & Baird, 1999). Two key aspects of metacognition have been identified (Yussen, 1985; Wells, 2000): metacognitive knowledge and metacognitive regulation. *Metacognitive knowledge* is the library of information that individuals have in memory about their own cognition and about strategies that influence it. Some of this knowledge extends beyond facts and provides a plan or guide for processing, the rules of which may be explicit or implicit. *Metacognitive regulation* refers to the execution of strategies to control the activities of the cognitive system. Metacognition theory and research started out in developmental psychology and have more recently been applied across various domains, including aging, memory, and neuropsychology (Nelson & Narens, 1990).

Over the last two decades, metacognition has been developed as a basis for understanding and treating psychological disorders (Wells, 2009). Wells and colleagues have argued for a move away from content-oriented cognitive-level explanations to an account of psychological dysfunction based on the way individuals relate to and regulate their own internal cognitive environment (Wells & Matthews, 1994, 1996; Wells, 2000). Wells and Matthews (1994, 1996) set out the *self-regulatory executive function (S-REF) model*, in which psychological disorder is associated with extended thinking on a particular topic, a thinking style called *cognitive attentional syndrome (CAS)*. CAS takes the form of attentional bias toward threat, maladaptive coping behaviors, thought suppression, and extended thinking (e.g., desire thinking, rumination, and worry). CAS produces paradoxical effects, maintaining rather than alleviating negative affect and a sense of threat. For instance, worrying focuses processing on potential future danger, so anxiety symptoms persist, and using alcohol to control distressing thoughts may lead to negative affect and perseverative thinking about the experience.

According to the S-REF model, CAS is activated by underlying metacognitive knowledge. Two broad content domains of such knowledge are important: positive and negative metacognitive beliefs. *Positive metacognitive beliefs* are those that motivate the use of CAS elements such as rumination and worry. They include beliefs such as *Analyzing why I'm a failure will help me succeed* and *Worrying means I can act before it's too late*. *Negative metacognitive beliefs* concern the significance, uncontrollability, or danger of thoughts. Examples include *Some thoughts could make me lose control* and *My thoughts are uncontrollable*.

The S-REF model has led to the development of disorder-specific formulations and treatments for depression (Wells, 2009), generalized anxiety disorder (Wells, 1995), obsessive-compulsive disorder (Wells, 2000; Wells & Matthews, 1994), post-traumatic stress disorder (Wells, 2000; Wells & Sembi, 2004), and social anxiety disorder (D. M. Clark & Wells, 1995). Metacognitive therapy or techniques based on such models have been evaluated across a series of studies for each of these disorders, with promising results (Fisher & Wells, 2005, 2008; Papageorgiou & Wells, 2000; Wells & King, 2006; Wells & Papageorgiou, 2001; Wells & Sembi, 2004; Wells et al., 2009; Wells et al., 2010).

The Nature of and Evidence for Metacognitive Processes in Problem Drinking

Although the S-REF model is likely to apply broadly to the area of substance abuse, the evidence base accrued has almost exclusively been in the area of problem drinking, so that is the focus of the present chapter. In the next three sections we will outline how the elements of the S-REF model apply to problem drinking.

Cognitive Attentional Syndrome Configurations in Problem Drinking

In problem drinking, CAS configurations involve predominantly uncontrolled alcohol use, suppression of alcohol-related thoughts, and extended thinking in the form of desire thinking, rumination, and worry. *Desire thinking* has been characterized as a voluntary process involving the elaboration of a desired target at a verbal level (repetitive self-talk regarding the need to attain the desired target and self-motivating statements; Caselli & Spada, 2010) and at an imaginal level (construction of mental images of the desired target or of its context of use; Kavanagh, May, & Andrade, 2009). The target of desire thinking may be an activity, an object, or a state (Kavanagh, Andrade, & May, 2004, 2005; Kavanagh et al., 2009). Research on problem drinkers has shown that desire thinking is positively associated with level of craving and alcohol use (Caselli, Ferla, Mezzaluna, Rovetto, & Spada, 2012) and leads to escalations in craving (Caselli, Soliani, & Spada, in press).

Rumination and worry are characterized by heightened self-focused attention involving persistent, recyclic, and predominantly verbal internal questioning about the causes, meaning, and consequences of one's internal experiences. Rumination is focused on depressive symptoms and their consequences (Nolen-Hoeksema & Morrow, 1991), while worry is characterized by an apprehensive expectation of possible negative outcomes in the future (Borkovec, 1994). Research has demonstrated that rumination is higher for problem drinkers compared to social drinkers

(Caselli, Bortolai, Leoni, Rovetto, & Spada, 2008) and that it prospectively predicts alcohol use in community and clinical samples (Caselli et al., 2010). Several studies have also supported an association between high levels of worry and the tendency to drink in order to reduce the worry process itself, especially among clients with alcohol use disorder (Goldsmith, Tran, Smith, & Howe, 2009; Smith & Book, 2010). Rumination and worry thus contribute to the escalation and persistence of negative cognitive-affective states that can trigger maladaptive coping strategies, including excessive alcohol use. Conversely, excessive alcohol consumption often results in substance-induced anxiety and depression, which may, in turn, sustain the tendency to ruminate and worry.

Metacognitive Beliefs or Knowledge in Problem Drinking

Evidence of the links between extended thinking (desire thinking, rumination, and worry) and metacognitive knowledge is wide-ranging. For example, research by Caselli and Spada (2010, 2011) found that individuals who misuse alcohol hold both positive and negative metacognitive beliefs about desire thinking. The positive metacognitive beliefs concern the usefulness of desire thinking in controlling negative thoughts and affect, in increasing positive sensations, in improving executive control over behavior, and in planning how to reach goals. Examples of these beliefs include *Imagining my desired activity will give me pleasure* and *Imagining my desired activity will help me avoid engaging in it*. Positive metacognitive beliefs about desire thinking are thought to play a role in the initiation and maintenance of the desire thinking process as a form of coping with cognitive-affective triggers (Caselli & Spada, 2010).

Negative metacognitive beliefs about desire thinking concern the uncontrollability of the desire thinking process and its negative impact on executive control over behavior, self-image, and cognitive performance. Examples of these beliefs include *Imagining the desired activity worsens my craving* and *I have no control over my desire thinking*. Negative metacognitive beliefs about desire thinking carry a strong negative valence, which may play a role in propagating negative affect once a desire thinking episode has started. This in turn may lead to the perseveration of desire thinking (because the goal of affect regulation is never reached) and a greater likelihood of alcohol use as a last-resort strategy to halt the growing sense of deprivation (Caselli & Spada, 2010)

Support for the link between metacognitive beliefs, on the one hand, and rumination and worry, on the other, has emerged from a wide range of studies showing cross-sectional and longitudinal relationships (e.g., Cartwright-Hatton & Wells, 1997; Papageorgiou & Wells, 2003; Wells & Papageorgiou, 1998). In these studies the role of metacognitive beliefs has been principally explored using the Metacognitions Questionnaire 30 (MCQ-30; Cartwright-Hatton & Wells, 1997; Wells & Cartwright-Hatton, 2004), which was developed to assess metacognitions related to psychopathology more generally. Recent research using this measure has shown that metacognitive beliefs are elevated in problem drinking, supporting the view that their activation may contribute to alcohol use, perhaps as a means of interrupting CAS processes and achieving, albeit temporarily, a degree of mental control. For example, in a study of drinkers from the community, Spada and Wells (2005) found a positive association between beliefs about the need to control thoughts and alcohol use that was independent of negative affect. In later research, Spada, Zandvoort, and Wells (2007) observed that these same beliefs, as well as beliefs relating to lack of cognitive confidence (negative evaluation of one's cognitive functioning), predicted classification as a problem drinker independently of negative affect. More recently, data from a prospective study found that beliefs about the need to control thoughts predicted levels of alcohol use and relapse in problem drinkers (Spada, Caselli, & Wells, 2009).

The results of these studies, taken together, indicate that problem drinking can be viewed as a strategy for controlling rumination and worry that is driven by metacognitive beliefs that certain thoughts need to be controlled. Among problem drinkers, negative thoughts and affective states (e.g., thoughts about drinking or low mood) are likely to be especially prominent and to be misinterpreted as indicating loss of self-control. The individual may ruminate and worry about these thoughts and affective states, monitor them, and try to suppress them (basically, CAS), leading to the exacerbation of negative affect and a greater likelihood of using alcohol.

Research exploring the nature of metacognitive beliefs in problem drinkers (Spada & Wells, 2006) has also identified positive and negative metacognitive beliefs about alcohol use. Positive metacognitive beliefs about alcohol use broadly relate to using alcohol as a means of controlling and regulating cognition (e.g., *Drinking helps me to control my thoughts*) and affect (e.g., *Drinking will improve my mood*). From a metacognitive standpoint, such beliefs are thought to play a central role in motivating individuals to engage in alcohol use as a means of cognitive-affective regulation (Spada & Wells, 2006, 2008, 2009, 2010). Negative metacognitive beliefs about alcohol use concern the perception of lack of executive control over alcohol use (e.g., *My drinking persists no matter how I try to control it*), uncontrollability of thoughts related to alcohol use (*The thought of alcohol use is stronger than my will*), thought-action fusion (*Thinking about using alcohol can make me drink*), and the negative impact of alcohol use on cognitive functioning (*Drinking will damage my mind*). From a metacognitive standpoint, such beliefs are thought to play a crucial role in the perpetuation of alcohol use, becoming activated during and following a drinking episode, and triggering negative affective states and biased mental regulation strategies (e.g., rumination) that compel a person to drink more (Caselli et al., 2010; Hoyer, Hacker, & Lindenmeyer, 2007; Spada & Wells, 2006, 2008, 2009, 2010).

Spada and Wells (2008) have developed measures of positive and negative metacognitive beliefs about alcohol use, and both measures have been found to predict alcohol use and problem drinking independently of negative affect in both community and clinical samples (Spada & Wells, 2008). Further research in a large community sample has confirmed that both positive and negative metacognitive beliefs about alcohol use predict alcohol use and problem drinking (Spada, Moneta, & Wells, 2007).

In a recent study, Spada and Wells (2010) observed that alcohol-dependent drinkers scored higher than problem drinkers and non-problem drinkers on both positive and negative metacognitive beliefs about alcohol use. Furthermore, problem drinkers scored higher on positive metacognitive beliefs about alcohol use than non-problem drinkers. In another recent study, which was controlled for personality dimensions and gender, Clark and colleagues (A. Clark et al., 2012) found that positive metacognitive beliefs about alcohol use predicted levels of alcohol use in binge-drinking university students. This finding highlights the role of metacognitive beliefs in predicting alcohol use, extending beyond aspects of personality that have traditionally been found to be associated with alcohol use.

The Role of Metacognitive Monitoring in Problem Drinking

The metacognitive model of psychological disorder proposes that failures or a breakdown in self-regulation resulting from the effects of using alcohol contribute to the development and maintenance of problem drinking (Wells & Matthews, 1994). It is widely accepted that alcohol impacts cognitive processes. In particular, impairment of attentional functioning appears to play a fundamental role in determining alcohol effects. For example, Steele and Josephs (1990) have argued that alcohol's pharmacological properties disrupt attentional processes (through the narrowing of perception to immediate cues and reduction of cognitive abstracting capacity), and Hull (1981) has advocated that alcohol use reduces self-awareness (corresponding to the encoding of information in terms of self-relevance).

We propose that both of these processes are likely to play a crucial role in impairing the effectiveness of monitoring of internal states during a drinking episode (Spada & Wells, 2006; Spada et al., 2007). The disruption of this monitoring process (termed *metacognitive monitoring;* Spada & Wells, 2006) is likely to lead to a continuation in alcohol use because the individual does not attend to information on affective change (e.g., feeling relaxed) and proximity to goals of alcohol use (e.g., achieving a greater degree of relaxation). In other words, the more problem drinkers consume alcohol, the greater the impairment of their capacity to monitor affective changes that indicate the goal of using alcohol has been achieved (feeling better, less stressed, etc.) and that it is okay to stop using.

In support of this view, evidence suggests that using alcohol affects metacognitive systems involved in monitoring internal states, increasing the likelihood of perseverative alcohol use (Nelson et al., 1998). In addition, semistructured interviews of problem drinkers (Spada & Wells, 2006) have shown that the majority of participants in these studies used alcohol as a coping strategy to regulate unpleasant cognitive or affective states (e.g., to reduce stress and enhance concentration). Furthermore, an internal signal (e.g., feeling calmer or more focused) was the indicator that their goal had been reached, but in most cases they did not know if the goal had been achieved. This could be explained by the fact that, for the majority of participants, their attention was predominantly focused externally (e.g., on the environment or a task at hand), reducing the flow of information (changes in cognition and affect) that could enable the cessation of drinking. Such external focus may be the direct result of alcohol or may be caused by drinking-related behavior.

Studies on monitoring internal states during drinking episodes (the process of metacognitive monitoring) have used the Alcohol Metacognitive Monitoring Scale (AMMS; Spada, 2006). Lower scores on this scale indicate lower levels of monitoring of internal states (units being drunk and attention to the effects of alcohol on affect, performance, and thoughts). AMMS scores have been found to be negatively correlated with alcohol use and problem drinking in both community and clinical samples. These data support the assertion that the less individuals monitor their internal states, the more they are likely to use alcohol in general.

A Triphasic Metacognitive Formulation of Problem Drinking

On the basis of the findings from these and other studies, we have proposed a formulation of problem drinking (presented in figure 4.1) that offers a bridge from the S-REF model to clinical practice (Spada, Caselli, & Wells, 2012). In this formulation, metacognitive beliefs and CAS can be mapped across three phases of a drinking episode: pre-alcohol use, alcohol use, and post-alcohol use. Common and specific processes and interactions between metacognitive beliefs and CAS operate in each of these phases.

Figure 4.1

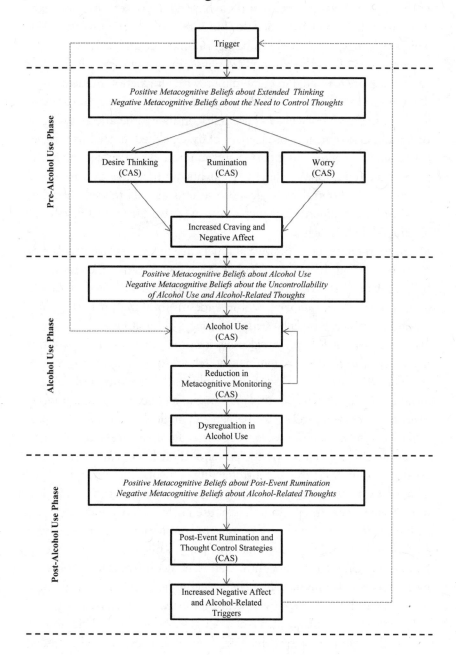

In the pre-alcohol use phase, cognitive-affective triggers in the form of cravings, images, memories, or thoughts lead to the activation of meta-cognitive beliefs about extended thinking or the need to control thoughts, which in turn activate desire thinking, rumination, and worry or a combination thereof. In the alcohol use phase, metacognitive beliefs about alcohol use are activated in combination with a reduction in metacognitive monitoring. This leads to dysregulation in alcohol use. In the post-alcohol use phase, once alcohol use is discontinued, the affective, cognitive, and physiological consequences of dysregulated alcohol use trigger metacognitive beliefs about post-event rumination and processing in the form of analyzing one's behavior, thoughts, and feelings as a means of trying to gain control over alcohol use and alcohol-related thoughts. This leads to a paradoxical increase in negative affect and associated alcohol-related thoughts.

In each phase, both positive and negative metacognitive beliefs may guide processing. In the pre-alcohol use phase, positive metacognitive beliefs relate to the benefits of extended thinking, such as *If I imagine using alcohol, I can gain control over it* (desire thinking), *If I analyze my craving experience, I will know what is causing it* (rumination), and *Worrying about alcohol will help me avoid using it in the future* (worry). Negative metacognitive beliefs predominantly relate to the need to control thoughts that arise from extended thinking (*I have to control thoughts about alcohol or they will control me*). In the alcohol use phase, positive metacognitive beliefs relate to the benefits of alcohol use (*Drinking will help me control my thoughts*). Negative metacognitive beliefs in this phase pertain to three domains: (1) the power of thoughts to cause uncontrollable alcohol use, (2) the uncontrollability of alcohol use once it is initiated, and (3) the need to continue using alcohol in order to avoid withdrawal symptoms. In the post-alcohol use phase, positive metacognitive beliefs relate to the benefits of post-event rumination (*If I analyze why I am feeling this way, I will understand why I use*), while negative metacognitive beliefs relate to the uncontrollability of alcohol-related thoughts (*I have no control over my thoughts about using alcohol*). As can be seen, there is overlap in the metacognitive themes activated in each phase.

The nature of CAS, which is characterized by attentional bias toward threat, maladaptive coping behaviors, thought suppression, and extended thinking (e.g., desire thinking, rumination, and worry), has similarities and differences across the three phases. In the pre-alcohol use phase,

CAS takes the form of desire thinking, rumination, and worry. In the alcohol use phase, CAS is characterized by a reduction in metacognitive monitoring resulting from the use of strategies aimed at using alcohol, which divert attention away from monitoring changes in affective states (e.g., feeling more relaxed) that may indicate that it is okay to stop using alcohol. Moreover, once alcohol use is initiated, it has chemical effects that lead to a disruption in metacognitive monitoring. As metacognitive monitoring is further reduced, individuals are increasingly unable to identify the stop signal that could motivate them toward cessation of alcohol use. In the post-alcohol use phase, CAS is characterized by extended thinking in the form of analyzing one's behavior, thoughts, and feelings as a means of trying to gain control over alcohol use and alcohol-related thoughts, together with intermittent attempts to suppress such thoughts. These attempts may be characterized by efforts to push away thoughts through distraction or trying to think about something else, leading to a "rebound effect" in the form of an increase in frequency of alcohol-related thoughts.

Metacognitive Therapy for Problem Drinking

Adrian Wells (2000, 2009) developed metacognitive therapy (MCT) as a transdiagnostic treatment approach for a range of psychological disorders. Empirical evidence supports the application of MCT for the treatment of generalized anxiety disorder, major depressive disorder, obsessive-compulsive disorder, and post-traumatic stress disorder (Wells, 2009). MCT consists primarily of a series of treatment components aimed at interrupting CAS processes, including metalevel socialization procedures, shifting to a metacognitive mode of processing, modifying metacognitive beliefs, attention modification (attention training and situational attentional refocusing), detached mindfulness, and development of new plans for processing. The order in which these treatment components are delivered varies depending on clinical presentation. What follows is an outline of MCT assessment and case formulation with problem drinking and examples of how the different treatment components of MCT can be used.

Assessment of Metacognition

The primary purpose of the assessment phase is to gather information that will enable the development of an idiosyncratic case formulation based on the triphasic formulation of the S-REF model applied to problem drinking. Three forms of assessment are relevant for problem drinking: the AMC analysis, metacognitve profiling, and a variety of psychometric instruments with a metacognitive focus.

THE AMC ANALYSIS

The AMC analysis provides a stepwise approach to assessment and case formulation. The "A" represents a thought or internal event (classically termed the "activating event"). This is followed by "M," the activation of a metacognitive plan. The plan consists of the individual's metacognitive beliefs and proceduralized blueprints that guide coping and may contribute to CAS. This in turn leads to "C," the affective consequences. In a brief example, the thought or internal event (A) might be an intrusive thought about being socially inadequate. The metacognitive plan (B) that is activated consists of (1) evaluating the thought as a significant event that needs to be controlled, (2) worrying about whether the thought will persist, (3) being guided by beliefs about the benefits of using alcohol to control the thought, and (4) focusing on obtaining alcohol to the exclusion of focusing on one's internal state. The consequences (C) include feeling anxious and, ultimately, using alcohol.

METACOGNITIVE PROFILING

The main goal of metacognitive profiling is to elicit the nature of the processing routines and metacognitive beliefs that are activated within the individual's metacognitive plan when faced with stressful or emotive situations. Metacognitive profiling may start by asking clients to describe a recent episode when they used alcohol, paying particular attention to cognitive-affective triggers experienced before use began. The assessment proceeds by focusing on metacognitive beliefs about the cognitive-affective triggers (e.g., "What were your thoughts about the triggers, such as cravings, images, or mood states, that led you to drink?") and alcohol use as a control strategy (e.g., "Before, during, and after the drinking episode, did you have any thoughts about the effect of alcohol use on your feelings or thinking?"). Coping strategies and goals are then considered. For example, clients may be asked to describe (1) whether alcohol was used as a coping strategy, and if so, what the main goal was; (2) how they knew if they had achieved their goal; and (3) what signaled that it was okay to stop using. Clients are also asked to recount what they typically focus on when using alcohol and whether there are any advantages and disadvantages of focusing their attention in the described manner.

PSYCHOMETRIC INSTRUMENTS WITH A METACOGNITIVE FOCUS

A variety of self-report instruments designed to capture metacognitive beliefs and aspects of CAS can aid the assessment process and facilitate the development of an idiosyncratic case formulation.

Desire Thinking Questionnaire (DTQ; Caselli & Spada, 2011). This is a ten-item self-report instrument designed to assess desire thinking. It consists of two factors with five items each. The first factor concerns the perseveration of verbal thoughts about desire-related content and experiences (Verbal Perseveration) and includes items such as "I mentally repeat to myself that I need to practice the desired activity" and "My mind is focused on repeating what I desire till I manage to satisfy it." The second factor concerns the tendency to prefigure images about desire-related content and experience (Imaginal Prefiguration) and includes items such as "I imagine myself doing the desired activity" and "I imagine myself involved in the desired activity as if it were a movie." Items are general in content and refer to the desired activity that may be specified in the instructions. Higher scores indicate higher levels of desire thinking. The DTQ total score and factor scores have shown good factor structure, internal consistency, test-retest reliability, and predictive and discriminative validity (Caselli & Spada, 2011).

Metacognitions Questionnaire 30 (MCQ-30; Wells & Cartwright-Hatton, 2004).This is a thirty-item self-report instrument designed to assess individual differences in metacognitive beliefs, judgments, and monitoring tendencies. It consists of five replicable factors assessed by six items each. The five factors measure the following dimensions of metacognition: (1) Positive Beliefs about Worry (e.g., "Worrying helps me cope"), (2) Negative Beliefs about Thoughts Concerning Uncontrollability and Danger (e.g., "When I start worrying I cannot stop"), (3) Lack of Cognitive Confidence (e.g., "My memory can mislead me at times"), (4) Beliefs about the Need to Control Thoughts (e.g., "Not being able to control my thoughts is a sign of weakness"), and (5) Cognitive Self-Consciousness (e.g., "I pay close attention to the way my mind works"). Higher scores indicate higher levels of maladaptive metacognitions. The MCQ-30 possesses good internal consistency and convergent validity, as well as acceptable test-retest reliability (Spada, Mohiyeddini, & Wells, 2008; Wells & Cartwright-Hatton, 2004).

Positive Alcohol Metacognitions Scale (PAMS; Spada & Wells, 2008). This is a twelve-item self-report instrument designed to assess positive metacognitive beliefs about alcohol use. It consists of two factors: (1) Positive Metacognitive Beliefs about Emotional Self-Regulation (e.g., "Drinking reduces my self-consciousness") and (2) Positive Metacognitive Beliefs about Cognitive Self-Regulation (e.g., "Drinking helps me to control my thoughts"). Higher scores represent higher levels of positive metacognitive beliefs about alcohol use. The PAMS possesses good internal and external reliability in both community and clinical populations (Spada & Wells, 2008).

Negative Alcohol Metacognitions Scale (NAMS; Spada & Wells, 2008). This is a six-item self-report instrument designed to assess negative metacognitive beliefs about alcohol use. It consists of two factors: (1) Negative Metacognitive Beliefs about Uncontrollability (e.g., "My drinking persists no matter how I try to control it") and (2) Negative Metacognitive Beliefs about Cognitive Harm (e.g., "Drinking will damage my mind"). Higher scores represent higher levels of negative metacognitive beliefs about alcohol use. The NAMS possesses good internal and external reliability in both community and clinical populations (Spada & Wells, 2008).

Case Formulation and Focus of Treatment

The triphasic formulation of the S-REF model of problem drinking is the basis for conceptualizing different CAS configurations and MCT pathways. Three key areas need to be specified across the triphasic spectrum: cognitive-affective triggers, metacognitive beliefs, and CAS configurations. These key areas then need to be synthesized into a model of the client's problem drinking and fed back to the client as a visual flowchart. This gives the client the opportunity to agree or disagree with the various components and modify them until a broad agreement is reached as to the formulation of the problem-drinking presentation.

The extent to which treatment focuses on a particular phase depends on the severity and duration of the problem-drinking presentation together with the client's level of awareness and treatment goals. For example, the pre-alcohol use phase typically features more prominently in occasional and irregular users, or those who are in the early stages of using to cope with negative affect. In this stage the link between negative affect and alcohol use will not yet be fully established, as the individual will most likely be experiencing the beginnings of the reinforcing effects of alcohol use in reducing extended thinking. Over time, as the link between alcohol use and the control of extended thinking strengthens, the individual may gradually move from occasional to more frequent use of alcohol and establishment of rigid metacognitive responses to negative internal states. The pre-alcohol use phase is also likely to play a central role for individuals attempting to remain abstinent who have not addressed their pre-alcohol use mode of processing, so that CAS remains as a residual symptom and a vulnerability factor that may be reactivated in response to feelings of deprivation (e.g., withdrawal symptoms) or negative affect.

The pre-alcohol use phase will typically be of less significance for individuals presenting with alcohol dependence or low levels of awareness. For these individuals, the alcohol use phase would be the primary focus of formulation and treatment. Thus, when obtaining alcohol has become a well-rehearsed response to negative affect, individuals may experience less pre-alcohol use extended thinking and may directly move to alcohol use as a response to the activation of metacognitive beliefs related to alcohol use.

Finally, the post-alcohol use phase will typically be of central importance when there is a chronic and persistent presentation with a history of relapses combined with awareness of the drinking problem. In this case, individuals who have tried to remain abstinent without changing their post-alcohol use CAS are likely to be more vulnerable to lapse episodes and long-term relapse. This is because the occurrence of a lapse in connection with the awareness of a drinking problem may activate positive metacognitive beliefs about post-event rumination as a strategy aimed at understanding the lapse, its causes, and its consequences. However this strategy is likely to lead to a paradoxical exacerbation of negative affect and increase the likelihood of using.

Treatment Components

An overarching goal in MCT is to socialize clients (metalevel socialization) to the role of CAS in maintaining their current difficulties. In the case of problem drinking, this means a specific focus on (1) how extended thinking (desire thinking, rumination, and worry) deepens distress and may lead to uncontrolled alcohol use, (2) how failures of metacognitive monitoring lead to alcohol overuse, and (3) how extended thinking about alcohol use and other alcohol-related thoughts (including thought suppression) increase negative affect and the possibility of further use. It is also important to highlight how behavior prevents the person from modifying unhelpful metacognitive beliefs, for instance, that alcohol use or thought suppression in response to negative thoughts stops the individual from discovering that such inner events are inconsequential.

Specific interventions are applied to the beliefs and processes in the principal target phase. All phases use basic treatment techniques (detached mindfulness, attention modification, modifying metacognitive beliefs, and developing new plans for processing, defined below), but there are differences in focus in each phase.

Interventions for the pre-alcohol use phase need to focus on interrupting extended thinking, particularly desire thinking, and associated metacognitive beliefs. Interventions for the alcohol use phase need to primarily target attention modification (in particular the enhancement of metacognitive monitoring) and challenge positive and negative metacognitive beliefs about alcohol use. Developing new plans for processing to cope with negative thoughts is central to both this phase and the pre-alcohol use phase. Finally, interventions for the post-alcohol use phase aim to promote a direct change in alcohol-related negative thinking (rumination and worry) and modify associated metacognitive beliefs.

SHIFTING TO A METACOGNITIVE MODE OF PROCESSING AND DETACHED MINDFULNESS

Shifting to a metacognitive mode and developing detached mindfulness will create new forms of awareness of cognitive events and processes. This helps clients see that the problem is not the occurrence of internal events but their relationship to those events, their metacognitive appraisal of the impact of those events on self-control, and the strategies they use to manage such events. Salient internal events can range from cravings and memories to thoughts, feelings, and physiological sensations. Detached mindfulness (Wells & Matthews, 1994; Wells, 2009) strategies are aimed at helping clients move to an observing stance (which is a metacognitive mode) with respect to their internal events. Detached mindfulness comprises two features: (1) mindfulness—an awareness of one's internal experience, and (2) detachment—separation of sense of self from internal experience and the suspension of any conceptual or coping activity in response to internal experiences. Detached mindfulness is not a symptom management technique; it is intended to facilitate engaging in an array of flexible responses to internal events. It involves encouraging clients to observe their cravings, images, memories, and thoughts without trying to control or change them. These strategies are introduced using metaphors, Socratic dialogue, and direct experiential techniques, such as the free-association task (Wells, 2009). In the free-association task, clients are asked to sit quietly and watch the ebb and flow of thoughts and memories that are triggered spontaneously by verbal stimuli. Verbal stimuli are random words that are said by the therapist at regular intervals (about twenty seconds), for example, "apple," "job," "tree," "restaurant," and so on. The aim of this technique is to help patients shift from perceiving thoughts and emotions as object-mode events depicting reality to seeing them as events in the mind that can be observed from a detached or metacognitive mode.

ATTENTION MODIFICATION

Direct attention modification strategies are a component of MCT. In 1990, Wells developed the *attention training technique* (ATT), which aims to improve the individual's executive control over the allocation of attention and prioritization of processing. This strategy involves asking clients to focus on a visual fixation point and to keep their gaze on this point. While doing this, clients are directed to focus their attention on individual sounds among an array of seven or more sounds and spatial locations. They are instructed to identify individual sounds, then to rapidly switch attention between them, and finally to divide attention among them. They are asked to practice ATT at least twice a day for ten to fifteen minutes each time. The rationale for the technique is important and emphasizes that no matter what thoughts or inner or outer events occur, these are examples of "noise" that individuals can learn to see as separate from their thinking.

A second strategy, developed in 2000 by Wells, involves *situational attentional refocusing* (SAR). It aims to increase the flow of adaptive information in awareness, increasing clients' ability to regulate cognition and behavior and modify erroneous metacognitive beliefs (e.g., about uncontrollability). One application of SAR entails encouraging clients to purposefully direct their attention to alcohol cues and refrain from conceptual elaboration of pleasant alcohol-related memories and images (e.g., focusing on how many drinks they have consumed rather than images of how pleasurable the next drink will be). An important application of SAR in the alcohol use phase is enhancement of metacognitive monitoring or awareness. The aim is to correct the failure of monitoring caused by alcohol-focused processing before more profound, chemical-induced failure occurs. The client is asked to focus on the impact of alcohol use on internal states as a drinking episode unfolds. This can be mapped as a timeline, helping clients see how they can choose to discontinue alcohol use as soon as they achieve a desired goal or in response to an external cue (e.g., quantity), whichever is most appropriate or occurs first. This scenario provides new goals and increases the flow of information about progress toward a goal that can be used as a basis for discontinuing alcohol use.

MODIFYING METACOGNITIVE BELIEFS

In MCT it is crucial to modify problematic metacognitive beliefs. Negative metacognitive beliefs are usually tackled first, as they tend to maintain CAS. Examples of negative metacognitive beliefs include *Angry thoughts will lead me to lose control of my mind*, *My craving experiences are uncontrollable*, and *Thoughts of using alcohol make me do it*. Strategies for tackling negative metacognitive beliefs include decatastrophizing their significance through verbal reattribution (e.g., "What is the evidence for and against the idea that your experience of craving needs to be controlled?"), strategies that directly change CAS processes (interventions aimed at interrupting desire thinking, rumination, and worry, such as the postponement of extended thinking), and practicing detached mindfulness.

Positive metacognitive beliefs (e.g., *If I imagine the object I desire, my mood will lift, If I ruminate, I will find a solution,* or *Using will help me gain control of my mind*) are linked to the activation of unhelpful coping strategies. Modifying these beliefs starts with verbal reattribution, such as an advantages-disadvantages analysis (e.g., "What are the advantages and disadvantages of thinking that drinking helps you gain control?"). This is followed by the exploration of better methods for achieving the advantages highlighted. Continuing with a similar theme, clients can be asked to explore the effectiveness of their chosen strategies in achieving their goal (e.g., cognitive-affective regulation).

In addition to these interventions, clients are asked to conduct behavioral experiments to test their metacognitive beliefs. For example, clients often present with a metacognitive belief that if they experience a cognitive-affective trigger (e.g., a craving), they need to act on it. An experiment is devised in which clients apply detached mindfulness and response postponement in response to a cognitive-affective trigger. After this experiment, clients are encouraged to reflect on their reactions and their predictions regarding the power or persistence of the trigger.

DEVELOPMENT OF NEW PLANS FOR PROCESSING

Clients are encouraged to identify the coping strategies they typically use and then not engage in them, substituting healthy alternatives instead. This is done initially in session and then between sessions when clients experience internal states associated with use.

For example, clients are encouraged to enter situations that trigger craving or discomfort and to apply a new set of strategies that have been learned and consolidated in treatment. In one case, the therapist accompanied the client to a bar and asked the client to implement a new processing plan of focusing on feelings of thirst while drinking a beer. When the feeling of thirst disappeared, the therapist asked the client to pause in drinking until the feeling returned. The client was surprised that the feeling did not return immediately. The process reduced the craving and reinforced the client's belief in his ability to control his drinking.

Summary and Future Directions for Research and Application

Metacognitive theory applied to psychopathology argues that the development and maintenance of psychological dysfunction is linked to the monitoring, appraisal, and attempted control of internal cognitive processes. The S-REF model provides a conceptual framework for expressing how stored knowledge and beliefs about thinking processes influence the choice of plans and regulation of coping. In our application of this model to problem drinking, we have argued for a triphasic formulation and approach to treatment that guides the clinician in identifying the most salient aspects of CAS and associated metacognitive beliefs.

In each phase, both positive and negative metacognitive beliefs may guide processing. In the pre-alcohol use phase, positive metacognitive beliefs relate to the benefits of extended thinking, whereas negative metacognitive beliefs predominantly relate to the need to control thoughts that arise from extended thinking. In the alcohol use phase, positive metacognitive beliefs relate to the benefits of alcohol use, and negative metacognitive beliefs pertain to the uncontrollability of alcohol use and alcohol-related thoughts. In the post-alcohol use phase, positive metacognitive beliefs relate to the benefits of post-event rumination, while negative metacognitive beliefs relate to the uncontrollability of alcohol-related thoughts.

The nature of CAS has some similarities and differences across the three phases. In the pre-alcohol use phase, CAS takes the form of desire thinking, rumination, and worry. In the alcohol use phase, CAS is characterized by alcohol use and a reduction in metacognitive monitoring. In the post-alcohol use phase, CAS is characterized by extended thinking in the form of analyzing one's behavior, thoughts, and feelings as a means of trying to gain control over alcohol use and thoughts related to alcohol use, along with intermittent attempts to suppress alcohol use thoughts.

Metacognitive therapy has been shown to be effective in the treatment of various psychological disorders. Further work using this treatment framework will lead to refinements in the key treatment components for problem drinking. At present, treatment incorporates techniques that interrupt extended thinking, challenge and restructure metacognitive beliefs, modify attention, and aid the development of novel ways to react to negative internal states.

The triphasic formulation of problem drinking is supported by empirical data; however, some of its aspects require further testing, such as examining the interaction of metacognitive knowledge and plans for extended thinking, as well as the relationship with internal and external triggers. Directions for future research also include testing versions of MCT for problem drinking specific to different presentations (e.g., binge drinkers, heavy drinkers, or alcohol-dependent drinkers) and different treatment goals (e.g., prevention, controlled drinking, or relapse prevention). It would also be valuable to examine whether changes in CAS components and related metacognitive beliefs occur during the process of problem drinking and alcohol dependence treatment, and if so, whether they are associated with relapse in longitudinal studies.

A further direction for future research would consist of expanding the triphasic formulation of the S-REF model of problem drinking to other addictive behaviors. Preliminary but as yet unpublished findings support the triphasic formulation as a good fit for nicotine dependence and pathological gambling. Notwithstanding this, it is likely that some of the triphasic components may differ on the basis of the substance or activity and its physiological effects. In conclusion, the triphasic formulation offers an alternative way of understanding and treating problem drinking and may eventually be extended to other addictive behaviors.

References

Borkovec, T. D. (1994). The nature, functions, and origins of worry. In G. C. L. Davey & F. Tallis (Eds.), *Worrying: Perspectives on theory, assessment, and treatment*. New York: Wiley.

Cartwright-Hatton, S., & Wells, A. (1997). Beliefs about worry and intrusions: The Metacognitions Questionnaire and its correlates. *Journal of Anxiety Disorders, 11*, 279-315.

Caselli, G., Bortolai, C., Leoni, M., Rovetto, F., & Spada, M. M. (2008). Rumination in problem drinkers. *Addiction Research and Theory, 16,* 564-571.

Caselli, G., Ferla, M., Mezzaluna, C., Rovetto, F., & Spada, M. M. (2012). Desire thinking across the continuum of drinking behavior. *European Addiction Research, 18,* 64-69.

Caselli, G., Ferretti, C., Leoni, M., Rebecchi, D., Rovetto, F., & Spada, M. M. (2010). Rumination as a predictor of drinking behaviour: A prospective study. *Addiction, 105,* 1041-1048.

Caselli, G., Soliani, M., & Spada, M. M. (in press). The effect of desire thinking on craving: An experimental investigation. *Psychology of Addictive Behaviors.*

Caselli, G., & Spada, M. M. (2010). Metacognitions in desire thinking: A preliminary investigation. *Behavioural and Cognitive Psychotherapy, 38,* 629-637.

Caselli, G., & Spada, M. M. (2011). The Desire Thinking Questionnaire: Development and psychometric properties. *Addictive Behaviors, 36,* 1061-1067.

Clark, A., Tran, C., Weiss, A., Caselli, G., Nikčević, A. V., & Spada, M. M. (2012). Personality and alcohol metacognitions as predictors of weekly levels of alcohol use in binge drinking university students. *Addictive Behaviors, 37,* 537-540.

Clark, D. M., & Wells, A. (1995). A cognitive model of social phobia. In R. Heimber, M. Liebowitz, D. A. Hope, & F. R. Schneier (Eds.), *Social phobia: Diagnosis, assessment, and treatment.* New York: Guilford Press.

Fisher, P. L., & Wells, A. (2005). Experimental modification of beliefs in obsessive-compulsive disorder: A test of the metacognitive model. *Behaviour Research and Therapy, 43,* 821-829.

Fisher, P. L., & Wells, A. (2008). Psychological models of worry and generalized anxiety disorder. In M. Antony & M. Stein (Eds.), *Handbook of anxiety and the anxiety disorders.* Oxford, UK: Oxford University Press.

Flavell, J. H. (1979). Metacognition and cognitive monitoring: A new area of cognitive-developmental inquiry. *American Psychologist, 34,* 906-911.

Goldsmith, A. A., Tran, G. Q., Smith, J. P., & Howe, S. R. (2009). Alcohol expectancies and drinking motives in college drinkers: Mediating effect on the relationship between generalized anxiety and heavy drinking in negative-affect situations. *Addictive Behaviors, 34,* 505-13.

Hoyer, J., Hacker, J., & Lindenmeyer, J. (2007). Metacognition in alcohol abusers: How are alcohol-related intrusions appraised? *Cognitive Therapy and Research, 31,* 817-831.

Hull, J. G. (1981). A self-awareness model of the causes and effects of alcohol consumption. *Journal of Abnormal Psychology, 90,* 586-600.

Kavanagh, D. J., Andrade, J., & May, J. (2004). Beating the urge: Implications of research into substance-related desires. *Addictive Behaviors, 29,* 1399-1372.

Kavanagh, D. J., Andrade, J., & May, J. (2005). Imaginary relish and exquisite torture: The elaborated intrusion theory of desire. *Psychological Review, 112,* 446-467.

Kavanagh, D. J., May, J., & Andrade, J. (2009). Tests of the elaborated intrusion theory of craving and desire: Features of alcohol craving during treatment for an alcohol disorder. *British Journal of Clinical Psychology, 48,* 241-254.

Moses, L. J., & Baird, J. A. (1999). Metacognition. In R. A. Wilson & F. C. Keil (Eds.), *The MIT Encyclopedia of the Cognitive Sciences*. Cambridge, MA: MIT Press.

Nelson, T. O., Graf, A., Dunlosky, J., Marlatt, A., Walker, D., & Luce, K. (1998). Effect of acute alcohol intoxication on recall and on judgments of learning during the acquisition of new information. In G. Mazzoni & T. O. Nelson (Eds.), *Metacognition and cognitive neuropsychology: Monitoring and control processes*. Mahwah, NJ: Lawrence Erlbaum Associates.

Nelson, T. O., & Narens, L. (1990). Metamemory: A theoretical framework and some new findings. In G. H. Bower (Ed.), *The psychology of learning and motivation*. New York: Academic Press.

Nolen-Hoeksema, S., & Morrow, J. (1991). A prospective study of depression and post-traumatic stress symptoms after a natural disaster: The 1989 Loma Prieta earthquake. *Journal of Personality and Social Psychology, 61*, 115-121.

Papageorgiou, C., & Wells, A. (2000). Treatment of recurrent major depression with attention training. *Cognitive and Behavioral Practice, 7*, 407-413.

Papageorgiou, C., & Wells, A. (2003). An empirical test of a clinical metacognitive model of rumination and depression. *Cognitive Therapy and Research, 27*, 261-273.

Smith, J. P., & Book, S. W. (2010). Comorbidity of generalized anxiety disorder and alcohol use disorders among individuals seeking outclient substance abuse treatment. *Addictive Behaviors, 35*, 42-45.

Spada, M. M. (2006). *Metacognition and problem drinking*. Unpublished PhD thesis, University of Manchester, UK.

Spada, M. M., Caselli, G., & Wells, A. (2009). Metacognitions as a predictor of drinking status and level of alcohol use following CBT in problem drinkers: A prospective study. *Behaviour Research and Therapy, 47*, 882-886.

Spada, M. M., Caselli, G., & Wells, A. (2012). *A triphasic metacognitive formulation of problem drinking*. Manuscript submitted for publication.

Spada, M. M., Mohiyeddini, C., & Wells, A. (2008). Measuring metacognitions associated with emotional distress: Factor structure and predictive validity of the Metacognitions Questionnaire 30. *Personality and Individual Differences, 45*, 238-242.

Spada, M. M., Moneta, G. B., & Wells, A. (2007). The relative contribution of metacognitive beliefs and expectancies to drinking behaviour. *Alcohol and Alcoholism, 42*, 567-574.

Spada, M. M., & Wells, A. (2005). Metacognitions, emotion, and alcohol use. *Clinical Psychology and Psychotherapy, 12*, 150-155.

Spada, M. M., & Wells, A. (2006). Metacognitions about alcohol use in problem drinkers. *Clinical Psychology and Psychotherapy, 13*, 138-143.

Spada, M. M., & Wells, A. (2008). Metacognitive beliefs about alcohol use: Development and validation of two self-report scales. *Addictive Behaviors, 33*, 515-527.

Spada, M. M., & Wells, A. (2009). A metacognitive model of problem drinking. *Clinical Psychology and Psychotherapy, 16,* 383-393.

Spada, M. M., & Wells, A. (2010). Metacognitions across the continuum of drinking behaviour. *Personality and Individual Differences, 49,* 425-429.

Spada, M. M., Zandvoort, M., & Wells, A. (2007). Metacognitions in problem drinkers. *Cognitive Therapy and Research, 31,* 709-716.

Steele, C. M., & Josephs, R. A. (1990). Alcohol myopia: Its prized and dangerous effects. *American Psychologist, 45,* 921-933.

Wells, A. (1990). Panic disorder in association with relaxation induced anxiety: An attention training approach to treatment. *Behavior Therapy, 21,* 273-280.

Wells, A. (1995). Worry and the incubation of intrusive images following stress. *Behaviour Research and Therapy, 33,* 579-583.

Wells, A. (2000). *Emotional disorders and metacognition: Innovative cognitive therapy.* Chichester, UK: Wiley.

Wells, A. (2009). *Metacognitive therapy for anxiety and depression.* London: Guilford Press.

Wells, A., & Cartwright-Hatton, S. (2004). A short form of the Metacognitions Questionnaire: Properties of the MCQ-30. *Behaviour Research and Therapy, 42,* 385-396.

Wells, A., Fisher, P., Myers, S., Wheatley, J., Patel, T., & Brewin, C. R. (2009). Metacognitive therapy in recurrent and persistent depression: A multiple-baseline study of a new treatment. *Cognitive Therapy and Research, 33,* 291-300.

Wells, A., & King, P. (2006). Metacognitive therapy for generalized anxiety disorder: An open trial. *Journal of Behavior Therapy and Experimental Psychiatry, 37,* 206-212.

Wells, A., & Matthews, G. (1994). Attention and emotion: A clinical perspective. Hove, UK: Lawrence Erlbaum Associates.

Wells, A., & Matthews, G. (1996). Modelling cognition in emotional disorder: The S-REF model. *Behaviour Research and Therapy, 34,* 881-888.

Wells, A., & Papageorgiou, C. (1998). Relationships between worry and obsessive-compulsive symptoms and meta-cognitive beliefs. *Behaviour Research and Therapy, 36,* 899-913.

Wells, A., & Papageorgiou, C. (2001). Brief cognitive therapy for social phobia: A case series. *Behaviour Research and Therapy, 39,* 713-720.

Wells, A., & Sembi, S. (2004). Metacognitive therapy for PTSD: A preliminary investigation of a new brief treatment. *Journal of Behavior Therapy and Experimental Psychiatry, 35,* 207-318.

Wells, A., Welford, M., King, P., Papageorgiou, C., Wisely, J., & Mendel, E. (2010). A pilot randomized trial of metacognitive therapy vs. applied relaxation in the treatment of adults with generalized anxiety disorder. *Behaviour Research and Therapy, 48,* 429-434.

Yussen, S. R. (1985). The role of metacognition in contemporary theories of cognitive development. In D. L. Forrest-Presley, G. E. MacKinnon, & T. G. Waller (Eds.), *Metacognition, cognition, and human performance.* New York: Academic Press.

CHAPTER 5

Motivational Interviewing: A Cousin to Contextual Cognitive Behavioral Therapies

Christopher C. Wagner
Virginia Commonwealth University

Karen S. Ingersoll
University of Virginia

Stephen Rollnick
Cardiff University

Motivational interviewing and the cognitive behavioral therapies can be seen as cousins, sharing family resemblances. As extended family members, they have more similarities to each other than to unrelated strangers, and they share some clear, overlapping family values and perspectives. However, cousins have different parents and somewhat different histories, norms, and developmental influences despite the family resemblances.

In this chapter, we introduce motivational interviewing (MI; Miller & Rollnick, 2012) and its theoretical model of addiction, clinical approach, and evidence base. We then consider how it and the contextual ("third-wave") cognitive behavioral therapies have important similarities, along with some key differences, in philosophical tradition, therapeutic stance, technique, and treatment focus.

MI has a basic, if unstated, premise: clients are able to consider, decide upon, and implement changes that help them move toward more fulfilling lives. This premise leads MI practitioners to approach clients with a productive and efficient focus: to simply help them determine how things could be better and how to move toward that end.

We consider MI to be a *direct* method of helping, focusing on discrete, specific changes rather than on underlying psychological patterns. Instead of presuming pathology, deficits, or inability, MI practitioners instead assume that clients are probably stuck, confused, or unclear. Their situations have gotten complicated enough that they may be stuck in a state of paralysis, or alternatively, they may be trying to make changes without having a clear sense of direction. In this context, MI practitioners combine a client-centered empathic approach with skill in guiding clients to focus on defining and implementing valued changes. This combination of empathy and direction helps clients simplify confusing situations, move into a state of greater calmness and clarity, and develop momentum toward a better future.

MI has its feet planted firmly in humanistic soil, presuming client competence and natural movement toward well-being. Generally, the focus is on client problems only to the extent needed to define goals for change and enhance motivation to work toward achieving them. Otherwise, the primary focus is on developing movement toward a better future and resolving any ambivalence that keeps clients stuck in their current situation or dilemma.

This is not a naive view; the suggestion is not that change simply involves applying willpower (Miller, 2006). Instead, we see it as a rationale for using a stepped-care approach, in which we first provide direct services to help mobilize or activate clients in moving toward positive growth or change, and add educational, skill-building, or reparative methods only when valuable for extending the benefits gained from direct change. For some clients, this MI work can be done in a few traditional-length sessions before transitioning to other approaches, although MI can also be used as an overarching model of helping.

With its focus on direct change, MI primarily uses an *eliciting and reflecting strategy* to help clients explore issues and possibilities, decide what to do, and begin (or increase) doing it. MI can start at any level of specificity regarding the target of change and can pick up from any point along a pathway of change. Regardless of the starting point, MI eventually focuses on specific changes that clients can make in order to move toward their preferred outcomes.

The therapeutic work in MI can have a relatively simple focus: addressing client inertia and ambivalence and other resolvable barriers, while also promoting the desire to change and increasing confidence about plans. It can also expand into greater complexity when direct decision making and planning stall out, addressing more general areas such as prioritizing client values as they relate to the client's current situation and desired outcomes (Wagner & Ingersoll, 2009).

MI Perspective on Addictive Behaviors, Habits, and Patterns

From an MI perspective, addiction is viewed as "fundamentally a problem of motivation" (Miller, 2006, p. 134). Cravings, urges, temptations, expectancies, problem recognition, perceived social norms and contingencies, perceived importance of and ability to change, and other addiction-related constructs all have significant motivational components. The development of addiction involves a process of diminishing volitional control of the addictive behaviors involved. As addiction intensifies, capacity for self-regulation diminishes—never below retrievable levels, but enough that it becomes ever more difficult for the person to consistently behave in consciously chosen ways (Miller, 1998).

Because MI is a therapy with a humanistic core, the basis of its conceptualization of addiction is that a person's process of natural growth and development is being blocked and the person has become stuck. The process of helping the person is not one of curing a disorder or altering a learning history, but releasing growth and development (Rogers, 1961). Like releasing a river that has become dammed, the process of helping may be as simple as opening up a channel to allow the flow to begin again; the river itself often takes care of the rest. Unresolved ambivalence makes up the core of the dam, slowing the river's momentum. Removing the barrier of unresolved ambivalence allows for a return to the natural flow toward health and well-being.

Ambivalence

Motivation can be understood as a multidimensional phenomenon including direction, effort, and persistence (Arnold & Randall, 2010). Ambivalence is highly prevalent in addiction, as in other health and habitual behaviors, and can interfere with all three elements of motivation. The targets or content of ambivalence may differ significantly across people, but the view in MI is that being stuck in ambivalence keeps people from changing.

The classic MI model casts unresolved ambivalence as a stalemate between motivation to change and motivation to maintain the status quo. In response to this stalemate, the person may experience inertia (lack of momentum), inconsistency in choices and behavior patterns as the person's perspective or emotions shift (lack of direction), or instability in change (lack of persistence). Ambivalence is not merely a cognitive phenomenon, but has emotional and behavioral elements as well (Wagner & Ingersoll, 2008, 2009). Cognitively, ambivalence can pull people back and forth, from argument to counterargument about continuing to live as they are versus trying something new. Emotionally, people can experience excitement, confidence, and determination about the possibilities in front of them, while also feeling dread, anger, or grief about the difficulties ahead and the comforts they may have to leave behind, along with disabling guilt or shame about the things they've done during their period of addiction. Behaviorally, some people make halting steps forward, unsure about moving at all or backtracking at the first sign of potential failure. Others rush forward in a desire to change as quickly as possible, only to discover that they weren't prepared for the challenges they face and possibly prompting a relapse.

Values Conflicts in Addiction

Ambivalence can also involve an internal conflict in personal values (Wagner & Sanchez, 2002), which can be seen as either behavioral ideals or preferences for experiences. As ideals, values provide judgments about what is good and not good. As preferences for experiences, values guide individuals toward seeking situations in which they may experience excitement, relaxation, novelty, competition, comfort, security, a sense of belonging, and so on.

Problematic addictive behaviors can involve behaviors that, while stimulating or relaxing, are ultimately shortsighted, overly self-oriented, or inconsistent with higher-order values. Shortsighted behavior produces short-term benefits at the cost of longer-term damage. The costs may be mildly impairing, such as a hangover that intrudes upon the following day's tasks, or more severe, such as the loss of belongings, home, or job due to extended patterns of unreliability or overextension of resources. Self-oriented behavior involves pursuing interests that are good or pleasurable for the individual at the expense of harming others. For example, a relationship may be harmed by lying to avoid social consequences of engaging in addictive behaviors, parenting may suffer due to being impaired or distracted, or loved ones may be harmed by impaired driving. Finally, ambivalence can be a battle between meeting basic physiological, emotional, or immediate social needs and developing higher-order social esteem and self-esteem or self-actualization, as proposed by Maslow (1970). A person with addiction may sacrifice self-growth opportunities in order to maintain the soothing or stimulating physical effects provided by the addictive behavior, the numbing of or escape from emotional pain, or the social reinforcement provided by friends with similar addictive patterns.

One implication of Maslow's hierarchy of needs is that when a person is forced to choose between a behavior that exclusively fulfills a lower-order value and one that only fulfills a higher-order value, it is natural to choose the former. When addictive behavior helps a person escape pain or gain pleasure, then it is natural for the person to continue that behavior, despite social rejection. When the problem behavior meets both biological and social needs, such as belonging to a peer group, it is natural for the person to continue the behavior even when it interferes with the pursuit of higher-order strivings toward achievement or self-actualization. To choose a healthy behavior that meets these higher-level values in place of an addictive behavior that meets lower-order values requires a transcendence of the natural order of motivations. Thus, addictive processes by their nature may contain inherent values conflicts that are difficult to resolve.

MI practitioners assume that a discrepancy between values and behavior probably exists, and therefore one therapeutic task is to help the person develop greater awareness of the discrepancy. Once some part of the behavior or its consequences becomes perceived as inconsistent with underlying values, the person is likely to become more motivated to change.

Emotions and Ambivalence Conflicts in Addiction

Ambivalence conflicts can take several forms, including *approach-approach conflicts*, *avoidance-avoidance conflicts*, and *approach-avoidance conflicts* (Lewin, 1951; Miller & Rollnick, 2012). These conflicts represent, respectively, being attracted to two different or opposing alternatives, being repelled by two different alternatives, and being simultaneously attracted to and repelled by a single option that is bittersweet in nature, containing both positive and negative elements. While any of these can generate anxiety and unresolved ambivalence, conflicts containing avoidance elements can be more difficult to resolve and may motivate a person to escape from the conflict altogether through distraction, inebriation, or psychological defenses.

Emotions are presumed to mediate these conflicts (Wagner & Ingersoll, 2008). A person in an approach-approach conflict is drawn to choose the pathway that promises the greatest hope, excitement, calm, or the like. An avoidance-avoidance conflict involves choosing the outcome that produces the least negative emotions among choices that all threaten to produce negative emotions. A common pattern in addiction is the approach-avoidance conflict. When viewed in relation to the addictive behavior, an approach-avoidance conflict may be one in which the person experiences positive emotions from engaging in addictive behaviors, followed by shame or other negative emotions in the aftermath of binge episodes. The negative emotions can evoke temporary commitments to avoid repeating the behavior in order to escape the negative emotional state of its aftermath. Alternately, the person may engage in distracting behaviors to escape the bad feelings. These waves of positive emotions followed by negative emotions create instability in motivations that increases the person's sense of lacking control over his or her own behavior. Additionally, the person's conflicts and contrasting emotional states can distance significant others, who react negatively to feeling pushed and pulled around by the addiction.

When considered in relation to a goal of change, the approach-avoidance conflict in addiction may involve desiring to change, whether through abstinence or control of the addictive behavior, and seeking to achieve that goal. However, as the person moves toward commitment regarding establishing a new, healthier pattern, the negatives about changing and the positives about continuing the addictive pattern become prominent in the person's mind and press him or her back toward a state of ambivalence. This, combined with the approach-avoidance conflict regarding continued use, results in a *double approach-avoidance conflict*, which is thought to be the most intractable type of conflict. MI is intended to resolve just such ambivalence conflicts.

Multivalence and Co-occurring Disorders

The term "ambivalence" implies a conflict between two choices. However, real life is often not so simple and involves multiple competing choices that may go beyond even the double approach-avoidance conflict. Barth and Näsholm (2006) refer to this as *multivalence*—in other words, simultaneous ambivalence conflicts about multiple issues and options.

One of the most common contexts in which multivalence may exist is in co-occurring disorders, whether mental or physical. For example, anxiety disorders may create a highly punishing situation that the person attempts to escape by using substances, gambling, or engaging in other potentially addictive behaviors. These behaviors reduce anxiety over the short term but also bring regret about the actions engaged in, which can then further exacerbate the underlying anxiety disorder. Subsequently, the person feels an even stronger desire to escape by a return to the addictive behavior. Recurring patterns such as these can lead to additional problems, such as depression, relational difficulties, or reductions in self-esteem. Although others may think that the person lacks motivation to change, the person is actually experiencing multiple conflicting motivations.

MI can help people see these invisible tides pulling them back and forth. If they have lost their footing and are adrift, motivational interviewing helps them relax, regain their wits and perspective, and take measured action to move in a productive direction. We now turn to how this is done in MI by describing its clinical approach.

The Clinical Approach of Motivational Interviewing

MI is a compassionate approach to helping based on forming a respectful partnership focused on the needs of the client (Miller & Rollnick, 2012). Clients are accepted as they are, and goals are elicited from them rather than provided or suggested by the practitioner. Because MI supports and respects the autonomy of clients, the solutions that are developed during the process of counseling fit well for the client.

MI practitioners elicit more information than they provide. The clients do more of the talking, explaining, exploring, and considering, while practitioners help them focus and clarify their perspectives, goals, and plans by reflecting, questioning, and supporting clients' efforts. MI practitioners show curiosity rather than expertise, even when they have substantial expertise in the area of the client's concern. It is more important that the MI practitioner develop an understanding of the client than it is to provide information, education, or persuasion about clinical problems or change options, which may provoke resistance or reluctance.

MI practitioners use a style described as *guiding* (Rollnick, Miller, & Butler, 2008), which involves collaborating, eliciting, encouraging, assisting, and focusing. Like a guide who helps hikers explore a mountain region, a good clinical guide listens closely to clients' desires, fears, and hopes and attempts to help them achieve their goals, both by accompanying them and by serving as an information resource along the way, while leaving the final choice or decision making to the clients.

Resolving Ambivalence in Favor of Change

Understanding and resolving ambivalence is a central goal of MI and is accomplished through elicitation rather than persuasion. Practitioners elicit clients' ideas and feelings about their current behaviors, how the behaviors fit in with their longer-term hopes and broader values, and whether there might be more optimal choices from the clients' perspectives. Practitioners elicit the client's own reasons and rationale for possible change, referred to as *change talk*. In the MI model, the opposite of change talk is *sustain talk*: client discussion of the positives of the current status quo or negatives about changing. Generally, MI practitioners respectfully acknowledge sustain talk but do not elicit or explore it unless the client seems to need to do so in order to let go of attachments or burdens and progress toward change.

Change talk focuses on the importance of change, confidence about change, and readiness to change. The various elements of change talk are summarized by the acronym DARN-CAT. *Importance of change* includes discussion of clients' desires (D), reasons (R), and need to change (N). *Confidence about change* includes clients' discussion of their current ability (A) to change. Altogether, these DARN elements are considered *preparatory change talk*, because practitioners elicit and reinforce them as part of the process of helping clients prepare to implement changes.

Once clients' ambivalence about change is mostly resolved, MI switches to a focus on *mobilizing change talk*, focused on clients' *readiness to change*. The CAT elements of mobilizing change talk are commitment (C), activation (A), and taking steps (T). Though the acronym is convenient, these elements are slightly out of order in comparison to how they usually occur in MI sessions. After clients discuss why they might make a change (desires, reasons, and/or needs), the typical focus shifts toward how they would go about it and their confidence in doing so (ability). Once clients feel that change is important and something they have sufficient confidence to attempt, they may begin expressing openness to activation (A), such as being ready or eager to change. As a part of change planning, they may make a commitment (C) to specific change attempts, followed by taking initial steps (T) toward the change goals they have set for themselves.

While this serves as a general plan for helping clients resolve ambivalence in favor of change, reality is often more complex. Clients sometimes have difficulty deciding what it is they want, struggle to let go of things they like about their current way of being, get defensive about changing habits that are not serving them well, delay implementing new habits that would help them reach their goals, and make halting, temporary progress before falling back into old patterns. Typical social reactions to such developments are to persuade, cajole, encourage, and even pressure individuals toward changing. However, while such interactions may influence a person to get past inertia, they rarely provide a basis for sustained attempts to change.

While MI practitioners tend not to focus their efforts on eliciting all sides of client ambivalence equally, putting more emphasis on change than the status quo, they also respectfully accept client hesitations, reservations, and defenses about change. Change is hard. It involves giving up valued parts of life and of oneself. New habits may feel awkward and may not pay off in the short term. Sometimes unanticipated challenges or disadvantages appear along the pathway to change. Old habits may also compensate for other difficulties that do not fully reveal themselves until change is attempted. MI practitioners strive to come alongside clients as they meet the inevitable challenges and setbacks. Rather than applying pressure to change, they instead protect the negative side of ambivalence, which can help liberate clients from the need to protect it, allowing them to explore alternatives more freely. By remaining empathic and accepting that change involves loss and hardships that clients may not choose to endure, MI practitioners communicate that change is the client's choice, and that no one but the client can decide whether change is worth the effort or can make change happen. By communicating recognition of the difficulties and losses involved, as well as acceptance of clients' autonomy in choosing and implementing change, MI practitioners help clients become more accepting of the struggles they experience, of their own ambivalence about making changes, and of the reality that if they do not actively choose to structure their lives in ways that fit with their values and goals, their lives will be shaped passively, by circumstances and by others. While MI is not didactic and does not attempt to teach perspectives or lessons, a broad goal is to help clients gain greater ownership of their own lives, becoming the authors of their own life stories. Thus, descriptions of MI often focus on the spirit of the approach more than the techniques.

Acceptance

One reason that people experience unresolved ambivalence is an inability to accept that certain past possibilities are no longer available and some past hopes should be left behind. Helping clients achieve acceptance is in itself a kind of change and can be approached in the same way that MI approaches other changes. Sometimes the situation is unchangeable; only the person's reaction to it can be changed. For example, others may have attitudes about the client that are intractable, and therefore the only choice for the client is whether to accept these or continue to be bothered by them. In this case, acceptance is change.

Other times, acceptance leads to change. Rejection by others often leads to rejection of oneself, which can then lead to a kind of paralysis. As Rogers indicated, "The curious paradox is that when I accept myself just as I am, then I can change" (Rogers, 1961, p. 17). In MI, self-acceptance is facilitated in large part by the deep acceptance offered by the practitioner, who lends a supportive presence and optimism about the future.

MI Core Communication Skills

While MI microcommunications are consistent with good client-centered counseling skills generally, they are used strategically in MI. The core communication methods are summarized as OARS: open questioning (O), affirming (A), reflective listening (R), and summarizing (S).

OPEN QUESTIONING

Open questions serve to show the counselor's interest in the client's perspective and give the client opportunities to cover whatever territory is important. However, open questions can also provide significant structure that helps the client to focus, as in "Tell me more about how drinking fits into your everyday life," or guides them toward thinking ahead, as in "Where might you go from here?"

AFFIRMING

Affirming means appreciating something about the person, such as "Given what you have going on, you put a lot of effort into coming here today" or "I appreciate how honest you're being, especially because this can be a tough subject to share with others." These affirmations focus on specific noticeable behaviors. Alternatively, affirmations can be more global in nature, appreciating a client strength or value put into action— for example, "Your dedication really paid off" or "It sounds like you work hard to be a good parent." While all are positive, affirmations differ from agreeing with client perspectives or approving their choices.

Too much affirmation can backfire, especially in more emotionally restrained cultures. Like salt in a recipe, affirmation can add flavor to the conversation, but just as too much salt can ruin food, excessive affirmations can come across as insincere.

REFLECTIVE LISTENING

Reflective listening has several intertwined components. *Listening attentively*, without judgment and with the intent to understand, is a key skill. *Reflections* are statements that capture the essence of what clients are saying. *Simple reflections* are restatements of what was said, usually paraphrasing. The statements sound like facts, mirroring what you heard and understood, and generally result in clients elaborating their perspectives. *Complex reflections* add something, such as recognition of an unspoken meaning, or capture the conflicting feelings clients have. Complex reflections can include metaphors that deepen the discussion when clients are focusing on superficial matters, that broaden the focus when clients are thinking narrowly about very specific behavior changes that might be more usefully bundled together into a larger lifestyle change, or that slow the momentum when clients appear to be rushing toward change in an unprepared fashion (Wagner & Ingersoll, in press).

Selecting what to reflect and what to ignore is an MI-specific skill that helps guide the conversation, may elicit or underscore change talk, and keeps the session moving. *Selective reflections* may be used to narrow the conversation toward a more productive focus, increase the forward momentum of a conversation, or bring clients back to a practical focus when conversation threatens to become a detached existential discussion (Wagner & Ingersoll, in press).

One specific MI reflection is the *double-sided reflection*, in which practitioners reflect both sides of clients' ambivalence (typically reflecting the sustain talk or status quo side of ambivalence first and ending with a focus on change, which subtly prompts clients to further explore the change side). A *continuing-the-paragraph reflection* guesses where the client was going next and helps keep momentum going (assuming the practitioner is right). While perhaps technically not a reflection, since it states something as yet unstated, this can help clients keep moving forward at times when the negative side of ambivalence appears to interrupt positive momentum. Reflections that convert clients' descriptions into images or metaphors can be quite powerful, often capturing dilemmas in memorable, emotion-laden ways that clients can easily recall, allowing clients to draw clarity and strength from them when they are in difficult situations. In MI, we particularly target reflections toward client change talk.

SUMMARIZING

Summaries go beyond reflections by linking several different parts of clients' experiences together in an integrative whole. Summaries help clients stand back and look at the big picture, pulling together their interests and concerns about different patterns and possibilities. Summaries help clients see the forest, not just the trees. The *collecting summary* brings together various client statements, often ending with an open question that has some momentum or direction built in, such as an invitation for clients to add more to the list or to comment on what they want to do next. A *linking summary* connects a current conversation with a previous conversation, perhaps on a different topic, often highlighting a shared theme, feeling, or dilemma. A *transitional summary* is used to wrap up a topic and shift to a new focus.

MI Clinical Processes and Strategies

MI does not focus exclusively on momentary interactions. Instead, it incorporates larger conversational strategies in the context of four general therapeutic processes: engaging, focusing, evoking, and planning (Miller & Rollnick, 2012). In our discussion of each of these areas below, we briefly define the domain and then give examples of strategies that are used within it in MI.

ENGAGING

The first key process is *engaging*: fostering a deep trust between practitioner and client that allows for the development of client-centered goals. MI is dependent on the development of a collaborative relationship between client and practitioner. Engaging has two essential functions in MI: enlisting clients in the process of opening up and discussing personal issues, and involving them in developing a meaningful relationship with the practitioner in which both arrive at a shared understanding through this psychological contact.

Clients typically have a range of interests and concerns when entering treatment. For example, they might wonder *How helpful will counseling be? Will the counselor respect me and my perspective or criticize and pressure me? How much of the truth should I tell, and how much should I keep to myself?* Clients may be embarrassed about things they've done or haven't done, critical of themselves for having to talk to a counselor, angry and blaming others, or fearful about their ability to gain enough self-control to manage their lives more productively going forward.

These issues may limit clients' ability to explore concerns and reveal themselves to practitioners, or limit their ability to envision a better future and make progress toward enacting it. To help reduce these distractions, the first process in MI is engaging clients in a trusting relationship and an empathic, supportive atmosphere.

Engagement can be undermined by prematurely focusing on exploring clinical issues before developing a bond and level of openness in the discussion, or by taking an expert stance, communicating implicitly that the client's role is to answer questions, provide information, pose problems, and so on for the professional to sort out, solve, and render advice on. Beginning an MI interaction with a formal psychological assessment risks combining both of these traps: focusing on problems and psychological status before developing a relationship, and implicitly communicating to clients that their job is to provide information in order to receive expert guidance. Thus, in MI, assessment typically would not be done at the outset of interactions, and it would be used as a means of eliciting client reactions and ideas rather than as a means of providing clients with expert feedback or recommendations. One approach is to sandwich assessments between two brief MI-oriented conversations about the person's concerns and interests.

Engagement can be accomplished through a skillful mix of open questions and reflections directed toward developing an empathic understanding of clients' perspectives and experiences. Open questions not only indicate to clients that the practitioner is interested in their perspectives and experiences but also, by their very structure, prompt clients to elaborate, which is an essential part of engaging.

While reflective listening is the core microcommunication in MI, reflections are used for different purposes at different times. While engaging clients, using frequent simple reflections of a key word or idea demonstrates that you are listening carefully and understand the key elements of their messages. Given that many clients of addiction services enter therapy in a defensive posture, these regular simple reflections can be more important than they may seem upon first glance.

Reflections can sometimes be confused with closed questions. Often the surface difference between the two is only a matter of voice inflection. Sometimes counselors believe it is more respectful to ask a question than to presume to make a statement about clients' experiences or perspectives. However, clients seem generally quite willing to correct off-target reflections, and seem to appreciate the effort to try to understand. Conversely, clients who are feeling defensive or unsure of themselves can easily hear closed questions as veiled judgments or accusations. For example, consider the following two practitioner comments:

- "You don't see your cocaine use as a problem?"

- "You don't see your cocaine use as a problem."

The first, a closed question, puts a demand on the client to answer the practitioner's inquiry and is ripe for misinterpretation as a judgmental statement, given a probable history of judgment by others. The second example, a reflection (delivered in an accepting manner without any sense of sarcasm), is more likely to come across as a respectful reflection of the client's current perspective, and communicates a nonjudgmental and nonhierarchical stance on the practitioner's part.

Throughout the course of MI, the goal is to average two to three reflections for every question (with other forms of communication much less frequent). This helps avoid a *question-answer trap*, in which you rely too much on asking questions (especially closed questions), essentially training clients to become more passive, answer the questions asked, avoid doing their own creative brainstorming, and wait for you to dispense expert advice following the series of questions. This is contrary to the process MI aims to develop to help clients move through lingering ambivalence about change.

The experience of ambivalence, with its alternating pushes and pulls, its instability, and the demands it makes on a person's thoughts and feelings, is nearly the opposite of the experience fostered through mindfulness. While MI does not teach mindfulness practice, it can help clients become more grounded, reducing their experience of swinging between the emotional pulls of different change possibilities. MI evokes a careful consideration of the choices people face, and in its pacing and focus, it can resemble a mindful process. Clients become calm and focused, considering various angles and detaching from automatic reactions in order to consciously choose their path forward.

Although the process of engaging clients should be firmly established before turning attention to the process of focusing, engaging is never fully finished. At the start of each session, whenever you are opening up new issues or deepening the discussion of vulnerable matters, or anytime clients become overwhelmed, intellectualized, defensive, or detached, returning to engagement can help reestablish the bond and clear mental clutter that competes for clients' focus or threatens their sense of well-being.

FOCUSING

The second key process is *focusing*, which is the process of directing attention toward the issue of client change. A variety of questions can inform how the practitioner guides the conversation during focusing: What does the client not like about his or her life? What might be different or better? What might the client like to keep while moving forward, and what can be left behind? MI focuses on the future that the client would like to bring into being.

Clients may initially present with nothing more than a vague sense of dissatisfaction, or they may have a clear focus, with several potential issues to choose between or focus on sequentially. The goal is to join clients wherever they are and focus conversations from there.

Often clients present with a number of concerns that compete for their focus. It can be unclear which areas are the most important, which are the most urgent, or which could be the most easily resolved in order to reduce stress and distraction and build momentum toward change.

One way to approach this dilemma is to do *agenda mapping*. This metaconversation is a way of mapping out how to proceed. A first step is to do some structuring, agreeing to work together to map out a plan and touching on issues but not delving into any of them until the mapping process is complete. Next, develop a list of topics that you might consider together going forward, without committing to any of them. Spend most of this time eliciting ideas from the client, providing support and affirmation, extending client ideas when inspired, and suggesting a few of your own once the client has finished, if the options seem incomplete and asking permission to introduce any ideas that you think may elicit defensiveness.

Once a basic list is established, focus in on a few topics that could use more fleshing out; then return to a bird's-eye view to see how they fit together and begin to lay out a plan for the journey ahead. If you need to take different roles regarding different issues (for example, if you must report on urine screenings in addition to counseling the client about relapse), this is a good time to clarify that as well. Optionally, you can supplement the conversation with a piece of paper on which you jot ideas in thought bubbles and connect the bubbles in the order in which you plan to proceed. The agenda is not fixed, of course, but having it allows you to draw attention to times when topics seem to diverge from the plan, in order to see if the agenda needs to be revisited and perhaps revised. Revisiting the agenda can also be useful when discussion seems to get bogged down and forward progress seems too slow.

At times, clients may only report that they are unhappy or express a number of dissatisfactions. Their addictive behaviors may exist alongside these complaints, but the connection isn't clear and clients may not seem to respond to invitations to explore. Rather than battling clients over focus, you can allow things to be vague for a while and establish momentum by working on other issues the client is interested in, gradually setting a general goal toward greater happiness or life satisfaction. That goal may narrow to better health or sleep or better relationships, and eventually connect rather naturally to changes in addictive behaviors. Developing these goals collaboratively over the course of conversation allows for a more thorough grounding of addictive behavior change goals in changes clients are already motivated to make (Wagner, 2012).

There may be times when you and the client have different ideas about what to focus on. For example, a client may want to focus on the specific circumstances that led to a DUI charge, while you may think it's important to discuss the more general drinking patterns that led up to that event and that may lead to similar events in the future. Or a client may want to talk about how unfair cannabis laws are, while you may want to focus on the possible connection between his cannabis use and the cocaine use he also acknowledges. The MI model suggests avoiding the "righting reflex" that counselors can fall into, wanting to fix things that are not going well. Rather than pressing your preferred focus, you might instead try to back up into a broader focus, find subtle connections between the areas, and then work forward from there, attempting to get the client to explore things in such a way that both focus areas are integrated.

If it isn't possible to integrate the competing areas of focus, an option is to provide information that clients may not be aware of using an *elicit-provide-elicit strategy*. In this strategy, you first elicit clients' current awareness, knowledge, or perspective on a topic. Then you provide information that fills in the blanks and corrects any misinformation the client holds. Rather than bombarding clients with details they already know and possibly having them miss the details they're unaware of or misunderstand, you can use this strategy to tailor the information you share to that which they truly are missing and can use. This also cues clients to be ready to take in information that they might otherwise miss if they are thinking about other things at the time. Finally, you then elicit their reactions to the information you shared, and if or how they might want to use it in relation to their own situation.

MI occasionally incorporates advice giving but limits it to situations in which the practitioner has the client's permission to offer it. This can be done directly by asking for permission (and not giving the advice if permission is refused), or indirectly by giving the suggestion, then following it with a clear acknowledgment that it is up to the client to follow it or not. Generally, we have found that giving advice is rarely needed if we are engaged with clients and focused on exploring their ideas.

EVOKING

The third central MI process is *evoking* clients' perspectives and ideas about change. With many addictive behaviors, people already are well aware of the risks and hazards involved. MI focuses attention on clients' autonomous motivation to change as the core clinical target. Long-term change occurs when it is substantially motivated by internal values or preferences, independently chosen by the person even though there may be external reinforcers involved (cf. self-determination theory; Markland, Ryan, Tobin, & Rollnick, 2005).

The process of evoking is the core of motivational interviewing. Key tasks include eliciting and responding to change talk in order to build momentum toward making positive change, accepting and responding to sustain talk in ways that prevent either defensiveness or inertia, enhancing hope for success, and heightening clients' awareness of any discrepancies between their current choices and their goals or values in order to encourage greater convergence. Evidence (reviewed later) is accumulating that the counselor's therapeutic style and focus on eliciting and reinforcing change talk do in fact increase change talk, commitment to change, and subsequent action.

The first thing you need to do is hear change talk when clients speak it. So much of professional training is targeted toward listening for problems and pathology that it can be difficult to even notice change talk in the middle of a conversation. Often, early change talk can be quite mild and buried in the midst of sustain talk and defensiveness. For example, "I'm sick of being lectured to. People don't really even know me that well, so a lot of their advice seems pretty stupid. Maybe there are a couple things I could think about a little more, but maybe not. It's not like people are making it out to be. I'm not addicted or powerless or whatever, and it's ridiculous that I have to do this." In the midst of this client's complaining, discounting others' impressions and ideas, and denying having an addiction is the gem, "Maybe there are a couple things I could think about a little more." Although mild, tentative, and only focused on "thinking about" a few things, it is still an opening, and a good MI response might be "It sounds like if you could get people off your back, you might feel a little freer to explore some things you might consider changing. What are some of the things you might think about more?" While such an exchange may take place earlier in the counseling process, such as while engaging or focusing, it is important to hear change talk whenever it occurs and to steer the conversation in that direction by evoking further thoughts (and backing off anytime the client resists).

Increasing Importance of Change

Within the process of evoking, a number of simple strategies can be used to increase clients' sense of the importance of change. The first is to discuss the habit or situation and the things that are good or not so good about it. While it may not be necessary to explore the status quo side of ambivalence (expressed as sustain talk), we find that initially exploring it can help increase the practitioner's understanding of clients' perspectives and allow them to vent about the difficulties or drawbacks of change so that they can later focus their energies on change. It can also help the practitioner learn about perceived obstacles for later reference when helping clients plan their change efforts.

Evocative questions, like the example above ("What are some of the things you might think about more?") are simple, yet they invite clients to consider change. You can use the categories of change talk to generate evocative questions, such as "How do you want things to be different?" (desire), "What are some ways things would be better if you did cut back on gambling?" (reasons), or "What would you say is the most important thing you could do to prevent things from getting worse?" (need).

Importance scaling is a strategy for discovering how important change is to the client and eliciting change talk. This strategy has three parts. First, elicit clients' sense of the importance of a specific change (or change in general) on a scale of 0 to 10. Next, ask what makes clients give that answer rather than 0 (assuming their answer isn't 0). This elicits change talk, which you then reflect and explore until clients run out of reasons to discuss. This may be the most important part of this strategy, and one that is often overlooked. Finally, if appropriate, you can ask what might make change even more important, focusing attention on additional risks or potential consequences to watch out for going forward. However, you may want to avoid this step if clients are defensive.

Another important strategy for increasing the importance of change is *looking back*, exploring how things were before the current problem developed as a potential reference point for improving things again. You can trace from that point to the present as a kind of summary that helps clients step back to gain a broader perspective and see things more clearly. For example, clients may share how their use progressed from having fun using substances to using them as an escape, then as a solution, and finally as a necessity. If clients' current problems are not as bad as things were previously, you can explore what has improved and how they accomplished that. *Looking forward* involves imagining how things might evolve if no changes are made, and its counterpart, *envisioning*, asks clients to imagine a better life ahead, how it would look, what would be different, and how they would feel.

There are typically some discrepancies between clients' values or goals and their current behavioral choices (actually, this is typical for all of us). One strategy is to *explore clients' values* in this light. Because people can easily become defensive about such discrepancies, we prefer to focus on this in a positive way, eliciting and exploring their values (and goals if they identify any), then exploring how they could live even more closely in line with those values or goals. We emphasize how everyone does some things that they probably wouldn't consider ideal, and invite clients to focus on what they are moving toward rather than on any current shortcomings.

Increasing Confidence for Change

Once clients are interested in making specific changes, it is time to help them gain momentum toward taking action by helping build their confidence that they can succeed. Once again, you can use evocative questions to elicit change talk (aimed at ability) in this regard, asking, "What's something you'd feel pretty confident about trying now?" or "What would help you feel more confident about getting started?" and then reflecting and exploring their perspectives. You can also use *confidence scaling*, again eliciting a rating on a scale from 0 to 10, and then asking clients why they assigned that rating rather than 0, thus eliciting change talk regarding their ability to meet their goals. In addition, you can ask what would boost their confidence by a couple of points, which helps build a treatment plan.

Another strategy to increase confidence involves helping clients generalize from past experiences so they can see how strengths they used in handling those challenges might help with their current difficulties. This can involve *reviewing past successes*, in which they describe previous accomplishments, how they prepared, what strategies they used, what barriers they faced, and how they worked around them. If the success was a change they made, you can ask how they maintained it. You can also help them by *reframing perceived failures* as steps along the way to eventual change.

More generally, you can elicit client conversation about personal strengths and external supports provided by others. Even if not directly applicable to the current change topic, building clients' sense that they are competent, worthwhile people with strengths and accomplishments, no matter how minor, can help them make difficult changes.

A final strategy to increase confidence about change is *brainstorming hypothetical change*. People seem to find it easier to imagine what-if scenarios about change without the pressure of committing and therefore are less likely to get caught up in a crisis of confidence. You can guide them to imagine what thoughts and feelings they would have if they were ready to change, which can feel less threatening.

PLANNING

Planning strategies are used once attention shifts from the whether and why of change to how. The shift may be sudden; perhaps a client who has been pondering possibilities declares, "I've got to change," or "I can't go on like this anymore." Other times the shift may be gradual, almost unnoticeable, as clients go back and forth between changing one way or another, or staying the same, considering hypothetical possibilities, and then talking about how each possibility might work and what they could do toward that end.

When people have mostly resolved their ambivalence and are interested in figuring out how to get started, you can use planning strategies to help them prepare for and initiate change. You can provide a *recapitulation*, or summary of the issues, focused on clients' perspectives on the importance of making changes and their confidence. Follow this with a question like "What now?" or "Where does this leave you?" Don't ask for commitment to a specific plan; leave it open. Next, you might clarify the goals of changing, then explore options for change with questions such as "What choices might you make?" or "What is on the list of likely approaches for your problem?" or "Which options seem easier to try and more likely to succeed?"

As you talk, listen for *mobilizing change talk*, and reflect and explore it. Mobilizing change talk relates to activation, or beginning to do something, and might sound like "I'm thinking about trying...," "I might...," or "I could...." As always, dance the dance one step at a time and don't press for firm commitment if clients are still tentative—keep building momentum instead of risking turning them back from change.

Another strategy to get started is to plan the steps toward change: What should happen in what sequence? What supports can be rallied? When should various steps happen? What rewards can the client imagine will result? What might be some challenges that could interfere with the plan? Some clients like to develop a written change plan, while others prefer to make plans through conversations only.

At this stage, it may be more useful to set interim action goals rather than longer-term outcome goals. Eating better and exercising are interim action goals (which still need to be further developed to specify discrete behaviors), whereas losing twenty pounds and being in better shape are outcome goals. Although it can be reinforcing to look down at the scale and see the numbers dropping, adopting new habits (through interim action goals) is often the key to long-term change. The new habits bring the outcome along with them.

Lastly, you can help clients get started by exploring their level of confidence in the specific plans they are considering and assessing their commitment to the change. When clients express doubt that plans can work as developed, it is helpful to modify the plan. Similarly, if they report low commitment even if their plans seem solid, it is possible that their rating of the importance of change has decreased and you should return to evoking strategies.

As clients move into action, it can be helpful to continue to provide support and guidance, assisting them in self-monitoring their progress or finding a supportive mutual monitoring situation, such as a group or buddy. Part of moving into action may involve learning new skills, and it can be useful to bring in other therapies, classes, or practice opportunities at this point.

Co-occurring Disorders

Addictive disorders frequently co-occur with both mental disorders and medical disorders. From an MI perspective, co-occurring disorders can be addressed using the same general approach outlined above. Adaptations for a particular disorder may be useful, but they are not necessary because the focus is on helping clients identify behaviors and habits they want to change, not on addressing symptoms. When there are multiple targets, clients' preferences for where to start are followed, based on the belief that even if the first target is not the most important change from the practitioner's perspective, it may ignite a desire to change and build momentum across target areas (Wagner & Ingersoll, 2009). Thus, co-occurring disorders can be handled using an agenda-mapping approach, as described above. In some cases, clients come to believe that a particular change is pivotal for all of the others and may therefore decide to tackle that one first based on the idea that the others will then more easily fall into place. Other times, it can be useful to tackle a small change in order to build momentum for making more challenging changes.

MI Groups

MI was developed as an individual counseling approach. However, the adaptation of MI to groups is an emerging model for facilitating change (Wagner & Ingersoll, in press). Groups are a frequent treatment modality, useful both for their unique ability to tackle interpersonal and social difficulties directly and for cost savings. MI groups are increasingly used as an alternative to dyadic MI to harness the power of a group of people who are "in it together" and who can provide support and encouragement to each other and learn from each other. These groups can be facilitated by those with skills in MI and in group counseling, and may vary considerably depending on how homogeneous or heterogeneous group members' presenting problems are. Some MI group leaders introduce topics and facilitate group discussion, while others facilitate the emergence of a group process that builds cohesion among members, who navigate their way toward change with the support of the group.

Evidence of MI Efficacy and Mechanisms

The scientific literature on MI has grown exponentially over the past decade, across many languages and cultures. MI delivered in an individual counseling format has the largest evidence base, second only to CBT, among all addiction-specific psychological treatments. Because this literature is now so large, it is useful to view it through published syntheses and meta-analyses.

Evidence about the Efficacy of MI

MI and its most common adaptation, *motivational enhancement therapy* (MET), a four-session version of MI plus personalized feedback, are listed as evidence-based practices in the U.S. National Register of Evidence-Based Programs and Practices (Substance Abuse and Mental Health Services Administration, 2007a, 2007b).

There have been over a dozen systematic reviews and meta-analyses focusing on MI, including several that focus on addictive behaviors and populations, such as people with substance abuse problems (Smedslund et al., 2011), adolescents who use substances (e.g., Grimshaw & Stanton, 2006), college students who drink (Carey, Scott-Sheldon, Carey, & DeMartini, 2007), adults who drink (Vasilaki, Hosier, & Cox, 2006), smokers (e.g., Heckman, Egleston, & Hofmann, 2010; Hettema & Hendricks, 2010; Lai, Cahill, Qin, & Tang, 2010), and mentally ill patients who use substances (Bechdolf et al., 2005). These studies consistently find that MI results in improved substance use outcomes across a range of behaviors and populations, equal to other, longer treatments and superior to advice, feedback alone, no treatment, or other weak comparison conditions, particularly when delivered with fidelity to the model. The average researched dose (less than two hours) tends to place MI and its adaptations in the category of a brief intervention (Burke, Arkowitz, & Menchola, 2003), with small to medium effect sizes for substance use, and larger effects for engagement in substance abuse treatment (Hettema, Steele, & Miller, 2005). Effects of MI appear early and tend to diminish over time, with more persistent effects when MI is added to another form of treatment (Hettema et al., 2005). About 75% of MI study participants experience positive gains, with 25% experiencing moderate to large gains (Lundahl, Kunz, Brownell, Tollefson, & Burke, 2010; Lundahl & Burke, 2009). Meta-analyses have raised concerns over methodological issues, however (Smedslund et al., 2011).

Evidence about MI Processes and Relationships with Outcomes

MI process studies can be categorized as those that look at processes within sessions, those that look at session processes in relation to client outcomes, and those that examine a purported causal path from practitioner behaviors to outcomes.

STUDIES OF WITHIN-SESSION PROCESSES

Practitioner acceptance, egalitarianism, empathy, warmth, and spirit are positively related to clients' within-session involvement (Miller, Moyers, Ernst, & Amrhein, 2001). In a study aimed at reducing smoking among urban African-Americans (Boardman, Catley, Grobe, Little, & Ahluwalia, 2006), MI-consistent communications were positively related to client-practitioner collaboration, while global practitioner ratings, MI-consistent communications, and MI strategies were related to more client change talk and client expression of affect, cooperation, self-disclosure, and engagement. Providing advice without permission was negatively correlated with change talk.

STUDIES OF MI PROCESSES AND CLIENT OUTCOMES

Several studies have examined MI microcommunications and their associations with outcomes in target behaviors. A study investigating college student drinking outcomes found that open questions and complex reflections predicted positive change, while closed questions and simple reflections tended to stall change (Carey et al., 2007). Other studies have found that increasing rates of commitment language (Amrhein, Miller, Yahne, Palmer, & Fulcher, 2003) and action-oriented change talk (Strang & McCambridge, 2004) predict later reduced drug use.

STUDIES OF POSSIBLE CAUSAL CHAINS

Researchers have begun to examine the links in a potential causal chain from practitioner behaviors to within-session client behaviors to client outcomes. A recent study (Moyers et al., 2007) of the relationship between practitioner behaviors, client in-session behavior, and client alcohol use outcomes in Project MATCH found that MI-consistent microcommunications (reflecting and affirming) and strategies (emphasizing personal choice and control and asking permission before raising concerns) were related to more within-session client change talk. In contrast, when practitioners used MI-inconsistent behaviors (such as warning or advising without permission), the immediate probability of clients producing sustain talk was increased. Additionally, client change talk and sustain talk were related to outcomes in the expected directions. This suggests that practitioner behaviors evoke client behaviors that are predictors of outcome.

A recent review examining these links among nineteen controlled studies of MI (Apodaca & Longabaugh, 2009) found support for outcomes being influenced positively by client change talk or intention language, as well as client perceptions of a discrepancy between values and behavior, and negatively by MI-inconsistent practitioner behaviors. In the few studies reporting specific techniques, only a decisional balance exercise was related to better outcomes.

Motivational Interviewing and Cognitive Behavioral Therapy

As we described in the opening section, we see MI as a close cousin to the cognitive behavioral therapies. In recent years, humanistic and behavioral traditions have grown increasingly closer to one another and can complement each others' strengths (Bricker & Tollison, 2011).

Although atheoretically derived, MI includes elements of both humanistic therapies and behavioral therapies. While we think there are ways that MI is substantially different from the other therapies described in this volume, we see it as similar in having a focus on making discrete changes (Wagner & Ingersoll, 2009). This focus is not surprising, given that Bill Miller, one of the creators of MI, was a behavior therapy researcher focusing on controlled drinking before he developed MI. There are other major areas of overlap, including a focus on the therapeutic relationship, an accepting stance on the part of the clinician, and an orientation toward values. We also think MI may provide a useful lead-in to the other therapies described in this book, given the evidence for MI as an engagement tool that serves to increase participation and outcomes.

That being said, we see two primary differences. One is that MI uses a direct approach to change. It does not focus on resolving underlying pathologies, limitations, or dysfunctions as a means to enabling change. Instead, it focuses directly upon defining and implementing desired changes, with little or no focus on functional limitations that may serve as obstacles to change. Cognitive behavioral therapies tend to use more indirect approaches to change, resolving underlying pathologies or cognitive dysfunctions that can be barriers to change, or at least freeing clients from the constraining influence of these underlying problems.

The other primary difference we see is within clinical interactions. In MI, practitioners serve as facilitators of a constructive conversation about change. While occasionally practitioners provide information meant to help clients set their own path forward, the intent is not to provide clients with expert information on healthy psychological functioning or a conceptual model to follow. MI primarily uses elicitation of client ideas and emotions, reinforced by selective reflections that help clients focus on why and how they want to change. Cognitive behavioral therapies also incorporate substantial use of elicitation and reflection, especially early on, yet these are often used to provide practitioners with enough information to help personalize the presentation of the psychological model and skills they then teach clients in order to help them move forward. Prototypically, in the MI therapeutic model, practitioners elicit both problems and solutions from clients, while in CBT models, practitioners elicit problems from clients, then provide expert solutions, framing, or suggestions. This difference between eliciting and providing, between building on competencies and correcting deficits, between drawing out and inserting, may be one that is relatively difficult to notice at times, as modern CBT approaches involve considerable attention to engaging clients and building a healthy alliance and relationship. However, these distinctions do reflect different philosophies about how clients change and what is key in therapeutic interactions. Thus, we believe that an essential distinction between MI and the contextual cognitive behavioral therapies is their focus on using eliciting strategies versus provision strategies, respectively.

While a direct approach to change is often effective, we also understand that sometimes client pathology or patterned cognitive distortions are barriers to making direct change. This pathology may be disorder specific, as addressed in dialectical behavior therapy (Dimeff & Sayrs, chapter 2 of this volume), or generalized, resulting from the disabling influences of language, as addressed in acceptance and commitment therapy (Wilson, Schnetzer, Flynn, & Kurz, chapter 1 of this volume). Clients may not always be able to autonomously define their goals. Some may be able to define goals in session, but not on their own. They may be able to make some temporary progress, yet be pulled back to a disabling state by underlying cognitive, behavioral, or emotional problems.

In these instances, a strategy that is primarily limited to eliciting, reflecting, and amplifying elements that emanate from clients may not be enough. Clients may need additional interventions that alter or remove entrenched barriers to making direct change. These methods may involve education or skills training, or helping clients incorporate new models, paradigms, and skills to reduce barriers to long-lasting change.

MI allows for some movement down this path, including strategies for providing or exchanging information and for providing advice (with client permission). MI practitioners may at times take an active role in helping clients set direction, consider possibilities, and try behaviors they might otherwise not have tried. Once we move to more than minimal inclusion of provision strategies, however, we leave the prototypical MI approach and venture into complementary approaches, such as the other therapies considered in this book. MI streamlines the focus so that no significant attention is given to unhelpful ways of thinking or acting unless this serves to identify patterns that clients don't like and want to move away from. MI focuses instead on what clients like and dislike about their lives and how they would like their lives to become.

We think the simple, direct, eliciting focus of MI may be more useful and efficient than is widely recognized, and that this approach may take many clients a long way toward their goals, and possibly all the way. For those who are unable to get all the way there through this direct approach, we believe the more comprehensive approaches described elsewhere in this volume are quite complementary.

References

Amrhein, P. C., Miller, W. R., Yahne, C. E., Palmer, M., & Fulcher, L. (2003). Client commitment language during motivational interviewing predicts drug use outcomes. *Journal of Consulting and Clinical Psychology, 71,* 862-878.

Apodaca, T. R., & Longabaugh, R. (2009). Mechanisms of change in motivational interviewing: A review and preliminary evaluation of the evidence. *Addiction, 104,* 705-715.

Arnold, J., & Randall, R. (2010). *Work psychology: Understanding human behaviour in the workplace.* Harlow, UK: Pearson Education.

Barth, T., & Näsholm, C. (2006). *Motivational interviewing (MI). Helping people to change on their terms.* [Book in Norwegian]. Lund, Sweden: Studentlitteratur.

Bechdolf, A., Pohlmann, B., Geyer, C., Ferber, C., Klosterkotter, J., & Gouzoulis-Mayfrank, E. (2005). Motivational interviewing for patients with comorbid schizophrenia and substance abuse disorders: A review. [Article in German]. *Fortschritte der Neurologie-Psychiatrie, 73,* 728-735.

Boardman, T., Catley, D., Grobe, J. E., Little, T. D., & Ahluwalia, J. S. (2006). Using motivational interviewing with smokers: Do therapist behaviors relate to engagement and therapeutic alliance? *Journal of Substance Abuse Treatment, 31,* 329-339.

Bricker, J., & Tollison, S. (2011). Comparison of motivational interviewing with acceptance and commitment therapy: A conceptual and clinical review. *Behavioural and Cognitive Psychotherapy, 39,* 541-559.

Burke, B. L., Arkowitz, H., & Menchola, M. (2003). The efficacy of motivational interviewing: A meta-analysis of controlled clinical trials. *Journal of Consulting and Clinical Psychology, 71,* 843-861.

Carey, K. B., Scott-Sheldon, L. A., Carey, M. P., & DeMartini, K. S. (2007). Individual-level interventions to reduce college student drinking: A meta-analytic review. *Addictive Behaviors, 32,* 2469-2494.

Grimshaw, G. M., & Stanton, A. (2006). Tobacco cessation interventions for young people. *Cochrane Database of Systematic Reviews, 4,* CD003289.

Heckman, C. J., Egleston, B. L., & Hofmann, M. T. (2010). Efficacy of motivational interviewing for smoking cessation: A systematic review and meta-analysis. *Tobacco Control, 19,* 410-416.

Hettema, J. E., & Hendricks, P. S. (2010). Motivational interviewing for smoking cessation: A meta-analytic review. *Journal of Consulting and Clinical Psychology, 78,* 868-884.

Hettema, J. E., Steele, J., & Miller, W. R. (2005). Motivational interviewing. *Annual Review of Clinical Psychology, 1,* 91-111.

Lai, D. T., Cahill, K., Qin, Y., & Tang, J. L. (2010). Motivational interviewing for smoking cessation. *Cochrane Database of Systematic Reviews, 1,* CD006936.

Lewin, K. (1951). *Field theory in social science.* New York: Harper and Row.

Lundahl, B. W., & Burke, B. W. (2009). The effectiveness and applicability of motivational interviewing: A practice-friendly review of four meta-analyses. *Journal of Clinical Psychology, 65,* 1232-1245.

Lundahl, B. W., Kunz, C., Brownell, C., Tollefson, D., & Burke, B. (2010). A meta-analysis of motivational interviewing: Twenty-five years of empirical studies. *Research on Social Work Practice, 20,* 137-160.

Markland, D., Ryan, R. M., Tobin, V., & Rollnick, S. (2005). Motivational interviewing and self-determination theory. *Journal of Social and Clinical Psychology, 24,* 785-805.

Maslow, A. H. (1970). *Motivation and personality.* New York: Harper and Row.

Miller, W. R. (1998). Enhancing motivation for change. In W. R. Miller, & N. Heather (Eds.), *Treating addictive behaviors: Processes of change.* New York: Plenum Press.

Miller, W. R. (2006). Motivational factors in addictive behaviors. In W. R. Miller & K. M. Carroll (Eds.), *Rethinking substance abuse: What science shows and what we should do about it*. New York: Guilford Press.

Miller, W. R., Moyers, T. B., Ernst, D., & Amrhein, P. (2001). *Manual for the motivational interviewing skill code (MISC) version 2.1*. Albuquerque: Center on Alcoholism, Substance Abuse, and Addictions, University of New Mexico.

Miller, W. R., & Rollnick, S. (2012). *Motivational interviewing: Facilitating change* (3rd ed.). New York: Guilford Press.

Moyers, T. B., Martin, T., Christopher, P. J., Houck, J. M., Tonigan, J. S., & Amrhein, P. C. (2007). Client language as a mediator of motivational interviewing efficacy: Where is the evidence? *Alcoholism, Clinical and Experimental Research, 31*, 10 Suppl, 40s-47s.

Rogers, C. R. (1961). On becoming a person. Boston: Houghton Mifflin.

Rollnick, S., Miller, W. R., & Butler, C. (2008). *Motivational interviewing in health care: Helping patients change behavior*. New York: Guilford Press.

Smedslund, G., Berg, R. C., Hammerstrom, K. T., Steiro, A., Leiknes, K. A., Dahl, H. M., et al. (2011). Motivational interviewing for substance abuse. *Cochrane Database of Systematic Reviews, 5*, CD008063.

Strang, J., & McCambridge, J. (2004). Can the practitioner correctly predict outcome in motivational interviewing? *Journal of Substance Abuse Treatment, 27*, 83-88.

Substance Abuse and Mental Health Services Administration. (2007a, September). *Motivational enhancement therapy*. Retrieved January 5, 2012, from www.nrepp.samhsa.gov/ViewIntervention.aspx?id=107.

Substance Abuse and Mental Health Services Administration. (2007b, December). *Motivational interviewing*. Retrieved January 5, 2012, from www.nrepp.samhsa.gov/ViewIntervention.aspx?id=130.

Vasilaki, E. I., Hosier, S. G., & Cox, W. M. (2006). The efficacy of motivational interviewing as a brief intervention for excessive drinking: A meta-analytic review. *Alcohol and Alcoholism, 41*, 328-335.

Wagner, C. C. (2012). Client-centered direction: Or how to get there when you're not sure where you're going. *Motivational Interviewing: Training, Research, Implementation, Practice, 1*, 36-38.

Wagner, C. C., & Ingersoll, K. S. (2008). Beyond cognition: Broadening the emotional base of motivational interviewing. *Journal of Psychotherapy Integration, 18*, 191-206.

Wagner, C. C., & Ingersoll, K. S. (2009). Beyond behavior: Eliciting broader change with motivational interviewing. *Journal of Clinical Psychology, 65*, 1180-1194.

Wagner, C. C., & Ingersoll, K. S. (Eds.). (in press). *Motivational interviewing in groups*. New York: Guilford Press.

Wagner, C. C., & Sanchez, F. (2002). The role of values in motivational interviewing. In W. R. Miller & S. Rollnick (Eds.), *Motivational interviewing: Preparing people for change* (2nd ed.). New York: Guilford Press.

PART 2

Clinical Issues and Populations

CHAPTER 6

Mindfulness, Acceptance, and Values-Based Interventions for Addiction Counselors: The Benefits of Practicing What We Preach

Jennifer H. R. Sayrs

Evidence Based Treatment Centers of Seattle

*B*ill has been a counselor for ten years. He primarily works with young adults who are dependent on substances. In the last two years, he has noticed that he dreads going to work. He feels tired frequently and thinks that work takes up his whole life. And, worst of all, he feels frustrated with his clients. He even dislikes a few of them. Whenever a client relapses, Bill feels angry and irritated, and thinks that nothing he does works anymore. He worries that these feelings might threaten his own recovery. Many days, Bill wakes up and wonders if he needs a change of career. He just wants to feel optimistic again.

The importance of mindfulness, acceptance, and values for clients and patients has been increasingly highlighted in recent years. A growing number of evidence-based treatments include mindfulness and acceptance as core components, including mindfulness-based stress reduction (MBSR; Kabat-Zinn, 1990), acceptance and commitment therapy (ACT; Hayes, Strosahl, & Wilson, 1999; Hayes, 2005; see also Wilson, Schnetzer, Flynn, & Kurz, chapter 1 of this volume), dialectical behavior therapy (DBT; Linehan, 1993a, 1993b; see also Dimeff & Sayrs, chapter 2 of this volume), mindfulness-based cognitive therapy (MBCT; Segal,

Williams, & Teasdale, 2002), mindfulness-based relapse prevention (Marlatt & Gordon, 1985; Witkiewitz, Marlatt, & Walker, 2005; see also Bowen, Witkiewitz, & Chawla, chapter 3 of this volume), and acceptance-based behavior therapy (Orsillo, Roemer, & Segal, 2011). In addition, a number of clinically based texts describe the integration of mindfulness practice in psychotherapy more broadly (e.g., Shapiro & Carlson, 2009).

Despite the recent proliferation of clinical interventions using mindfulness, surprisingly less attention has been paid to the potential of mindfulness practice for providers. Although many providers clearly attest to the benefits of these practices for their clients, the field has provided little guidance on how to harness the power of the practices for clinicians themselves (for exceptions, see, for example, Siegel, 2010; Shapiro & Carlson, 2009; and Epstein, 1999).

The application of mindfulness for providers likely has value in many areas and may be particularly useful to those of us who work with substance-abusing clients. Our work with these clients is difficult. We frequently experience disappointment, frustration, sadness, and loss when clients make choices that are not beneficial for them. We become emotionally attached and feel each twist and turn in their paths acutely. Alternatively, we can become detached, particularly when clients' paths are painful. Such detachment may serve to protect us, but it also can lead to providing less effective care and missing out on the successes the treatment may bring. Or we may bend over backward to provide the best care possible, burning bright, and then not have any energy left to give, and therefore leave our careers prematurely, when our expertise is still needed by the field.

This is no light matter. When providers become stressed, overwhelmed, and burned out, the cost can be high both to the clients and to the providers (e.g., Maslach, Schaufeli, & Leiter, 2001). Finding peace, fulfillment, and meaning that persist throughout one's career remains elusive for many. But in a very fundamental way, we are no different from our clients. What may bring them healing and relief can also work for us as their providers. By learning to tolerate our pain, minimize our suffering, and fully appreciate pleasant moments, we can be less reactive and impulsive, more effective, and more at peace with work and at home. Mindfulness practice for providers may be a powerful method for achieving these benefits. Studies have provided preliminary evidence that mindfulness practice is associated with decreased perceived stress and increased self-compassion (Shapiro, Astin, Bishop, & Cordova, 2005; Shapiro, Brown, & Biegel, 2007); decreased negative affect, anxiety, and rumination, as well as increased self-compassion and positive affect (Shapiro et al., 2007); decreased emotional exhaustion (Cohen-Katz, Wiley, Capuano, Baker, & Shapiro, 2005); improved sleep quality (Klatt, Buckworth, & Malarkey, 2009); increased empathy, improved mood, and decreased burnout (Krasner et al., 2009); and improved psychological health under stress (Rosenzweig, Reibel, Greeson, Brainard, & Hojat, 2003).

This chapter provides a conceptual and practical framework for engaging in mindfulness as a personal practice among therapists, counselors, social workers, case managers, physicians, and others who work with substance-abusing clients. It is based on clinical experience with substance-abusing clients and supervision with providers using behavioral treatments that incorporate mindfulness, acceptance, and a focus on values as core components (specifically, ACT and DBT). It is intended to provide practical strategies for providers in the field and to stimulate future research and innovation about the ways in which the provider's use of mindfulness skills may be beneficial. Challenges to adopting a mindfulness practice and integrating it into one's clinical work will also be discussed. Specific recommendations and ways to practice will be provided in order to decrease burnout, impulsivity, and reactivity, in session and out; decrease lapses or relapses on the provider's part, if relevant; and increase effective client care, effective self-care, joy, and mastery, at work and more broadly. As befits the purposes of the chapter, I will use a more personal tone (first and second person) than much of the rest of the present volume.

The Skills of Mindfulness and Acceptance

There are many definitions of mindfulness available, from complex Buddhist texts to very straightforward instructions that teach mindfulness practice. These definitions converge on similar points, succinctly encapsulated by Kabat-Zinn (2003): Mindfulness is "awareness that emerges through paying attention on purpose, in the present moment, and nonjudgmentally to the unfolding of experience moment by moment" (p. 145). While this definition is frequently used and very concise, it may still feel overwhelming. The question may remain: how does one become more mindful?

Linehan (1993b) offered a solution to this problem. After intensive training and practice in Zen meditation, she analyzed exactly what behaviors were occurring when she meditated. She carefully observed the practice and distilled it into behavioral instructions, or operationally defined activities, that teach what to do to become mindful and how to practice such activities. Because these are behavioral definitions, removed from any spiritual tradition, they are compatible with any spiritual practice or a purely secular context. They may be used while meditating, but they are completely separate from meditation and may also be used in daily life. These skills, along with the closely related practices of acceptance and living a values-based life, are outlined in table 6.1 and discussed in the sections that follow.

Table 6.1 The Skills of Mindfulness and Acceptance

Skill	Brief definition
Mindfulness "what" skills (Linehan, 1993b):	What to do to become mindful; these skills can only be used one at a time.
Observe	Just noticing; taking in what is there without adding words.
Describe	Putting words on an experience without adding assumptions or concepts; sticking to the facts.
Participate	Throwing oneself in; becoming one with an experience.

Mindfulness "how" skills (Linehan, 1993b):	How to be mindful; these skills are to be engaged in simultaneously while observing, describing, or participating.
Nonjudgmentally	Removing evaluations of "good" and "bad" and focusing on the facts and one's preferences.
One-mindfully	Focusing on one thing at a time.
Effectively	Doing what works rather than what seems fair or right, or what one thinks *should* work.
Wise mind (Linehan, 1993b)	The above mindfulness skills are used as a vehicle to reach wise mind, a state where one can incorporate one's logic and one's emotions to reach wisdom; one can trust one's instincts and make wise decisions in this state.
Acceptance (e.g., Hayes et al., 1999) and radical acceptance (Linehan, 1993b)	Taking in what is there; accepting one's reality completely.
Living a valued life (e.g., Hayes et al., 1999; Linehan, 2012)	Determining one's values; setting goals that facilitate engaging in behavior in line with one's values over the course of time, rather than acting on short-term impulses.

Observing and Describing

One of the main components of a mindful stance is the ability to simply observe what is happening without reacting, fixing, changing, or *doing* anything. When practicing observing, one practices letting go of attachment to particular outcomes and is therefore able to see what is actually there, rather than what one wants or expects to see. This is not the same as being detached; feelings of disappointment or relief are all part of the experience. It merely means one is allowing reality. Nor is this the same as being passive, where one sits back and stops trying to shape one's life. Observation is merely the ability to pause and take in data before responding. It means having patience to wait until the data are collected before choosing a course of action, which in certain situations is extremely difficult. One may notice external events, thoughts, urges, physical sensations associated with emotions, and so on. Observation is a main focus of mindfulness-based therapies and many meditation practices.

Once one has observed, or noticed, something, it is possible to put words on the experience. Mindfully labeling an event ("physical sensation," "thought," "interpersonal interaction," etc.) is called *describing*. Such description involves sticking to only what can be noticed: emotions, thoughts, urges, environmental events, and so on. This excludes mental constructs such as assumptions, judgments, and concepts. For example, upon noticing that another person has a particular facial expression, "You are angry" would not be a description, as it adds a great deal of assumption. Instead, description would include such phrases as "eyebrows pressed together," "lips thinned," and so on. This might mean someone was angry, or it might mean that person had a stomachache; many other explanations might be possible, as well. It is not until we actually check our facts that we can say confidently that this is indeed anger.

Teaching our clients to observe and then describe helps them slow down, become less impulsive, and understand their environment and their reactions better. They learn to see what is really in front of them, and see the difference between these raw elements of experience and the assumptions and interpretations they add. This same skill is essential for providers. Without this skill, providers may not be able to distinguish between what is occurring in session and their added assumptions and interpretations. As a result, they may have difficulty seeing patterns clearly and may intervene less effectively. This could lead to increased demoralization, frustration, and exhaustion. With observation and description, many doors open for client and therapist alike, because they have more information, less reactivity, and more ability to identify and implement solutions. This, in turn, may help decrease distress and burnout for providers, as they stop adding in assumptions that make the situation worse and see the benefits of their efforts more clearly. Three examples closely related to provider burnout and self-care are described below: urge surfing, responding to a hostile client, and observing a provider's limits.

URGE SURFING

One example of the use of observing and describing, called *urge surfing*, comes from relapse prevention (Marlatt, 1985) and is also used in Linehan's DBT for substance use disorders treatment (DBT-SUD; McMain, Sayrs, Dimeff, & Linehan, 2007; see also Dimeff & Sayrs, chapter 2 of this volume). In these treatments, one observes an urge to use drugs as if riding a surfboard on a wave, allowing the urge to build, peak, and pass. One could also describe or label the experience as a wave, which can provide additional perspective. This skill is not just useful for clients, but can be extremely helpful for therapists, as well. Recently, a client of mine who was dependent on marijuana had worked with me to create a detailed plan for abstinence. He had made steady progress on the plan, and then one week he simply ignored the plan and used multiple times per day. My first urge was to fix the problem, to change him or perhaps lecture him to be sure he understood how harmful it was to him and frustrating it was to me. I wanted my distress to disappear, and quickly. Had I not used urge surfing, I would have engaged in these behaviors, which typically served to distance him, often resulting in a missed session and more drug use. Instead, I simply noticed the urge to fix the situation and the sensations associated with fear and frustration. I let the experience hang out for a while as I watched. I did not try to get rid of it, think it away, or squash it down. This allowed me to slow down, examine the situation, and then assess and intervene more skillfully. It provided me with a red flag, signaling that I could respond ineffectively if I were not paying attention, and helped me respond strategically instead of impulsively.

RESPONDING TO HOSTILITY

Many times I have had therapists come to me for consultation very upset because their clients told them they were incompetent, selfish, or uncaring. I, too, have been accused of these upon occasion. It is important to listen to such feedback from clients, albeit challenging! Mindfulness can be an extremely helpful aid at such times. Observing the situation mindfully, rather than reacting from an intense desire to defend oneself or change the client's mind, can support listening fully to the client's experience. This is yet another situation in which a provider could benefit from observing and describing, and allowing what is noticed to inform a plan of action.

When Darren, a therapist in training, discussed his most recent session with me, he was visibly distressed. He said he had focused on recent drug use with his client Kate. In response, Kate cursed at him and told him he had no idea how hard it was, that he wasn't helpful, and that he was a bad therapist. Darren alternated between feeling ashamed that he had done something wrong in the therapy session and feeling angry that Kate would be so ungrateful as to dismiss his hard work. At the moment of Kate's outburst, Darren moved out of a mindful stance and into an automatically reactive stance. He was no longer listening to her communication and was focused only on how to convince her that she was wrong so he could escape his emotional state.

The ability to remain mindful in the face of such client anger takes a great deal of practice. Darren began working on taking one step back in his mind when clients said such things (and in role-plays in supervision, as well). He noted his own emotion, the client's emotion, and the difficulty of the situation without moving forward to fix it. He watched the client's reactions and his reactions as if they were on a conveyor belt, each one coming toward him and then passing away, allowing him to carefully separate, label, and choose to which ones he would respond. After practicing this repeatedly, he noticed that the occasions on which Kate accused him of not understanding were those when he made a difficult request; Kate's words were functioning to communicate her fear and actually had nothing to do with Darren's capability or skill. Saying to himself *She is experiencing the emotion of fear* helped him remember what was going on for her, and also helped him remember that this was a temporary experience he and his client were having, not the permanent state of their relationship. He also noticed, and was able to communicate to Kate, that when she expressed herself in this way, he was significantly less effective, but if she could say, "That scares me," he had many ideas about how to help. This moved their therapy forward significantly.

OBSERVING A PROVIDER'S LIMITS

Yet another place where the ability to observe and describe can be extremely helpful is in setting boundaries with clients. Most providers are taught to set boundaries in order to protect themselves from the intrusions of clients. These boundaries help make sure providers' lives stay separate from their clients' lives, and that clients' needs and demands are kept in their proper place, all to minimize burnout and maximize self-care and effective treatment. As an alternative to setting boundaries, Linehan (1993a) emphasizes the importance of observing limits. Setting boundaries involves, in essence, drawing a line in the sand that the client is not to cross. Boundaries are typically predetermined rules that govern therapist and client behaviors across all moments and contexts in treatment. They are established at the beginning of the relationship and are consistent across clients. Examples of common boundaries that therapists set at the outset of treatment include not taking phone calls from clients, not talking about one's children, or not accepting small gifts. Although some rules are clearly important in treatment (e.g., no sexual contact with a client), an emphasis on setting boundaries rather than observing limits can make a therapist miss subtleties and act out of context. For example, accepting a small gift from a client who has a very difficult history of rejection may be critical in maintaining the relationship and could be therapeutically important despite the fact that it "breaks a rule."

Observing limits, by contrast, can be viewed as an exercise in mindfulness. The "observe" in observing limits is aimed at getting therapists to pay attention moment to moment, rather than establishing rules in advance. By doing so, the therapist can monitor his or her own reaction to the situation and make adjustments as necessary. The therapist can design a plan of action based on his or her own life situation and the client's behavior at that particular time. The therapist monitors his or her own reaction to the client, notices when demands feel too great or are uncomfortable in some other way, examines this nonjudgmentally, and determines if the benefits of stretching his or her limits temporarily outweigh the cost of feeling stretched—and if not, the therapist discusses making a change with the client.

This approach takes significantly more energy, as therapists must constantly monitor their emotions and thoughts to determine if a limit has been stretched. But the benefits can be significant, as well. Of particular importance is the benefit of allowing clinicians the flexibility to engage in therapy as effectively as possible, and allowing them to move in and out of certain situations purposefully, maximizing the benefit while minimizing the cost to both parties. Therapists may discover and identify new limits as their lives change (for example, a therapist's limits may change after having a child). This stance also allows for the nonjudgmental acceptance of those moments when one's limits are more narrow, and opens the door to changing the treatment when therapists notice that they have been pushed too far. The close attention therapists pay to their own reactions can be invaluable in adjusting the treatment and keeping themselves as motivated as possible.

To make this more concrete, consider Jo, a therapist treating an alcohol-dependent client who, despite much willingness in session, continued to drink. Some therapists in this situation set boundaries for no contact outside of sessions in order to keep work and home separate. Instead, Jo chose to observe her limits and agreed to phone coaching between sessions. Jo wanted to facilitate generalization of the therapy to the client's natural environment by having contact when urges to drink arose during the week. Jo closely monitored her reactions to the phone calls, as she had with other clients in the past. Previously, this strategy had worked well. Jo could see the progress clients made with each phone contact, and as they made progress, the calls were faded out until they were unnecessary.

With this particular client, however, Jo noticed that she felt dread when her phone rang. She had no sense of progress or success. Because she was paying close attention to her reactions and avoided judging herself and the client, she realized that the client was benefiting from the calls in the moment but no overall progress was occurring. She explained to the client that this type of phone call was outside of her limits and that a change was needed. Based on her ongoing nonjudgmental observations, she pinpointed that she needed to have calls that moved clients forward and contributed to progress in therapy; if they were not contributing to progress, then she was no longer willing to take the call. This level of specificity and context-driven change was important for Jo, and it also helped the client to make gradual changes toward accepting coaching more effectively, and then eventually implement the skills without immediate contact with Jo.

Participating One-Mindfully

One-mindfulness is the skill of focusing on just one thing. Our society reveres multitasking, encouraging us to divide our attention in multiple ways. Although multitasking is thought to have many benefits, the actual effects can be harmful. Examples of its costs abound in the clinical setting, including sending e-mails to the wrong recipient, not remembering where we put things, and not remembering what we assigned for a client's homework, as well as giving less than full attention to the people who are important to us, such as family members, friends, and clients. One-mindfulness can be implemented in combination with other mindfulness skills (i.e., one can one-mindfully observe, one-mindfully describe, or one-mindfully participate).

This section will focus on one-mindfulness while participating: throwing oneself into a particular situation and being completely present and at one with what is happening in the moment without giving attention to the running chatter of judgments, self-consciousness, or other thoughts. Most people have experienced one-mindful participation when dancing or singing (oftentimes when no one is watching), engaging in sports, or playing a musical instrument. One-mindfulness is the moment when we know exactly what to do, when effective behavior comes smoothly and without intense effort, and when we are fully present, not judging or worrying about what others think. Although it is easiest to one-mindfully participate in fun, engaging activities, these skills can be helpful even in the most difficult situations, such as challenging interpersonal conflicts. Thus, these skills may have value not just to enhance pleasure, but also to help us wake up, experience the moment, and feel more free of the pressure of judgments and other thoughts in any context.

One-mindfully participating can be extremely useful for providers. Being more present with clients, dealing with our own frustration and apathy, noticing progress, and enjoying life outside of work are all examples of how these skills can be implemented in providers' work and more broadly.

BEING MORE PRESENT WITH CLIENTS

Clients often notice when we are not fully present. When we aren't tracking what they're saying, or we're forgetting important details, they feel invalidated and misunderstood. Being fully focused on a particular client in a particular moment can be challenging, especially when we are tired and overworked. Who hasn't thought about what to eat for dinner or where to take their next vacation during a therapy session? Exerting the energy necessary to wake up, focus, and be fully present for our clients is difficult. And yet it may be just this level of one-mindful participation that is needed to help them engage in treatment, trust the clinician and the process, and make change.

These skills are not just important for our clients' benefit, however. This level of attention is also very relevant for promoting providers' wellbeing and preventing burnout. Not only does noticing clients' progress decrease burnout, but being present, fully participating in the session, and becoming one with the moment, instead of yearning for it to end, can change our level of engagement in the session. It is difficult to be bored in a session if one is truly awake. It is difficult to be detached or disengaged if one is truly awake. The motivation to help the person in the therapy room is significantly stronger if one is truly awake. Throwing oneself into the current session and the current moment transforms the moment into something compelling and rewarding, rather than one more thing we have to slog through before we can go home for the night.

DEALING WITH FRUSTRATION AND APATHY

One-mindfulness allows one to enter into a situation as if one had never experienced it before, taking in the information as if one had never seen or heard it—in short, participating anew. This allows providers to experience their clients in a fresh, novel way, without bringing along the baggage of the previous sessions. It can also allow providers to respond to clients in a novel way because it involves actually listening to what is being said prior to deciding how to respond. This stance can be taken too far if one ceases to learn from previous experience due to only taking in data from the present moment. This is truly a dialectic, where one learns from the past yet experiences the present as a brand-new moment. Engaging in treatment with a challenging client in this manner can be extremely helpful in reducing burnout.

For example, Bill, the counselor described at the start of this chapter, often begins sessions thinking *This client is going to be frustrating* again today. *I am going to have to endure his hostility and his lack of progress* again.

Every time I see him, he says he'll do things, and then he doesn't follow through. I can't wait for the end of the day. If Bill were to engage one-mindfully, he would focus instead on the present moment. He would approach the lack of progress with curiosity rather than exasperation, thinking *Today, I'm going to throw myself into this session. What have I been missing?* Being one-mindful helps reduce boredom and frustration, and this can increase the level of participation and engagement. Bill would not want to ignore the fact that changes are not occurring—that would be taking this skill too far—but assuming things will always go the same way leaves him more helpless and disengaged.

NOTICING PROGRESS

One-mindfulness allows one to notice little changes, which can increase mastery. If Bill is busy focusing on the escape he will enjoy in a few hours, he may miss a small shift in a client in session, when a door for change opens just slightly. Not only will he miss the chance to reinforce the new behavior for the client's benefit, he will miss the enjoyment that progress brings for both of them. Mastery and a sense of accomplishment are essential to enjoying one's work and staving off burnout, and if one is not awake for it, one will miss that sense of mastery.

ENJOYING LIFE OUTSIDE OF WORK

One-mindful participation can also be very helpful if it increases one's engagement in life outside of work. I have met countless therapists who begin to dread the workweek by Sunday afternoon. In effect, they waste half of their weekend by focusing on the future. Similarly, those who are on call may experience every moment when the phone is not ringing as a moment when the phone could ring. They watch their phones, waiting for a distressing phone call from a client. They do not embrace the moment when their phones are quiet or embrace the fact that there are no work demands on them on Sunday afternoons. Being fully focused on one's free time, away from work, provides a needed break that many providers miss. Practicing one-mindfulness when engaging with one's family, pets, or hobbies can function as a mini vacation, renewing the provider.

Cultivating a Nonjudgmental Stance and Compassion

The Dalai Lama defines compassion as the desire that others become free of suffering (Dalai Lama & Vreeland, 2001). His Holiness writes that in order to develop compassion, we must first develop our empathy for others and recognize the gravity of their suffering. However, for providers working with very difficult clients, this can be unbearable at times. The extent of the suffering of our clients can be intense and overwhelming, and to truly focus on it may be very aversive. Without our own mindfulness practice, this focus can be difficult enough that we focus away from the suffering, which can interfere with our effectiveness. One way His Holiness suggests for dealing with this is to begin with focusing on our own suffering, in a mindful way, and then expand that focus onto others (Dalai Lama & Vreeland, 2001). This is the opposite of pushing away our awareness of our own suffering and our clients' suffering, as we may want to do. Instead of pushing away either the awareness of suffering or the interactions with these clients, we open our hearts to their suffering, a painful process that can ultimately reduce our suffering.

This is very relevant to the skill of maintaining a nonjudgmental stance. A nonjudgmental stance is one in which we move away from evaluations of "good" and "bad" and instead describe simply what is there. We may still have opinions, values, morals, and such that make us want certain outcomes, but these preferences do not become a means to judge ourselves or others. Judgments significantly interfere with compassion, as well as with understanding suffering and moving toward solutions. If someone is judged as "bad," we stop short of investigating what led to a particular behavior, since we assume that the behavior is completely explained by the person being "bad." This leaves us with insufficient information, as well as a host of emotions that can land providers in a world of suffering. Certain problems associated with judging our clients and judging ourselves are discussed below.

WHEN WE JUDGE OUR CLIENTS

One means of judging is using "shoulds." Such language implies that people are bad (stupid, inferior, pathological, etc.) when they take a path other than the one that *should* be taken. Take a simple example of driving in heavy traffic. When we think *She should not cut me off!* our irritability and frustration increase, and our compassion is nonexistent. If instead we think that the person driving in front of us has some reason for cutting us off, that perhaps she did not see us or she is experiencing a medical emergency, we have a completely different experience: one full of compassion, minimizing our suffering. Or we can focus on our preference that others not cut us off—even that we intensely dislike it. This simple change of language into nonjudgmental terms, casting "shoulds" as preferences, takes some heat out of the situation, allowing us to think more clearly about the other person's situation, reducing our stress, and increasing our compassion.

As providers, we may think that our clients *should* make better choices, work harder, or get over certain problems. Even when we know things are not as simple as this, we may engage such thoughts because they help us cope with the distress of dealing with such difficult problems. "Shoulds" may be a form of avoiding clients' suffering, because such suffering can be unbearably intense. These "shoulds," however, decrease our compassion significantly and increase our irritability and frustration. "Shoulds" really come down to our own preferences: we would prefer that clients make effective choices so we would not have to feel pain and see them suffer the consequences of their actions. When we reduce a problem to the simplicity of a person not behaving as he or she should, we lose all the reasons why that person is behaving in that way, forgetting that the person is behaving exactly as expected, given his or her biology and learning history.

Bill, the clinician from the start of the chapter, found the suffering of his clients so difficult to tolerate that he focused on suppressing thoughts and emotions related to their suffering. He did so by frequently thinking about how his clients *should* act: they *should* follow his suggestions, do their homework, and focus on abstinence. Bill pathologized his clients when they did not. Of course, a number of his clients often did not do what he suggested, and by approaching their problems in this way, he felt frustrated much of the time. He started to believe he was ineffectual in treating these clients, and to some extent this was true because his irritation with his clients was interfering with his ability to treat them effectively. This judgmental stance left him feeling significantly worse, with much less compassion for his clients and their behavior.

Practicing the skill of taking a nonjudgmental stance involves assuming there are logical reasons for clients' challenging behavior. This does not imply that they do not need to change. Quite the opposite, as looking for the reasons for their behavior (e.g., they used drugs because they had contact with a former dealer, or they experienced an emotion that was so strong that they believed they had to escape) can facilitate change. A nonjudgmental, compassionate stance allows for the unbiased collection of data that promotes behavior change, whereas focusing on how our clients *should* act keeps us from learning and openly understanding their situation. Taking a nonjudgmental stance also allows us to keep our heads in the game, without the long-standing deleterious effects of ongoing frustration and exasperation with those we are trying to help. In addition, it can facilitate mastery, because with better assessment we become better problem solvers, and with less irritability we become better at convincing our clients to try something different.

WHEN WE JUDGE OURSELVES

A nonjudgmental stance is useful with our own behavior, as well. Judging our own behavior, in session and out, interferes with our ability to have compassion for our own struggles. If we do become irritable or frustrated with a client, miss an important piece of information, or periodically provide care that is below our standards, it is all too easy to judge ourselves as bad at our jobs or to think we should be different. This judgment prevents us from learning what the obstacles are. If we assume our mistakes are due to being "bad," we will not delve deeper and we risk losing an opportunity to reach creative solutions. Self-judgments can also lead to misery, burnout, and dissatisfaction, creating a vicious circle of judgments and unhappiness.

A nonjudgmental stance is particularly useful when we fail. From a nonjudgmental stance, "failing" simply means doing something that doesn't work. From this perspective, we fail regularly. If failure becomes the catalyst for highly judgmental thinking, burnout will soon follow. Seeing failure nonjudgmentally and simply collecting data about the strategies that did not work is an approach that allows us to understand how we can provide better care.

Cultivating Acceptance

Acceptance is emphasized heavily in mindfulness-based treatments. The primary focus of acceptance and commitment therapy is on responding differently to pain by ending the struggle to get rid of it and instead simply accepting, or taking in, what is there (Hayes et al., 1999). ACT, like other mindfulness-based treatments, emphasizes the notion of accepting all of reality in this moment, not only the parts we prefer. This does not mean accepting one's future, as the future has not occurred yet; however, one's history and one's present moment are already here. Failing to accept one's reality, no matter how painful, can only add suffering, which is even more distressing than the original pain and is an obstacle to resolving or reducing one's pain.

RADICAL ACCEPTANCE

One of the most powerful (and challenging) lessons to learn about acceptance is that it needs to be complete. Linehan (1993b) uses the term "radical acceptance," "radical" meaning complete, or 100%. Similarly, Hayes (2005; Hayes et al., 1999) emphasizes willingness to feel anything that comes up, completely and willingly, with the goal not being to feel better, but to be present and alive. I used to work toward acceptance in order to feel better about a situation. This, of course, did not work, and it was pointed out to me that while I was working on accepting the situation, I had not accepted that the situation came with a multitude of distressing emotions and thoughts, which were part and parcel of the situation and weren't going anywhere. It was not until I was able to mindfully observe the situation *and* my reactions, that I was able to truly move into acceptance.

Here is a simple example: A coworker slights me during a consultation meeting. My first instinct is to work on accepting that it happened, and that my coworker is either upset with me or has something else going on. I would open my heart and try to accept that this was simply reality, with the full expectation that as soon as I reached acceptance I would no longer feel hurt and frustrated. This, of course, doesn't work! Until I can truly accept that I feel hurt and frustrated, and that I am having thoughts (some of which might be ineffective)—and accept this without any judgment, just noticing these experiences and the associated physical sensations—I will still be stuck. Noticing that these emotions and thoughts have already been fired, that they are a core part of what happened in the meeting, and that they will pass but in the meantime I will be very uncomfortable moves this into radical acceptance, where I can come to peace with uncomfortable events.

ACCEPTANCE OF PAINFUL EMOTIONS ABOUT CLIENTS

Seeing clients make decisions we believe will harm them, or seeing our best, most scientifically driven strategies fail to work, causes emotion. It would be nearly impossible to engage in this work and not feel the highs and lows, particularly the lows, acutely. This is another area where it may help to practice what we preach. Although we teach clients how to experience emotions effectively, we do not always follow our own advice. When we notice we are irritable or judgmental, it is possible that we are experiencing a distressing emotion.

I had a client who had been clean for many months. When she chose to use heroin again, I had a brief moment of feeling extremely frightened and sad. I cared deeply about her and was very concerned that she would not recover from this decision. My fear and sadness were intense and difficult to tolerate. Without making any overt decision to do so, I switched to feeling angry at her instead. I was mad at her for wasting all of our hard work, for dragging me along on a roller-coaster ride, and for not taking advantage of the wonderful opportunity she was receiving (psychotherapy, opiate replacement medication, etc.). Feeling angry provided me with relief. It was easier to judge her, and at times judge myself, than to allow myself to feel the more painful emotions related to the state of her life. However, I subsequently realized that I needed to allow the fear and sadness to be, without pushing them away, and doing so motivated me to act in a different way. It helped me grieve, process the emotion, and get back in the game. It prevented a tear in the therapeutic relationship and kept me curious about why the lapse had occurred. This does not imply that anger is never appropriate or skillful, but in this case it was not, because it served to help me avoid my sadness and interfered with effective work.

When we lack acceptance, it can sometimes be useful to ask, "What's the threat?" or "What is so threatening about this moment?" (M. M. Linehan, personal communication, September, 2000). In other words, if you truly accept what is right in front of you, what catastrophe will happen? This question can result in some very interesting answers. Recently I was coaching a therapist who, while more generally was quite accepting, felt very willful, in the sense of not willing to tolerate or do what was needed in the moment (Linehan, 1993b), about a particular client's behaviors in session. When asked, "What's the threat?" the therapist considered the question carefully, then concluded that the threat was that if she accepted this client's interpersonal behavior in session, she would have to directly address it, which she found strongly aversive. She realized that she had been fighting reality in order to avoid turning therapy toward this topic and experiencing her own associated emotions. She was distressed as she accepted reality, and at the same time she realized it was the only way forward in treatment.

Of course, when one has particularly strong emotional reactions in session, there is always the possibility that the session will become more about the therapist's needs than the client's. The ability to be aware of and stay in contact with such emotional reactions will help alert the therapist to this situation, allowing for additional help, such as supervision or consultation. If one is unable to tolerate the emotional reaction, the chances of becoming ineffective in session become quite high, so this is an important red flag.

Living a Values-Driven Life

Values are a primary focus in ACT (Hayes et al., 1999). Moving attention onto what is meaningful in one's life can be extremely powerful in changing one's relationship with pain and suffering. Linehan has also incorporated the concept of valued living into DBT (Linehan, 2012). Determining what matters to oneself in domains such as spirituality, family, career, the larger community, or self-care, and then mindfully choosing a path of action based on those values can be transformational. It is easy to fall out of accordance with one's values if one mindlessly reacts in response to distress and does not reflect on what brings meaning and importance to one's life. Paying attention to how one's actions fit within one's values can vastly improve satisfaction, increase the effectiveness of one's decisions, and provide meaning to one's actions.

We work with our clients to identify their values, evaluate which behaviors are consistent with their values and which are not, and help them shape their behaviors to increase values-based living. This is thought to increase their joy, fulfillment, and satisfaction in their lives, increasing effectiveness and decreasing behaviors that are causing harm. But how often do providers themselves engage in this activity?

When providers enter the field of mental health, most will say they do so because it is consistent with their values. Helping others, individually and on a broader level; advancing the field's understanding of behavior change and substance use; and alleviating suffering are common reasons why providers choose to treat substance dependence. However, we often lose sight of this motivation. After many years, we can forget why we're in this business. Becoming mindful of our values and the ways our work provides us with meaning and satisfaction can reduce the level of burnout even with the most difficult clients.

We need constant reminders of our values. We must remain mindful of what keeps us going, what gives us that sense of satisfaction and meaning. Reviewing our values formally, even writing about them periodically, will fuel our desire to do our work. Without that, we may only see that particular clients frustrate us to no end, losing sight of why we keep coming back to fight the fight against substance dependence and other chronic, difficult problems.

Reviewing our values can also help us build up our lives outside of work. One significant source of burnout is the belief that work takes over our lives, that we do not have enough time to relax, be with our children, or engage in other interests. Reviewing our values reminds us that work is only one piece of a fulfilling life. It can encourage us to take the gardening class we've been meaning to take, take more vacations, spend more time with friends and family, or further our academic education. Without pausing to notice where we spend our time and what is meaningful to us, we can wake up years later realizing that opportunities have passed and we missed them.

Effectiveness

The final mindfulness skill—effectiveness—is doing what works, not what seems right or fair or just. Effectiveness is really the thrust behind this entire chapter. The goal is to help therapists become more effective in their work and in their lives by practicing each of the other mindfulness and acceptance skills. Burnout, lack of self-care, lapses, distress, and stress all interfere with effectively providing treatment and having peace in one's life. It is effective to change one's relationship to suffering such that one can tolerate pain and reduce the fight against reality, and thereby minimize suffering. The hope is that these skills move one toward effective changes. If one remains observant, collects data without reacting, monitors what works, and implements solutions strategically, one can build a valued life and find joy.

Integrating Mindfulness into One's Life and One's Practice

There are clear challenges to integrating mindfulness into one's life. The compatibility of mindfulness with your treatment approach, and the treatment approaches of other providers with whom you may work, may be a concern—but this entire book addresses that issue. Of more direct relevance to the scope of the present chapter is the compatibility of mindfulness practice with one's personal beliefs.

Concerns about Compatibility with Personal Views

When contemplating practicing mindfulness and acceptance, powerful concerns about compatibility with personal views often arise. Those who are unfamiliar with mindfulness practice may have a range of beliefs and assumptions that can serve as barriers to exploring developing a mindfulness practice. Following are some of the more common concerns, as well as perspectives that may help elucidate points of convergence:

- *Being nonjudgmental and accepting of clients who don't act as they "should" is enabling; it will only give them license to do it more.* Aversive consequences do not teach new behaviors and, further, can result in concealment rather than elimination of problem behaviors. Clients need to be empowered to make new choices. Modeling how to take a course of action based on mindfully reviewing one's values encourages change that is meaningful, satisfying, and self-reinforcing.

- *This is too unfamiliar, strange, esoteric, or "woo-woo."* This chapter, and indeed this entire book, has emphasized concrete and practical presentations and uses of mindfulness. Counselors interested in trying these methods for themselves can rely on their own experience as a guide. No "woo woo" is needed.

- *This might conflict with my religious beliefs or practices.* Mindfulness is a set of behavioral skills, not a religious or spiritual activity. These skills can be used in the context of any spiritual practice and are also available to those without a spiritual practice. All major religions include forms of contemplation, silence, reflection, meditation, or prayer—practices that are compatible with the behaviors taught in mindfulness practice. For example, there is significant convergence between Christian contemplative prayer and the skills of mindfulness practice.

- *I can't be still; this approach isn't for me.* Many people say they cannot practice mindfulness because they can't sit still, but sitting is not actually a requirement of mindfulness. There are many movement-based ways to be mindful, including yoga and walking meditation, and one may choose to practice mindfulness without any sitting. One may also find that the ability to be still improves with practice. Others may be concerned that they cannot hold their attention still long enough to be mindful. Understanding that the aim is not to become so focused that one's mind never wanders, but to notice each wandering and gently return, means that even those who are extremely distractible can effectively practice mindfulness.

- *This conflicts with 12-step practices.* The qualities of acceptance, greater awareness, and values-based living are central to both the skills outlined in this chapter and 12-step approaches. There is no known incompatibility between the two (see Jacobs-Stewart, 2010, for a detailed discussion).

Building One's Practice

The importance of a therapist's personal practice of mindfulness is a central question in the area of mindfulness-based or mindfulness-informed clinical practice. This is relevant to substance abuse care providers in general and may have particular salience for those who are in recovery themselves. Many individuals with a history of substance use disorders wish to help others with similar problems. In one study, 30% of the 575 responding staff in fifty-one substance abuse treatment centers identified themselves as in recovery (Stoffelmayr, Mavis, & Kasim, 1998). Mindfulness may be all the more important if you as a provider are dealing with substance abuse or dependence issues yourself. It could be argued that providers with such a history are in a unique position to help clients, given their own experiences and ability to understand, empathize, and promote change. With this opportunity comes danger, however, in that these providers can do more harm with their clients if their own substance use problems are not under control. When clients see or sense that their own provider is struggling with substance issues, this can damage the client's willingness and hope more than anything else. This makes it all the more important to notice early warning signs of urges to lapse and get help immediately. Facing our own fears and ineffective habits, and wrestling with how the skills discussed in this chapter can benefit us, can improve our own lives and help us be more empathic and skillful teachers for our clients. Evidence from several studies indicates that acceptance and mindfulness make practitioners less likely to burn out and more able to learn how to help clients change (e.g., Hayes et al., 2004; Varra, Hayes, Roget, & Fisher, 2008).

Does one need to have a mindfulness practice to teach mindfulness to one's clients or to infuse one's treatment with mindfulness? Does one need to practice mindfulness specifically through the form of meditation? Is it possible to teach mindfulness out of a workbook, having no practice of one's own and no experiential understanding of what one is asking clients to do? Mindfulness can appear deceptively simple in CBT workbooks. The truth is, it is incredibly difficult, and providers simply must know, not just intellectually but experientially, what their clients will go through in attempting to learn it. It is essential to integrate one's intellectual understanding of mindfulness with an experiential understanding. Many treatments that incorporate mindfulness require the provider to have some type of mindfulness practice (e.g., DBT; Linehan, 1993a), and approaches that incorporate meditation typically require therapists to have their own meditation practice (e.g., MBSR; Kabat-Zinn, 1990).

This chapter has emphasized the potential benefits of a therapist's own mindfulness practice; however, it does so with recognition that developing such a practice can be challenging. Offered here are some guidelines and suggestions for starting or continuing one's own mindfulness practice as a foundation for using mindfulness-based clinical approaches.

CONSISTENCY IS VALUABLE

Regular practice is necessary. Some amount of frequency and duration of practice is important in allowing a quieting of the mind and allowing one to be accustomed to the feared, dreaded, difficult content that floats to the surface when one is silent. With regular practice, particularly if one adds in some type of ritual, such as a bell or a certain sitting position, one can become conditioned and more easily enter a mindful state. Experimentation and mindful observation are needed to determine how much time one will require to gain the benefits of practice. A few minutes of silence once per week is likely to be insufficient; however, it probably is not necessary to practice many hours per week.

PRACTICE IN THE CONTEXT OF REGULAR DAILY LIFE

Combining quiet, formal practice with many attempts at active practice—with clients, with one's children, with one's pets, or while walking in the park—can be quite effective. Actively working at being one-mindful, fully present, nonjudgmental, and accepting in any situation not only will provide benefits to oneself, but also facilitate use of these skills in the therapy room. Getting these skills to generalize to one's daily life is the best part! Supplementing daily, active practice with periodic episodes of more intense practice, such as attending a retreat, can provide additional learning and experience to help one's practice progress.

FIND A MINDFULNESS TEACHER

Working with a teacher may be extremely helpful in learning to implement mindfulness at home and in the workplace. Reading about mindfulness does provide intellectual information, but having a teacher guide one through practice, helping to be sure one is not straying too far from the intended path, may significantly advance one's practice.

SPECIFIC SUGGESTIONS

Below are some specific suggestions for beginning or developing a mindfulness practice. They include ideas for various levels of intensity. Experiment with these techniques, rather than choosing just one to focus on. Try things that might make you uncomfortable, just to see if your assumptions are accurate. Remember, this is about mindfully observing and doing what works, which will require stepping out of your comfort zone and trying new things:

- Each time you brush your teeth, try noticing exactly what the bristles feel like and how the toothpaste tastes.

- Try noticing an urge to do anything—drink water, go to the bathroom, tell someone to do something differently—and just observe it for ten minutes. This means not acting on the urge and not trying to get rid of it. Just be curious about what an urge feels like when you don't give in to it.

- Fully participate in an interaction with a client for ten minutes. Be one-mindful, completely present, and open to what the client is saying. This means not looking at the clock or thinking about what you'll do afterward, but really directing all of your attention toward the client.

- The next time you judge someone, try getting curious about why the judged behavior showed up. Instead of thinking the action or the person is bad, see if you can make sense of why the behavior showed up and just notice that it would be your preference to have it go differently.

- The next time you feel irritable, see if you might be experiencing fear. Is there some reality you simply do not want to face? If so, what is the threat? What are you trying to avoid? See if asking these questions helps you increase your acceptance.

- Write out your values. List five ways your behavior is not consistent with your values and pick one to change.

- If you are in recovery, try monitoring urges after particularly difficult sessions. See if observing physical sensations, thoughts, feelings, and so on helps you notice when your substance plan is threatened.

- Create a mindfulness group at work to practice meditating, read about mindfulness, and discuss your experience. This could be fifteen minutes every week.

- Attend a meditation retreat.

- Try an audio guided MBSR program (Kabat-Zinn, 2005, accompanied by Kabat-Zinn, 1990).

- Discuss these ideas with colleagues, supervisors, and administrators at your agency. Identify obstacles and, if possible, begin problem solving.

Summary

There is growing evidence that mindfulness strategies may offer substantial benefits to clients with substance use disorders. Although this area of research and practice is growing, there is surprisingly less emphasis placed on the benefits or value of providers having a mindfulness practice. Treating clients with substance use disorders presents many challenges. Skills pertaining to mindfulness, acceptance, and one's values may provide tools for coping with these difficulties. This chapter presented a number of strategies and suggestions to help providers integrate these practices into their own work and daily lives. The intention was to generate providers' interest and exploration of their own mindfulness practice, facilitate the growth of mindfulness in agencies providing treatment for clients with substance abuse problems, and, more broadly, stimulate research regarding how these practices may be beneficial.

Acknowledgments

The author would like to thank Sona Dimidjian, PhD, for comments on an earlier draft of this chapter.

References

Cohen-Katz, J., Wiley, S. D., Capuano, T., Baker, D. M., & Shapiro, S. (2005). The effects of mindfulness-based stress reduction on nurse stress and burnout, part II: A quantitative and qualitative study. *Holistic Nursing Practice, 19,* 26-35.

Dalai Lama & Vreeland, N. (2001). *An open heart: Practicing compassion in everyday life.* New York: Back Bay Books.

Epstein, R. M. (1999). Mindful practice. *Journal of the American Medical Association, 282,* 833-839.

Hayes, S. C., with Smith, S. (2005). *Get out of your mind and into your life: The new acceptance and commitment therapy.* Oakland, CA: New Harbinger.

Hayes, S. C., Bisset, R., Roget, N., Padilla, M., Kohlenberg, B. S., Fisher, G., et al. (2004). The impact of acceptance and commitment training and multicultural training on the stigmatizing attitudes and professional burnout of substance abuse counselors. *Behavior Therapy, 35,* 821-835.

Hayes, S. C., Strosahl, K. D., & Wilson, K. G. (1999). *Acceptance and commitment therapy: An experiential approach to behavior change.* New York: Guilford Press.

Jacobs-Stewart, T. (2010). *Mindfulness and the 12 steps: Living recovery in the present moment.* Center City, MN: Hazelden.

Kabat-Zinn, J. (1990). *Full catastrophe living: Using the wisdom of your body and mind to face stress, pain, and illness.* New York: Delacorte.

Kabat-Zinn, J. (2003). Mindfulness-based interventions in context: Past, present, and future. *Clinical Psychology: Science and Practice, 10,* 144-156.

Kabat-Zinn, J. (2005). *Guided mindfulness meditation* [CD]. Available from www.mindfulnesscds.com.

Klatt, M. D., Buckworth, J., & Malarkey, W. B. (2009). Effects of low-dose mindfulness-based stress reduction (MBSR-ld) on working adults. *Health Education and Behavior, 36*, 601-614.

Krasner, M. S., Epstein, R. M., Beckman, H., Suchman, A. L., Chapman, B., Mooney, C. J., et al. (2009). Association of an educational program in mindful communication with burnout, empathy, and attitudes among primary care physicians. *Journal of the American Medical Association, 302*, 1284-1293.

Linehan, M. M. (1993a). *Cognitive behavioral treatment of borderline personality disorder.* New York: Guilford Press.

Linehan, M. M. (1993b). *Skills training manual for treating borderline personality disorder.* New York: Guilford Press.

Linehan, M. M. (2012). *Dialectical behavior therapy skills training manual.* Manuscript in preparation.

Marlatt, G. A. (1985). Cognitive assessment and intervention procedures for relapse prevention. In G. A. Marlatt & J. R. Gordon (Eds.), *Relapse prevention: Maintenance strategies in the treatment of addictive behaviors.* New York: Guilford Press.

Marlatt, G. A., & Gordon, J. R. (Eds.). (1985). *Relapse prevention: Maintenance strategies in the treatment of addictive behaviors.* New York: Guilford Press.

Maslach, C., Schaufeli, W. B., & Leiter, M. P. (2001). Job burnout. *Annual Review of Psychology, 52*, 397-422.

McMain, S., Sayrs, J. H. R., Dimeff, L. A., & Linehan, M. M. (2007). Dialectical behavior therapy for individuals with borderline personality disorder and substance dependence. In L. A. Dimeff & K. Koerner (Eds.), *Dialectical behavior therapy in clinical practice: Applications across disorders and settings.* New York: Guilford Press.

Orsillo, S. M., Roemer, L., & Segal, Z. V. (2011). *The mindful way through anxiety: Break free from chronic worry and reclaim your life.* New York: Guilford Press.

Rosenzweig, S., Reibel, D. K., Greeson, J. M., Brainard, G. C., & Hojat, M. (2003). Mindfulness-based stress reduction lowers psychological distress in medical students. *Teaching and Learning in Medicine, 15*, 88-92.

Segal, Z. V., Williams, M. G., & Teasdale, J. D. (2002). *Mindfulness-based cognitive therapy for depression: A new approach to preventing relapse.* New York: Guilford Press.

Shapiro, S. L., Astin, J. A., Bishop, S. R., & Cordova, M. (2005). Mindfulness-based stress reduction for health care professionals: Results from a randomized trial. *International Journal of Stress Management, 12*, 164-176.

Shapiro, S. L., Brown, K. W., & Biegel, G. M. (2007). Teaching self-care to caregivers: Effects of mindfulness-based stress reduction on the mental health of therapists in training. *Training and Education in Professional Psychology, 1*, 105-115.

Shapiro, S. L., & Carlson, L. E. (2009). *The art and science of mindfulness: Integrating mindfulness into psychology and the helping professions.* Washington, DC: American Psychological Association.

Siegel, D. J. (2010). *The mindful therapist: A clinician's guide to mindsight and neural integration.* New York: W. W. Norton.

Stoffelmayr, B. E., Mavis, B. E., & Kasim, R. M. (1998). Substance abuse treatment staff: Recovery status and approaches to treatment. *Journal of Drug Education, 28,* 135-145.

Varra, A. A., Hayes, S. C., Roget, N., & Fisher, G. (2008). A randomized control trial examining the effect of acceptance and commitment training on clinician willingness to use evidence-based pharmacotherapy. *Journal of Consulting and Clinical Psychology, 76,* 449-458.

Witkiewitz, K., Marlatt, G. A., & Walker, D. (2005). Mindfulness-based relapse prevention for alcohol and substance use disorders. *Journal of Cognitive Psychotherapy: An International Quarterly, 19,* 211-228.

CHAPTER 7

Self-Stigma and Shame in Addictions

Jason B. Luoma

Portland Psychotherapy Clinic, Research, and Training Center

Barbara S. Kohlenberg

University of Nevada School of Medicine

I magine the experience of an individual who is addicted to drugs or alcohol. Addiction can be all-consuming. Substance use dominates attention, while other important aspects of life are neglected and tainted with failure. In contrast, recovery is a process of disconnecting from the solace found in substance use and contacting that which has been neglected or destroyed. This disorienting process is often infused with shame and stigmatizing judgments by both self and others, making recovery all the more difficult. Lightening the burden of shame and stigma on those in recovery is the focus of this chapter. Our goals are to outline the application of a psychological flexibility model of human behavior and to identify new methods that might help reduce the impact of shame and stigma.

Surveys show that attitudes in the United States and Europe toward people with alcohol and drug problems are at least as negative as those toward mental illness, and probably more negative (Corrigan, River, & Lundin, 2000; Crisp, Gelder, Rix, Meltzer, & Rowlands, 2000). A common stereotype is that substance users lack willpower and are unable to recover. People with substance abuse problems are often thought to be fundamentally different from others, worthless, morally weak, incompetent, blameworthy, violent, unreliable, shameful, and deceitful (Luoma et al., 2011). Stigma manifests structurally in public disapproval for funding addiction treatment (Schomerus, Matschinger, & Angermeyer, 2007), resulting in underfunded treatment systems with high turnover (Kimberly & McLellan, 2006). At the individual level, enacted stigma (i.e., acts of discrimination based on stigma) often occurs in the form of interpersonal rejection, housing discrimination, and barriers to employment (Luoma, 2011).

In addition to experiencing the direct effects of being stigmatized, people suffering from addiction internalize the pejorative attitudes of the public, resulting in what has been termed *self-stigma* (Corrigan, Watson, & Barr, 2006; Luoma, Kohlenberg, Hayes, Bunting, & Rye, 2008). While research on self-stigma in addiction is relatively sparse, there is a great deal of literature on the impact of stigma on psychological conditions more generally. This data shows that stigma leads to delays in seeking treatment or complete avoidance of treatment (Livingston & Boyd, 2010), diminished self-esteem or self-efficacy (Corrigan et al., 2006; Schomerus et al., 2011), increased mental health symptoms (Ritsher & Phelan, 2004), and lower quality of life (Lysaker, Davis, Warman, Strasburger, & Beattie, 2007). To further deepen the problem, people with addiction frequently carry stigma related to other aspects of their identity, such as mental illness, a diagnosis of HIV or hepatitis, homelessness, poverty, sexual minority status, ethnic or racial minority status, or a history of incarceration. All of these identities must be managed, and each can add to a sense of worthlessness, powerlessness, and being held back by others. Fortunately, an acceptance- and mindfulness-based treatment modality provides a new and useful approach to untangling this problem. That is the focus of the present chapter.

How Stigma and Self-Stigma Develop

Figure 7.1 presents a model for how stigma and self-stigma begin to affect an individual. Through their social context, people inevitably learn the stereotypes that relate to groups that are socially relevant to them (Devine, 1989). When stereotypes about people with addiction are initially learned, the corresponding attributes appear to apply to others who are misusing substances. However, as people develop an addiction, they may begin to see themselves as part of this conceptual group of addicts, alcoholics, or substance abusers. For many, this labeling process often begins around the time of entry into treatment (Link, Struening, Neese-Todd, Asmussen, & Phelan, 2002), and many people avoid treatment to avoid being labeled as part of an undesirable social group (e.g., Cunningham, Sobell, Sobell, Agrawal, & Toneatto, 1993). As people begin to see themselves as part of the conceptual group, basic language processes result in the application of stereotypes about the conceptualized group to the self. The result is self-stigma, which refers to difficult thoughts and feelings (e.g., shame, negative self-evaluative thoughts, or fear of enacted stigma) and the resulting behavioral impacts that emerge from identification with a stigmatized group (Luoma et al., 2007).

Figure 7.1. Model of the Initiation of Stigma

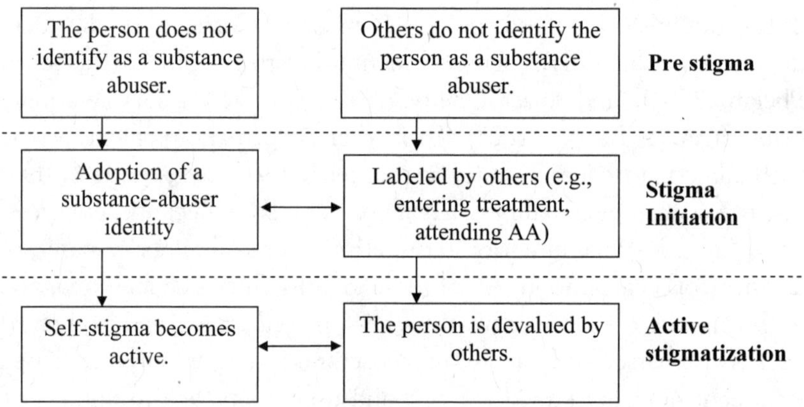

In parallel, enacted stigma begins when *others* label a person as a substance abuser and begin to respond to the person in ways influenced by stereotypes of the stigmatized group (Link & Phelan, 2001). In addition, enacted and self-stigma also interact. Self-stigma can lead to behaviors (e.g., failure in social roles or further drug use) that evoke stigmatizing responses. Conversely, experiences of enacted stigma (e.g., hearing loved ones say, "You are a failure") can result in increases in self-stigma (e.g., "I *am* a failure").

Shame and Addiction

In addition to being the emotional core of self-stigma, shame has long been seen as important to address in addiction treatment. Studies show that people with substance use problems experience more shame compared to those not using substances (Dearing, Stuewig, & Tangney, 2005) or compared to people with many other mental health difficulties (O'Connor, Berry, Inaba, Weiss, & Morrison, 1994). Shame may be influential in the development of drug use, as suggested by research showing that fifth graders with a tendency toward shame were more likely to be using drugs at age eighteen (Tangney & Dearing, 2002). Furthermore, shame also appears to play a role in the maintenance of drug use. For example, research on moods that trigger substance use suggests that shame may be particularly powerful compared to other moods (Mohr, Brannan, Mohr, Armeli, & Tennen, 2008), and shame predicts relapse among Alcoholics Anonymous participants (Wiechelt & Sales, 2001).

As with other nontechnical terms, definitions of shame vary; however, definitions generally include the idea that shame occurs when the self is perceived as flawed in the eyes of oneself or others (Gilbert, 1998; Tangney, Stuewig, & Mashek, 2007). Theorists often argue that shame can be distinguished from guilt in that people experience guilt when they have a negative evaluation of their *behavior* or *actions*, whereas shame involves a negative evaluation of the *self* (Barrett, 1995). While shame has generally been shown to be related to negative outcomes, "shame-free" guilt has generally been shown to be more adaptive, often predicting fewer substance use problems (Dearing et al., 2005; Stuewig, Tangney, Mashek, Forkner, & Dearing, 2009).

Shame is one of the so-called self-conscious emotions, as it requires the ability to reflect on one's self and how others might perceive one's self (Lewis, 1997). Not only is shame extremely aversive, but when people feel shame, there is a tendency to focus on their negative conceptualized self rather than specific behavior. This is often accompanied by feeling inferior, helpless, and exposed. This increased self-focus disrupts the ability to connect empathically with others and has been associated with anger and increased defensive blaming and externalizing (Tangney et al., 2007; Tracy & Robins, 2006). People experiencing shame are typically motivated to avoid, hide from, deny, or escape shame-inducing situations (Tangney et al., 2007).

People with addiction typically enter treatment at a low place in their lives. They are often highly marginalized and lacking in power. Both stigma and their own behavior may have led to a loss of social resources such as employment, friendships, and family. These people have often violated important personal values as a result of their addictive behavior or have failed to meet role expectations across many domains of living. Such violations of social norms, violations of personal values, and loss of social standing are likely to result in high levels of shame. While there is potential for people to have adaptive responses to shame (e.g., reparation of relationships), the internalized negative stereotypes connected to a stigmatized identity as a substance user can serve to further reinforce a shame-prone self-concept that is easily triggered by a variety of common life events.

Potential Adaptive Functions of Shame

While shame has often been perceived as a largely maladaptive negative emotion with little useful function (Tangney & Dearing, 2002), other perspectives do exist. From an evolutionary perspective, emotions such as shame are adaptive patterns of coordinated sets of organismic responses that both shape the behavior of others through emotion expression and regulate the person's own behavior. From this perspective, shame is triggered when people perceive that they have violated social norms or moral standards. If left unmitigated, such transgressions could lead to judgment by others, loss of social standing, and a loss of resources. Shame appears to have evolved to communicate appeasement, maintain social status, prevent rejection by the group, reinforce social hierarchies, and reduce conflict (Keltner & Harker, 1998; Kemeny, Gruenewald, & Dickerson, 2004; Tracy & Robins, 2004).

Functionally, shame reduces social ostracism and rejection, solidifies social roles, and appeases others when a violation of social norms has occurred (Keltner & Harker, 1998; Kemeny et al., 2004; Tracy & Robins, 2004). Shame is displayed in Caucasian US populations through a fairly reliable pattern of gaze and postural changes that includes hunched shoulders, touching one's face, blushing, downward gaze and head movements, decreased levels of expressive behavior, avoidance of eye contact, and other appeasement behaviors (Keltner, 1995). When displayed, shame tends to elicit sympathy, cooperation, and prosocial responding in others (Beer & Keltner, 2004; Keltner & Harker, 1998). Intrapersonally, shame is thought to function to alert people to actual or anticipated deviations from societal norms that may lead to judgment by others and potential loss of social standing, thereby motivating corrective action (Keltner & Harker, 1998; Kemeny et al., 2004; Tracy & Robins, 2004).

A Psychological Flexibility Model of Stigma and Shame

From a psychological flexibility perspective, the harmful effects of self-stigma and shame do not come simply from the content, intensity, frequency, or situational specificity of the emotions or thoughts involved, but also depend on other contextual and historical features that determine how shame and self-stigma function for the individual (Luoma et al., 2008). In this section, we outline three of the contexts that shape the function of shame and self-stigma.

Experiential Avoidance

Much of the harm of self-stigma comes not simply from the presence of shame, painful self-evaluations, or fear of stigmatization, but from understandable yet costly attempts to avoid events that elicit these experiences and the experiences themselves. Research has shown that when people who identify with a stigmatized social group encounter a situation where they could be devalued based on a verbally construed membership in that group, they devote some of their resources to defending against that devaluation at a cost to their performance (Steele, Spencer, & Aronson, 2002). For example, a person in recovery might search for signs of being seen as immoral (a common stereotype), resulting in interpersonal disruption. Similarly, people in stigmatized groups often disengage their efforts in areas of living where they perceive the potential for devaluation based on a stereotype (Major & Schmader, 1998). For instance, a person in recovery might give up parenting in part to avoid possibly confirming the stereotype of unreliability. Yet experimental research shows that people asked to avoid or suppress stereotype-congruent thinking can paradoxically experience increases in those very attributions (Wenzlaff & Wegner, 2000), suggesting that suppression of shame- and stigma-related thinking may contribute to the maintenance of those ways of thinking.

Substance use as a form of experiential avoidance can be fueled by shame and negative self-evaluation. Substance use appears to serve as a form of negative reinforcement (Stewart & Conrod, 2003), with short-term reductions in negative affect leading to escalating drug use. However, high levels of drug use cannot be maintained, and withdrawal leads to an exacerbation of negative affect. In addition, escalating drug or alcohol use also leads to failures in role functioning and violations of personal values, and therefore more shame.

The perception that shame is a largely maladaptive, negative emotion could lead to the conclusion that shame must be quickly reduced in order to deal with its problematic effects (Dearing et al., 2005). However, clinicians need to be cautious in order to not contribute to the tendency to suppress shame that already exists in Western culture (Wiechelt, 2007). Considering that shame serves as punishment following transgressions or as anticipatory feedback when considering potential deviations from societal norms or personal values, avoidance or suppression of shame could allow people to continue deviant behavior, such as problematic drug use, or allow them to violate personal values without feeling the shame that would ordinarily accompany those actions. In addition, suppressing the expression of shame may inhibit its tendency to evoke sympathy and prosocial responding in others and therefore inhibit its social repair function. Appropriate expression of shame could play a role in repairing disrupted relationships, increasing social inclusion, and building social support.

A psychological flexibility model suggests experiential acceptance as an alternative to suppression and avoidance. Rather than trying to avoid, suppress, or otherwise change unwanted shame, self-devaluing thoughts, or fears of enacted stigma, acceptance fosters the ability to compassionately notice difficult experiences, accept them as they are, and nonavoidantly shift attention toward values-based actions.

Cognitive Fusion

Self-stigma depends upon some of the most basic functions of language and cognition, such as categorical and evaluative processes. We are pervasively evaluating and classifying everyone in our social world, including ourselves. When we are fused with these thoughts, the result is objectification, in which behavior toward others and ourselves is dominated by verbal categories (Hayes, Niccolls, Masuda, & Rye, 2002; Luoma et al., 2008). For example, people fused with the thought *I'm bad* will be largely unaware of the *process* of verbal evaluation (put into words, they won't see the experience as *I'm having the thought* I'm bad); instead, they will interact with others and themselves on the basis of *being* bad.

Two problems emerge from this type of cognitive fusion. Evaluations of self and others tend to be global and negative, undermining the ability to respond flexibly. When a person is fused with the thought *I'm bad*, that thought says little about what to do next. And while it is logical to want to directly change the negative thinking that is part of shame and stigma, this may be difficult and largely counterproductive. Information disconfirming stereotypes tends to be forgotten if the new information conflicts with older stereotypes. In addition, stereotype-congruent behavior tends to be inferred to dispositional causes, while stereotype-incongruent behavior tends to be inferred to situational causes (Hewstone, 1990). Finally, if a person learns new ways of thinking in a situation, the old ways of thinking will reemerge if the new ways are frustrated or punished (e.g., Wilson & Hayes, 1996).

A psychological flexibility approach suggests that a more rapid path to decreasing the influence of negative self-evaluations is to encourage a process called *cognitive defusion*. In cognitive defusion, people are taught to notice the ongoing process of thinking and to see thoughts (including self-evaluations) as thoughts, rather than what they seem to be (a truth about oneself). As people learn to notice the process of thinking in flight, their overt behavior is less influenced by the products of thinking, allowing them to take more effective actions that align with their values and longer-term life goals and plans, such as engagement in a recovery process.

Rigid Self-Processes

Through interaction with our social and verbal community, we learn to generate coherent stories about ourselves that seem to describe the nature of who we are and the causes of our behavior. When we observe problematic behavior, we often explain this behavior through reference to dispositional causes (e.g., *I was fired from my job because I am unreliable*) or group membership (e.g., *I was fired because I'm an addict*). The search for coherence in self-concept can reinforce further unworkable behavior tied to the person's identity (e.g., *I'm unreliable, so why bother to look for a job?*). This can result in a self-defeating cycle wherein failures in role functioning and violations of personal values reinforce negative stories about the self, and then this negative sense of self leads to further unworkable behavior. In the context of self-stigma and shame, the content of this self-conceptualization is often very negative. People are often motivated to hide the "damaged" self in order to avoid rejection, leading to withdrawal and secrecy about their problems with addiction. Unfortunately, secrecy in the context of substance misuse has been related to poor outcomes and lowered social support (e.g., Luoma et al., 2007).

People experiencing shame tend to have a rigid focus on the self and less ability to experience empathy for others or take another's perspective on an event (Leith & Baumeister, 1998). In general, deficits in perspective taking have been linked to severe social dysfunction in the case of autism (Baron-Cohen, 1995), and to arrogant, self-centered, or aggressive styles of interpersonal responding with milder deficits in perspective taking (Richardson, Hammock, Smith, Gardner, & Signo, 1994). Shame, in particular, has been associated with anger and increased defensive blaming and externalizing (Tangney et al., 2007; Tracy & Robins, 2006).

In contrast to the rigid defense of immutable facts about the self, a psychological flexibility model suggests that helping people loosen their attachment to their conceptualized self can free them to respond more flexibly to situational demands and align their behavior with longer-term life goals and values. If people increase their range of potential psychological perspectives on their experience, they can relate to their self-devaluing thoughts from a more distanced position; develop a repertoire of kinder and more compassionate reactions to themselves; and increase their awareness of the others' perspectives in interpersonal situations, an ability that is related to effective interpersonal functioning (Galinsky, Ku, & Wang, 2005).

A Brief ACT Group Protocol Targeting Self-Stigma and Shame

With a few exceptions (Gilbert & Procter, 2006; Rizvi & Linehan, 2005), there has been little study of treatments focusing on shame. The addictions literature discusses interventions for shame (Cook, 1991; Potter-Efron, 2002), but to our knowledge the only treatment that has been systematically developed (Luoma et al., 2008) and evaluated is the ACT group protocol described below (Luoma, Kohlenberg, Hayes, & Fletcher, 2012). The ACT protocol involves three two-hour group sessions that employ a mixture of instruction, discussion, metaphor, and experiential activities to help people with shame, self-devaluation, and fear of judgment and rejection from others. This protocol was tested in a residential treatment program that was largely based in a 12-step approach but also included a wide variety of other elements, such as training in life skills, relapse prevention, parenting skills, recreational therapy, and anger management.

Shame and self-stigma were targeted together because they tend to be elicited by similar contexts, despite some differences in how they manifest. To illustrate, stigma is often described as "an attribute that is deeply discrediting" and reduces a person from "a whole and usual person to a tainted, discounted one" (Goffman, 1963, p. 3). In contrast, shame is thought to result when the self is perceived as undesirable or flawed in the estimation of others (Gilbert & Tarrier, 2006). In self-stigma, people fear being condemned, rejected, or judged by others because of their membership in the marginalized group, while in shame, they see themselves as inferior and fear that others will reject them (Gilbert, 1998). While a client's current negative self-conceptualization and fear of rejection could reflect either self-sigma, shame, or both, the intervention is essentially the same because the eliciting contextual stimuli are highly overlapping.

Process and Orientation

Because shame and self-stigma are particularly likely to be elicited in social interactions, the group process itself offers an essential learning opportunity (for general recommendations on the process and structure of ACT groups, see Walser & Pistorello, 2004). Group leaders helped participants notice instances where stigma, stereotyping, and shame occurred during the group process. Fusion with these events as they occur in session can derail the group process and feed avoidance, whereas noticing, accepting, and gently observing judgment and shame as they occur can create opportunities to deepen the effectiveness of the treatment.

As an example of this process, participants' private and public assumptions about and evaluations of the group leaders were used as an opportunity for learning. The content of these judgments might have included whether or not the group leaders have a personal history with substance misuse, whether they were seen as for or against 12-step participation, whether they were too intellectual, and so on. When such evaluations occurred, group leaders tried to show participants how these in-session judgments might interfere with benefiting from the intervention. An example of a therapist statement in this context might be "Can you have that thought, that I am not in recovery and therefore cannot understand and help you, and also be open to the possibility that I might be able to understand and help you?" or "If you listened to these thoughts, where would that take you?" or "What about allowing the thought to happen and also staying in the room and being open to something new happening?"

Judgment and stereotyping also occurred between group members. Participants often labeled one another—for example, "She has a hard time expressing herself," "He is always in his head," "She can't help it; she has ADHD," "She's a meth addict," and so on. Group leaders encouraged participants to notice such thoughts while at the same time responding to them in a nonjudgmental manner. For example, a leader might say, "Isn't it interesting? Our minds are doing it right here—evaluating, assessing, judging—and here you are, brave enough to let us see it right here!" Then the leader could relate it to the topic of the session by saying something like "We will be exploring this very human process and tendency to label for the rest of the sessions." In addition, group leaders might note these judgments as they occur for use in later exercises.

Session-by-Session Outline

The following outline delineates the general principles involved in each session, as well as selected metaphors and exercises. A detailed protocol is available online (at www.contextualpsychology.org/treatment_protocols). Groups were structured so that each session targeted two to three core principles, with flexibility to utilize a range of exercises and metaphors as needed. The protocol was designed to fit within an eclectic treatment setting, with a primary focus of the group being to enhance participants' engagement with other facets of their treatment.

SESSION 1

The purpose of this session was to build an awareness of enacted stigma and self-stigma, and their effects. Participants were invited to describe a few experiences of being stigmatized. Leaders then introduced how stigmatizing attitudes are internalized and how people with substance problems can begin to limit themselves due to self-stigma. If examples of stereotyping had already emerged during the group, these were identified as examples of the tendency to stigmatize.

Passengers on the Bus (Hayes, Strosahl, & Wilson, 1999) served as a core metaphor for the group sessions. In this metaphor, the individual is described as the driver of a bus, intending to travel in the direction of his or her values. Various passengers, consisting of difficult thoughts, feelings, memories, sensations, or urges, try to threaten, convince, reason, or otherwise encourage the driver to turn away from the valued direction. In this metaphor, the goal is not to find a way to kick all the difficult passengers off the bus; it is to find a way to accept the presence of the passengers while continuing to move in a valued direction. Participants were encouraged to identify particular passengers that would be on their bus, with a focus on self-critical and judgmental thoughts that might represent instances of self-stigma. Through the remainder of the sessions, difficult or constricting thoughts, feelings, and memories that showed up were frequently cast as passengers on the person's bus.

In addition, session 1 focused on helping participants appreciate the pervasive tendency of humans to judge, evaluate, and predict. Common ACT exercises were used to help participants notice the ease, automaticity, and pervasiveness of evaluation. A novel exercise, which we called the Crosscutting Categories exercise, was used if the participants were relatively new to each other. In this exercise, volunteers served as subjects, and the other members of the group were invited to notice the ease with which they had evaluations, predictions, and judgments about the volunteers based on very little information. The volunteers then responded to a series of fairly personal questions that were intended to elicit a sense of empathy in observers, such as "Would you be willing to share something that you're concerned about that has to do with a member of your extended family?" or "Would you be willing to tell us about a time when you let somebody down?" or "Tell us about the last time you cried." The exercise was then debriefed with a focus on noticing how judgments tended to dissolve as the complexity of the person's experience was recognized and a shared sense of common humanity emerged.

During the first session, participants were also introduced to the concept that experiential control is the problem, not the solution. A variety of standard ACT exercises, such as the Rule of Private Events, the Polygraph metaphor, the Chocolate Cake exercise, and the Person in the Hole metaphor (all in Hayes et al., 1999), were utilized to sensitize participants to the paradoxical effects of efforts at mental control. In some groups, participants were encouraged to participate in an expressive writing exercise focusing on contacting and allowing feelings and thoughts related to a past experience of failure or shame. For homework, participants were encouraged to simply notice how their minds worked, particularly in response to difficult thoughts and feelings. They were encouraged not to try to do anything differently, just directed to notice mental processes.

SESSION 2

The primary focus of session 2 was introducing the concepts of acceptance and defusion, and practicing related skills. Defusion was introduced as an alternative to changing evaluations and judgments, with an emphasis on self-stigma. The bus metaphor was again referenced to suggest that there might be other ways to respond to these kinds of thoughts. We also introduced a metaphor of a bubble over the head, saying something like "Thoughts are like see-through plastic bubbles on our heads. When you have a blue plastic bubble, you can't see it; you can only see through it. And when it's blue, things look a particular way—for example, blue and white objects appear to be the same color. Now, we're not suggesting that what you want to do is get rid of the bubbles. However, we'll do some exercises that might help you take them off your head so that you can look at them and see them clearly." This was typically acted out by the leader so that there was also a visual component to the metaphor. This was followed by an exercise in which a word was repeated, out loud, for a brief period of time, such as thirty seconds, while participants were coached to notice what happens. This exercise has been shown to rapidly reduce the believability of self-referential evaluative thoughts (e.g., Masuda et al., 2009). In this protocol, the exercise was introduced using a neutral word, then repeated using a self-evaluative word identified by a volunteer.

This session also addressed the cultural assumption of control versus the alternative of acceptance. Participants were taught to distinguish between the capacity to control the external world of objects, where direct action and effort tend to pay off, and attempts to control the internal world of thoughts and feelings, where direct action often does not work and may actually create additional difficulties. Various exercises were used, with the most central being a role-play of the Tug-of-War with a Monster metaphor (Hayes et al., 1999). In this exercise, a volunteer identifies a shame-inducing thought or situation, and identifies a variety of thoughts and feelings that arise in response to shame. In the ensuing role-play, the therapist acts out the part of the "shame monster" in a tug-of-war with the client where winning the tug-of-war means pulling the opponent into a bottomless pit. Clients are encouraged to experience what it is like to struggle against the shame monster, and to consider and observe the effects of letting go of the struggle by dropping the rope.

In the latter part of this session, members practiced defusion, acceptance, and letting go of attachment to their conceptualized self in the context of stigma and self-judgment. The core exercise in this section was acting out the Passengers on the Bus metaphor. A volunteer played the bus driver and was coached to identify a valued direction in which he or she wished to head, and other members played the various passengers (i.e., thoughts, feelings, urges, etc.) that threatened the driver and tried to convince him or her to turn away from the value direction. The exercise proceeded in several rounds, including role-plays of arguing with the passengers, compromising with the passengers, and accepting the passengers and driving the bus with all of the passengers along for the ride.

In another exercise focused on letting go of attachment to self-evaluation, participants wrote negative self-judgments on name tags that they wore on their chests. In a final exercise, participants sat in pairs and looked into each others' eyes while the therapists coached them to notice their judgments and thereby achieve a more accepting stance toward the other and the self. The homework assignment following this session was typically for participants to watch for places where they turned the driving over to their thoughts or times when they got hooked by thoughts.

SESSION 3

The primary focus of session 3 was defining and contacting core values and fostering commitments to valued action. Exercises were aimed at helping participants consider and clarify their core values. They were guided through a process of identifying intentions for future actions, developing goals, and making plans. They were also given an opportunity to articulate their values, discuss past avoidance, and publicly commit to a new direction.

A particular focus was treatment- and recovery-related values. Therapists defined values as akin to a direction versus a goal, reflecting that values are part of an ongoing quality of action and therefore something that can be instantiated through the process of living, whereas goals specify events or actions that can be completed. The metaphor of values as a compass was used, with participants being encouraged to choose in what direction they wished to travel. Group leaders posed questions such as "Have you ever wondered what your life would be like if your addiction and fears didn't rule you? What would you be doing? That's what we want to focus on today."

One of two exercises was used to help participants contact their most central life values. In one version, a large tombstone was drawn on a whiteboard, and participants were encouraged to identify what they would most want the epitaph on their tombstone to say about them when they died (similar to Eifert & Forsyth, 2005).

In the second, often more emotionally intense, exercise, participants were asked to visit their own funeral in their imagination and consider what they were most afraid their loved ones would say about them. This was followed by an exercise in which a volunteer role-played attending his or her own funeral while other participants played the roles of loved ones and friends giving brief eulogies. The role-play proceeded in two rounds. In the first round, the volunteer talked about what he or she thought each loved one might say if the volunteer were to die today, and this was then enacted in a eulogy by another participant. This often evoked experiences of shame and self-devaluation, bringing the target of the intervention into the room. In the second round, the volunteer imagined what that same loved one might say if the volunteer were to make a change in his or her life and get a second chance in the relationship with that person; this was then enacted in a eulogy by another participant, allowing the volunteer to powerfully and visually contact the valued direction in which he or she would like to head in the future.

Finally, participants identified actions that aligned with their values and intentions for future actions, and made commitments to specific actions. The goal of this last part of the session was to help participants translate their more general valued directions into concrete goals, and to help them make a commitment to actions that would honor their most central values. Typically, the session ended with an exercise in which participants first completed a values worksheet about their values, goals, and barriers, including those related to treatment and recovery. Group leaders then conducted an exercise in which participants took turns mindfully standing in front of the group and publicly stating what they had been doing that wasn't working (e.g., "What I've been doing is…"), what the cost of that behavior had been (e.g., "What that has cost me is…"), and their commitment (e.g., "What I will do from here is…").

Data Relating to a Psychological Flexibility Model of Self-Stigma and Shame in Addiction

The group protocol described above has been examined in two studies. In the first study, the protocol was developed and refined in an iterative fashion across nine groups of clients ($n = 88$) participating in a twenty-eight-day residential substance misuse treatment program (Luoma et al., 2008). The group intervention was inserted in place of six hours of their normal group therapy programming. Assessments were conducted one week apart, which coincided with pre- and post-intervention. Medium to large effect size improvements were found across a variety of outcome measures, including internalized shame.

Following on the preliminary results of the open trial, a randomized controlled trial was conducted (Luoma et al., 2012). In this trial, the six-hour protocol developed in the open trial was compared to treatment as usual. The design was similar to an additive design, except the ACT intervention *replaced* six hours of regular programming during a twenty-eight-day residential program. Assessments were at pretreatment, post-treatment, and four-month follow-up. A total of sixteen groups ($n = 133$) were assigned in a pairwise random fashion to the two conditions. Analyses showed that the ACT condition resulted in smaller reductions in shame at post-treatment, but larger reductions in shame at follow-up. Those attending the ACT group also reported fewer days of substance use and more treatment attendance at follow-up. Effects of the ACT intervention on treatment utilization at follow-up were mediated by post-treatment levels of shame, in that those evidencing higher levels of shame at post-treatment were more likely to be attending treatment at follow-up. Intervention effects on substance use at follow-up were mediated by treatment utilization at follow-up, suggesting that the intervention may have had its effects, at least in part, through improving treatment attendance. Together, these two trials provide preliminary evidence for the effectiveness of an intervention focused on improving psychological flexibility in relation to shame.

A study examining self-stigma in relation to weight also provides some support for this model of intervention (Lillis, Hayes, Bunting, & Masuda, 2009). At the three-month follow-up, those who received the ACT intervention showed greater improvements across a variety of dimensions, including quality of life, stigma, and weight. Mediational analyses indicated that changes in weight-specific psychological flexibility mediated outcomes.

Future Directions in Research and Applications

Health care professionals, like the rest of the public, hold many stigmatizing attitudes toward substance users, including the idea that substance-misusing clients are unlikely to recover (McLaughlin & Long, 1996). Health care providers may be a particularly promising target of stigma-reduction interventions, as stigmatizing attitudes tend to have a greater impact when one group has power over another (Link & Phelan, 2001). In addition, some researchers have cautioned that shame-inducing treatment methods are common in the clinical world (e.g., O'Connor et al., 1994) and could contribute to poor outcomes (Wiechelt, 2007). The utility of an intervention based on a psychological flexibility model in this context has been tested successfully in one pilot study (Hayes et al., 2004) designed to reduce entanglement with stigmatizing attitudes among counselors working with clients with alcohol and drug abuse problems.

A second important domain for future research in this area is the development of new measures of stigma, shame, and relevant contextual variables, such as fusion or experiential avoidance. One effort (presently unpublished) is the development of a self-report measure based on a psychological flexibility model, the Substance Abuse Self-Stigma Scale. This measure consists of four subscales measuring self-devaluation and shame, fear of enacted stigma, stigma avoidance, and stigma-related disengagement from valued actions. Initial psychometric evaluation suggested that the first three subscales had good reliability and validity, while the fourth scale had a more mixed pattern of results (Luoma et al., 2011).

However, because shame leads to a desire to hide, valid self-reports are difficult to obtain. Thus, there is a need for other methods of measurement, particularly those such as implicit measures, which may be less influenced by social presentation biases (de Houwer, Teige-Mocigemba, Spruyt, & Moors, 2009).

Conclusion

People with addictions suffer from the direct effects of their substances of choice and the pervasive losses that result from addictive behavior. These losses can result in chronic feelings of shame and worthlessness, which may be further magnified by a community that can curtail the person's choices and opportunities through stigma. Attenuating enacted stigma is not the subject of this chapter. However, the reach of negative social judgments, echoing in the heart and mind of the person with the addiction problem, can create self-imposed barriers to living a valued life.

We are guided by a conviction that the lives of those with addiction problems need not be limited by their history, and that the contribution that those in recovery can make to their families and communities is deep and vast. Early data seem to indicate that facilitating clients in recovery in relating to their shame and negative self-judgment with compassion and mindful awareness, and turning their attention toward values-based action may be helpful to them. We hope that this work can lead to more compassionate and effective treatments for people with addiction problems, freeing them from imprisonment by shame and stigma.

References

Baron-Cohen, S. (1995). *Mindblindness: As essay on autism and theory of mind.* Cambridge, MA: MIT Press.

Barrett, K. C. (1995). A functionalist approach to shame and guilt. In J. P. Tangney & K. W. Fischer (Eds.), *Self-conscious emotions: The psychology of shame, guilt, embarrassment, and pride.* New York: Guilford Press.

Beer, J. S., & Keltner, D. (2004). What is unique about self-conscious emotions? *Psychological Inquiry, 15,* 126-128.

Cook, D. R. (1991). Shame, attachment, and addictions: Implications for family therapists. *Contemporary Family Therapy, 13,* 405-419.

Corrigan, P. W., River, L. P., & Lundin, R. K. (2000). Stigmatizing attributions about mental illness. *Journal of Community Psychology, 28,* 91-102.

Corrigan, P. W., Watson, A. C., & Barr, L. (2006). The self-stigma of mental illness: Implications for self-esteem and self-efficacy. *Journal of Social and Clinical Psychology, 25,* 875-884.

Crisp, A. H., Gelder, M. G., Rix, S., Meltzer, H. I., & Rowlands, O. J. (2000). Stigmatisation of people with mental illnesses. *British Journal of Psychiatry, 177,* 4-7.

Cunningham, J. A., Sobell, L. C., Sobell, M. B., Agrawal, S., & Toneatto, T. (1993). Barriers to treatment: Why alcohol and drug-abusers delay or never seek treatment. *Addictive Behaviors, 18,* 347-353.

Dearing, R. L., Stuewig, J., & Tangney, J. P. (2005). On the importance of distinguishing shame from guilt: Relations to problematic alcohol and drug use. *Addictive Behaviors, 30,* 1392-1404.

De Houwer, J., Teige-Mocigemba, S., Spruyt, A., & Moors, A. (2009). Implicit measures: A normative analysis and review. *Psychological Bulletin, 135,* 347.

Devine, P. (1989). Stereotypes and prejudice: Their automatic and controlled components. *Journal of Personality and Social Psychology, 56,* 5-18.

Eifert, G. H., & Forsyth, J. P. (2005). *Acceptance and commitment therapy for anxiety disorders.* Oakland, CA: New Harbinger.

Galinsky, A. D., Ku, G., & Wang, C. S. (2005). Perspective-taking and self-other overlap: Fostering social bonds and facilitating social coordination. *Group Processes and Intergroup Relations, 8,* 109-124.

Gilbert, P. (1998). What is shame? Some core issues and controversies. In P. Gilbert & B. Andrews (Eds.), *Shame: Interpersonal behavior, psychopathology, and culture.* Oxford, UK: Oxford University Press.

Gilbert, P., & Procter, S. (2006). Compassionate mind training for people with high shame and self-criticism: Overview and pilot study of a group therapy approach. *Clinical Psychology and Psychotherapy, 13,* 353-379.

Gilbert, P., & Tarrier, N. (2006). A biopsychosocial and evolutionary approach to formulation with a special focus on shame. In N. Tarrier (Ed.), *Case formulation in cognitive behavior therapy: The treatment of challenging and complex cases.* New York: Routledge/Taylor and Francis Group.

Goffman, E. (1963). *Stigma: Notes on the management of spoiled identity.* Englewood Cliffs, New Jersey: Prentice Hall.

Hayes, S. C., Bissett, R., Roget, N., Padilla, M., Kohlenberg, B. S., Fisher, G., et al. (2004). The impact of acceptance and commitment training and multicultural training on the stigmatizing attitudes and professional burnout of substance abuse counselors. *Behavior Therapy, 35,* 821-835.

Hayes, S. C., Niccolls, R., Masuda, A., & Rye, A. K. (2002). Prejudice, terrorism, and behavior therapy. *Cognitive and Behavioral Practice, 9,* 296-301.

Hayes, S. C., Strosahl, K. D., & Wilson, K. G. (1999). *Acceptance and commitment therapy: An experiential approach to behavior change.* New York: Guilford Press.

Hewstone, M. (1990). The "ultimate attribution error"? A review of the literature on intergroup causal attribution. *European Journal of Social Psychology, 20,* 311-335.

Keltner, D. (1995). Signs of appeasement: Evidence for the distinct displays of embarrassment, amusement, and shame. *Journal of Personality and Social Psychology, 68,* 441-454.

Keltner, D., & Harker, L. (1998). The forms and functions of the nonverbal signal of shame. In P. Gilbert & B. Andrews (Eds.), *Shame: Interpersonal behavior, psychopathology, and culture*. Oxford, UK: Oxford University Press.

Kemeny, M. E., Gruenewald, T. L., & Dickerson, S. S. (2004). Shame as the emotional response to threat to the social self: Implications for behavior, physiology, and health. *Psychological Inquiry, 15*, 153-160.

Kimberly, J. R., & McLellan, A. T. (2006). The business of addiction treatment: A research agenda. *Journal of Substance Abuse Treatment, 31*, 213-219.

Leith, K. P., & Baumeister, R. F. (1998). Empathy, shame, guilt, and narratives of interpersonal conflicts: Guilt-prone people are better at perspective taking. *Journal of Personality, 66*, 1-37.

Lewis, M. (1997). The self in self-conscious emotions. *Annals of the New York Academy of Sciences, 818*, 119-142.

Lillis, J., Hayes, S. C., Bunting, K., & Masuda, A. (2009). Teaching acceptance and mindfulness to improve the lives of the obese: A preliminary test of a theoretical model. *Annals of Behavioral Medicine, 37*, 58-69.

Link, B. G., & Phelan, J. C. (2001). Conceptualizing stigma. *Annual Reviews in Sociology, 27*, 363-385.

Link, B. G., Struening, E. L., Neese-Todd, S., Asmussen, S., & Phelan, J. C. (2002). On describing and seeking to change the experience of stigma. *Psychiatric Rehabilitation Skills, 6*, 201-231

Livingston, J. D., & Boyd, J. E. (2010). Correlates and consequences of internalized stigma for people living with mental illness: A systematic review and meta-analysis. *Social Science and Medicine (1982), 71*, 2150-61.

Luoma, J. B. (2011). Substance abuse stigma as a barrier to treatment and recovery. In B. A. Johnson (Ed.), *Addictive medicine: Science and practice*. New York: Springer.

Luoma, J. B., Kohlenberg, B. S., Hayes, S. C., Bunting, K., & Rye, A. K. (2008). Reducing self-stigma in substance abuse through acceptance and commitment therapy: Model, manual development, and pilot outcomes. *Addiction Research and Theory, 16*, 149-165.

Luoma, J. B., Kohlenberg, B. S., Hayes, S. C., & Fletcher, L. B. (2012). Slow and steady wins the race: A randomized clinical trial of acceptance and commitment therapy targeting shame in substance use disorders. *Journal of Consulting and Clinical Psychology, 80*, 43-53.

Luoma, J. B., Nobles, R. H., Drake, C. E., Hayes, S. C., O'Hair, A., Fletcher, L., & Kohlenberg, B. S. (2011). *Self-stigma in substance abuse: Development of a new measure*. Unpublished manuscript.

Luoma, J. B., Twohig, M. P., Waltz, T., Hayes, S. C., Roget, N., Padilla, M., et al. (2007). An investigation of stigma in individuals receiving treatment for substance abuse. *Addictive Behaviors, 32*, 1331-46.

Lysaker, P. H., Davis, L. W., Warman, D. M., Strasburger, A., & Beattie, N. (2007). Stigma, social function, and symptoms in schizophrenia and schizoaffective disorder: Associations across 6 months. *Psychiatry Research, 149*, 89-95.

Major, B., & Schmader, T. (1998). Coping with stigma through psychological disengagement. In J. K. Swim and C. Stangor (Eds.), *Prejudice: The target's perspective*. San Diego, CA: Academic Press.

Masuda, A., Hayes, S. C., Twohig, M. P., Drossel, C., Lillis, J., & Washio, Y. (2009). A parametric study of cognitive defusion and the believability and discomfort of negative self-relevant thoughts. *Behavior Modification, 33,* 250-262.

McLaughlin, D., & Long, A. (1996). An extended literature review of health professionals' perceptions of illicit drugs and their clients who use them. *Journal of Psychiatric and Mental Health Nursing, 3,* 283-288.

Mohr, C. D., Brannan, D., Mohr, J., Armeli, S., & Tennen, H. (2008). Evidence for positive mood buffering among college student drinkers. *Personality and Social Psychology Bulletin, 34,* 1249-59.

O'Connor, L. E., Berry, J. W., Inaba, D., Weiss, J., & Morrison, A. (1994). Shame, guilt, and depression in men and women in recovery from addiction. *Journal of Substance Abuse Treatment, 11,* 503-510.

Potter-Efron, R. T. (2002). *Shame, guilt, and alcoholism: Treatment issues in clinical practice.* Binghamton, NY: Haworth Press.

Richardson, D. R., Hammock, G. S., Smith, S. M., Gardner, W., & Signo, M. (1994). Empathy as a cognitive inhibitor of interpersonal aggression. *Aggressive Behavior, 20,* 275-289.

Ritsher, J. B., & Phelan, J. C. (2004). Internalized stigma predicts erosion of morale among psychiatric outpatients. *Psychiatry Research, 129,* 257-265.

Rizvi, S. L., & Linehan, M. M. (2005). The treatment of maladaptive shame in borderline personality disorder: A pilot study of "opposite action." *Cognitive and Behavioral Practice, 12,* 437-447.

Schomerus, G., Corrigan, P. W., Klauer, T., Kuwert, P., Freyberger, H. J., & Lucht, M. (2011). Self-stigma in alcohol dependence: Consequences for drinking-refusal self-efficacy. *Drug and Alcohol Dependence, 114,* 12-17.

Schomerus, G., Matschinger, H., & Angermeyer, M. C. (2007). Familiarity with mental illness and approval of structural discrimination against psychiatric patients in Germany. *Journal of Nervous and Mental Disease, 195,* 89.

Steele, C. M., Spencer, S. J., & Aronson, J. (2002). Contending with group image: The psychology of stereotype and social identity threat. *Advances in Experimental Social Psychology, 34,* 379-440.

Stewart, S. H., & Conrod, P. J. (2003). Psychosocial models of functional associations between posttraumatic stress disorder and substance use disorder. In. P. Ouimette & P. J. Brown (Eds.), *Trauma and substance abuse: Causes, consequences, and treatment of comorbid disorders.* Washington, DC: American Psychological Association.

Stuewig, J., Tangney, J. P., Mashek, D., Forkner, P., & Dearing, R. (2009). The moral emotions, alcohol dependence, and HIV risk behavior in an incarcerated sample. *Substance Use and Misuse, 44,* 449-71.

Tangney, J. P., & Dearing, R. L. (2002). *Shame and guilt.* New York: Guilford Press.

Tangney, J. P., Stuewig, J., & Mashek, D. J. (2007). Moral emotions and moral behavior. *Annual Review of Psychology, 58,* 345-372.

Tracy, J. L., & Robins, R. W. (2004). Putting the self into self-conscious emotions: A theoretical model. *Psychological Inquiry, 15,* 103-125.

Tracy, J. L., & Robins, R. W. (2006). Appraisal antecedents of shame and guilt: Support for a theoretical model. *Personality and Social Psychology Bulletin, 32,* 1339.

Walser, R. D., & Pistorello, J. (2004). ACT in group format. In S. C. Hayes, K. Wilson, & K. Strosahl (Eds.), *A practical guide to acceptance and commitment therapy.* New York: Springer.

Wenzlaff, R. M., & Wegner, D. M. (2000). Thought suppression. *Annual Review of Psychology, 51,* 59-91.

Wiechelt, S. A. (2007). The specter of shame in substance misuse. *Substance Use and Misuse, 42,* 399-409.

Wiechelt, S. A., & Sales, E. (2001). The role of shame in women's recovery from alcoholism: The impact of childhood sexual abuse. *Journal of Social Work Practice in the Addictions, 1,* 101-116.

Wilson, K. G., & Hayes, S. C. (1996). Resurgence of derived stimulus relations. *Journal of the Experimental Analysis of Behavior, 66,* 267-281.

CHAPTER 8

Detoxification: Challenges and Strategies from an Acceptance and Mindfulness Perspective

Angela L. Stotts

University of Texas Medical School at Houston

Akihiko Masuda

Georgia State University

The purpose of detoxification in substance abuse is to manage withdrawal symptoms and help clients adjust to a substance-free state so that further treatment may begin. When a drug is stopped, the body typically responds by overreacting in the opposite direction to the effects of the drug of abuse, producing psychologically distressing and sometimes physically dangerous withdrawal symptoms. Detoxification can be highly variable in intensity and duration depending on the individual and the drug of abuse, but it generally occurs over a one- to two-week period. In most cases, it requires daily visits with a medical health care provider to monitor and manage withdrawal symptoms.

Substances with the most challenging detoxification are alcohol, benzodiazepines (e.g., alprazolam or lorazepam), and opiates (e.g., heroin or hydrocodone). The challenge is both physical and psychological. For example, about 10% of alcohol-dependent patients will have delirium or grand mal seizures, and symptoms can last up to six months (Hernandez-Avila & Kranzler, 2011). Similarly, withdrawal from long-term benzodiazepine dependence can be dangerous, with severe symptoms including delirium, seizures, psychosis, and severe depression.

Withdrawal from opioids results in flu-like symptoms that are extremely uncomfortable and distressing, yet not life-threatening. Symptoms such as sweating, watery eyes, chills, muscle aches, nausea or vomiting, diarrhea, and fever can last from one to three weeks; longer-acting opioids are most often tapered over an eight- to twenty-four-week period, with the most severe symptoms appearing toward the end of the taper. Some signs of opioid withdrawal (increased blood pressure, increased metabolic rate, and lowered body weight) may continue for about six months and are often accompanied by dysphoria and vulnerability to relapse. The early prodromal symptoms of withdrawal are sufficient to drive even the most committed patients back to previous levels of opioid use. Success rates for detoxification from opioids are low, ranging from 12% to 25% (Dunn, Sigmon, Strain, Heil, & Higgins, 2011).

The most effective treatment available for opioid dependence is sustained, long-term agonist replacement therapy with methadone or buprenorphine medication (Amato, Davoli, Ferri, Gowing, & Perucci, 2004). Methadone maintenance (MM) treatment reduces heroin use and criminal activity, and improves social functioning (Marsch, 1998). However, permanent use is controversial (Magura & Rosenblum, 2001) due to its financial burden, life-limiting restrictions, and unpleasant stigma. The majority of MM clients state a preference for abstinence (Lenne et al., 2001), and clients in various stages of MM treatment request detoxification or attempt to detoxify themselves (Latowsky, 1996). About 10% to 15% of MM clients are in the process of detoxification at any one time.

Detoxification Treatment

Comparatively little research has been done to identify effective psychological and behavioral treatments targeting detoxification. Systematic desensitization has demonstrated some success (Cheek, Tomarchio, Standen, & Albahary, 1973; Hollands & Turecek, 1980). Contingency management has resulted in a decrease of opiate use during early phases of detoxification but not long-term gains (Robles, Stitzer, Strain, Bigelow,

& Silverman, 2002). Individual or group therapy has resulted in higher illicit opiate use and higher dropout rates when compared to sustained MM treatment (Sees et al., 2000).

Very little research has been conducted on the psychological or behavioral mechanisms that play a role in poor detoxification outcomes. An older literature has shown that fear of anticipated withdrawal symptoms may amplify the negativity of the perceived detoxification experience beyond withdrawal symptoms themselves (Eklund, Hiltunen, Melin, & Borg, 1997; Phillips, Gossop, & Bradley, 1986). Milby, Garrett, and Meredith (1980) found an "iatrogenic detoxification phobia" in at least 30% of MM participants. These clients were more likely to be in MM treatment longer and make fewer detoxification attempts (Milby et al., 1994). Detoxification-related anxiety increases as dose decreases (Hall, Loeb, & Kushner, 1984), and fear of anticipated withdrawal is the predominant reason for discontinuation of a dose-reduction program among MM clients (Berger & Schwegler, 1973). This older literature has provided a general basis for some of the more recent attempts to examine the psychological aspects of detoxification.

An Acceptance- and Mindfulness-Based Theoretical Model for Approaching Detoxification

The acceptance- and mindfulness-based account of detoxification presented in this chapter is grounded in a contemporary behavioral framework of psychological health called *psychological flexibility* (Hayes, Luoma, Bond, Masuda, & Lillis, 2006; Hayes, Villatte, Levin, & Hildebrandt, 2011). Broadly speaking, psychological flexibility is a global behavioral pattern of approaching one's experience with openness and awareness, and of persisting in or changing behavior when doing so serves valued ends. From this conceptual perspective, detoxification is a time during which the promotion of more open, flexible, and values-consistent living is crucial (Stotts, Masuda, & Wilson, 2009).

Psychological flexibility in the context of detoxification can be understood as the extent to which a client openly allows withdrawal symptoms and associated psychological triggers (e.g., anticipatory fear or diminished self-confidence) to occur without acting to change them and while flexibly engaging in values-consistent living (Wilson & Murrell, 2004). In other words, psychological well-being depends on choosing a values-based action in the presence of difficult psychological events. This is a much different experience for most substance-abusing clients, for whom previous treatments have focused primarily on their substance use patterns and consequences.

Struggles are inevitable in life, and these clients are likely to experience the rise and fall of challenges associated with detoxification for many months or even years. As such, the psychological flexibility model implies that there is nothing pathological about having an urge to use, lacking confidence in staying abstinent, or feeling overwhelmed or depressed even after being abstinent for some time. Excessive and inflexible efforts to eliminate, decrease, or regulate withdrawal symptoms and associated triggers are at the core of the detoxification struggle. This inflexible pattern, often called *experiential avoidance*, is negatively reinforced as such efforts result in temporary alleviation of negative affect and distress (Gifford et al., 2004; Hayes, Wilson, Gifford, Follette, & Strosahl, 1996).

During detoxification, some signs of experiential avoidance are readily apparent, while others are quite subtle. It is easy to identify a brief relapse episode as an indicator of a negatively reinforced regulation pattern, in that illicit substances or alcohol are taken to alleviate distress. On the other hand, clients' positive self-statements (e.g., *Stay strong!*), although seemingly aligned with flexible and values-directed living, can be a part of rigid avoidance- and control-based efforts. In the context of detoxification treatment, such self-talk is often used to push away associated fear and anxiety, paradoxically resulting in greater distress. In fact, pertinent literature suggests that this tendency is associated with premature termination of detoxification therapy (Kavanagh, Andrade, & May, 2004; Lejuez et al., 2008). Given the inevitability of withdrawal experiences, learning to stay open to the rise and fall of these experiences—for example, using urge surfing (Bowen & Marlatt, 2009)—may be an alternative behavioral choice that is realistic and effective.

Developing awareness of and openness to experiencing urges to use and other difficult private experiences may appear counterintuitive, and it is important to note that not all efforts to eliminate and downregulate urges are counterproductive in all circumstances. Rather, such efforts become problematic when clients become preoccupied with them, using them exclusively, and particularly if those efforts begin to interfere with values-based living (Wilson & Murrell, 2004). For example, consider engaging in exercise as a way to cope with the unpleasant physical symptoms; although this strategy has merit, if it becomes rigid and excessive, it may begin to interfere with other important life activities, such as relationships and work.

Furthermore, the elimination of negative affect and psychological triggers is not necessary to successfully complete detoxification. These events play a problematic role in the maintenance of substance abuse. However, the behavior-regulatory function of these events is not inherent, but *learned*. As suggested above, clients can learn alternative ways of responding to these unpleasant feelings, without making efforts to eliminate or reduce them.

In sum, the psychological flexibility model is a good fit in the context of detoxification. Its primary contribution is a more workable stance in regard to the physical and psychological discomfort and pain inevitable in detoxification. Many pharmacological and behavioral interventions are developed with the hope of reducing and minimizing these difficult experiences to facilitate treatment completion and maintenance of recovery. However, this is often not possible, as efforts to escape amplify the discomfort even further and ultimately result in relapse to the abused substance. Interestingly, opiate detoxification conducted under general anesthesia to help patients avoid experiencing withdrawal symptoms has not resulted in better outcomes post-detoxification (Gold, Cullen, Gonzales, Houtmeyers, & Dwyer, 1999).

An Acceptance- and Mindfulness-Based Intervention to Promote Detoxification

The primary goal of an acceptance- and mindfulness-based intervention targeting detoxification is to promote quality of life through building mindfulness skills and promoting values-consistent actions (Hayes et al., 2006; Hayes et al., 2011). It is important to emphasize several factors in this approach.

First, given the difficulty involved in initiating and completing detoxification, it is extremely important to tailor the program individually and flexibly to each client and to monitor progress. The strategies clients have used in previous detoxification attempts and their consequences, the motivation behind the current detoxification attempt, clients' expectations about the course of detoxification, and their social support and stability in life should inform the process of planning treatment. Also, as clients experience the rise and fall of detoxification fear and withdrawal symptoms over time, it is important to implement the treatment plan flexibly.

Second, because detoxification treatment is often provided in an interdisciplinary setting, it is important for all members of the treatment team to be in agreement and functioning similarly in regard to treatment goals and adherence to the protocol. Acceptance- and mindfulness-based approaches may be new to treatment staff, and therefore staff training and monitoring are crucial for treatment success.

Third, from a functional and contextual perspective, physical and psychological symptoms are treated as functionally similar: both can elicit control- and avoidance-based coping. When clients insist that their physical symptoms are real, often they mean that they "can't stand it" and thus the symptoms must go away; however, "I can't stand it" is, in part, a psychological reaction. A major treatment goal is to undermine the functional association of both physical and psychological symptoms with control- and avoidance-based coping. The therapist assists in breaking rigid responses (e.g., drug use or treatment dropout) to unpleasant internal experiences while increasing psychological flexibility.

Finally, the therapeutic relationship is crucial for behavior change when using acceptance- and mindfulness-based interventions (Gifford, Ritsher, McKellar, & Moos, 2006). Such a relationship can facilitate therapy sessions that are intimate, personal, and empowering for both clients and therapists, and increase motivation for behavior change (Hayes & Wilson, 1994; Wilson & Murrell, 2004).

An Acceptance- and Mindfulness-Based Treatment Protocol

The following example of an acceptance- and mindfulness-based protocol is primarily drawn from our six-month methadone dose-reduction program for methadone maintenance clients who were willing to enter a research-based detoxification program (Stotts et al., 2009). The content of the protocol is largely based on existing acceptance and commitment therapy manuals (ACT; Hayes, Strosahl, & Wilson, 1999) and previous ACT projects targeting substance use problems (Hayes et al., 2004; Smout et al., 2010). Modifications were made to reflect issues specific to methadone detoxification. As seen in table 8.1, the protocol consisted of three phases, reflecting a typical course of detoxification treatment. Components in these phases should be delivered additively throughout the course of therapy, rather than separately or independently.

Table 8.1 Overview of ACT Components and Strategies

Phase	Components/Strategies	Goals/Purposes
1 Pre-dose-reduction phase	Informed consent and normalizing challenges in detoxification	Clients develop realistic expectations about the course of detoxification (e.g., anticipating varying levels of confidence, withdrawal symptoms, and detoxification fear over time).
	Building the therapeutic relationship	Clients and therapists develop treatment alliances and goals consistent with an acceptance- and mindfulness-based intervention.
	Choosing a valued direction (values clarification)	Clients identify values, begin to align their behavior with a values-directed life, and commit to detoxification.
2 Dose-reduction phase	Shifting perspective	Clients identify difficult psychological events (e.g., anxiety, self-doubt, fear, negative bodily sensations, etc.) and typical coping styles that might serve as obstacles to persistence in dose-reduction and values-consistent actions.
		Clients learn that these coping strategies are control- and avoidance-based, and that efforts to control and avoid problematic private events are counterproductive, functioning as barriers to values-consistent activities.

Phase	Component	Description
	Letting go of struggles	Clients notice that controlling or avoiding difficult private events is not necessary for persisting in detoxification.
		Clients consider an alternative approach to their difficult private events, such as fear of uncertainty or fear of failure.
	Acceptance and mindfulness	Clients learn psychological acceptance as an alternative to avoidance and control.
		Clients choose to be open to or to allow whatever they are experiencing as it is (i.e., acceptance), even difficult physical events.
		Clients learn to observe their private events from a more detached perspective.
		Clients learn not to get sidetracked by their difficult psychological events.
	Commitment to behavior change	Clients progress toward a committed, values-directed life (e.g., the completion of detoxification and early recovery phase).
3 Post-dose-reduction phase and follow-up	Acceptance and behavior change as a whole	Clients continue to practice mindfulness and acceptance in order to live wisely and effectively and to pursue values-consistent actions even when difficult private events occur.

The protocol was designed to utilize twenty-four weekly, fifty-minute individual sessions spanning the six months of the program—a traditional model of therapy. However, the number of treatment sessions and the dose-reduction schedule (rapid vs. gradual dose reduction) can vary depending on factors such as clients' physical safety during detoxification and levels of psychological openness at the outset. The intervention should begin at least a few weeks prior to the beginning of the dose-reduction phase and continue through the post-detoxification period.

Although this protocol utilizes individual sessions, other therapy modalities should be considered. For example, previous studies of ACT for substance abuse have combined individual and group therapy (Hayes et al., 2004), while ACT studies with different populations have had success with more intensive, workshop-based treatments (Gregg, Callaghan, Hayes, & Glenn-Lawson, 2007).

Generally, each session starts with a five- to ten-minute mindfulness exercise (e.g., breathing, sitting still, or noticing and observing thoughts, feelings, or bodily sensations). This exercise is designed to promote a present-moment focus. Session-specific components are introduced using the client's personal experiences related to dose reduction or other life events.

Pre-Dose-Reduction Phase

The stance of acceptance- and mindfulness-based approaches is often counterintuitive to clients, and thus it is important to establish treatment goals and a solid therapeutic relationship at the outset. We inform clients that they may find the treatment program confusing or counterproductive, but that these reactions are expected (Hayes et al., 1999; Hayes et al., 2004). Clients should also be informed that they are likely to experience ups and downs in various psychological and physical challenges (urges, detoxification fear, withdrawal symptoms, lack of confidence, etc.).

Values-focused interventions are also used early, prior to beginning the dose reduction. It is critical to establish the client's personal rationale for entering detoxification for several reasons. For one, clarifying the client's personal values gives the therapy an overarching purpose based on what the client deems most important, and this dignifies the suffering that is inevitable. Further, focusing on values will allow the client to see that detoxification itself is not the end goal; rather, it is a step toward a more fulfilling life. In addition, values and goals clarification, as well as the ACT treatment rationale, are introduced prior to dose reduction to increase motivation and commitment to enter into and persist in detoxification.

Dose-Reduction Phase

As clients enter the dose-reduction phase, they begin to experience emotional distress, sometimes before any significant withdrawal symptoms occur. This is conceptualized as anticipatory fear of detoxification. Because habitual coping reactions to this fear are strongly rooted and often lead directly back to drug use, this phase of the intervention primarily focuses on the workability of avoidant coping strategies and on shifting perspective from avoiding and controlling aversive private events to observing these events and relinquishing the struggle with them (i.e., psychological acceptance). As mentioned elsewhere (Stotts et al., 2009), this is likely the most challenging task for clients who are entering detoxification and facing inevitable suffering. Many clients believe, as most people do, that having negative thoughts and feelings will automatically lead to treatment failure, so they make excessive efforts to not have them by engaging in distraction and self-talk (e.g., *I just have to stay positive!*). Some clients even refuse to talk about their distress in session. Thus, the first step is shifting perspective to the possibility that eliminating these experiences isn't necessary to successfully continuing detoxification. Useful activities during this phase include a series of experiential exercises (e.g., the metaphor Take Your Keys with You; Hayes et al., 1999) and insightful awareness of previous experiences where clients demonstrated values-consistent behavior while having incongruent thoughts and feelings. For example, the therapist might process the client's experience of not using a drug even when having the urge to do so.

Following the shift in perspective, the stance of acceptance and mindfulness is introduced, especially as fears and withdrawal symptoms intensify. Given that the term "acceptance" already has an established nuance implying emotional tolerance ("Suck it up") and being defeated, this word must be used carefully. In therapy, the stance of acceptance is introduced as a behavioral *skill* of willingness or openness to one's internal experiences, including detoxification fear and withdrawal symptoms. The skill is to allow oneself to have these experiences without reacting to them. Experiential exercises, such as Contents on Cards (Hayes et al., 1999), are useful for teaching clients the stance of acceptance through their own experiences. In one version of the Contents on Cards exercise, clients are given an index card with a difficult thought or feeling written on it (e.g., "You can't make it") and are asked to carry it with them at all times, perhaps in a pocket, and to take it out and look at it occasionally. This exercise highlights that acceptance simply means allowing oneself to have a difficult thought without trying to challenge or act on it. Strong negative reactions toward carrying the card are not uncommon. Such reactions fade if clients persist with the exercise.

Commitment to values-directed activities is addressed throughout the detoxification program but becomes particularly crucial when dose reduction results in highly distressing withdrawal symptoms and related emotional struggles (e.g., loss of confidence, fear, pain, or anger). These difficult experiences should be identified, validated, and normalized, and should also be put into context with the aspects of life the client finds most important (i.e., values). Personal values are revisited repeatedly throughout detoxification to strengthen values-directed behavior, including commitment to finishing the program. Additionally, even engagement in ordinary daily activities (e.g., getting out of bed or coming to the treatment clinic) should be acknowledged and encouraged.

Post-Dose-Reduction and Follow-Up Phase

Detoxification in the absence of subsequent treatment is neither cost-effective nor helpful (Epstein, Phillips, & Preston, 2011). Detoxification in and of itself does not typically result in sustained abstinence and should not be considered effective treatment in isolation. Rather, it should be considered the initial stage of treatment, to be followed by further treatment or, at the very least, formal assessment and referral. Relapse is extremely common post-detoxification, making follow-up sessions crucial for monitoring clients' condition, solidifying acceptance and mindfulness skills, and intervening during or following any relapse episodes.

Empirical Evidence for an Acceptance- and Mindfulness-Based Model of Detoxification

This entire volume provides extensive evidence of the effectiveness of ACT and other acceptance- and mindfulness-based interventions for substance use, making a review of those studies superfluous. However, the similarity between a psychological flexibility approach to withdrawal symptoms experienced in detoxification and the growing literature on the use of acceptance strategies in coping with chronic pain is worth noting. Common control-based strategies designed to reduce or eliminate acute or chronic pain (e.g., thought suppression, imaginative distraction, or controlled breathing) are being called into question, particularly when looking beyond the immediate effects of these methods. McCracken (1998) found that greater acceptance of pain was associated with less pain-related anxiety and avoidance, less depression, less physical and psychosocial disability, more daily uptime, and better work status, even after accounting for pain intensity per se. The number of successful randomized trials of ACT for pain has led the American Psychological Association to acknowledge it as an evidence-based treatment for pain (APA Division 12, n.d.).

Specific hypothesized theoretical mechanisms relevant to the detoxification process have also been studied. Individuals who engage in chronic opiate use tend to have greater fear of anxiety and anxiety-related sensations, or anxiety sensitivity (Lejuez, Paulson, Daughters, Bornovalova, & Zvolensky, 2006; Tull, Schulzinger, Schmidt, Zvolensky, & Lejuez, 2007), and MM patients have been shown to be intolerant of distress (Brown, Lejuez, Kahler, & Strong, 2002; Compton, Charuvastra, & Ling, 2001). Avoidance and inflexibility have been found to mediate the effects of ACT on smoking outcomes, while negative affect and withdrawal symptoms did not (Gifford et al., 2004).

Studies of acceptance- and mindfulness-based treatments during the detoxification period per se are just beginning. We conducted a stage I pilot study (Stotts et al., 2009), funded by the National Institute on Drug Abuse, to examine whether an ACT-based intervention targeting relevant mechanisms (i.e., experiential avoidance and detoxification fear) would improve detoxification success rates in MM. The study was a twenty-four-week, randomized, controlled, parallel group pilot trial in which fifty-six male and female opioid-dependent patients currently enrolled in a methadone clinic and seeking detoxification were assigned to one of two possible treatment conditions: an ACT-based opiate detoxification therapy following the protocol described here, or drug counseling (Crits-Christoph et al., 1999). Both were individual therapies and began during a four-week pre-dose-reduction phase, continued through an eighteen-week linear methadone dose-reduction phase, and extended two weeks into the post-dose-reduction period. At the end of twenty-four weeks, all participants were contacted to complete end-of-treatment assessments.

Rates of treatment success (opiate-negative urine drug screen at the end of treatment with no reenrollment in a methadone clinic) were almost double for participants who received the ACT treatment (36.7% for the ACT group vs. 19.2% for the drug counseling group), and were higher than rates reported in previous opiate detoxification studies, which typically have success rates lower than 30% (Dunn et al., 2011). Detoxification fear and psychological inflexibility were higher for participants who failed to successfully complete the detoxification program. These are only preliminary data, but they offer initial support for an approach to detoxification based on building psychological flexibility.

Unique Issues and Challenges

The detoxification phase of treatment can be highly challenging, particularly for patients dependent on opioids, alcohol, or benzodiazepines. Detoxification in and of itself does not typically result in sustained abstinence and should not be considered effective treatment in isolation. Clients who become dependent on one or more drugs, and therefore are in need of detoxification, tend to have extensive substance use histories and long-standing psychological difficulties. These clients find it extremely challenging to bring themselves in contact with thoughts, feelings, and other experiences related to past consequences of drug use, such as trauma, abuse, job or relationship failure, or legal issues. This level of avoidance and an often defensive stance make acceptance- and mindfulness-based therapy highly relevant and applicable, yet quite challenging. These clients are very skilled at avoiding heartfelt discussion about difficult private experiences. In our opiate detoxification treatment study, several clients were unable to tolerate even a five-minute mindfulness exercise. Although at times progress was slow, the experiential exercises and metaphors common to ACT protocols were ideal strategies for working with these avoidance issues.

Many clients entering detoxification have lost jobs, ruined careers, had difficulties with spouses, and have angered children, making identification and clarification of values complicated. In the detoxification phase, clients often experience intense emotions, typically anger, fear, and sadness, related to the consequences of their substance abuse that resulted in entering into treatment. Working constructively to identify values during this initial stage takes patience, persistence, and creativity on the part of the therapist. With some of our clients, the only value they could connect with initially was the potential for personal satisfaction from following through and completing something (the program). Values work tends to be a shaping process wherein the therapist must start with something small and immediately tangible and, over time, work toward uncovering more emotionally and contextually difficult values. Despite these challenges, as discussed earlier, values work is critical to dignifying the suffering client's experience during the detoxification phase of treatment.

Conclusion

Detoxification is a highly challenging experience for both clients and therapists. It is important to remember that in detoxifying from substances, clients are eliminating one of their primary emotion regulation strategies. The idea of being drug-free may be appealing, yet it is sure to be accompanied by anxiety, fear, pain, and sadness. Acceptance and mindfulness theory and strategies bring a unique perspective that can be very powerful in this context.

References

Amato, L., Davoli, M., Ferri, M., Gowing, L., & Perucci, C. A. (2004). Effectiveness of interventions on opiate withdrawal treatment: An overview of systematic reviews. *Drug and Alcohol Dependence, 73,* 219-226.

APA Division 12, Society of Clinical Psychology. (n.d.). Acceptance and commitment therapy for chronic pain. Retrieved February 29, 2012, from www.div12 .org/PsychologicalTreatments/treatments/chronicpain_act.html.

Berger, H., & Schwegler, M. J. (1973). Voluntary detoxification of patients on methadone maintenance. *International Journal of the Addictions, 6,* 1045-1047.

Bowen, S., & Marlatt, A. (2009). Surfing the urge: Brief mindfulness-based intervention for college student smokers. *Psychology of Addictive Behaviors, 23,* 666-671.

Brown, R. A., Lejuez, C. W., Kahler, C. W., & Strong, D. R. (2002). Distress tolerance and duration of past smoking cessation attempts. *Journal of Abnormal Psychology, 111,* 180-185.

Cheek, F. E., Tomarchio, T., Standen, J., & Albahary, R. S. (1973). Methadone plus—a behavior modification training program in self-control for addicts on methadone maintenance. *International Journal of the Addictions, 8,* 969-996.

Compton, P., Charuvastra, V. C., & Ling, W. (2001). Pain intolerance in opioid-maintained former opiate addicts: Effect of long-acting maintenance agent. *Drug and Alcohol Dependence, 63,* 139-146.

Crits-Christoph, P., Siqueland, L., Blaine, J., Frank, A., Luborsky, L., Onken, L. S., et al. (1999). Psychosocial treatments for cocaine dependence: National Institute on Drug Abuse Collaborative Cocaine Treatment Study. *Archives of General Psychiatry, 56,* 493-502.

Dunn, K. E., Sigmon, S. C., Strain, E. C., Heil, S. H., & Higgins, S. T. (2011). The association between outpatient buprenorphine detoxification duration and clinical treatment outcomes: A review. *Drug and Alcohol Dependence, 119,* 1-9.

Eklund, C., Hiltunen, A. J., Melin, L., & Borg, S. (1997). Abstinence fear in methadone maintenance withdrawal: A possible obstacle for getting off methadone. *Substance Use and Misuse, 32,* 779-792.

Epstein, D. H., Phillips, K. A., & Preston, K. L. (2011). Opioids. In P. Ruiz & E. Strain (Eds.), *Substance abuse: A comprehensive textbook.* Philadelphia, PA: Lippincott Williams and Wilkins.

Gifford, E. V., Kohlenberg, B. S., Hayes, S. C., Antonuccio, D. O., Piasecki, M. M., Rasmussen-Hall, M. L., et al. (2004). Acceptance-based treatment for smoking cessation. *Behavior Therapy, 35,* 689-705.

Gifford, E. V., Ritsher, J. B., McKellar, J. D., & Moos, R. H. (2006). Acceptance and relationship context: A model of substance use disorder treatment outcome. *Addiction, 101,* 1167-1177.

Gold, C. G., Cullen, D. J., Gonzales, S., Houtmeyers, D., & Dwyer, M. J. (1999). Rapid opioid detoxification during general anesthesia: A review of 20 patients. *Anesthesiology, 91,* 1639-1647.

Gregg, J. A., Callaghan, G. M., Hayes, S. C., & Glenn-Lawson, J. L. (2007). Improving diabetes self-management through acceptance, mindfulness, and values: A randomized controlled trial. *Journal of Consulting and Clinical Psychology, 75,* 336-343.

Hall, S. M., Loeb, P. C., & Kushner, M. (1984). Methadone dose decreases and anxiety reduction. *Addictive Behaviors, 9,* 11-19.

Hayes, S. C., Luoma, J. B., Bond, F. W., Masuda, A., & Lillis, J. (2006). Acceptance and commitment therapy: Model, processes, and outcomes. *Behaviour Research and Therapy, 44,* 1-25.

Hayes, S. C., Strosahl, K. D., & Wilson, K. G. (1999). *Acceptance and commitment therapy: An experiential approach to behavior change.* New York: Guilford Press.

Hayes, S. C., Villatte, M., Levin, M., & Hildebrandt, M. (2011). Open, aware, and active: Contextual approaches as an emerging trend in the behavioral and cognitive therapies. *Annual Review of Clinical Psychology, 7,* 141-168.

Hayes, S. C., & Wilson, K. G. (1994). Acceptance and commitment therapy: Altering the verbal support for experiential avoidance. *Behavior Analyst, 17,* 289-303.

Hayes, S. C., Wilson, K. G., Gifford, E. V., Bissett, R., Piasecki, M., Batten, S. V., et al. (2004). A preliminary trial of twelve-step facilitation and acceptance and commitment therapy with polysubstance-abusing methadone-maintained opiate addicts. *Behavior Therapy, 35,* 667-688.

Hayes, S. C., Wilson, K. G., Gifford, E. V., Follette, V. M., & Strosahl, K. D. (1996). Experimental avoidance and behavioral disorders: A functional dimensional approach to diagnosis and treatment. *Journal of Consulting and Clinical Psychology, 64,* 1152-1168.

Hernandez-Avila, C. A., & Kranzler, H. R. (2011). Alcohol use disorders. In P. Ruiz & E. Strain (Eds.), *Substance abuse: A comprehensive textbook.* Philadelphia, PA: Lippincott Williams and Wilkins.

Hollands, G. B., & Turecek, J. R. (1980). An evaluation of behaviour therapy programme as an intervention treatment for the fear of withdrawal with heroin-dependent persons. *Drug and Alcohol Dependence, 5,* 153-160.

Kavanagh, D. J., Andrade, J., & May, J. (2004). Beating the urge: Implications of research into substance-related desires. *Addictive Behaviors, 29,* 1359-1372.

Latowsky, M. (1996). Improving detoxification outcomes from methadone maintenance treatment: The interrelationship of affective states and protracted withdrawal. *Journal of Psychoactive Drugs, 28,* 251-257.

Lejuez, C. W., Paulson, A., Daughters, S. B., Bornovalova, M. A., & Zvolensky, M. J. (2006). The association between heroin use and anxiety sensitivity among inner-city individuals in residential drug use treatment. *Behaviour Research and Therapy, 44,* 667-677.

Lejuez, C. W., Zvolensky, M. J., Daughters, S. B., Bornovalova, M. A., Paulson, A., Tull, M. T., et al. (2008). Anxiety sensitivity: A unique predictor of dropout among inner-city heroin and crack/cocaine users in residential substance use treatment. *Behaviour Research and Therapy, 46,* 811-818.

Lenne, M., Lintzeris, N., Breen, C., Harris, S., Hawken, L., Mattick, R., et al. (2001). Withdrawal from methadone maintenance treatment: Prognosis and participant perspectives. *Australian and New Zealand Journal of Public Health, 25,* 121-125.

Magura, S., & Rosenblum, A. (2001). Leaving methadone treatment: Lessons learned, lessons forgotten, lessons ignored. *Mount Sinai Journal of Medicine, 68,* 62-74.

Marsch, L. A. (1998). The efficacy of methadone maintenance interventions in reducing illicit opiate use, HIV risk behavior, and criminality: A meta-analysis. *Addiction, 93,* 515-532.

McCracken, L. M. (1998). Learning to live with the pain: Acceptance of pain predicts adjustment in persons with chronic pain. *Pain, 74,* 21-27.

Milby, J. B., Garrett, C., & Meredith, R. (1980). Iatrogenic phobic disorders in methadone maintenance treated patients. *International Journal of the Addictions, 15,* 737-747.

Milby, J. B., Hohmann, A. A., Gentile, M., Huggins, N., Sims, M. K., McLellan, A. T., et al. (1994). Methadone maintenance outcome as a function of detoxification phobia. *American Journal of Psychiatry, 151,* 1031-1037.

Phillips, G. T., Gossop, M., & Bradley, B. (1986). The influence of psychological factors on the opiate withdrawal syndrome. *British Journal of Psychiatry, 149,* 235-238.

Robles, E., Stitzer, M. L., Strain, E. C., Bigelow, G. E., & Silverman, K. (2002). Voucher-based reinforcement of opiate abstinence during methadone detoxification. *Drug and Alcohol Dependence, 65,* 179-189.

Sees, K. L., Delucchi, K. L., Masson, C., Rosen, A., Clark, H. W., Robillard, H., et al. (2000). Methadone maintenance vs. 180-day psychosocially enriched detoxification for treatment of opioid dependence: A randomized controlled trial. *Journal of the American Medical Association, 283,* 1303-1310.

Smout, M. F., Longo, M., Harrison, S., Minniti, R., Wickes, W., & White, J. M. (2010). Psychosocial treatment for methamphetamine use disorders: A preliminary randomized controlled trial of cognitive behavior therapy and acceptance and commitment therapy. *Substance Abuse, 31,* 98-107.

Stotts, A. L., Masuda, A., & Wilson, K. G. (2009). Using acceptance and commitment therapy during methadone dose reduction: Rationale, treatment description, and a case report. *Cognitive and Behavioral Practice, 16,* 205-213.

Tull, M. T., Schulzinger, D., Schmidt, N. B., Zvolensky, M. J., & Lejuez, C. W. (2007). Development and initial examination of a brief intervention for heightened anxiety sensitivity among heroin users. *Behavior Modification, 31,* 220-242.

Wilson, K. G., & Murrell, A. R. (2004). Values work in acceptance and commitment therapy: Setting a course for behavioral treatment. In S. C. Hayes, V. M. Follette, & M. M. Linehan (Eds.), *Mindfulness and acceptance: Expanding the cognitive-behavioral tradition.* New York: Guilford Press.

CHAPTER 9

Contextual Cognitive Behavioral Therapies for Smoking Cessation: Motivational Interviewing and Acceptance and Commitment Therapy

Jonathan B. Bricker

*Fred Hutchinson Cancer Research Center
and University of Washington*

Christopher M. Wyszynski

Fred Hutchinson Cancer Research Center

Cigarette smoking is a major problem worldwide. In the United States, an estimated 19.3% of adults smoke, and cigarette smoking continues to be the leading cause of preventable death, accounting for approximately 443,000 deaths per year (Centers for Disease Control and Prevention, 2011). Worldwide, there are about 1.4 billion smokers, and cigarette smoking accounts for nearly 6 million annual deaths (Shafey, Eriksen, Ross, & Mackay, 2009). If current smoking trends continue, cigarette smoking will be the cause of an estimated 8 million annual deaths by the year 2030 (Shafey et al., 2009).

To address this problem, pharmacotherapy is often the first method used to help people quit smoking. The most common pharmacological intervention is the nicotine patch (a form of nicotine replacement therapy; NRT), which is designed to reduce nicotine cravings and withdrawal symptoms (Fiore et al., 2008). Other medications include bupropion and nicotine partial agonists, such as varenicline, which are designed to undermine the positively reinforcing functions of cigarette smoking (Cahill, Stead, & Lancaster, 2011). However, varenicline use is associated with a 72% increased risk for cardiovascular complications (Singh, Loke, Spangler, & Furberg, 2011), and the effect sizes for medications are not large. Prescription and over-the-counter NRT have an average six-month quit rate of 7% (Shiffman et al., 2002), and a recent Cochrane Review found the risk ratio of successful abstinence using varenicline versus NRT to be 1.13, suggesting the two treatments may have similar effectiveness (Cahill et al., 2011). The limited effectiveness and serious side effects of pharmacotherapy motivate the need for alternatives. Psychological interventions may be the answer.

Psychological approaches to smoking cessation generally focus on enhancing motivation and social support for quitting, providing basic health information about smoking and quitting, teaching coping skills, and helping smokers set a quit date (Fiore et al., 2008). However, calculations from four Cochrane Reviews of behavioral interventions for smoking cessation have demonstrated that the weighted average of the thirty-day point prevalence quit rates (i.e., not smoking at all in the past thirty days) at the one-year post-intervention follow-up are 14%, and 20% for counseling and a combination of counseling and pharmacotherapy, respectively, *across all modes of intervention delivery* (Lancaster & Stead, 2005; Silagy, Lancaster, Stead, Mant, & Fowler, 2004; Stead & Lancaster, 2005, updated 2009; Stead, Perera, & Lancaster, 2006). While these quit rates are considerably greater than the 4% success rate of those who try to quit on their own (Fiore et al., 2008), the fact that current interventions are failing 80% to 86% of smokers suggests the need for innovative behavioral interventions.

The present chapter will examine motivational interviewing (MI; Miller & Rollnick, 1991, 2002; see also Wagner, Ingersoll, & Rollnick, chapter 5 of this volume) and acceptance and commitment therapy (ACT; Hayes, Strosahl, & Wilson, 2011; see also Wilson, Schnetzer, Flynn, & Kurz, chapter 1 of this volume), two contemporary contextual psychotherapies that hold great promise in helping boost the success of cessation programs. Specifically, MI and ACT share a focus on enhancing commitment to behavior change, working in the medium of clients' language processes to achieve this goal, and using clients' values as a means of enhancing commitment (Hayes et al., 2011; Miller & Rollnick, 1991, 2002). Our primary focus will be on how MI and ACT apply to smoking cessation. We will then examine each intervention's approach to smoking cessation in both face-to-face and non–face-to-face treatment contexts.

Motivational Interviewing: Theory and Clinical Application

Although MI was "not derived from theory, but rather arose from specification of principles underlying intuitive clinical practice" (Hettema, Steele, & Miller, 2005, p. 106), it is consistent with self-perception theory (SPT; Bem, 1972), which posits that individuals infer their attitudes from observing their behavior (e.g., speech), and speech act theory (SAT; Austin, 1962; Searle, 1969), which explains how obligatory language (e.g., "I will stop smoking") can lead to actual behavior change. MI applies SPT by having clients generate arguments for behavior change (change talk) and reduce arguments against change (counter-change talk), and applies SAT by engendering client commitment language. Research has shown that these applications are indeed linked, with client commitment language serving as a mediator of the relationship between change talk and behavior change (Miller & Rose, 2009).

Therapeutic Relationship

In the MI therapeutic relationship, clients are accepted for who they are and are viewed as already possessing the tools necessary for change. As in ACT, any resistance met in the therapist-client interaction is seen not as a flaw of the client, but as a signal that the current interactive process is not conducive to change. If a client says, "I don't need to quit smoking right now," the MI therapist might respond with a reflection that meets the client where that individual is in the change process. For example, the therapist might say "It sounds like you aren't ready to quit smoking now. What do you think you do need now?"

Language in Therapy

MI redirects the client's speech about problematic behaviors through a method summarized by the acronym OARS (Miller & Rollnick, 2002): *open-ended* questions, *affirmation*, listening *reflectively*, and *summarizing*. The therapist asks open-ended questions (e.g., "What are your reasons to quit smoking?"), affirms clients to help them see their strengths and give themselves credit for the progress made in the change process (e.g., "You're doing a great job with not smoking in the car"), listens reflectively to act as a mirror of the client's thoughts (e.g., "You say that a pack of cigarettes is 'big bucks.' And you say you are 'just not sure' if you want to quit"), and summarizes the discussion (e.g., "You say that you are 'just not sure' if you want to quit. And smoking is 'big bucks,' driving your wife 'up the walls' and making you 'winded when going up the stairs.' So what do you make of that?"). Hearing their own arguments for change increases the likelihood that clients will engage in change talk (Moyers, Martin, Houck, Christopher, & Tonigan, 2009).

Values in Therapy

The MI therapist also works with clients to articulate their values, defined as behavioral ideals, preferences for experiences, and how people define themselves (Wagner & Sanchez, 2002) and amplifies the discrepancy between current behavior and clients' values. For example, an MI therapist might say, "You said earlier that you care a lot about your health and your children. And you mentioned just now that you are concerned about how smoking is impacting those areas of your life. What is that telling you?"

Acceptance and Commitment Therapy: Theory and Clinical Application

ACT's theoretical framework is relational frame theory (RFT; Hayes, Barnes-Holmes, & Roche, 2001), which views cognition as learned and

arbitrarily applicable relational responding. RFT suggests that it is difficult to control these relations and that some deliberate control efforts
will result in paradoxical effects and exacerbate the obstacles impeding
behavior change. Accordingly, ACT focuses instead on using acceptance
and mindfulness methods to reduce the automatic impacts of thoughts,
emotions, memories, and sensations on behavior, and works to increase
clients' ability to focus on and engage in behaviors consistent with their
long-term values (for a review, see Hayes et al., 2001).

Therapeutic Relationship

The ACT therapist expresses a sense of shared suffering, values, and
humanity. ACT therapists may use self-disclosure to model an accepting
stance toward their own struggles while maintaining the ability to act in
accordance with their values. For example, if a client is struggling with
thoughts or judgments about quitting, the therapist might say, "Before I
quit smoking, I had a lot of self-doubting thoughts, like *I'm going to fail at
quitting.* The more I believed those thoughts, the more I struggled at quitting smoking. So, I have a feel for what it's like to walk in your shoes."

Language in Therapy

ACT focuses on the use of metaphors and experiential exercises in
order for clients to directly experience ACT processes (Hayes et al.,
2011). An example of a metaphor we use for smoking cessation is the car
journey: "You're the driver and I'm a front-seat passenger, helping you
navigate your way. In the backseat and trunk, like baggage, are all of the
urges, thoughts, and feelings that trigger you to smoke. The goal of this
program to quit smoking is to help you drive in directions that matter to
you, like quitting because of your love for your children, while making
room for the baggage that will come along for the ride."

Values in Therapy

Work on values is the primary method that ACT uses to enhance
motivation to change. Much like driving east in a car, where you never

actually arrive at "east" but you can reach specific destinations (e.g., achieving a goal), values are the directions an individual is headed in life (Hayes, 2005, pp. 153-155). For example, a therapist could ask, "What would you love to do with other people, such as your partner, children, or friends? And how might that help you quit smoking?"

Comparing MI and ACT in Context: Face-to-Face Interventions

While there are differences between MI and ACT, their overlap is noteworthy. MI and ACT can be used as complementary interventions for smoking cessation, and each can utilize the methods of the other to support the aim of creating collaborative, empathetic therapeutic relationships in which nonprescribing language is used to clarify clients' values in order to motivate quitting smoking. These therapies can also be delivered flexibly; in addition to face-to-face interventions, which we explore first, they can also be delivered via phone or the Internet.

Clinical Application of Face-to-Face MI for Smoking Cessation

In a clinical setting, MI therapists focus on exploring the client's feelings, beliefs, and values regarding smoking with the goal of eliciting ambivalence. Once this ambivalence is identified, the clinician will selectively elicit and support change talk (i.e., reasons to quit) and commitment language (e.g., plans to not smoke in the car), with the goal of overcoming ambivalence. To achieve these goals, the MI therapist follows four general principles: expressing empathy, developing discrepancy, rolling with resistance, and supporting self-efficacy. Expressing empathy includes normalizing concerns (e.g., "A lot of people worry about gaining weight after quitting") and supporting the client's right to choose (e.g., "You say you aren't ready to quit; I'm here to help when you are ready"). Developing discrepancy includes reinforcing both change talk (e.g., "You are realizing how smoking is affecting your health") and commitment language (e.g., "You say you really want to quit smoking"). Rolling with resistance includes using reflections when a client expresses resistance (e.g., "Sounds like you're under pressure to quit smoking"). Supporting self-efficacy includes identifying past successes (e.g., "You were able to stay smoke-free from pregnancy until your baby was three months old").

Empirical Evidence for the Effectiveness of Face-to-Face MI for Smoking Cessation

Meta-analyses suggest that, compared to brief advice, MI demonstrates modest but significant increased cessation rates (Hettema & Hendricks, 2010; Lai, Cahill, Qin, & Tang, 2010). However, many of the current MI studies have methodological limitations, such as lack of treatment fidelity and lack of comparable treatment intensity (e.g., Soria, Legido, Escolano, Lopez Yeste, & Montoya, 2006).

Clinical Application of Face-to-Face ACT for Smoking Cessation

An illustration of how ACT is applied in face-to-face clinical contexts is the recently published pilot test of ACT for smoking cessation in a group format (Hernandez-Lopez, Luciano, Bricker, Roales-Nieto, & Montesinos, 2009). The program focused on the following four key components:

- **Analyzing the personal costs of smoking as an attempt to control private events.** The program looked at how smoking was a control strategy that, in the short run, served to reduce urges or distress. The therapist illustrated how trying to control thoughts, emotions, and sensations, in this case by smoking, might have negative effects on certain valued life domains (e.g., health, family).

- **Values clarification and commitment with personal choices.** The program helped participants articulate how quitting would help them live a more meaningful life. They were shown how to take specific actions to quit (e.g., setting a quit date) and to notice psychological barriers to these actions (e.g., fear of withdrawal).

- **Defusion and willingness to experience and accept private aversive events.** The program helped participants notice internal triggers (e.g., urges) and external triggers (e.g., other people who smoke) that led them to smoke and to differentiate among those they could change (e.g., throwing away ashtrays) and those they could not (e.g., being sad). The goal was to break the link between triggers and smoking behavior—to see urges as urges, not as the cause of smoking.

- **Relapse as part of the process of quitting.** No explicit distinction was made between lapse and relapse. Participants were helped to notice when they weren't moving in the direction they wanted to travel and then to get back to moving in that direction regardless of the intensity of lapse.

Empirical Evidence for the Effectiveness of Face-to-Face ACT for Smoking Cessation

Although empirical evidence for face-to-face ACT for smoking cessation is limited, the results that do exist are promising. One study compared group therapy ACT plus bupropion with physician-delivered bupropion (Gifford et al., 2011). The intent-to-treat twelve-month analysis showed that the ACT intervention had a quit rate of 32%, versus 18% in the comparison group. The second study compared group therapy ACT to CBT (both without pharmacotherapy) for adult smoking cessation (Hernandez-Lopez et al., 2009). The intent-to-treat twelve-month thirty-day point prevalence quit rate was 30% in the ACT group, versus 13% in the CBT group. Finally, an individual plus group therapy ACT intervention with no nicotine patch was compared to the nicotine patch with no behavioral treatment (Gifford et al., 2004). ACT participants demonstrated higher levels of acceptance of internal smoking cues and had a twenty-four-hour biochemically supported abstinence rate of 21%, versus 9% in the nicotine patch group. Each of these studies had methodological limitations (e.g., the lack of a behavioral control group or having a small number of subjects). We are now developing and testing a group-delivered ACT intervention in a fully powered randomized trial.

Comparing MI and ACT in Context: Telephone Interventions

Smoking cessation interventions delivered by telephone are an exciting application of MI and ACT. Smoking cessation telephone quitlines are an important and cost-effective part of US tobacco control programs. Additionally, telephone interventions save millions of dollars in medical costs and productivity losses (Fiore et al., 2004), and are relatively brief, with an average total intervention length of ninety minutes (Stead et al., 2006). Smoking cessation quitlines are available in all fifty US states, Canada, western Europe, and Australia, and their availability continues to grow throughout the world.

Clinical Application of Telephone-Delivered MI for Smoking Cessation

MI for smoking cessation has been delivered via telephone—for example, in a recent study that focused on high-school seniors who smoked at least monthly (Peterson et al., 2009). Using MI, the counselor strategically led discussions with the goal of moving the smoker toward making a quit attempt. Building motivation was focused on enhancing both the importance of quitting and the confidence to quit. To increase the importance of quitting, the therapist might say, "Sounds like it's important to you to not smoke around your younger sister. Tell me more about that." To build confidence to quit smoking, the therapist might say, "You said you once stopped smoking for three days. That's great. What helped you do that?" There was no preset timeline for the quit attempt to occur. The pace was set by the participant, as was the decision to quit.

Empirical Evidence for the Effectiveness of Telephone-Delivered MI for Smoking Cessation

One study of telephone-delivered MI for smoking cessation compared three randomly assigned groups: one fifteen-minute MI call, one thirty- to forty-minute initial call and one brief follow-up call, and one thirty- to forty-minute initial call and up to four follow-up calls (Hollis et al., 2007). All three interventions were done in two conditions: with and without nicotine replacement therapy. The results showed that the two more intense interventions resulted in increased cessation rates, with the NRT condition producing a similar proportional increase of quit rates across all levels of the behavioral intervention.

In a second study of telephone-delivered MI, participants were drawn from fifty different Washington state high schools and were randomized into either a proactive phone intervention with MI and cognitive behavioral skills training components, or a no-intervention control group (Peterson et al., 2009). Among adolescent daily smokers, the group receiving the intervention had greater six-month abstinence rates (10.1%) than the control group (5.9%). A follow-up mediational analysis found that the MI component might have increased commitment to quitting (Bricker, Liu, et al., 2010). While results from both studies are encouraging, it is unclear whether the effects were due to MI per se or a result of more contact time with the interventionist.

Clinical Application of Telephone-Delivered ACT for Smoking Cessation

We recently developed an initial version of a telephone-based ACT intervention for smoking cessation (Bricker, Mann, Marek, Liu, & Peterson, 2010). The intervention provided up to five scheduled counseling sessions (an average of thirty minutes for the first call and an average of fifteen minutes for all following calls), with a total of ninety minutes per participant. Scheduling was flexible, though the calls usually occurred every seven days at the same time each day. Delivery was conversational, and each core ACT process was flexibly covered according to the immediate needs of the participant. Nonetheless, each call focused on specific core ACT processes, as outlined below.

Call 1 focused on the core ACT processes of values (i.e., life purposes driving quitting), acceptance (i.e., willingness to experience smoking triggers without acting on them), and committed action (i.e., specific action plans in the service of values that support quitting). To learn clients' values, we started by asking two questions: "Why do you want to quit now?" and "What makes that important to you?" To address acceptance and committed action, we asked a question like "Each time you have an urge this week, can you ask yourself this question: 'How willing am I to have an urge and not smoke?'"

Call 2 focused on the ACT processes of being present (i.e., nonjudgmentally noticing, in the present moment, sensations, thoughts, and emotions that act as triggers for smoking) and committed action. The counselor led a five-minute exercise in being present using the breath as a focus: "Now just take some slow, deep breaths in and out. (Pause.) Notice the feeling of the air as it comes in and goes out."

Call 3 focused on the ACT processes of cognitive defusion (i.e., recognizing thoughts as just words and pictures, not as reality) and committed action. For example, if stress was a trigger for smoking, the counselor might have suggested that, together, they repeat the word "stress" on the phone for ninety seconds. The counselor would then suggest that the participant repeat the exercise on the phone.

Call 4 focused on the ACT processes of self-as-context (i.e., the unchanging part of the self that observes what one experiences) and committed action. For example, the counselor would build on exercises in being present by adding a focus on the process of noticing (e.g., "noticing breathing," "noticing thinking," "noticing feeling").

Call 5 reviewed material from prior calls and finalized a committed action plan for quitting. For example, the counselor might say, "Our goal today is to keep you on course as you continue to travel on your journey of quitting smoking and staying quit. Staying on course means making a plan that ties together all of the work we've done up until now. Remember those action plans we developed in our prior calls? Well, now we're going to take those plans that worked best for you and put them all on one piece of paper. How does that sound to you?"

Empirical Evidence for the Effectiveness of Telephone-Delivered ACT for Smoking Cessation

The first-ever study of telephone-delivered ACT was recently conducted in a small single-arm feasibility study of smoking cessation (Bricker, Mann, et al., 2010). Participants showed a potential increase in acceptance of physical cravings, emotions, and thoughts that cue smoking and were more committed to quitting. The twelve-month post-treatment intent-to-treat analysis found that 29% of participants had not smoked within the past twelve months. This is similar to the face-to-face results for ACT reported earlier and is over double the 14% average cessation rate for telephone interventions (Stead et al., 2006). We also found that our ACT intervention could be delivered with fidelity by telephone (Schimmel-Bristow, Bricker, & Comstock, 2012). A randomized trial of telephone ACT is now underway.

Comparing MI and ACT in Context: Web-Based Interventions

Smoking cessation websites are now reaching millions of adults twenty-four hours a day (Fiore et al., 2000; Fiore et al., 2008). Cessation websites that utilize the U.S. Clinical Practice Guidelines offer quit planning, skills training, advice on FDA-approved pharmacotherapy, and social support for quitting (Fiore et al., 2000; Fiore et al., 2008). Currently, 77% of US adults use the Internet, and historical trends show that this proportion will increase (Pew Internet and American Life Project, 2011). Web-based interventions provide a viable intervention modality for smokers who want to quit, especially because of their high reach: They are a highly accessible alternative to traditional modalities (e.g., group or individual counseling); they can be accessed anytime and anywhere if an Internet connection is available; and they don't require health insurance (Civljak, Sheikh, Stead, & Car, 2010; Hutton et al., 2011).

Web-Delivered MI for Smoking Cessation

We are not aware of any published study of web-delivered MI intervention for smoking cessation. However, a study investigating the efficacy of an online MI smoking cessation intervention as compared to a more prescriptively toned web-based intervention is in development (J. B. McClure, personal communication, July 27, 2011).

Web-Delivered ACT for Smoking Cessation

No studies to date have been reported on web-based ACT for smoking cessation. However, we are now developing and pilot testing a self-paced, eight-part web-based smoking cessation intervention program. A major theme is self-compassion. Several metaphors and exercises emphasize the message that quitting smoking is a difficult process, and invite users to be patient and forgiving of themselves.

- To target ACT's core process of values and how they might guide quitting, part 1 contains a series of web-based video testimonials from former smokers describing how quitting smoking has changed their lives in fundamental ways.

- To target ACT's process of committed action, part 2 has users apply core values that guide quitting toward a personalized plan for quitting; this part includes a flexible menu of options for stopping smoking and current best-practice–based advice on choosing medications to quit smoking. Users can update this plan as they progress through the program.

- To target ACT's core processes of acceptance, present-moment awareness, cognitive defusion, and self-as-context, in parts 3 through 7 we developed a series of videos in which former smokers model key ACT exercises and metaphors focused on accepting the urges, emotions, and thoughts that trigger smoking. Users are invited to practice each set of exercises daily for seven days and then return to the website to learn the next set of exercises. In addition to watching the videos, users can also read texts of the testimonials, metaphors, and exercises. In parts 3 through 7, relapse is presented as part of the process of quitting. Participants are invited to notice when they have detoured from the direction they wanted to follow, and then to get back to traveling in their valued direction regardless of the intensity of the lapse (i.e., whether they had smoked a single puff or resumed smoking for some time). Participants are informed that if they lapse, they can set another quit date, and that each attempt will give them opportunities to practice ACT skills on the path to quitting.

- Part 8 invites users to review their progress in learning skills and in quitting smoking. Users can complete several worksheets and exercises to apply what they learned from the videos.

Future Directions

Better controlled research is needed to provide confidence in the utility of these new methods. Methodological issues such as measurement of treatment fidelity, high recruitment and retention, equalizing dosing, and adequate statistical power need to be addressed. Data on theory-based mechanisms of these smoking cessation interventions would provide insights into how to improve their effectiveness. The combination of MI and ACT provides another exciting future direction in smoking cessation interventions.

Another key direction is applying technology to deliver the treatments. With approximately 71% of developed countries using the Internet (International Telecommunication Union, 2010), web-based programs might prove to be an effective vehicle for delivering smoking cessation interventions. Randomized controlled trials comparing MI-based and ACT-based web interventions with popular online smoking cessation programs would help developers effectively structure websites to increase cessation rates. Similarly, 35% of Americans use smartphones (Smith, 2011), and about 65% of Americans are expected to have a smartphone or tablet in 2015 (In-Stat, 2011, as cited in Reisinger, 2011). Developing and testing MI and ACT smoking cessation applications for smartphones would provide a convenient, handheld medium through which to deliver these interventions.

Conclusion

MI and ACT show great promise in improving the quit rates of smoking cessation interventions. If well-designed studies prove MI and ACT to be effective, then both therapies stand to make a strong impact by increasing abstinence rates and providing current smokers with new options to help them quit.

Acknowledgments

This chapter was written with support from NIH Grants 5R01CA151251 -02 and 1R21DA030646-01A1.

References

Austin, J. L. (1962). *How to do things with words.* Cambridge, MA: Harvard University Press.

Bem, D. J. (1972). Self-perception theory. In L. Berkowitz (Ed.), *Advances in experimental social psychology* (Vol. 6). New York: Academic Press.

Bricker, J. B., Liu, J., Comstock, B. A., Peterson, A. V., Kealey, K. A., & Marek, P. M. (2010). Social cognitive mediators of adolescent smoking cessation: Results from a large randomized intervention trial. *Psychology of Addictive Behaviors, 24,* 436-445.

Bricker, J. B., Mann, S. L., Marek, P. M., Liu, J., & Peterson, A. V. (2010). Telephone-delivered acceptance and commitment therapy for adult smoking cessation: A feasibility study. *Nicotine and Tobacco Research, 12,* 454-458.

Cahill, K., Stead, L. F., & Lancaster, T. (2011). Nicotine receptor partial agonists for smoking cessation. *Cochrane Database of Systematic Reviews, 2,* CD006103.

Centers for Disease Control and Prevention. (2011). Vital signs: Current cigarette smoking among adults aged $\geq$ 18 years—United States, 2005–2010. *Morbidity and Mortality Weekly Report, 60,* 1207-1212.

Civljak, M., Sheikh, A., Stead, L. F., & Car, J. (2010). Internet-based interventions for smoking cessation. *Cochrane Database of Systematic Reviews, 9,* CD007078.

Fiore, M. C., Bailey, W. C., Cohen, S. J., Dorfman, S. F., Goldstein, M. G., Gritz, E. R., et al. (2000). *Treating tobacco use and dependence.* Clinical practice guideline. Rockville, MD: U.S. Department of Health and Human Services, Public Health Service.

Fiore, M. C., Croyle, R. T., Curry, S. J., Cutler, C. M., Davis, R. M., Gordon, C., et al. (2004). Preventing 3 million premature deaths and helping 5 million smokers quit: A national action plan for tobacco cessation. *American Journal of Public Health, 94,* 205-210.

Fiore, M. C., Jaén, C. R., Baker, T. B., Bailey, W. C., Benowitz, N. L., Curry, S. J., et al. (2008). *Treating tobacco use and dependence: 2008 update.* Clinical practice guideline. Rockville, MD: U.S. Department of Health and Human Services, Public Health Service.

Gifford, E. V., Kohlenberg, B. S., Hayes, S. C., Antonuccio, D. O., Piasecki, M. M., Rasmussen-Hall, M. L., et al. (2004). Acceptance-based treatment for smoking cessation. *Behavior Therapy, 35,* 689-705.

Gifford, E. V., Kohlenberg, B. S., Hayes, S. C., Pierson, H. M., Piasecki, M. P., Antonuccio, D. O., et al. (2011). Does acceptance and relationship focused behavior therapy contribute to bupropion outcomes? A randomized controlled trial of functional analytic psychotherapy and acceptance and commitment therapy for smoking cessation. *Behavior Therapy, 42,* 700-715.

Hayes, S. C., with Smith, S. (2005). *Get out of your mind and into your life: The new acceptance and commitment therapy.* Oakland, CA: New Harbinger.

Hayes, S. C., Barnes-Holmes, D., & Roche, B. (2001). *Relational frame theory: A post-Skinnerian account of human language and cognition.* New York: Plenum Press.

Hayes, S. C., Strosahl, K. D., & Wilson, K. G. (2011). *Acceptance and commitment therapy: The process and practice of mindful change* (2nd ed.). New York: Guilford Press.

Hernandez-Lopez, M., Luciano, M. C., Bricker, J. B., Roales-Nieto, J. G., & Montesinos, F. (2009). Acceptance and commitment therapy for smoking cessation: A preliminary study of its effectiveness in comparison with cognitive behavioral therapy. *Psychology of Addictive Behaviors, 23,* 723-730.

Hettema, J. E., & Hendricks, P. S. (2010). Motivational interviewing for smoking cessation: A meta-analytic review. *Journal of Consulting and Clinical Psychology, 78,* 868-884.

Hettema, J. E., Steele, J., & Miller, W. R. (2005). Motivational interviewing. *Annual Review of Clinical Psychology, 1,* 91-111.

Hollis, J. F., McAfee, T. A., Fellows, J. L., Zbikowski, S. M., Stark, M., & Riedlinger, K. (2007). The effectiveness and cost effectiveness of telephone counselling and the nicotine patch in a state tobacco quitline. *Tobacco Control, 16,* Suppl 1, i53-i59.

Hutton, H. E., Wilson, L. M., Apelberg, B. J., Tang, E. A., Odelola, O., Bass, E. B., et al. (2011). A systematic review of randomized controlled trials: Web-based interventions for smoking cessation among adolescents, college students, and adults. *Nicotine and Tobacco Research, 13,* 227-238.

International Telecommunication Union. (2010). The world in 2010. Retrieved March 1, 2012, from http.itu.int/ITU-D/ict/material/FactsFigures2010.pdf.

Lai, D. T., Cahill, K., Qin, Y., & Tang, J. L. (2010). Motivational interviewing for smoking cessation. *Cochrane Database of Systematic Reviews, 1,* CD006936.

Lancaster, T., & Stead, L. F. (2005). Individual behavioural counselling for smoking cessation. *Cochrane Database of Systematic Reviews, 2,* CD001292.

Miller, W. R., & Rollnick, S. (1991). *Motivational interviewing: Preparing people to change addictive behavior.* New York: Guilford Press.

Miller, W. R., & Rollnick, S. (2002). *Motivational interviewing: Preparing people for change* (2nd ed.). New York: Guilford Press.

Miller, W. R., & Rose, G. S. (2009). Toward a theory of motivational interviewing. *American Psychologist, 64,* 527-537.

Moyers, T. B., Martin, T., Houck, J. M., Christopher, P. J., & Tonigan, J. S. (2009). From in-session behaviors to drinking outcomes: A causal chain for motivational interviewing. *Journal of Consulting and Clinical Psychology, 77,* 1113-1124.

Peterson, A. V., Jr., Kealey, K. A., Mann, S. L., Marek, P. M., Ludman, E. J., Liu, J., et al. (2009). Group-randomized trial of a proactive, personalized telephone counseling intervention for adolescent smoking cessation. *Journal of the National Cancer Institute, 101,* 1378-1392.

Pew Internet and American Life Project. (2011). Demographics of Internet users. Retrieved July 25, 2011, from http.pewinternet.org/Static-Pages/Trend-Data/Whos-Online.aspx.

Reisinger, D. (2011). In-Stat: Majority in U.S. to have smartphones, tablets by 2015. CNET News, August 23, 2011. Retrieved November 17, 2011, from http://news.cnet.com/8301-13506_3-20095949-17/in-stat-majority-in-u.s-to-have-smart phones-tablets-by-2015/.

Schimmel-Bristow, A. G., Bricker, J. B., & Comstock, B. A. (2012). Can acceptance and commitment therapy be delivered with fidelity as a brief telephone-intervention? *Addictive Behaviors, 34,* 517-520.

Searle, J. R. (1969). *Speech acts: An essay in the philosophy of language.* London: Cambridge University Press.

Shafey, O., Eriksen, M., Ross, H., & Mackay, J. (2009). *The tobacco atlas* (3rd ed.). Atlanta, GA: American Cancer Society.

Shiffman, S., Rolf, C. N., Hellebusch, S. J., Gorsline, J., Gorodetzky, C. W., Chiang, Y. K., et al. (2002). Real-world efficacy of prescription and over-the-counter nicotine replacement therapy. *Addiction, 97,* 505-516.

Silagy, C., Lancaster, T., Stead, L., Mant, D., & Fowler, G. (2004). Nicotine replacement therapy for smoking cessation. *Cochrane Database of Systematic Reviews, 3,* CD000146.

Singh, S., Loke, Y. K., Spangler, J. G., & Furberg, C. D. (2011). Risk of serious adverse cardiovascular events associated with varenicline: A systematic review and meta-analysis. *Canadian Medical Association Journal, 183*, 1359-1366.

Smith, A. (2011). Smartphone adoption and usage. Pew Internet and American Life Project. Retrieved July 21, 2011, from http://pewinternet.org/Reports/2011 /Smartphones.aspx.

Soria, R., Legido, A., Escolano, C., Lopez Yeste, A., & Montoya, J. (2006). A randomised controlled trial of motivational interviewing for smoking cessation. *British Journal of General Practice, 56*, 768-774.

Stead, L. F., & Lancaster, T. (2005, updated 2009). Group behaviour therapy programmes for smoking cessation. *Cochrane Database of Systematic Reviews, 2*, CD001007.

Stead, L. F., Perera, R., & Lancaster, T. (2006). Telephone counselling for smoking cessation. *Cochrane Database of Systematic Reviews, 3*, CD002850.

Wagner, C. C., & Sanchez, F. P. (2002). The role of values in motivational interviewing. In W. R. Miller & S. Rollnick (Eds.), *Motivational interviewing: Preparing people for change* (2nd ed.). New York: Guilford Press.

CHAPTER 10

Mindfulness-Based Therapy for Problem Gambling

Tony Toneatto

University of Toronto

With prevalence estimates of pathological gambling ranging between 1% and 2% of the population of the United States and Canada (Shaffer, Hall, & Vander Bilt, 1999), and an additional 5% to 6% of the population experiencing significant gambling problems, there is a need for effective treatments for this increasingly common disorder. Recent critical reviews of controlled research of gambling (e.g., Hodgins & Holub, 2007) have concluded that cognitive behavioral treatments show the greatest therapeutic benefits and promise. These reviews have demonstrated that most gambling treatments typically include a *behavioral* component, directed at reducing the stimulus cue properties of gambling activities and venues, and a *cognitive* component, directed at the maladaptive beliefs frequently held by gamblers. While cognitive behavioral therapies for problem gambling can be effective (Pallesen, Mitsem, Kvale, Johnsen, & Molde, 2005), significant proportions of gamblers who receive these treatments do not make substantial progress. A recent review of randomized trials of cognitive behavioral therapy showed that substantial improvements were obtained by less than half of the participants. While much remains to be learned about the most effective ways to treat problem gambling (Toneatto & Millar, 2004), it is known that the gamblers' responses to gambling-related thoughts and emotions play a significant role in treatment outcomes. For example, irrational beliefs and negative affect are predictive of treatment failure among problem gamblers (Daughters, Lejuez, Lesieur, Strong, & Zvolensky, 2003).

Limitations to Current Treatments for Problem Gambling

Reviews of the treatment literature (Pallesen et al., 2005; Petry, 2005; Toneatto & Ladouceur, 2003) have identified several limitations to traditional cognitive or cognitive behavioral approaches to treating problem gamblers. A major challenge in the development of effective treatments for gambling problems is the presence of rigid and dysfunctional beliefs and attitudes about gambling (e.g., Hodgins & el-Guebaly, 2004; Toneatto, 1999). Many gambling-related distortions can be very resistant to restructuring (e.g., *I still believe I will find a winning system* or *God will help me win*), despite intellectual understanding and efforts at cognitive restructuring (Toneatto & Gunaratne, 2009). Gamblers may not always be aware of all the various distortions that could influence their gambling behavior, since many may be ego-syntonic and consistent with their worldview (e.g., *If you really want something, you will get it*). Some gambling distortions may express dysfunctional schemas related to the gambler's self-concept or character pathology, and these may not be easily identified or modified within a brief treatment (e.g., exaggerated belief in one's uniqueness or a sense of entitlement). Despite the relative efficacy of cognitive behavioral treatments (Petry, 2005), substantial numbers of gamblers continue to drop out of treatment prematurely, even from very brief treatments, or report high rates of relapse. Thus, additional approaches to engaging and treating problem gamblers should be explored.

Cognitive Psychology of Problem Gambling

Gambling-related cognitive psychopathology is a well-substantiated feature of problem gambling (e.g., Joukhador, Maccallum, & Blaszczynski,

2003; Petry, 2005; Toneatto & Nguyen, 2007). The core or primary cognitive distortion or schema among problem gamblers may be defined as the conviction that there exists a reliable method to either predict or control gambling outcomes. This core distortion may give rise to a multitude of erroneous gambling beliefs (e.g., related to luck, winning systems, chasing losses, attribution biases, or memory distortions), which can lead to persistence in gambling (e.g., Benhsain, Taillefer, & Ladouceur, 2004) and precipitate relapse (Hodgins & el-Guebaly, 2004).

It is often difficult to modify or restructure these beliefs or reduce gamblers' convictions regarding the validity of gambling-related cognitions using traditional, content-focused therapies such as cognitive behavioral therapy. Problem gamblers typically have a high level of belief in the validity of their gambling-related cognitions, increasing the likelihood of engaging in gambling behavior even when it is highly imprudent (Ladouceur, 2004). Untreated, such beliefs may reduce the impact of treatment and serve as potent triggers for relapse (e.g., Hodgins & el-Guebaly, 2004).

In order to improve gambling treatment outcomes, alternative conceptualizations of problem gambling, gambling-related cognitions, and effective therapy need to be considered. Instead of directly modifying gambling-related cognitions, an alternative approach might address how such cognitions are construed. One such alternative focuses on the nature of the relationship between the gambler and gambling-related beliefs and attitudes that can be described as cognitive fusion or thought-action fusion, wherein cognitive events are responded to literally or with the conviction that beliefs and thoughts can directly influence external events (Hayes, Strosahl, & Wilson, 1999).

This alternative typifies mindfulness approaches to clinical disorders, which strive to reduce cognitive fusion and teach clients that their own cognitive processes are neither veridical nor necessarily related to, or reflective of, external, objective reality. Some of the methods covered in the present volume, such as motivational interviewing (Wagner, Ingersoll, & Rollnick, chapter 5 of this volume), have been tested in randomized controlled trials with problematic gambling (e.g., Diskin & Hodgins, 2009), but the focus of the present chapter will be explicitly on mindfulness-based methods.

Mindfulness Meditation: Core Characteristics and Possible Relevance to Problem Gambling

Mindfulness and meditation, although often conflated and equated, describe distinct activities and processes. Not all meditation is mindful, as meditation encompasses a range of mental disciplines, while the development of mindfulness does not necessarily require formal meditation (Hayes, Follette, & Linehan, 2004). Buddhist teachings on classical mindfulness, recognized in all Buddhist traditions, identify two major types of meditative practice: concentration or tranquility meditation, and insight or mindfulness meditation. While different Buddhist traditions may emphasize either concentration or insight, in practice mindfulness meditation typically combines both.

Traditionally, concentration practices are intended to regulate attention; to this end, practitioners learn to sustain bare attention on the breath as the object of meditation while remaining simultaneously aware of the body and mind (Wallace, 1999). Such bare attention permits the awareness of subjective experience devoid of the projections and associations with which we automatically perceive such experience (Thera, 1973). When a cognitive event distracts attention from the breath (or any other object of meditation), introspective awareness is applied to label the distraction, and attention is then once again returned to the breath. Through such repeated labeling, the process of the arising of subjectivity is separated from the specific content of that subjectivity. On their own, concentration practices do not directly enhance mindfulness but actually encourage the opposite (i.e., fusion, merger, or one-pointed focus), and as a result they are associated with tranquility and calm. However, such practices form the necessary context within which mindfulness meditative practices, discussed next, are rooted.

Meditation can also take the form of introspective awareness directed toward subjective experience in order to discern its intrinsic or veridical nature or quality. Understood this way, the insight or mindfulness aspect of meditation is stressed. Through the moment-to-moment experience of subjectivity within the context of the mental stability and tranquility induced by concentration practices, the transient, conditioned, and constructed nature of subjective experience is directly observed. In this way, mindfulness practice can enhance awareness of habitual patterns of preoccupation with maladaptive mental content.

When the cultivation of sustained, repeated, and increasingly extended periods of attention on an object through concentration practices (bare attention) is integrated with introspective insight awareness, a deeper understanding of the moment-to-moment arising of subjectivity is achieved (Rapgay & Bystrisky, 2009).

Both the concentration and insight aspects of mindfulness meditation can have clinical benefits for individuals struggling with problem gambling, especially if problem gambling is construed as a cognitive disorder. Although contemporary psychiatry defines problem gambling as an impulse disorder, there has been considerable confusion and inconsistency in developing an accurate conceptualization of problem gambling (Petry, 2005). This is not surprising given the clinical heterogeneity of this disorder, which likely reflects several distinct aspects of psychopathology (e.g., impulsive, compulsive, obsessional, and addictive). For the purposes of this chapter, problem gambling can most profitably be considered a cognitive disorder insofar as the most unique feature of problem gambling is not the gaming behaviors, per se, which are legal, widely available, and socially acceptable behaviors, but the highly dysfunctional beliefs, attitudes, and thoughts that problem gamblers maintain about this activity. While interventions that do not address the cognitive basis of problem gambling tend to be less successful, the empirically supported treatments that do target cognitive variables show considerable room for improvement. This provides a compelling rationale for considering mindfulness-based approaches, since this family of interventions also focuses on the cognitive aspects of problem gambling; however, instead of directly attempting to modify or restructure gambling-related thoughts and feelings, the emphasis is on developing a decentered attitude to these thoughts and feelings.

Learning to relate differently to gambling cognitions may be as important as, if not more important than, challenging the specific contents of the thoughts as in traditional cognitive behavioral therapy. In a sample of video lottery players, Ladouceur (2004) showed that the raw frequency of erroneous perceptions related to gambling did not distinguish problem from non-problem gamblers. Instead, problem gamblers were more convinced of, or attached to, the seeming truth of their erroneous gambling-related perceptions than non-problem gamblers, and their conviction increased as they gambled.

Mindfulness Meditation and Recovery from Problem Gambling

Promising approaches for applying mindfulness to problem gambling include mindfulness-based stress reduction (MBSR; Kabat-Zinn, 1990), mindfulness-based relapse prevention (MBRP; Bowen, Chawla, & Marlatt, 2011; see also Bowen, Witkiewitz, & Chawla, chapter 3 of this volume), and acceptance and commitment therapy (ACT; Hayes et al., 1999; see also Wilson, Schnetzer, Flynn, & Kurz, chapter 1 of this volume), all of which have been shown to reduce psychological morbidity associated with chronic illnesses, as well as emotional and behavioral disorders (see Shapiro & Carlson, 2009, and Chiesa, 2010, for reviews of the mindfulness literature). Bowen and colleagues (2011) have described the application of MBSR to addictive behaviors in general and, by extension, to problem gambling.

While no studies to date have evaluated the effectiveness of mindfulness in specifically reducing problem gambling, there are correlational and treatment studies showing a connection between mindfulness and gambling. A key point is that dispositional mindfulness and gambling pathology are related. Lakey, Campbell, Brown, and Goodie (2007) found that trait mindfulness was inversely correlated with gambling pathology and positively predicted more successful judgment and risk-taking performance on the Iowa Gambling Task (IGT; Bechara, Damasio, Damasio, & Anderson, 1994). Most significantly, the link between mindfulness and lower gambling pathology was partially mediated by better performance on these measures of gambling-related judgment and decision-making processes. Furthermore, a recent matched intervention trial (Alfonso, Caracuel, Delgado-Pastor, & Verdejo-García, 2011) compared treatment as usual to mindfulness meditation plus goal management training for polysubstance abusers. Those in the mindfulness condition improved on the IGT, suggesting that mindfulness meditation improves executive functions and decision making relevant to problem gambling.

Despite the absence of a body of empirical research, the highly cognitive nature of problem gambling would indicate that mindfulness meditation can be considered a potentially important component of treatment, for five key reasons.

First, the emphasis on modifying the relationship between individuals and their subjectivity rather than focusing on the content of cognitions is a particularly beneficial contribution of mindfulness interventions for this disorder (de Lisle, Dowling, & Allen, 2011). Mindfulness meditation facilitates a detached awareness of subjective experiences (e.g., thoughts, feelings, and sensations), an especially beneficial skill for those in early gambling recovery, for whom subjective awareness can be unpleasant, overwhelming, and distressing (due to realization of devastating financial ruin or damaged interpersonal relationships, for example). Concentration practices in particular may help problem gamblers learn to shift their awareness to the present, away from dwelling on negative consequences, and interrupt ruminative patterns that can exacerbate negative affective states.

Mindfulness also encourages an attitude of skepticism regarding the veridicality of gambling-related cognition and reduces the intensity of the conviction that such thoughts, as compelling as they may appear, are true and valid reflections of empirical reality (de Lisle et al., 2011). Mindfulness practice can help distinguish between mental events and responses to them, providing the gambler with a choice about how to best respond to gambling-related cognition, rather than simply reacting to them.

Second, the tendency for gamblers to rapidly and impulsively modify aversive subjective experiences (e.g., negative affect, urges, or boredom) by relying on the cognition-altering qualities of gambling activity can be modified through mindfulness practice, which encourages subjectivity, especially toward undesirable experiences, focusing on observation, description, awareness, and nonjudgment of such experience. Through guided mindfulness practice, insight into the impermanent and transitory nature of gambling-related cognitions is facilitated (e.g., Toneatto, Vettese, & Nguyen, 2007). The outcome of such practice is an awareness-based response in the presence of gambling triggers and high-risk situations, rather than behavior that is merely reactive, conditioned, impulsive, or automatic.

Third, mindfulness may improve the ability to cope with urges and cravings, which present an inevitable and serious threat to stable recovery, by applying a nonjudgmental, accepting, patient response to urges that demonstrates their vicissitudes and impermanence (Marlatt, 2002). Mindfulness meditation can be considered a form of counterconditioning in which a state of present-moment awareness and relaxation is invoked in the midst of a strong impulse to reject the subjective experience underlying the craving (e.g., anxiety, anger, or stress), weakening the conditioned association between a craving and gambling (Witkiewitz, Marlatt, & Walker, 2005).

Fourth, mindfulness meditation can, through concentration on the breath as an anchor for awareness, enhance the ability to concentrate and focus attention, and reduce the tendency toward distraction and rumination that can characterize the early phases of recovery, when the overwhelming consequences of gambling dominate the gambler's concerns (Sinha, 2001). This is especially beneficial in maintaining a positive therapeutic motivation to remain engaged in treatment despite the tendency to ruminate on the losses that have accrued as a result of problem gambling. To counter this tendency, the concentrative aspects of mindfulness practice can assist individuals in shifting their awareness to the immediate present and can also interfere with and terminate the onset of negative emotions and feelings of demoralization that might result from prolonged attention to the harmful consequences of problem gambling.

Fifth, mindfulness-based interventions have increasingly been proven effective in reducing the intensity of variables implicated in addiction relapse (e.g., negative affective states, such as depression and anxiety; Witkiewitz & Villarroel, 2009), whether through attentional regulation, reperceiving, cognitive defusion, or decentering. In all of these processes, mindfulness facilitates an attitude of reflexivity, perspective, and insight into the conditioned but arbitrary connection between subjective experiences and behavioral activity. As a result, impulsive, spontaneous, compulsive, or otherwise automatic response patterns are attenuated and replaced with the discernment that, in the face of compelling subjective experiences, the individual has choices and alternatives to act in ways other than gambling.

Issues in the Introduction of Mindfulness-Based Interventions for Problem Gambling

Since gambling may regulate an array of negative mental states, especially anxiety, depressed affect, stress, and boredom, clients may have considerable difficulty initially tolerating such states during mindfulness practice. Bowen and colleagues (2011) highlight some of the challenges in teaching mindfulness to individuals struggling with addiction, all of which would certainly be of significance in integrating mindfulness-based interventions into the treatment of problem gamblers. These challenges, or obstacles, include coping with the emergence of cognitive and affective experiences while practicing mindfulness that, if not properly responded to, may interfere with the benefits of practice and lead to premature dropout from treatment.

Many of these obstacles occur early in the gambler's exposure to mindfulness practice. Among the most important are aversion to mindfulness practice; restlessness, anxiety, and agitation; extreme drowsiness or lethargy, and possibly feelings of boredom and depression; doubt about the value of mindfulness exercises; and strong desires and urges related to reinforcement of gambling behavior. It is imperative that these early and potentially serious impediments to mindfulness practice among problem gamblers be identified and addressed through ongoing monitoring of their practice by clinicians skilled in teaching mindfulness and knowledgeable about the psychology of gambling.

Prior to commencing a mindfulness-based intervention, gamblers should be educated that such emotional responses are highly likely and quite normal. They should be encouraged to note the vicissitudes of their attention and observe how sensations, feelings, and thoughts arise and pass. By observing and noting these everyday aspects of experience, they gain skills in observing them with reduced impulsivity or reactivity (Toneatto, 2002).

It is also worthwhile to instruct problem gamblers that the mental states they may encounter while they practice mindfulness are precisely those that may be associated with the onset and maintenance of gambling behavior. That is, aversive emotions, such as anxiety, depression, stress, boredom, and anger, that occur while practicing mindfulness may be the same emotional states associated with an increased likelihood of problem gambling or aroused by high-risk gambling situations. Thus, to encounter them while practicing mindfulness provides a valuable opportunity for a transformational therapeutic experience. In fact, since these emotions represent some of the specific challenges gamblers will face as they learn to cope with gambling-related triggers and stimuli, becoming familiar with these mental events through mindfulness practice is a potent therapeutic experience that can teach problem gamblers about the nature of cognitive experience and provide insight into more effective ways to cope with gambling-specific mental processes.

Due to the tendency for problem gamblers to relapse, skills acquisition may require repeated and prolonged practice, taking into consideration the likelihood that gamblers may at times be unable to effectively maintain a mindfulness attitude and therefore could revert to highly conditioned gambling responses. These challenges highlight the necessity of combining mindfulness interventions with a comprehensive cognitive behavioral treatment (see below).

In sum, rather than reacting to thoughts and attempting to control them directly by altering their content, as in standard cognitive behavioral therapy, in mindfulness practice problem gamblers learn to passively but alertly observe their mental activity and cultivate mindful attention to the links between thinking and impulsively acting out. Mindfulness practice also facilitates cognitive defusion.

Issues in the Empirical Study of Mindfulness Meditation and Problem Gambling

Investigators wishing to evaluate the efficacy of mindfulness interventions for problem gambling would be prudent to heed the results of the review by Zgierska and colleagues (2009), examining seventeen studies of mindfulness meditation for psychoactive substance abuse. A number of methodological issues that are pertinent for the conduct of gambling-related treatment research that integrates mindfulness approaches are highlighted. In addition to addressing the more common methodological weaknesses of this research area (Chiesa, 2010), the inclusion of measures of mindfulness outcomes such as the Mindful Attention Awareness Scale (Brown & Ryan, 2003) or the Five Facet Mindfulness Questionnaire (Baer et al., 2008) or measures of the process of mindfulness meditation (i.e., what subjects actually did while they practiced mindfulness meditation) would greatly enhance the internal validity of such studies. Surprisingly, the specific impact of mindfulness meditation on behavior (i.e., patterns of substance use) were infrequently assessed or reported, yet this is ostensibly the most important variable in evaluating the efficacy of mindfulness-based interventions for substance use and should be rectified in future empirical evaluations of mindfulness-based interventions, including those for problem gamblers.

Limitations of Mindfulness Interventions

It is unlikely that mindfulness meditation is sufficient as a stand-alone intervention for treating problem gambling. As with traditional mindfulness teachings, the benefits of such training are enhanced within a more comprehensive strategy of cognitive, affective, and behavioral change (as in Buddhism's eightfold path). Indeed, the majority of studies that have included mindfulness interventions (e.g., DBT, MBCT, or ACT) have done so within comprehensive cognitive behavioral treatments that include a large array of other important clinical techniques. In the case of problem gambling, it is critical to embed mindfulness interventions within empirically supported treatments (e.g., cognitive behavioral treatments).

At various stages of treatment, mindfulness interventions may play distinctly different roles. For example, in the commencement or assessment phase of treatment, mindfulness interventions can enhance self-awareness of mental events related to gambling (e.g., thoughts, fantasies, or feelings)—a form of self-awareness often avoided by gamblers, who may prefer to rapidly react to their own cognitions rather than experience them. During active phases of treatment, mindfulness interventions may serve to raise awareness of cognitive, behavioral, and affective resistance to implementing treatment strategies and coping with high-risk situations, urges, and temptations. Mindfulness practice during treatment might also identify the presence of obscure thoughts or beliefs (e.g., *I don't deserve to get better*) that may mask core beliefs about the self and the world (e.g., a sense of entitlement or feelings of omniscience). Finally, in the maintenance or relapse phase of treatment, the identification of perceptions and cognitions that predict lapse or relapse can be identified through ongoing mindfulness practice.

Throughout the various phases of treatment, the essential characteristics of mindfulness practice remain operative (i.e., an open, broad, decentered, and defused awareness of all aspects of cognition) but are directed at the unique challenges faced by the problem gambler at the current stage of the treatment process.

Conclusion

Mindfulness-based interventions for emotional and physical disorders have become widespread. While their efficacy in the treatment of problem gambling has yet to be tested, there are strong justifications for the application of mindfulness interventions to treating problem gambling. These include the limited efficacy of cognitive behavioral treatments for gambling, the presence of significant cognitive psychopathology that is resistant to traditional cognitive treatments, and the role of gambling-related urges and impulsivity. However, until mindfulness-based approaches have been substantiated by empirical research, clinicians will need to take care in extrapolating from similar interventions applied to other addictive and mental disorders. Nevertheless, mindfulness interventions provide a hopeful avenue of exploration for dealing with this difficult problem.

References

Alfonso, J. P., Caracuel, A., Delgado-Pastor, L. C., & Verdejo-García, A. (2011). Combined goal management training and mindfulness meditation improve executive functions and decision-making performance in abstinent polysubstance abusers. *Drug and Alcohol Dependence, 117,* 78-81.

Baer, R. A., Smith, G. T., Lykins, E., Button, D., Krietemeyer, J., Sauer, S., et al. (2008). Construct validity of the Five Facet Mindfulness Questionnaire in meditating and nonmeditating samples. *Assessment, 15,* 329-342.

Bechara, A., Damasio, A. R., Damasio, H., & Anderson, S. W. (1994). Insensitivity to future consequences following damage to human prefrontal cortex. *Cognition, 50,* 7-15.

Benhsain, K., Taillefer, A., & Ladouceur, R. (2004). Awareness of independence of events and erroneous perceptions while gambling. *Addictive Behaviors, 29,* 399-404.

Bowen, S., Chawla, N., & Marlatt, G. A. (2011). *Mindfulness-based relapse prevention for addictive behaviors: A clinician's guide.* New York: Guilford Press.

Brown, K. W., & Ryan, R. M. (2003). The benefits of being present: Mindfulness and its role in psychological well-being. *Journal of Personality and Social Psychology, 84,* 822- 848.

Chiesa, A. (2010). Vipassana meditation: Systematic review of current evidence. *Journal of Alternative and Complementary Medicine, 16,* 37-46.

Daughters, S. B., Lejuez, C. W., Lesieur, H., Strong, D. R., & Zvolensky, M. J. (2003). Towards a better understanding of gambling treatment failure: Implications of translational research. *Clinical Psychology Review, 23,* 573-586.

De Lisle, S. M., Dowling, N. A., & Allen, J. S. (2011). Mindfulness-based cognitive therapy for problem gambling. *Clinical Case Studies, 10,* 210-228.

Diskin, K. M., & Hodgins, D. C. (2009). A randomized controlled trial of a single session motivational intervention for concerned gamblers. *Behaviour Research and Therapy, 47,* 382-388.

Hayes, S. C., Follette, V. M., & Linehan, M. M. (2004). *Mindfulness and acceptance: Expanding the cognitive-behavioral tradition.* New York: Guilford Press.

Hayes, S. C., Strosahl, K. D., & Wilson, K. G. (1999). *Acceptance and commitment therapy: An experiential approach to behavior change.* New York: Guilford Press.

Hodgins, D. C., & el-Guebaly, N. (2004). Retrospective and prospective reports of precipitants to relapse in pathological gambling. *Journal of Consulting and Clinical Psychology, 72,* 72- 80.

Hodgins, D. C., & Holub, A. (2007). Treatment of problem gambling. In G. Smith, D. Hodgins, & R. Williams (Eds.), *Research and measurement issues in gambling studies.* Burlington, MA: Academic Press.

Joukhador, J., Maccallum, F., & Blaszczynski, A. (2003). Differences in cognitive distortions between problem and social gamblers. *Psychological Reports, 92,* 1203-1214.

Kabat-Zinn, J. (1990). *Full catastrophe living: Using the wisdom of your body and mind to face stress, pain, and illness.* New York: Delacorte.

Ladouceur, R. (2004). Perceptions among pathological and nonpathological gamblers. *Addictive Behaviors, 29,* 555-565.

Lakey, C. E., Campbell, W. K., Brown, K. W., & Goodie, A. S. (2007). Dispositional mindfulness as a predictor of the severity of gambling outcomes. *Personality and Individual Differences, 43,* 1698-1710.

Marlatt, G. A. (2002). Buddhist philosophy and the treatment of addictive behavior. *Cognitive and Behavioral Practice, 9,* 44-50.

Pallesen, S., Mitsem, M., Kvale, G., Johnsen, B. H., & Molde, H. (2005). Outcome of psychological treatments of pathological gambling: A review and meta-analysis. *Addiction, 100*, 1412-1422.

Petry, N. M. (2005). *Pathological gambling: Etiology, comorbidity, and treatments.* Washington, DC: American Psychological Association.

Rapgay, L., & Bystrisky, A. (2009). Classical mindfulness: An introduction to its theory and practice for clinical application. *Annals of the New York Academy of Sciences, 1172*, 148-162.

Shaffer, H. J., Hall, M. N., & Vander Bilt, J. (1999). Estimating the prevalence of disordered gambling behavior in the United States and Canada: A research synthesis. *American Journal of Public Health, 89*, 1369-1376.

Shapiro, S. L., & Carlson, L. E. (2009). *The art and science of mindfulness.* Washington, DC: American Psychological Association.

Sinha, R. (2001). How does stress increase risk of drug abuse and relapse? *Psychopharmacology, 158*, 343-359.

Thera, N. (1973). *The heart of Buddhist meditation.* New York: Samuel Weiser.

Toneatto, T. (1999). Cognitive psychopathology of problem gambling. *Substance Use and Misuse, 34*, 1593-1604.

Toneatto, T. (2002). Cognitive treatment of problem gambling. *Cognitive and Behavioral Practice, 9*, 72-78.

Toneatto, T., & Gunaratne, M. (2009). Does the treatment of cognitive distortions improve clinical outcomes for problem gambling? *Journal of Contemporary Psychotherapy, 38*, 221-229.

Toneatto, T., & Ladouceur, R. (2003). The treatment of pathological gambling: A critical review of the literature. *Psychology of Addictive Behaviors, 17*, 284-292.

Toneatto, T., & Millar, G. (2004). The assessment and treatment of problem gambling: Empirical status and promising trends. *Canadian Journal of Psychiatry, 49*, 173-181.

Toneatto, T., & Nguyen, L. (2007). Individual characteristics and problem gambling behavior. In G. Smith, D. Hodgins & R. Williams (Eds.), *Research and measurement issues in gambling studies.* Burlington, MA: Academic Press.

Toneatto, T., Vettese, L., & Nguyen, L. (2007). The role of mindfulness in the cognitive-behavioral treatment of problem gambling. *Journal of Gambling Issues, 19*, 91-100.

Wallace, A. (1999). The Buddhist tradition of samatha: Methods for refining and examining consciousness. *Journal of Consciousness Studies, 6*, 175-187.

Witkiewitz, K., Marlatt, G. A., & Walker, D. D. (2005). Mindfulness-based relapse prevention for alcohol use disorders: The meditative tortoise wins the race. *Journal of Cognitive Psychotherapy, 19*, 221-228.

Witkiewitz, K., & Villarroel, N. A. (2009). Dynamic association between negative affect and alcohol lapses following alcohol treatment. *Journal of Consulting and Clinical Psychology, 77*, 633-644.

Zgierska, A., Rabago, D., Chawla, N., Kushner, K., Koehler, R., & Marlatt, A. (2009). Mindfulness meditation for substance use disorders: A systematic review. *Substance Abuse, 30*, 266-294.

CHAPTER 11

Contextual Cognitive Behavioral Therapy for Binge Eating

Jason Lillis

Weight Control and Diabetes Research Center,
The Miriam Hospital/Brown Alpert Medical School

B inge eating, and the chronic overconsumption of food more generally, represents a significant public health problem, and there is evidence that its prevalence is increasing (Flegal, Carroll, Odgen, & Curtin, 2010; Hudson, Hiripi, Pope, & Kessler, 2007). *Binge eating* refers to eating a large amount of food in a short period of time with an experience of loss of control. *Chronic overconsumption* refers to eating patterns that lead to obesity, including high-fat, high-calorie diets; subclinical binge eating; and general patterns of disinhibited or emotional eating. This chapter presents a theoretical model of binge eating and chronic overconsumption from a contextual perspective and examines how acceptance-, mindfulness-, and values-based interventions might be applied to this problem area.

Theoretical Model

Binge eating or chronic overconsumption is increasingly being viewed as an addictive behavior given its many functional similarities to more traditional addictive problem behaviors, such as drug abuse. Drug abuse and overeating are both harmful patterns of ingestive behavior that persist in part due to the powerful reinforcing properties of potent rewards and despite the threat of serious consequences. Researchers have suggested that overeating and illicit drug use may involve similar processes that lead to, maintain, and exacerbate these problems (e.g., Barry, Clarke, & Petry, 2009; Volkow, Wang, Fowler, & Telang, 2008; Volkow & Wise, 2005).

From a neurobiological perspective, food and drug intake both activate dopamine-containing neurons within brain reward circuitry (Wise & Rompré, 1989), and weight gain or obesity and chronic illicit drug use are both related to low D2 dopamine receptor expression in the ventral striatum (P. M. Johnson & Kenny, 2010; G. J. Wang, Volkow, Thanos, & Fowler, 2004). This may be in part due to the fact that illicit drug use and obesity can impact prefrontal cortex functioning through a reduction in D2 receptors, which has been shown to impact metabolism in the prefrontal cortex (Volkow et al., 2008). One aspect of cognitive functioning that is particularly affected by prefrontal cortex deregulation is the ability to inhibit a well-trained or overlearned behavior (Aron, Robbins, & Poldrack, 2004). In other words, prefrontal cortex deregulation may contribute to a person continuing to overconsume food or abuse drugs in the short-term despite long-term consequences.

From a behavioral perspective, binge eating and chronic overconsumption have recently been linked to a theoretical process known to impact addictive behavior: experiential avoidance (Kingston, Clarke, & Remington, 2010). Experiential avoidance is the tendency to try to change or avoid difficult thoughts, feelings, or bodily sensations even when doing so may produce harm (Hayes, Wilson, Gifford, Follette, & Strosahl, 1996). From an experiential avoidance perspective, overconsumption can serve as an attempt to regulate or change a negative thought or feeling by consuming food.

There is a growing literature supporting an experiential avoidance conceptualization of binge eating. Binge eating can be triggered by emotional distress (e.g., Fairburn, Cooper, & Shafran, 2003; Greeno, Wing, & Shiffman, 2000; Stein et al., 2007; Waters, Hill, & Waller, 2001), including in response to only moderately negative emotional states (W. G. Johnson, Schlundt, Barclay, Carr-Nangle, & Engler, 1995). Binge eating has also been shown to reduce extreme negative affect both during a binge (Hsu, 1990; Kaye, Gwirtsman, George, Weiss, & Jimerson, 1986) and immediately following a binge (Hsu, 1990; Schlundt & Johnson, 1990). Despite the fact that some evidence has shown that binge eating can be followed by negative feelings (often guilt), the new aversive state is experienced as more tolerable than the often more intense emotion that preceded the binge (e.g., depression or shame; Cooper et al., 1988; Lingswiler, Crowther, & Stephens, 1989). This is consistent with the literature on disinhibited or emotional eating (the general tendency to eat in an attempt to regulate emotion), which has been found to be related to overconsumption and obesity (Elfhag & Rossner, 2005; Fitzgibbon, Stolley, & Kirschenbaum, 1993).

Binge eaters also suffer from exaggerated high expectations, including both their own standards and their perceptions of what other people expect from them (e.g., physical attractiveness, body shape, or achievement), which in turn leads to a high frequency of self-judgment and associated negative emotions (for a review, see Heatherton & Baumeister, 1991). The evidence suggests that eating in response to emotions can foster a narrowing of attention or awareness to the immediate stimulus environment, thus allowing for avoidance or escape from self-critical thoughts (e.g., perceptions of inadequacy and failure) and associated negative emotions (e.g., depression, anxiety, or shame; Heatherton & Baumeister, 1991).

Binge eating has also been associated with the presence of situational stress (Greeno & Wing, 1994; Hansel & Wittrock, 1997). Coping with stress may be a particular problem for people who overeat more generally, as well. For example, one study found that people who reported excessive consumption of food used very few coping strategies other than eating (Grilo, Shiffman, & Carter-Campbell, 1994), while another found that they used a variety of coping strategies but that most of those strategies were avoidance-based (Wolff, Crosby, Roberts, & Wittrock, 2000).

Taken in sum, the neurobiological literature fits a model of eating as an addiction, and the behavioral literature supports experiential avoidance as a common core process involved in overeating behavior. In many cases, binge eating appears to be an attempt to escape or avoid negative thoughts and emotions, which in turn can produce harm by feeding a cycle of self-criticism.

Interventions and Evidence

Contextual cognitive behavioral therapy (CBT) or "third-wave" approaches have been shown to be particularly useful in targeting experiential avoidance (Baer, 2003; Hayes, 2004). These therapies use a combination of mindfulness, acceptance, and values processes to effect behavior change. The goals of treatment are usually some combination of the following: building client skills for becoming more deeply aware of or in touch with private experiences—thoughts, feelings, and bodily sensations (mindfulness); changing the way clients relate to their private experiences by promoting openness and a more accepting stance toward thoughts, feelings, and whatever is present (acceptance); and identifying and building on core values that are explicitly nonavoidant and promote healthy, vital living over the long term (values). This section samples and reviews contextual CBT intervention techniques designed to target binge eating or chronic overconsumption and related problems, and briefly reviews available evidence for these approaches.

Acceptance and Commitment Therapy

Acceptance and commitment therapy (ACT; Hayes, Strosahl, & Wilson, 1999; see also Wilson, Schnetzer, Flynn, & Kurz, chapter 1 of this volume) uses mindfulness, acceptance, and values processes to reduce patterns of experiential avoidance and increase psychological flexibility. It has been used to target binge eating or chronic overconsumption and related problems. ACT frequently utilizes metaphors and exercises to illustrate key processes. Generally the focus in such approaches for binge eating is not just on urges to eat (e.g., mindfully watching eating urges rise and fall as if each one were flowing down a stream on a leaf) but also on thoughts and feelings that may lead to the use of food as a method of avoidance, including unwanted emotions (e.g., imaging them as physical objects or experiencing each emotion and reaction one by one, like a chain of paper clips). Exercises such as these can serve to increase clients' flexibility in how they respond to thoughts, feelings, and sensations that typically have led to or maintained unhealthy eating patterns. Perhaps one of the more innovative components of ACT interventions for binge eating and overconsumption, however, has been addressing self-stigma and shame.

In one study, ACT with a particular focus on shame and self-stigma has been shown to reduce binge eating and improve weight maintenance relative to a wait list control group in a sample of eighty-three adults seeking weight-loss treatment (Lillis, Hayes, Bunting, & Masuda, 2009). Participants were taught mindfulness skills that helped them distinguish a transcendent sense of self from their self-judgments. For example, participants observed self-judgments and were asked to notice the part of themselves that was noticing the judgments. Participants also wrote down a judgment on a name tag and wore it during group—a physical metaphor for accepting or making room for judgments to occur without acting on them. Finally, participants were taught to defuse from negative judgments by noticing the distinction between treating thoughts as literal and having perspective on the process of thinking (e.g., imagining being close to versus far away from a computer screen that is generating self-judgments).

ACT has been shown to be helpful with related problems, including weight loss (Forman, Butryn, Hoffman, & Herbert, 2009), increasing physical activity (Tapper et al., 2009), and adjusting to bariatric surgery (Weinland, Arvidsson, Kakoulidis, & Dahl, 2012). In these studies, ACT was successful in reducing experiential avoidance or increasing distress tolerance (e.g., through breath holding experiments), which in turn led to changes in outcomes relevant to food consumption.

Dialectical Behavior Therapy

Dialectical behavior therapy (DBT) utilizes mindfulness, emotion regulation, and distress tolerance strategies to reduce problematic behaviors (see Dimeff, & Sayrs, chapter 2 of this volume). Although developed for the treatment of borderline personality disorder (Linehan, 1993), DBT has been adapted for a variety of clinical presentations, including eating disorders (Linehan & Chen, 2005).

When applied to binge eating, DBT focuses on the role of emotional dysregulation and the link between problematic emotions and eating. A study by Telch, Agras, and Linehan (2000) that lays out a framework for using DBT with this population is summarized here. Clients are taught to observe emotional experiences, thoughts, and urges to eat, and allow them to pass through their minds without suppressing them or judging them as good or bad. For example, clients are taught to label the feeling "shame" appropriately and become more mindfully aware of how it feels in their body (e.g., sick to one's stomach or wanting to hide). The link between distressing feelings and eating is discussed. Emotional regulation skills are taught as a way of dealing with eating urges. For example, clients are taught to act opposite to the urge to binge (i.e., engage in noneating behavior, such as exercise) and feelings of shame (e.g., seek others for support). They also learn to reduce their vulnerability by getting appropriate sleep and avoiding the use of alcohol. In addition, they learn distress tolerance skills in order to prevent further damage due to binge eating or overconsumption when facing already distressing situations. For example, clients are taught to replace the natural impulse to eat with a pleasant event, such as taking a warm bath or listening to soothing music, or to distract from eating urges by visiting with friends or taking a walk.

Research has shown preliminary support for the use of DBT for binge eating and related problems (e.g., Safer, Telch, & Agras, 2001; Salbach, Klinkowski, Pfeiffer, Lehmkuhl, & Korte, 2007). For example, a randomized trial of group DBT compared to a wait list control group showed 89% of DBT participants had stopped binge eating at the end of treatment (Telch, Agras, & Linehan, 2001). Another randomized controlled trial of a twenty-session DBT group for binge-eating disorder as compared to an active group treatment control found that DBT was more efficient in eliminating binge-eating behavior and had a significantly lower dropout rate (Safer, Robinson, & Jo, 2010).

Motivational Interviewing

Motivational Interviewing (MI) uses acceptance- and values-based interviewing techniques to help resolve ambivalence about change (Miller & Rollnick, 2002; see also Wagner, Ingersoll, & Rollnick, chapter 5 of this volume). When MI is applied to binge eating and overconsumption, clients may be asked to consider both the benefits and consequences of binge eating, to identify concerns about their own behavior, to become more aware of their ambivalence about change, and to identify important values (for an example, see Cassin, von Ranson, Heng, Brar, & Wojtowicz, 2008). For example, a MI therapist might ask clients to identify specific concerns they have about their eating and then have them write a statement of pros and cons about changing versus not changing their behavior. In addition, clients might be asked about their ideal life (to identify values) and guided to ponder the dissonance between their ideal and actual life, along with the possible role reducing binge eating might play in helping them achieve their ideal life.

MI has been used to address binge eating in clinical samples (e.g., Dunn, Neighbors, & Larimer, 2006). Cassin and colleagues (2008) tested a combination of one MI session plus a self-help handbook versus self-help alone in a group of 108 women with binge-eating disorder. Results showed that the MI group had a higher binge abstinence rate (27.8% vs. 11.1%) and a higher proportion of participants who no longer met criteria for binge-eating disorder (87.0% vs. 57.4%).

Mindfulness-Based Cognitive Therapy

Mindfulness-based cognitive therapy (MBCT; Segal, Williams, & Teasdale, 2002; Teasdale et al., 2000), builds mindfulness skills that promote nonjudgmental observation and acceptance of bodily sensations, perceptions, cognitions, and emotions. MBCT for problems with eating typically incorporates a series of mindfulness and traditional meditation practices. Often these protocols also emphasize broad mindfulness skills that can be used when problematic eating behavior emerges (for an example of the use of these methods in a successful case study, see Baer, Fischer, & Huss, 2005).

One example of a specific technique is the use of a mindful eating exercise, where clients eat a raisin with the goal of focusing attention on the sensations and movements of eating and the thoughts and emotions that come and go during eating. Another common technique is mindful stretching, where clients are encouraged to become more aware of physical sensations during slow, gentle movements. MBCT also utilizes mindfulness techniques for problematic automatic thoughts, both general (*I'm so weak*) and specific (*I'm unable to stop eating once I start*). In this case, clients are asked to notice these thoughts as they come up in the moment, watch them come and go, and refrain from trying to control or change them. It is important to note that MBCT therapists practice each mindfulness skill in the moment with their clients. Clients are also instructed to engage in daily mindfulness practice, for example, by spending three minutes noticing their breath (a skill initially taught in treatment).

Although the data are somewhat limited, mindfulness-focused therapies have shown some promise for treating binge eating and related problems (e.g., Kristeller & Hallett, 1999; Leahey, Crowther, & Irwin, 2008).

Summary of the Evidence for Contextual CBT

Taken as a whole, contextual CBT interventions have shown preliminary support for ameliorating problems related to the overconsumption of food by using mindfulness, acceptance, and values techniques, which are known to reduce patterns of experiential avoidance. Larger studies and more randomized trials are needed to evaluate the broad effectiveness of these interventions.

Special Issues

There are a number of additional factors that relate to binge eating and the chronic overconsumption of food. In particular, reward sensitivity in the brain, a toxic food environment, and self-stigma are key contributing factors and should be considered during intervention.

Reward Sensitivity

There is evidence to suggest that people who suffer from binge eating or chronic overconsumption of food display higher sensitivity to rewards in general (Davis et al., 2007; Franken & Muris, 2005). Neuroimaging studies have found that binge eaters showed more left prefrontal brain activity when exposed to a freshly cooked lunch relative to nonbingeing controls (Karhunen et al., 2000), along with stronger medial orbitofrontal cortex responses, indicating greater sensitivity to reward (Schienle, Schafer, Hermann, & Vaitl, 2009). It is not yet known if these differences are causal, but they do suggest that mindfulness methods should perhaps be focused on appetitive arousal in response to food or reward. For example, interventions might seek to increase mindful acceptance of cravings and appetite for food without acting on these urges, or focus on identifying and engaging in alternative valued activities that compete with the highly reinforcing qualities of eating unhealthy foods.

Food Environment

The past several decades have seen major changes in the food environment in the United States, including increasing caloric intake, larger portion sizes, increased consumption of food away from home, rising cost of healthy foods relative to unhealthy foods, decreased physical demands of occupational and environmental activities, massive promotional campaigns linked to unhealthy foods, and higher fat, salt, and sugar content in foods (S. S. Wang & Brownell, 2005; Yach, Stuckler, & Brownell, 2006). Animals are adept at maintaining a steady body weight, except when exposed to continuous availability of highly palatable, high-fat, high-sugar food (e.g., Gale, Van Itallie, & Faust, 1981; P. M. Johnson & Kenny, 2010), and several migration studies have shown similar patterns in humans (for a review, see S. S. Wang & Brownell, 2005), suggesting that binge eating and obesity are unlikely to occur in the absence of an unhealthy food environment.

Given the current cultural context, it is unlikely that individuals who struggle with binge eating or overconsumption can control their environment enough to eliminate eating cues and the presence of highly palatable, high-calorie foods. This suggests that acceptance methods may be helpful for dealing with inevitable food cravings and eating cues, while values methods may be helpful for orienting behavior toward long-term goals.

Weight Stigma

Overweight and obese people are seen as mean, stupid, ugly, less competent, lazy, and lacking in self-discipline, motivation, and personal control (Brylinskey & Moore, 1994; Crandall, 1994; Teachman, Gapinski, Brownell, Rawlins, & Jeyaram, 2003). Weight bias and discrimination appear to be increasing (Andreyeva, Puhl, & Brownell,

2008) and affect both men and women from moderately overweight to morbidly obese (Myers & Rosen, 1999; Puhl, Moss-Racusin, Schwartz, & Brownell, 2008). They can be found in employment settings; for example, 43% of overweight people report job discrimination, and obese people show a 24% reduction in salary for the same job (Maranto & Stencien, 2000; Puhl & Brownell, 2006). These biases are also present in the health care system, with 50% of physicians labeling overweight patients as ugly and noncompliant (Foster et al., 2003). These attitudes are evident among strangers, friends, family members, spouses, teachers, nurses, physicians, coworkers, and bosses, and are reinforced in the media. This situation is broadly referred to as "enacted stigma" (for reviews, see Puhl & Brownell, 2001, and Puhl & Heuer, 2009).

It is common for overweight individuals to internalize this powerful social stigma, possibly because weight is commonly seen by others as controllable, and because frequent failed attempts to lose weight reinforce stereotypes (e.g., fat people are lazy or incompetent; Rudman, Feinberg, & Fairchild, 2002; S. S. Wang, Brownell, & Wadden, 2004). This is often referred to as self-directed stigma, or weight self-stigma. Weight self-stigma is predictive of binge eating, discontinuation of efforts to improve diet, decreased ability to refrain from eating, and avoidance of exercise (Puhl & Brownell, 2001; Puhl & Heuer, 2009), behaviors that promote the overconsumption of food and are toxic to weight management. As noted earlier, there is already evidence that acceptance and mindfulness methods applied to self-stigma may be especially helpful in reducing binge eating (Lillis et al., 2009), a lead that might be usefully followed as contextual CBT methods are applied to this population.

Summary and Future Developments

Binge eating and the chronic overconsumption of food are multifaceted problems that represent a significant public health threat. Evidence suggests that problematic consumption of food can be viewed as an addictive behavior. In addition, problematic consumption appears to be fueled by experiential avoidance. Newer cognitive behavioral therapies that focus on mindfulness, acceptance, and values techniques are in a unique position to develop effective treatments for a range of problematic eating behaviors. As research expands our knowledge of the processes that underlie binge eating (e.g., reward sensitivity, the food environment, or weight stigma), mindfulness and acceptance methods can be more precisely targeted to the key issues that support and sustain eating disorders. While early treatment development studies have shown promising preliminary support, larger studies and more randomized trials are needed to test the efficacy and effectiveness of these methods.

References

Andreyeva, T., Puhl, R. M., & Brownell, K. D. (2008). Changes in perceived weight discrimination among Americans, 1995-1996 through 2004-2006. *Obesity, 16,* 1129-1134.

Aron, A., Robbins, T., & Poldrack, R. (2004). Inhibition and the right inferior frontal cortex. *Trends in Cognitive Science, 8,* 170-177.

Baer, R. A. (2003). Mindfulness training as a clinical intervention: A conceptual and empirical review. *Clinical Psychology: Science and Practice, 10,* 125-143.

Baer, R. A., Fischer, S., & Huss, D. B. (2005). Mindfulness-based cognitive therapy applied to binge eating: A case study. *Cognitive and Behavioral Practice, 12,* 351-358.

Barry, D., Clarke, M., & Petry, N. M. (2009). Obesity and its relationship to addictions: Is overeating a form of addictive behavior? *American Journal on Addictions, 18,* 349-451.

Brylinskey, J. A., & Moore, J. C. (1994). The identification of body build stereotypes in young children. *Journal of Research in Personality, 28,* 170-181.

Cassin, S. E., von Ranson, K. M., Heng, K., Brar, J., & Wojtowicz, A. E. (2008). Adapted motivational interviewing for women with binge eating disorder: A randomized controlled trial. *Psychology of Addictive Behaviors, 3,* 417-425.

Cooper, J. L., Morrison, T. L., Bigman, O. L., Abramowitz, S. I., Levin, S., & Krener, P. (1988). Mood changes and affective disorder in the bulimic binge-purge cycle. *International Journal of Eating Disorders, 7,* 469-474.

Crandall, C. S. (1994). Prejudice against fat people: Ideology and self-interest. *Journal of Personality and Social Psychology, 66,* 882-894.

Davis, C., Patte, K., Levitan, R., Reid, C., Tweed, S., & Curtis, C. (2007). From motivation to behaviour: A model of reward sensitivity, overeating, and food preferences in the risk profile for obesity. *Appetite, 48,* 12-19.

Dunn, E. C., Neighbors, C., & Larimer, M. E. (2006). Motivational enhancement therapy and self-help for binge eaters. *Psychology of Addictive Behaviors, 20,* 44-52.

Elfhag, K., & Rossner, S. (2005). Who succeeds in maintaining weight loss? A conceptual review of factors associated with weight loss maintenance and weight regain. *Obesity Reviews, 6,* 67-85.

Fairburn, C. G., Cooper, Z., & Shafran, R. (2003). Cognitive behavioral therapy for eating disorders: A "transdiagnostic" theory and treatment. *Behaviour Research and Therapy, 41,* 509-528.

Fitzgibbon, M. L., Stolley, M. R., & Kirschenbaum, D. S. (1993). Obese people who seek treatment have different characteristics than those who do not seek treatment. *Health Psychology, 12,* 342-345.

Flegal, K. M., Carroll, M. D., Odgen, C. L., & Curtin, L. R. (2010). Prevalence and trends in obesity among U.S. adults, 1998-2008. *Journal of the American Medical Association, 303,* 223-319.

Forman, E. M., Butryn, M. L., Hoffman, K. L., & Herbert, J. D. (2009). An open trial of an acceptance-based behavioral intervention for weight loss. *Cognitive and Behavioral Practice, 16,* 223-235.

Foster, G. D., Wadden, T. A., Markis, A. P., Davidson, D., Sanderson, R. S., Allison, et al. (2003). Primary care physicians' attitudes about obesity and its treatment. *Obesity Research, 11,* 1168-1177.

Franken, I. H., & Muris, P. (2005). Individual differences in reward sensitivity are related to food craving and relative body weight in healthy women. *Appetite, 45,* 198-201.

Gale, S. K., Van Itallie, T. B., & Faust, I. M. (1981). Effects of palatable diets on body weight and adipose tissue cellularity in the adult obese female Zucker rat (fa/fa). *Metabolism, 30,* 105-110.

Greeno, C. G., & Wing, R. R. (1994). Stress-induced eating. *Psychological Bulletin, 115,* 444-464.

Greeno, C. G., Wing, R. R., & Shiffman, S. (2000). Binge antecedents in obese women with and without binge eating disorder. *Journal of Consulting and Clinical Psychology, 68,* 95-102.

Grilo, C. M., Shiffman, S., & Carter-Campbell, J. T. (1994). Binge eating in normal-weight nonpurging females: Is there consistency? *International Journal of Eating Disorders, 16,* 239-249.

Hansel, S., & Wittrock, D. A. (1997). Appraisal and coping strategies in stress situations: A comparison of individual who binge eat to controls. *International Journal of Eating Disorders, 21,* 89-93.

Hayes, S. C. (2004). Acceptance and commitment therapy, relational frame theory, and the third wave of behavioral and cognitive therapies. *Behavior Therapy, 35,* 639-665.

Hayes, S. C., Strosahl, K. D., & Wilson, K. G. (1999). *Acceptance and commitment therapy: An experiential approach to behavior change.* New York: Guilford Press.

Hayes, S. C., Wilson, K. G., Gifford, E. V., Follette, V. M., & Strosahl, K. D. (1996). Experiential avoidance and behavioral disorders: A functional dimensional approach to diagnosis and treatment. *Journal of Consulting and Clinical Psychology, 64,* 1152-1168.

Heatherton, T. F., & Baumeister, R. F. (1991). Binge eating as escape from self-awareness. *Psychological Bulletin, 110,* 86-108.

Hsu, L. K. G. (1990). Experiential aspects of bulimia nervosa: Implications for cognitive behavioral therapy. *Behavior Modification, 14,* 50-65.

Hudson, J. I., Hiripi, E., Pope, H. G., & Kessler, R. C. (2007). The prevalence and correlates of eating disorders in the national comorbidity survey replication. *Biological Psychiatry, 61,* 348-358.

Johnson, P. M., & Kenny, P. J. (2010). Addiction-like reward dysfunction and compulsive eating in obese rats: Role for dopamine D2 receptors. *Nature Neuroscience, 13,* 635-641.

Johnson, W. G., Schlundt, D. G., Barclay, D. R., Carr-Nangle, R. E., & Engler, L. B. (1995). A naturalistic functional analysis of binge eating. *Behavior Therapy, 26,* 101-118.

Karhunen, L. J., Vanninen, E. J., Kuikka, J. T., Lappalainen, R. I., Tiihonen, J., & Uusitupa, M. J. I. (2000). Regional cerebral blood flow during exposure to food in obese binge eating women. *Psychiatry Research: Neuroimaging, 99,* 29-42.

Kaye, W. H., Gwirtsman, H. E., George, D. T., Weiss, S. R., & Jimerson, D. C. (1986). Relationship of mood alterations to bingeing behavior in bulimia. *British Journal of Psychiatry, 149,* 479-485.

Kingston, J., Clarke, S., & Remington, B. (2010). Experiential avoidance and problem behavior: A mediational analysis. *Behavior Modification, 34,* 145-163.

Kristeller, J. L., & Hallett, C. B. (1999). An exploratory study of a meditation-based intervention for binge eating disorder. *Journal of Health Psychology, 4,* 357-363.

Leahey, T. M., Crowther, J. H., & Irwin, S. R. (2008). A cognitive-behavioral mindfulness group therapy intervention for the treatment of binge eating in bariatric surgery patients. *Cognitive and Behavioral Practice, 15,* 364-375.

Lillis, J., Hayes, S. C., Bunting, K., & Masuda, A. (2009). Teaching acceptance and mindfulness to improve the lives of the obese: A preliminary test of a theoretical model. *Annals of Behavioral Medicine, 37,* 58-69.

Linehan, M. M. (1993). *Cognitive-behavioral treatment of borderline personality disorder.* New York: Guilford Press.

Linehan, M. M., & Chen, E. Y. (2005). Dialectical behavior therapy for eating disorders. In A. Freeman (Ed.), *Encyclopedia of cognitive behavior therapy.* New York: Springer.

Lingswiler, V. M., Crowther, J. H., & Stephens, M. A. P. (1989). Emotional and somatic consequences of binge episodes. *Addictive Behaviors, 14,* 503-511.

Maranto, C. L., & Stencien, A. F. (2000). Weight discrimination: A multidisciplinary analysis. *Employee Responsibilities and Rights Journal, 12,* 9-24.

Miller, W. R., & Rollnick, S. (2002). *Motivational interviewing: Preparing people to change* (2nd ed.). New York: Guilford Press.

Myers, A., & Rosen, J. C. (1999). Obesity stigmatization and coping: Relation to mental health symptoms, body image, and self-esteem. *International Journal of Obesity, 23,* 221-230.

Puhl, R., & Brownell, K. D. (2001). Bias, discrimination, and obesity. *Obesity Research, 9,* 788-805.

Puhl, R., & Brownell, K. D. (2006). Confronting and coping with weight stigma: An investigation of overweight and obese adults. *Obesity, 14,* 1802-1815.

Puhl, R., & Heuer, C. A. (2009). The stigma of obesity: A review and update. *Obesity, 17,* 941-964.

Puhl, R., Moss-Racusin, C. A., Schwartz, M. B., & Brownell, K. D. (2008). Weight stigmatization and bias reduction: Perspectives of overweight and obese adults. *Health Education Research, 23,* 347-358.

Rudman, L. A., Feinberg, J., & Fairchild, K. (2002). Minority members' implicit attitudes: Automatic ingroup bias as a function of group status. *Social Cognition, 20,* 294-320.

Safer, D. L., Robinson, A. H., & Jo, B. (2010). Outcome from a randomized controlled trial of group therapy for binge eating disorder: Comparing dialectical behavior therapy adapted for binge eating to an active comparison group therapy. *Behavior Therapy, 41,* 106-120.

Safer, D. L., Telch, C. F., & Agras, W. S. (2001). Dialectical behavior therapy for bulimia nervosa. *American Journal of Psychiatry, 158,* 632-634.

Salbach, H., Klinkowski, N., Pfeiffer, E., Lehmkuhl, U., & Korte, A. (2007). Dialectical behavior therapy for adolescents with anorexia and bulimia nervosa (DBT-AN/BN): A pilot study. [Article in German.] *Praxis der Kinderpsychologie und Kinderpsychiatrie, 56,* 91-108.

Schienle, A., Schafer, A., Hermann, A., & Vaitl, D. (2009). Binge-eating disorder: Reward sensitivity and brain activation to images of food. *Biological Psychiatry, 65,* 654-661.

Schlundt, D. G., & Johnson, W. G. (1990). *Eating disorders: Assessment and treatment.* Needham Heights, MA: Allyn and Bacon.

Segal, Z. V., Williams, J. M. G., & Teasdale, J. T. (2002). *Mindfulness-based cognitive therapy for depression: A new approach to preventing relapse.* New York: Guilford Press.

Stein, R. I., Kenardy, J., Wiseman, C. V., Dounchis, J. Z., Arnow, B. A., & Wilfley, D. E. (2007). What's driving binge eating disorder? A prospective examination of precursors and consequences. *International Journal of Eating Disorders, 40,* 195-203.

Tapper, K., Shaw, C., Ilsley, J., Hill, A. J., Bond, F. W., & Moore, L. (2009). Exploratory randomised controlled trial of a mindfulness-based weight loss intervention for women. *Appetite, 52,* 396-404.

Teachman, B. A., Gapinski, K. D., Brownell, K. D., Rawlins, M., & Jeyaram, S. (2003). Demonstrations of implicit anti-fat bias: The impact of providing causal information and evoking empathy. *Health Psychology, 22,* 68-78.

Teasdale, J. T., Williams, J. M. G., Soulsby, J. M., Segal, Z. V., Ridgeway, V. A., & Lau, M. A. (2000). Prevention of relapse/recurrence in major depression by mindfulness-based cognitive therapy. *Journal of Consulting and Clinical Psychology, 68,* 615-623.

Telch, C. F., Agras, W. S., & Linehan, M. M. (2000). Group dialectical behavior therapy for binge-eating disorder: A preliminary, uncontrolled trial. *Behavior Therapy, 31,* 569-582.

Telch, C. F., Agras, W. S., & Linehan, M. M. (2001). Dialectical behavior therapy for binge-eating disorder. *Journal of Consulting and Clinical Psychology, 69,* 1061-1065.

Volkow, N. D., Wang, G. J., Fowler, J. S., & Telang, F. (2008). Overlapping neuronal circuits in addiction and obesity: Evidence of systems pathology. *Philosophical Transactions of the Royal Society B, 363,* 3191-3200.

Volkow, N. D., & Wise, R. A. (2005). How can drug addiction help us understand obesity? *Nature Neuroscience, 8,* 555-560.

Wang, G. J., Volkow, N. D., Thanos, P. K., & Fowler, J. S. (2004). Similarity between obesity and drug addiction as assessed by neurofunctional imaging: A concept review. *Journal of Addictive Disorders, 23,* 39-53.

Wang, S. S., & Brownell, K. D. (2005). Public policy and obesity: The need to marry science with advocacy. *Psychiatric Clinics of North America, 28,* 235-252.

Wang, S. S., Brownell, K. D., & Wadden, T. A. (2004). The influence of the stigma of obesity on overweight individuals. *International Journal of Obesity, 28,* 1333-1337.

Waters, A., Hill, A., & Waller, G. (2001). Internal and external antecedents of binge eating episodes in a group of women with bulimia nervosa. *International Journal of Eating Disorders, 29,* 17-22.

Weinland, S., Arvidsson, D., Kakoulidis, T., & Dahl, J. (2012). Acceptance and commitment therapy for bariatric surgery patients, a pilot RCT. *Obesity Research and Clinical Practice, 6,* e21-e30.

Wise, R. A., & Rompré, P. P. (1989). Brain dopamine and reward. *Annual Review of Psychology, 40,* 191-225.

Wolff, G. E., Crosby, R. D., Roberts, J. A., & Wittrock, D. A. (2000). Differences in daily stress, mood, coping, and eating behavior in binge eating and nonbinge eating college women. *Addictive Behaviors, 25,* 205-216.

Yach, D., Stuckler, D., & Brownell, K. D. (2006). Epidemiologic and economic consequences of the global epidemics of obesity and diabetes. *Nature Medicine, 12,* 62-66.

CHAPTER 12

A Contextual Approach to Pornography Addiction

Jesse M. Crosby

Utah State University and
McLean Hospital/Harvard Medical School

Michael P. Twohig

Utah State University

Pornography addiction has been referred to as sexual addiction (Orzack & Ross, 2000), sexual impulsivity (Mick & Hollander, 2006), and sexual compulsivity (Cooper, Putnam, Planchon, & Boies, 1999), among other terms. Diagnostic criteria and terminology from substance use disorders (Schneider, 1994), impulse control disorders (Grant & Potenza, 2007), and obsessive-compulsive disorder (Black, 1998) have also been used to define pornography addiction. The theoretical debate in regard to understanding and diagnosing the behavior is far from settled, and this has proven to be a stumbling block in devoting focus to treatment research. In previous publications we have referred to this issue as "problematic pornography use" to highlight the functional and contextual nature of the issue (Crosby, 2011; Twohig & Crosby, 2010; Twohig, Crosby, & Cox, 2009), but for consistency with this book, we will refer to the problem as "pornography addiction."

Pornography addiction is characterized by an inability to control the use of pornography, an experience of negatively evaluated cognitions or emotions associated with viewing, and the resulting negative effects on quality of life or general functioning from these two experiences (McBride, Reece, & Sanders, 2007). Rough estimates of prevalence suggest that between 1.5% and 3% of the US adult population may experience this problem (Kuzma & Black, 2008). Similar to other addictive behaviors, the use of pornography may not be inherently addictive or problematic; it is addictive to the extent to which it becomes excessive and leads to problematic emotional, cognitive, or behavioral outcomes (Twohig et al., 2009).

Pornography addiction has been linked to depression, social isolation, damaged relationships, career loss or decreased productivity, and financial consequences (Schneider, 2000a). It has also been associated with anxiety, shame, guilt, potential legal problems, loneliness, and self-blame (McBride et al., 2007), as well as increased contacts with mental health providers (Cooper, Griffin-Shelley, Delmonico, & Mathy, 2001). Damage to intimate relationships has been linked to pornography use (Manning, 2006), including decreased interest in sexual activity between affected partners (Schneider, 2003) and marital separation and divorce (Schneider, 2000b). There are negative societal effects to consider as well, including the exposure of children to pornography (Schneider, 2000b) and use of work computers to access materials, leading to significant productivity and financial losses for businesses and risks of unemployment for the user (Cooper, Delmonico, & Burg, 2000). Additionally, pornography use has been linked to increased risk of sexual deviancy (Oddone-Paolucci, Genuis, & Violato, 2000), negative attitudes toward women (Garcia, 1986), behavioral aggression (Allen, D'Alessio, & Brezgel, 1995), and extramarital affairs and participation in prostitution (Stack, Wasserman, & Kern, 2004). It is clear that pornography use can be associated with a variety of negative outcomes, but it is important to highlight the functional nature of the behavior, as use is not inherently pathological. For example, it has been shown that there are many situations where pornography use is welcomed by couples (Bergner & Bridges, 2002).

The literature on the treatment of pornography addiction relies largely on clinical experience, rather than experimentation. Suggested treatments include motivational interviewing (Del Giudice & Kutinsky, 2007), cognitive behavioral therapy (Young, 2007), 12-step programs (Schneider, 1994), and emotion-focused therapy (Reid & Woolley, 2006). There is a clear need for controlled research.

A Theoretical Model of Pornography Addiction

The disorders to which pornography addiction is compared—substance abuse or dependence, impulse control, and obsessive-compulsive disorder (OCD)—inform our conceptualization of pornography addiction. As with all three of these disorders, pornography addiction involves the inability to control or regulate behavior that is excessive and interferes with functioning. Similar to these other disorders, pornography addiction is also influenced by private experiences such as thoughts (e.g., sexual fantasies), emotions (e.g., stress, fear, sadness, anger, or boredom), and physical sensations (e.g., sexual arousal), which play a functional role in the maintenance of the behavior. Indeed, pornography use often functions to help people appease or avoid these private experiences, just as seen in the diagnostic criteria for most anxiety and impulse control disorders.

Current research on the way private experiences (i.e., thoughts, emotions, physical sensations) are conceptualized in OCD and impulse control disorders may have important implications for understanding pornography addiction. The thought suppression literature (Wegner, 1994) has demonstrated that deliberate attempts to suppress thoughts can result in increases in both neutral thoughts and unwanted intrusive thoughts. Similarly, attempting to control thoughts can increase their intensity and influence over behavior (Abramowitz, Tolin, & Street, 2001).

Research on thought-action fusion has demonstrated the tendency of some individuals to assign unrealistic levels of influence to thoughts, so that thinking is viewed as comparable to actually performing the behavior or having the power to make an event more likely to happen (Rachman, Thordarson, Shafran, & Woody, 1995). This would influence both the distress caused by the thoughts and the need to respond behaviorally to the thoughts. This struggle with thoughts is an important part of how sexual compulsivity is defined and measured (Coleman, 1991). Indeed, a commonly used measure of sexual compulsivity addresses the struggle to control sexual thoughts and behaviors (Kalichman & Rompa, 1995). It is possible that attempts to control or avoid the urges to use pornography can lead to increased intensity and influence of the urges and, in a context where these thoughts are treated literally, an increased likelihood of a behavioral response such as using pornography to regulate these urges. This is supported by recent research with pornography addiction that demonstrated that the amount an individual struggles and attempts to control urges to use pornography mediates how problematic the viewing becomes (Twohig et al., 2009).

The paradoxical nature of attempts to control private experiences appears to be one of the underlying processes behind addictive pornography use. Traditional thought suppression or distraction techniques may actually be counterproductive in addressing this problem, as an increased focus on suppressing thoughts about pornography may lead to an increase in related private experiences (e.g., sexual fantasies or urges) and subsequent pornography use. This is an example of psychological inflexibility as conceptualized in ACT (Hayes, Luoma, Bond, Masuda, & Lillis, 2006) and suggests ACT may be an effective treatment for pornography addiction, because it targets processes that generally aim to decrease experiential avoidance and the effects of private experiences on behavior (urges to use pornography in this case).

The six core processes targeted in ACT—acceptance, defusion, self-as-context, present-moment awareness, values clarification, and committed action—are relevant in understanding and treating pornography addiction. The process of experiential avoidance is apparent in pornography addiction as an individual responds to urges to view with attempts to control or avoid the urges, which only serve to increase the intensity and frequency of the urges. Sometimes the control or avoidance behaviors are adaptive alternatives (e.g., exercising, socializing, or watching a movie), but they may produce the paradoxical effects of attempts to control thoughts (more intense and frequent urges, and greater influence of thoughts over actions). Individuals may also report frustration that their efforts to avoid or control urges are not working, and they may blame themselves for the failure. Often, the primary behavior used to avoid or control urges is viewing pornography. Not only is this behavior problematic, but it also serves to reinforce the urges and activate the paradoxical process of experiential avoidance. It is important to clarify that urges to view pornography are not limited to specific sexual arousal or curiosity. They include a variety of nonsexual thoughts, feelings, and physical sensations that are typically unwanted and avoided. For example, feelings of sadness due to social isolation accompanied by negative self-talk could be the private experience pornography is intended to avoid or control. This maladaptive experiential avoidance is addressed by fostering *acceptance* in the form of willingness to experience urges and not working to regulate them.

Cognitive fusion might also help explain the impact of certain private experiences, including sexual arousal, distressing emotions, and negative thoughts associated with urges to view pornography. Fusion with self-evaluations may exacerbate the impact of experiences that accompany pornography viewing, such as guilt, shame, or low self-esteem. If people take the thought *I'm a loser* literally, it makes sense that they would go to great effort to avoid this thought. Unfortunately, pornography use provides short-term avoidance of these internal experiences, fueling a cycle of addiction as the viewing provides temporary escape and then feeds the very internal content that was avoided. This process is addressed by work with cognitive *defusion*, through which the individual learns to experience internal content as it is, rather than allowing the meaning of a private experience to be determined by arbitrary verbal relations.

Individuals struggling with pornography addiction often define themselves as addicts and see it as something that is permanently part of them. They may believe they will never escape from the urges to engage in the behavior, and often settle for a life that is a compromise between their addiction and their true goals. This is the process of self-as-content, in which individuals define themselves by the literal content of their private experiences—content over which they have little, if any, control. This is addressed by work that defines the *self as the context* in which private experiences occur within the person; from this perspective, the individual is not defined by the experience of urges to view pornography.

When trying to resist an urge to view pornography, people may get caught up in thoughts that they *can't resist much longer* or *have never been able to control this behavior.* There is a tendency to get caught in fused interactions with fears about the future or rumination about the past, and not take action in the present moment, where they actually have a say in what happens. *Present-moment awareness* fosters a nonjudgmental relationship to private experiences as they occur. The ability to step back and watch one's inner experiences for what they are, while they are occurring, provides an opportunity to choose a response. When behaviors are dependent on an urge to view, it can feel like the only options are to view or not, when in reality there are many choices (watch television, go for a walk, call a friend, etc.).

Overall, the addictive behavior functions to regulate unwanted private experiences. From the client's perspective, viewing is governed by urges: as long as the urges occur, the behavior will occur. The ACT processes discussed above are meant to provide flexibility in responding to these urges, and once the behavior-regulating power of the urges is lessened, clients can shift their energy to more meaningful directions in life. The goals of *values clarification* are identifying how individuals really want to live their lives and establishing patterns of *committed action*— behaviors that are consistent with values and not controlled by private experiences. Ultimately, addressing these psychological processes fosters *psychological flexibility*, the ability to move in meaningful directions without allowing difficult inner experiences to serve as obstacles to valued actions (Hayes et al., 2006).

ACT Intervention for Pornography Addiction

Most ACT experiential exercises and metaphors can be adapted to work with pornography addiction (Hayes, Strosahl, & Wilson, 2011; see also Wilson, Schnetzer, Flynn, & Kurz, chapter 1 of this volume). Given the conceptual similarities, we have also found that the ACT work for trichotillomania is easily adapted for this problem (see Woods & Twohig, 2008). Additionally, the specific mindfulness-, acceptance-, and values-based approaches for addiction discussed in this book may also be helpful, with adaptations, for pornography addiction. The protocol outlined in table 12.1 provides general guidelines for implementation of the intervention. The key to successful adaptation is the conceptualization of "urges" (to view pornography) as a general term referring to the variety of private experiences that can influence behavior, including not just the obvious sexual urges but also thoughts, feelings, or physical sensations that may not appear to be directly connected to and regulated by viewing (e.g., thoughts of low self-esteem, feelings of anger, or even physical agitation).

Table 12.1 ACT Protocol for Pornography Addiction

Session	Treatment components	Session content
1	Values	• Identify treatment goals and link to values. • Support client goals of either no viewing or reduced and controlled amounts of viewing.
	Acceptance	• Identify the distinction between viewing and urges to view.
2	Acceptance	• Discuss short-term versus long-term effectiveness of attempts to control urges. • Identify the negative impacts of attempts to control urges. • Highlight the paradoxical nature of attempts to control urges using the *Person in the Hole* metaphor.
3	Acceptance	• Reinforce the futility of attempts to control urges. • Identify attempts to control urges as part of the problem using the *Polygraph* metaphor and the *Chocolate Cake* and *What Are the Numbers?* exercises. • Discuss the social contexts that support regulation of private events using the *Rule of Mental Events* dialogue. • Introduce acceptance as an alternative to control using the *Tug-of-War with a Monster* metaphor.

4	Acceptance	• Review acceptance by demonstrating that the willingness to experience urges is a chosen behavior and an alternative to control using the *Tug-of-War with a Monster* metaphor. • Identify the decrease in effort required to willingly experience urges.
	Values	• Briefly discuss client values to give purpose and meaning to acceptance. • Discuss what could be gained by letting go of the control agenda.
	Committed action	• Make behavioral commitments to gradually reduce viewing. • Make behavioral commitments to engage in values-based activities instead of attempting to control urges.
5-8	Defusion	• Teach the limits of language and its role in suffering. • Undermine cognitive fusion using the *Passengers on the Bus* metaphor.
	Self-as-context	• Identify the self as the context where inner experiences occur using the *Chessboard* metaphor. • Explain that the client can't choose what inner experiences occur but can choose what to do with them.
	Present-moment awareness	• Help the client be present with inner experiences. • Identify the importance of being present while not being heavily attached to inner experiences.

	Acceptance	• Identify opportunities for acceptance from out-of-session practice. • Encourage acceptance of any problematic inner experiences.
	Committed action	• Make behavioral commitments to continue to reduce viewing. • Make behavioral commitments to engage in values-based activities instead of attempting to control urges.
9-10	Values	• Define the concept of values. • Clarify the client's values and assess the consistency of his or her behavior with those values using the *Values Assessment* worksheet.
	Committed action	• Make behavioral commitments to continue reduced viewing. • Increase behavioral commitments to engage in valued living based on recent values work. • Discuss relapse management using ACT skills.
11-12	Termination	• Review any processes that still need attention. • Summarize the treatment using the *Joe the Bum* metaphor. • Apply ACT processes to relapse management. • Apply ACT processes to termination. • Suggest a self-help workbook for continued progress.

Note: Italicized elements are from Hayes et al., 2011.

Ultimately, from an ACT perspective it is important to recognize that the viewing is functioning to help clients escape, avoid, or control unwanted internal experiences and, as such, can be conceptualized as experiential avoidance, which is a clear target of ACT. This adds an educational component to the intervention as the functional nature of the behavior may not be readily apparent to clients. Thus, in addition to the focus on psychological inflexibility and experiential avoidance, an ACT intervention for pornography addiction also includes psychoeducation to identify the functional nature of the behavior, which may be unique for each individual. For example, for one client viewing could be functioning as a means to escape feelings of sadness and social isolation, while another client may be using the behavior to manage perfectionistic anxiety. This is a collaborative process, as the therapist has to work to identify the function and then help the client see it as well.

An intervention targeting the function of the behavior must be flexible, as the specific target of the work can shift from sexual urges to guilt about the behavior to depressive symptoms to whatever else is influencing the behavior. In other words, there may be times when an ACT intervention for pornography addiction looks very similar to ACT work with depression or anxiety. As the intervention progresses, there is a sense of broadening the application of the ideas. At first, the focus is exclusively on the urges to view and how to control the behavior. As the functional nature of the urges becomes more apparent, the scope of the work increases to help clients develop psychological flexibility with all private experience.

Empirical Evidence

Research has examined the effectiveness of ACT for pornography addiction. In a case series design, the feasibility of ACT for treating pornography addiction was tested in three male participants who endorsed distress due to pornography use (Crosby & Twohig, 2009). The intervention consisted of eight sessions of ACT delivered once a week for eight weeks, with a follow-up assessment after twelve weeks. The amount of reported viewing across participants decreased to zero at post-treatment, and this was maintained at follow-up. The psychological inflexibility process measure was consistent with behavioral outcomes, changing with the behaviors and therefore indicating that the behavior change could be attributed to the intervention. Participants also had improved quality of life at post-treatment and follow-up.

A multiple baseline design was used to test the effectiveness of ACT for pornography addiction in six adult males treated in eight 1.5-hour sessions (Twohig & Crosby, 2010). The participants all reported that their pornography use was affecting their quality of life. Treatment resulted in an 85% reduction in viewing at post-treatment, with results being maintained at a three-month follow-up (83% reduction). Increases were observed on measures of quality of life, and reductions were observed on measures of OCD and scrupulosity (a moral-based subtype of OCD). Weekly measures of ACT-consistent processes showed improvements that corresponded with reductions in viewing. Improvements were also observed on a measure of psychological flexibility.

A randomized clinical trial of ACT for the treatment of pornography addiction (Crosby, 2011) compared a twelve-session ACT protocol ($n = 14$) with a wait list control ($n = 14$). The results showed a significant decrease (93%) in self-reported hours viewed per week from pretreatment to post-treatment compared to the control condition, which experienced a 21% decrease. The treatment group maintained treatment gains at a twenty-week follow-up. Clinical effectiveness data showed that 54% of the participants completely stopped viewing at post-treatment, and another 39% of participants reduced viewing by at least 70% of pretreatment levels by post-treatment. These results provide the first randomized group evidence of an effective treatment for pornography addiction.

Unique Issues and Challenges

Several unique issues and challenges arise in the treatment of pornography addiction, two of which are related to how the problem is defined. A component of the definition of pornography addiction is that clients experience negative cognitions or emotions associated with the behavior. Viewing pornography is not inherently problematic, so if the behavior is manifested as an addiction, there is an evaluation by the individual that the behavior is unwanted and not consistent with personal values or standards. Often, the addictive nature of the behavior is defined by the excessive amount of the actual behavior, but this quantitative determination can also be influenced by religious or spiritual beliefs, or the commitments clients have made to a significant other in an intimate relationship. These factors influence the amount of viewing that individuals find to be problematic (e.g., they may be reporting significant distress from very little viewing) and the consequences of engaging in the behavior, which can be devastating. This can introduce a high-stakes atmosphere in treatment that can be particularly challenging in regard to relapse, which can lead to distressing thoughts and emotions. For example, the spouse may be threatening a divorce if the client is unable to stop engaging in the behavior. While challenging, these distressing thoughts and emotions can provide a unique opportunity to apply ACT skills in session to help clients experience both how the skills can be used to respond to relapse and how they can be applied generally to implement behavioral change. For example, conflict with the spouse while in treatment can introduce distressing private experiences that could have the potential to negatively influence behavior.

Working with clients who take this high-stakes approach to treatment can also put pressure on the therapist to deliver an effective treatment, which may ultimately lead to less effective work. For example, ACT work often involves repeated attempts to target the underlying processes. This often works best in an atmosphere where the client is open to new ideas and experiences and willing to explore some confusing territory. With the high-stakes attitude, it can be difficult to foster this open atmosphere because the client is looking for immediate results. Although instances of pornography use while in treatment can be a valuable therapeutic opportunity, with the high-stakes attitudes these instances can derail treatment and make it hard for clients to stay engaged, because they can be so unforgiving of themselves. The therapist should be aware of these challenges. It may also be helpful to point this out to clients to create some openness to the exploratory nature of the intervention and to continued struggles with pornography use as part of that process.

During initial work with the acceptance process, the religious or spiritual values of the client may pose another unique challenge. In many religious traditions, individuals are held accountable for thoughts as well as behaviors. This can provide a partial explanation for why some people respond to urges to view pornography as a private experience that must be controlled (i.e., for moral reasons). This can lead to distress when the idea of accepting their sexual thoughts and simply not acting on them is first presented. For many religious individuals, this is in opposition to their religious standards. You may find it tempting to engage such clients in an intellectual discussion about the subtleties of acceptance, but it may be better to express your commitment to helping them live their values, and just leave the door open for further exploration of the idea of acceptance later in the intervention. Once the client has experienced some defusion, it may then be appropriate to illustrate the subtle difference between automatic thoughts and thinking as a chosen behavior. This can be connected with the theological principle of temptation, the idea that they can expect to be tempted to sin but are judged on their response to the temptation.

A final consideration with pornography addiction is the nature of the urges. Sexual desire, arousal, and curiosity are part of a universal human experience that is natural and often a healthy part of intimate relationships. This can be a good starting point for a discussion of acceptance, as clients recognize that they may not want to totally get rid of all of their sexual urges, but rather wish learn to respond in a manner that is consistent with their personal values.

Conclusion and Future Directions

Research into the treatment of pornography addiction is in the beginning stages and receiving increased attention. There are still conceptual, theoretical, and treatment issues to work out, but conceptualizing the behavior from an ACT perspective allows for the application of a treatment with an established evidence base for functionally similar problems. Work specifically with pornography addiction has shown ACT to be an effective treatment, and future work in this area will include continued treatment research to improve generalizability. Dissemination is also a priority, as it is evident that this is a pressing issue for many individuals and the clinicians who are seeking resources for treatment.

References

Abramowitz, J. S., Tolin, D. F., & Street, G. P. (2001). Paradoxical effects of thought suppression: A meta-analysis of controlled studies. *Clinical Psychology Review, 21,* 683-703.

Allen, M., D'Alessio, D., & Brezgel, K. (1995). A meta-analysis summarizing the effects of pornography II: Aggression after exposure. *Human Communication Research, 22,* 258-283.

Bergner, R. M., & Bridges, A. J. (2002). The significance of heavy pornography involvement for romantic partners: Research and clinical implications. *Journal of Sex and Marital Therapy, 28,* 193-206.

Black, D. W. (1998). Recognition and treatment of obsessive-compulsive spectrum disorders. In R. P. Swinson, M. M. Antony, S. Rachman, & M. A. Richter (Eds.), *Obsessive-compulsive disorder: Theory, research, and treatment.* New York: Guilford Press.

Coleman, E. (1991). Compulsive sexual behavior: New concepts and treatments. *Journal of Psychology and Human Sexuality, 4,* 37-52.

Cooper, A., Delmonico, D. L., & Burg, R. (2000). Cybersex users, abusers, and compulsives: New findings and implications. *Sexual Addiction and Compulsivity, 7,* 5-29.

Cooper, A., Griffin-Shelley, E., Delmonico, D. L., & Mathy, R. M. (2001). Online sexual problems: Assessment and predictive variables. *Sexual Addiction and Compulsivity, 8,* 267-285.

Cooper, A., Putnam, D. E., Planchon, L. A., & Boies, S. C. (1999). Online sexual compulsivity: Getting tangled in the net. *Sexual Addiction and Compulsivity, 6,* 79-104.

Crosby, J. M. (2011). *Acceptance and commitment therapy for the treatment of compulsive pornography use: A randomized clinical trial.* Doctoral dissertation, Utah State University. Retrieved March 1, 2012, from http://digitalcommons.usu.edu/etd/999/.

Crosby, J. M., & Twohig, M. P. (2009, November). *Acceptance and commitment therapy for the treatment of problematic pornography use: A case series of low behavioral rates.* Poster presented at the annual convention of the Association for Behavioral and Cognitive Therapies, New York, NY.

Del Giudice, M. J., & Kutinsky, J. (2007). Applying motivational interviewing to the treatment of sexual compulsivity and addiction. *Sexual Addiction and Compulsivity, 14,* 303-319.

Garcia, L. T. (1986). Exposure to pornography and attitudes about women and rape: A correlational study. *Journal of Sex Research, 22,* 378-385.

Grant, J. E., & Potenza, M. N. (2007). Impulse control disorders. In J. E. Grant & M. N. Potenza (Eds.), *Textbook of men's mental health.* Arlington, VA: American Psychiatric Publishing.

Hayes, S. C., Luoma, J. B., Bond, F. W., Masuda, A., & Lillis, J. (2006). Acceptance and commitment therapy: Model, processes, and outcomes. *Behaviour Research and Therapy, 44,* 1-25.

Hayes, S. C., Strosahl, K. D., & Wilson, K. G. (2011). *Acceptance and commitment therapy: The process and practice of mindful change* (2nd ed.). New York: Guilford Press.

Kalichman, S. C., & Rompa, D. (1995). Sexual sensation seeking and sexual compulsivity scales: Reliability, validity, and predicting HIV risk behavior. *Journal of Personality Assessment, 65,* 586-601.

Kuzma, J. M., & Black, D. W. (2008). Epidemiology, prevalence, and natural history of compulsive sexual behavior. *Psychiatric Clinics of North America, 31,* 603-611.

Manning, J. C. (2006). The impact of Internet pornography on marriage and the family: A review of the research. *Sexual Addiction and Compulsivity, 13,* 131-165.

McBride, K. R., Reece, M., & Sanders, S. A. (2007). Predicting negative outcomes of sexuality using the Compulsive Sexual Behavior Inventory. *International Journal of Sexual Health, 19,* 51-62.

Mick, T. M., & Hollander, E. (2006). Impulsive-compulsive sexual behavior. *CNS Spectrums, 11,* 944-955.

Oddone-Paolucci, E., Genuis, M., & Violato, C. (2000). A meta-analysis of the published research on the effects of pornography. In C. Violato, E. Oddone-Paolucci, & M. Genius (Eds.), *The changing family and child development.* Aldershot, UK: Ashgate.

Orzack, M. H., & Ross, C. J. (2000). Should virtual sex be treated like other sex addictions? *Sexual Addiction and Compulsivity, 7,* 113-125.

Rachman, S., Thordarson, D. S., Shafran, R., & Woody, S. R. (1995). Perceived responsibility: Structure and significance. *Behaviour Research and Therapy, 33,* 779-784.

Reid, R. C., & Woolley, S. R. (2006). Using emotionally focused therapy for couples to resolve attachment ruptures created by hypersexual behavior. *Sexual Addiction and Compulsivity, 13,* 219-239.

Schneider, J. P. (1994). Sex addiction: Controversy within mainstream addiction medicine, diagnosis based on the *DSM-III-R,* and physician case histories. *Sexual Addiction and Compulsivity, 1,* 19-44.

Schneider, J. P. (2000a). A qualitative study of cybersex participants: Gender differences, recovery issues, and implications for therapists. *Sexual Addiction and Compulsivity, 7,* 249-278.

Schneider, J. P. (2000b). Effects of cybersex addiction on the family: Results of a survey. *Sexual Addiction and Compulsivity, 7,* 31-58.

Schneider, J. P. (2003). The impact of compulsive cybersex behaviors on the family. *Sexual and Relationship Therapy, 18,* 329-354.

Stack, S., Wasserman, I., & Kern, R. (2004). Adult social bonds and use of Internet pornography. *Social Science Quarterly, 85,* 75-88.

Twohig, M. P., & Crosby, J. M. (2010). Acceptance and commitment therapy as a treatment for problematic Internet pornography viewing. *Behavior Therapy, 41,* 285-295.

Twohig, M. P., Crosby, J. M., & Cox, J. M. (2009). Viewing Internet pornography: For whom is it problematic, how, and why? *Sexual Addiction and Compulsivity, 16,* 253-266.

Wegner, D. M. (1994). Ironic processes of mental control. *Psychological Review, 101,* 34-52.

Woods, D. W., & Twohig, M. (2008). *Trichotillomania: An ACT-enhanced therapy approach.* New York: Oxford University Press.

Young, K. S. (2007). Cognitive behavior therapy with Internet addicts: Treatment outcomes and implications. *CyberPsychology and Behavior, 10,* 671-679.

Editor **Steven C. Hayes, PhD**, is Nevada Foundation Professor at the Department of Psychology at the University of Nevada. An author of thirty-four books and more than 470 scientific articles, he has shown in his research how language and thought lead to human suffering, and has developed acceptance and commitment therapy, a powerful therapy method that is useful in a wide variety of areas. Hayes has been president of several scientific societies and has received several national awards, including the Lifetime Achievement Award from the Association for Behavioral and Cognitive Therapy.

Editor **Michael E. Levin, MA**, is a doctoral candidate in clinical psychology at the University of Nevada, Reno and a research associate with Contextual Change, LLC. He has been a principal investigator on two federally funded grants, seeking to develop and test web-based acceptance and mindfulness-based interventions for the prevention and treatment of mental health problems. Levin has published thirty articles and chapters related to addictive behaviors and acceptance and mindfulness-based interventions.

Index

A

absolute abstinence, 84–86

abstinence: dialectical approach to, 84–86; suppression strategy for, 11

abstinence violation effect, 85

acceptance: ACT approach to, 52–53, 308; addictive behavior and, 10–12; counselor cultivation of, 203–205; definition of, 191; mindfulness and, 203–205; motivational interviewing and, 162–163; radical, 203–204

Acceptance and Action Questionnaire (AAQ), 120

acceptance and commitment therapy (ACT), 27–63; acceptance practice in, 52–53; assessment process in, 42; binge eating and, 292–293; cognitive fusion and, 33–34; committed action and, 35–36, 57–59; defusion exercises used in, 54–55; detoxification protocol based on, 245–251; experiential avoidance and, 32–33; face-to-face interventions, 263–265; future directions for studying, 62–63; gambling problems and, 280; group process and orientation, 226–227; informed consent and opening session, 37–42; integration into current treatment settings, 59–61; mindfulness interventions and, 61; motivational interviewing and, 60; pornography addiction and, 307–313; Practicing Our Way to Stillness exercise, 43–47; present-moment processes and, 29–30, 48–49; psychological flexibility model of addiction, 28–36; research on efficacy of, 61–62, 231–232, 251–252, 264–265, 268, 313–314; self processes and, 30–32,

DBT. *See* dialectical behavior therapy
defusion, 54–55, 223–224, 308
denial, skillful use of, 91–92
depression, 30, 34, 36
description process, 192–196
desire thinking, 131, 141
Desire Thinking Questionnaire (DTQ), 141
detached mindfulness, 145
detoxification, 239–253; ACT treatment protocol for, 245–251; challenges in treating, 252–253; dose-reduction phase, 246–247, 249–250; efficacy of ACT for, 251–252; post-dose-reduction phase, 247, 250–251; pre-dose-reduction phase, 246, 248–249; psychological flexibility model of, 241–243; treatments targeting, 240–241, 243–244; values focus in, 248–249, 250; withdrawal symptoms from, 239–240
dialectical behavior therapy (DBT): binge eating and, 293–294; substance use disorders and, 69–97
dialectical behavior therapy for substance use disorders (DBT-SUD), 69–97; approach to abstinence in, 84–86; attachment strategies for, 86–88; borderline personality disorder and, 69, 70–72; clear mind as goal of, 79–80; dialectical philosophy and, 72–73; distress tolerance in, 89;

emotion regulation in, 90; interpersonal effectiveness in, 90; mindfulness skills in, 88–89; Path to Clear Mind in, 80–84; research on efficacy of, 95–97; skills specific to, 90–93; target hierarchy for, 77–78; treatment modes and functions, 74–77
dialectical philosophy, 72–73
Dimeff, Linda A., 69
Dimidjian, Sona, 213
discomfort, being with, 111
distress tolerance, 89
dose-reduction phase, 246–247, 249–250
double approach-avoidance conflict, 159
double-sided reflections, 164
drinking problems. *See* alcohol abuse
drug abuse: ACT-based study on, 62; binge eating compared to, 289–290; detoxification symptoms, 240; MBRP-based studies on, 119–121. *See also* substance use disorders
drug testing, 94

E

eating disorders. *See* binge eating
effectiveness, 207
eliciting and reflecting strategy, 154
elicit-provide-elicit strategy, 170
emotions: acceptance of painful, 204–205; ambivalence conflicts and, 158–159; binge eating and,

O

OARS acronym, 18, 163–165, 260
obese individuals, 297–298
observing and describing, 191–196
obsessive-compulsive disorder
   (OCD), 304, 306
one-mindfulness, 197–199
open questions, 163, 166, 260
opioid dependence: replacement
   medications, 94, 240;
   withdrawal symptoms, 240
options/cues to use, 82–83
overeating. See binge eating
overweight individuals, 297–298

P

pain: chronic drug use and, 81;
   distress tolerance and, 89;
   efficacy of ACT for, 251
Passengers on the Bus metaphor,
   227–228, 229–230
Path to Clear Mind, 80–84;
   decreasing capitulation to drug
   use, 83; decreasing options and
   cues to use, 82–83; decreasing
   physical discomfort, 81;
   decreasing substance abuse,
   80–81; decreasing urges and
   cravings to use, 81–82;
   increasing community
   reinforcement of clear mind
   behaviors, 83–84
perspective taking, 31, 50–51
pharmacological interventions.
   See medications
physical discomfort, 81
planning strategies, 174–175

pornography addiction, 304–316;
   ACT protocol for, 309–313;
   challenges in treating, 314–316;
   characteristics of, 304–305; core
   processes of ACT and, 307–
   309; efficacy of ACT for,
   313–314; problems linked to,
   305; religious values and,
   315–316; terms for describing,
   304; theoretical model of,
   306–309
Positive Alcohol Metacognitions
   Scale (PAMS), 142
positive metacognitive beliefs,
   129, 147
positive reinforcement, 106
post-alcohol use phase, 137,
   138–139, 143–144, 148
post-dose-reduction phase, 247,
   250–251
Practicing Our Way to Stillness
   (POWS) exercise, 43–47
pre-alcohol use phase, 137,
   138–139, 143, 144, 148
pre-dose-reduction phase, 246,
   248–249
prefrontal cortex deregulation,
   290
present-moment awareness: ACT
   practice of, 48–49, 308–309;
   difficulties related to, 29–30;
   mindfulness and, 9
problem drinking. See alcohol
   abuse
problem gambling. See gambling
   problems
prolapse concept, 85
providers. See counselors

S

Sayrs, Jennifer H. R., 69, 187
Schnetzer, Lindsay W., 27
selective reflections, 164
self processes: ACT practices
    based on, 49–52; addictive
    behavior and, 30–32; difficulties
    related to, 30–32, 224–225;
    pornography addiction and,
    308; self-stigma and shame and,
    224–225
self-as-content, 30, 308
self-as-context, 31, 308
self-as-process, 30–31
self-care, 114–115
self-compassion, 269
self-criticism, 291
self-judgments, 202–203, 291, 293
self-medication hypothesis,
    104–105
self-oriented behavior, 157
self-perception theory (SPT), 259
self-stigma: ACT group protocol
    targeting, 225–231; addiction
    and, 217; binge eating and,
    292–293; cognitive fusion and,
    223–224; development of,
    217–218; efficacy of ACT for,
    231–232; experiential avoidance
    and, 221–223; future directions
    for studying, 233; rigid self-
    processes and, 224–225; weight-
    related, 298
Serenity Prayer, 5, 20, 73
sexual addiction. See pornography
    addiction
shame: ACT group protocol
    targeting, 225–231; adaptive

functions of, 220–221; addiction
    and, 219–220, 234; binge eating
    and, 292–293; cognitive fusion
    and, 223–224; efficacy of ACT
    for, 231–232; experiential
    avoidance and, 221–223; future
    directions for studying, 233;
    rigid self-processes and,
    224–225
shortsighted behavior, 157
"should" language, 201
simple reflections, 164
situational attentional refocusing
    (SAR), 8–9, 146
situational stress, 291
Six Breaths on Purpose exercise,
    48–49
skills generalization, 75–76
smartphone applications, 270–271
smoking cessation, 257–271; ACT
    for, 260–262, 263–265, 266–
    268, 269–270; face-to-face
    interventions for, 262–265;
    future directions for studying,
    270–271; motivational
    interviewing for, 259–260,
    262–263, 265–266, 269;
    pharmacotherapy for, 257–258;
    psychological approaches to,
    258; research on ACT efficacy
    for, 61–62, 264–265, 268;
    research on MI efficacy for, 263,
    266; telephone interventions
    for, 265–268; web-based
    interventions for, 268–270
SOBER breathing space exercise,
    8, 112
social support, 115, 116

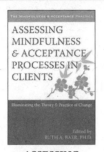
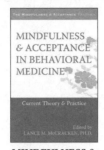

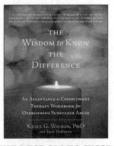